Handbook of Japanese Media and Popular Culture in Transition

Japan Documents Handbooks
This series focuses on the broad field of Japanese Studies, aimed at the worldwide English language scholarly market, published in Tokyo in English. Each Handbook will contain an average of 20 newly written contributions on various aspects of the topic, which together comprise an up-to-date survey of use to scholars and students. The focus is on Humanities and Social Sciences.

Titles in this series:
Handbook of Higher Education in Japan *(edited by Paul Snowden)*
Handbook of Confucianism in Modern Japan *(edited by Shaun O'Dwyer)*
Handbook of Japanese Media and Popular Culture in Transition *(edited by Forum Mithani and Griseldis Kirsch)*

Forthcoming titles in this series:
Handbook of Japanese Christian Writers *(edited by Mark Williams, Van Gessel and Yamane Michihiro)*
Handbook of Environmental History in Japan *(edited by Tatsushi Fujihara)*
Handbook of the Japanese Constitution: An Annotation *(edited by Colin P.A. Jones)*
Handbook of Modern and Contemporary Japanese Women Writers *(edited by Rebecca Copeland)*
Handbook of Japanese Feminisms *(edited by Andrea Germer and Ulrike Wöhr)*
Re-examining Postwar Japanese History: A Handbook *(edited by Simon Avenell)*
Handbook of Sport and Japan *(edited by Helen Macnaughtan and Verity Postlethwaite)*
Handbook of Japanese Martial Arts *(edited by Alexander Bennett)*
Handbook of Japanese Public Administration and Bureaucracy *(edited by Mieko Nakabayashi and Hideaki Tanaka)*
Handbook of Crime and Punishment in Japan *(edited by Tom Ellis and Akira Kyo)*
Handbook of Disaster Studies in Japan *(edited by Paola Cavaliere and Junko Otani)*
Handbook of Contemporary Japanese Diplomacy: The 2010s *(edited by Tosh Minohara)*
Handbook of Russia-Japan Relations *(edited by Kazuhiko Togo and Dmitry Streltsov)*
Handbook of Japan's Environmental Law, Policy, and Politics *(edited by Hiroshi Ohta)*
Handbook of Japanese Games *(edited by Rachael Hutchinson)*
Handbook of Human Rights and Japan *(edited by Tamara Swenson)*
Handbook of Europe-Japan Relations *(edited by Lars Vargö)*
Teaching Japan: A Handbook *(edited by Gregory Poole and Ioannis Gaitanidis)*
Handbook of Women in Japanese Buddhism *(edited by Monika Schrimpf and Emily Simpson)*
Handbook of Japanese Security *(edited by Leszek Buszynski)*
Handbook of Japanese Tourism *(edited by Hideto Fujii)*
Handbook on Japanese Civil Society *(edited by Simon Avenell and Akihiro Ogawa)*
Handbook of Japanese Labor Practices: Changing Perceptions *(edited by Robin Sakamoto)*
The Advent of Sound in Japanese Cinema: A Handbook *(edited by Sean O'Reilly)*
Handbook of Global Migration and Japan *(edited by Shinnosuke Takahashi and Yasuko Hassall Kobayashi)*
Handbook of Work and Leisure in Japan *(edited by Nana Okura Gagne and Isaac Gagne)*

Handbook of Japanese Media and Popular Culture in Transition

Edited by Forum Mithani and Griseldis Kirsch

Amsterdam University Press

First published 2022 By Japan Documents, an imprint of MHM Limited, Tokyo, Japan.

MHM Limited gratefully acknowledges K.K. Nihon Bunken Shuppan, and its owner-president, Mr. Sumio Saito, as the originator of the imprint "Japan Documents" and declares here that it is used under license and with the kind permission of Mr. Saito.

Cover design, layout, and typography: TransPac Communications, Greg Glover

ISBN   978 94 6372 889 8
NUR   718

Printed and bound by CPI Group (UK) Ltd, Croydon, CR0 4YY

Table of Contents

Contributors vii

Preface
Forum Mithani and Griseldis Kirsch xi

Introduction
Griseldis Kirsch and Forum Mithani xiii

Part 1: Reimagining History

1 Imagining Alternative Pasts: Imperial Nostalgia on Japanese Television
   Griseldis Kirsch 3

2 Truth and Limitations: Japanese Media and Disasters
   Christopher P. Hood 17

3 Solace or Criticism? The Representation of the Fukushima Nuclear Disaster in
   Television Dramas and Films
   Hilaria Gössmann 32

Part 2: Transitions and Transcultural Flows

4 *Red-Light Bases* (1953): A Cross-Temporal Contact Zone
   Irene González-López 47

5 Creating the Youth Star System in Japan: Transnational and Transmedia Phenomena
   Marcos P. Centeno-Martin 62

6 映画とテレビ: その歴史的相克を越えて Film and Television: Looking Beyond a Historic
   Rivalry
   北浦 寛之 *Hiroyuki Kitaura* 78

7 Remaking Revenge: Transnational Television Drama Flows and the Remaking of the
   Korean Drama *Mawang* in Japan
   Julia Stolyar 90

Part 3: Franchises and Formats

8 Media Mix: Theorizing and Historicizing Japanese Franchising
   Rayna Denison 107

9   Nihilistamina: Gloomy Heroisms in Contemporary Anime
    Artur Lozano-Méndez and Antonio Loriguillo-López 124

10 A Television Flagship Sailing the Currents of a Changing Media World: NHK's
    Morning Drama (*asadora*) in the 21st Century
    Elisabeth Scherer 140

Part 4: Gender and Media

11 Japanese Popular Fiction: Constraint, Violence and Freedom in Kirino Natsuo's *Out*
    Lyle De Souza 157

12 Intersections of Difference: Sex, Gender and Disability in Japanese Visual Media
    Forum Mithani 171

13 Marketing Men (,) Silencing Men: The Sapporo Beer-Mifune Campaign and
    Perspectives on Gender in Japanese Advertising
    James X. White 186

14 Japanese Men's Magazines: (Re)producing Hybrid Masculinities
    Ronald Saladin 201

Part 5: Audiences and Users

15 Japanese Audiences, and Japanese Audience Studies
    Jennifer Coates 217

16 The Serious Business of Song: Karaoke as Discipline and Industry in Japan
    Laurence Green 231

17 Studying Digital Media in the Diasporic Transnationalism Context: The Case of
    International Migrants in Japan
    Xinyu Promio Wang 244

Index 261

Contributors

Marcos Centeno-Martin is Lecturer in Media Studies at Universitat de València and Honorary Research Fellow in Japanese Studies at Birkbeck, University of London, where he has been the Japanese program director. Before that, Centeno was Lecturer in Film Studies in the Department of Japan and Korea at SOAS (London) where he convened the MA "Global Cinemas and the Transcultural." Centeno was also Guest Lecturer at Nanzan University in Nagoya and Ochanomizu University, and Research Associate at Waseda University and visiting researcher at Université Sorbonne Nouvelle-Paris 3 and Goethe Universität Frankfurt. His research interests revolve around Japanese documentary film, particularly issues related to memory and representation of minorities (mainly the Ainu people), diversity and transculturality in Japan. His research project "Japanese Transnational Cinema" was funded by several institutions including the Sasakawa and Daiwa foundations, Waseda University and the Japanese Ministry of Education.

Jennifer Coates is Senior Lecturer in Japanese Studies at the School of East Asian Studies, University of Sheffield. She is the author of *Making Icons: Repetition and the Female Image in Japanese Cinema, 1945–1964* (Hong Kong University Press, 2016) and co-editor of *Japanese Visual Media: Politicizing the Screen* (with Eyal Ben-Ari, Routledge, 2021) and *The Routledge Companion to Gender and Japanese Culture* (with Lucy Fraser and Mark Pendleton, Routledge, 2019). Her current ethnographic research focuses on early postwar film audiences in Japan.

Rayna Denison is Professor of Film and Digital Arts at the University of Bristol, with a focus on contemporary Japanese animation and cinema. Her publications include the monograph *Anime: A Critical Introduction* and the edited collection *Princess Mononoke: Understanding Studio Ghibli's Monster Princess*. She has also published a wide range of co-edited collections and special issues of journals, as well as having publications in leading journals including *Cinema Journal, Japan Forum, Animation: An Interdisciplinary Journal* and the *Velvet Light Trap*.

Lyle De Souza is a Lecturer in the Department of English Language and Literature at Kyoto Notre Dame University and a JSPS KAKENHI Researcher at the Institute for Research in Humanities, Kyoto University. His current research project, "The Literature of the Japanese Diaspora: Identity Beyond Japan," combines his interdisciplinary expertise across the social sciences (Japanese Studies, sociology) and humanities (literary theory, cultural studies). His work aims to improve understanding of minority identities through analysis of processes of racialization.

Irene González-López is Lecturer in Japanese Studies at Birkbeck, University of London, and Research Associate of the Visual and Material Culture Research Centre at Kingston University. Before pursuing a PhD in Film Studies at SOAS (University of London), Irene lived in Japan for eight years. Her research spans Japanese creative industries, with a special focus on postwar cinema and issues related to gender and sexuality, both in front of and behind the camera. Irene's publications include *Tanaka Kinuyo: Nation, Stardom and Female Subjectivity* (co-editor together with Michael Smith, Edinburgh University Press, 2018); "Marketing the *panpan* in Japanese popular culture: youth, sexuality, and power" (2018); "In Search of the Authentic Japanese Taste: *Solitary Gourmet* and Cultural Tourism" (2018); and "The Profound Desire of the Goddess: Sexuality and Politics in *The Insect Woman*" (2017).

Hilaria Gössmann is Professor for Japanese Studies at the University of Trier, Germany. The focus of her research and teaching is modern literature, television dramas and films. She has edited a book on gender and media in Japan and Germany together with Muramatsu Yasuko (in Japanese: *Media ga tsukuru gendā. Nichidoku no danjo kazokuzō o yomitoku*, Shinyōsha, 1998) and a book on the Fukushima nuclear accident in media, popular culture and literature (in German: *Schriften der Gesellschaft für Japanforschung, Band 4: Dokumentation, Trostspende oder Anklage? Die Atomkatastrophe von Fukushima in japanischen Medien, Populärkultur und Literatur*, Gesellschaft für Japanforschung eV, 2021).

Laurence Green is a 3rd year PhD Student at SOAS University of London. His current research focuses on the use of music within the Japanese animation industry, and his writing has previously been published in both *NEO Magazine* and the *Japan Society Review*, as well as in the recent edited volume *Japan beyond Its Borders: Transnational Approaches to Film and Media* (Seibunsha, 2020). He is currently serving as Managing Editor of the journal *Japan Forum* and is a recipient of the Meiji Jingu Japanese Studies Research Scholarship, Japan Research Centre Fuwaku Fund and the British Association of Japanese Studies John Crump Studentship.

Christopher Hood is a Reader in Japanese Studies at Cardiff University. He is the author of the books, *Japan: The Basics*; *Osutaka: A Chronicle of Loss in the World's Largest Single Plane Crash*; *Dealing with Disaster in Japan: Responses to the Flight JL123 Crash*; *Shinkansen: From Bullet Train to Symbol of Modern Japan* and *Education Reform in Japan: Nakasone's Legacy*. Connected to the chapter in this collection, he is the author of "Disaster Narratives by Design: Is Japan Different?" (*International Journal of Mass Emergencies and Disasters*, August 2020). He is also the author of the novels *Hijacking Japan*, *Tokyo 20/20 Vision* and *FOUR*. Homepage: http://hoodcp.wordpress.com Twitter: @HoodCP

Griseldis Kirsch is Reader in Contemporary Japanese Culture at SOAS University of London. She is the author of *Contemporary Sino-Japanese Relations on Screen. A History: 1989–2005* (Bloomsbury Academic, 2015) and co-editor of the volume *Assembling Japan: Technology, Modernity and Global Culture* (Peter Lang, 2015). Her research interests include nationalism, identity and memory in Japanese screen media and she has also published widely on these topics.

Hiroyuki Kitaura is Associate Professor of Film Studies in the Faculty of International Liberal Arts at Kaichi International University, Japan. He is the author of *Terebi seichōki no Nihon eiga: Media kan kōshō no naka no dorama* (Japanese movies during the growth period of television: The dramas in media interactions, Nagoya Daigaku Shuppankai, 2018) and has written extensively in the area of Japanese film and television history.

Antonio Loriguillo-López is Assistant Professor at the Universitat Jaume I (Spain). He teaches courses on Audiovisual Communication, Video Game Design and Development, as well as the Master's Degree in New Trends and Innovation Processes in Communication. He is a graduate of the first class of the Kadokawa Media Mix Summer Program organized by the University of Tokyo (2014). His interests focus on post-classical storytelling in contemporary audiovisuals and Japanese commercial animation. He is the author, editor and co-editor of several books and also author of scientific articles related to these topics in journals such as *Animation, Quarterly Review of Film and Video, Creative Industries Journal* and *International Journal on Media Management*.

Artur Lozano-Méndez has a PhD in Translation and Intercultural Studies and is a Serra Húnter Lecturer at the Department of Translation and Interpretation and East Asian Studies at Universitat Autònoma de Barcelona. He teaches about Japanese politics, philosophy, popular culture and social issues in Japan. His research is focused on those same areas as a member of the InterAsia research group (UAB). His publications include: "Techno-Orientalism in East-Asian Contexts: Reiteration, Diversification, Adaptation" (chapter in *Counterpoints: Edward Said's Legacy*, Cambridge Scholars Publishing, 2010); editor of *El Japón Contemporáneo. Una aproximación desde los Estudios Culturales* (Bellaterra, 2016); "Mamoru Oshii's Exploration of the Potentialities of Consciousness in a Globalised Capitalist Network" (in *ejcjs – Electronic Journal of Contemporary Japanese Studies* 15:3, 2015); co-editor (with Blai Guarné and Dolores Martinez) of *Persistently Postwar: Media and the Politics of Memory in Japan* (Berghahn Books, 2019).

Forum Mithani is a British Academy Postdoctoral Fellow at Cardiff University, where she has previously held the position of Lecturer in Japanese Studies. She received her PhD from SOAS University of London for her thesis on the representation of single motherhood in Japanese television drama. She is the author of "Maternal Fantasies in an Era of Crisis—Single Mothers, Self-Sacrifice and Sexuality in Japanese Television Drama," in F. Portier-Le Cocq ed. *Motherhood in Contemporary International Perspective: Continuity and Change* (Routledge, 2020) and "(De)Constructing Nostalgic Myths of the Mother in Japanese Drama *Woman*" in *Series—International Journal of TV Serial Narratives* 5 (2019). Her research interests include Japanese media and popular culture, gender, motherhood, feminism and social minorities.

Ronald Saladin is an Assistant Professor of Japanese Studies at the University of Trier, Germany. In 2019, he published his monograph, *Young Men and Masculinities in Japanese Media—(Un-)Conscious Hegemony*, which is a qualitative and quantitative analysis of Japanese men's magazines, with Palgrave Macmillan. In his research and teaching, he focuses on media, contemporary literature, gender and popular culture of Japan.

Elisabeth Scherer is a Japanese studies researcher and e-learning professional at Heinrich Heine University Düsseldorf. Her areas of research interest include popular culture, intermedia, rituals and gender studies. She is the editor of *Reconsidering the Cultural Significance of NHK's Morning Dramas* (special issue of the East Asian Journal of Popular Culture, 2019).

Julia Stolyar is a PhD researcher at SOAS, University of London. Her research interests include transnational media flows between Korea and Japan and transnational television more broadly, exploring notions of identity and national identity and the creation and circulation of national myths through television.

Xinyu (Promio) Wang is an assistant professor in Cultural Studies at the Department of Contemporary English, Ibaraki Christian University, Japan. Xin's research focuses on the transnational socio-cultural practices of Chinese digital migrants and Chinese queer digital migrants in the UK and Japan. Xin's latest publications include "Digital Technology, Physical Spaces, and the Notion of Belonging among Chinese Migrants in Japan" in *Asiascape: Digital Asia*, 7 (2020) and "Chinese Migrants' Sense of Belonging in Japan: Between Digital and Physical Spaces" in *Migration Research Series* No. 61 [online] Geneva: International Organization for Migration.

Elisabeth Scherer is a Japanese studies researcher and e-learning professional at Heinrich Heine University Düsseldorf. Her areas of research interest include popular culture, intermedia, rituals and gender studies. She is the editor of *Reconsidering the Cultural Significance of NHK's Morning Dramas* (special issue of the East Asian Journal of Popular Culture, 2019).

Julia Stolyar is a PhD researcher at SOAS, University of London. Her research interests include transnational media flows between Korea and Japan and transnational television more broadly, exploring notions of identity and national identity and the creation and circulation of national myths through television.

Xinyu (Promio) Wang is an assistant professor in Cultural Studies at the Department of Contemporary English, Ibaraki Christian University, Japan. Xin's research focuses on the transnational socio-cultural practices of Chinese digital migrants and Chinese queer digital migrants in the UK and Japan. Xin's latest publications include "Digital Technology, Physical Spaces, and the Notion of Belonging among Chinese Migrants in Japan" in *Asiascape: Digital Asia*, 7 (2020) and "Chinese Migrants' Sense of Belonging in Japan: Between Digital and Physical Spaces" in *Migration Research Series* No. 61 [online] Geneva: International Organization for Migration.

James White completed his PhD at the School of East Asian Studies at the University of Sheffield in 2019 with ESRC and Japan Foundation support. His thesis explored intellectual and critical definitions of gender in Japanese beer advertising across the postwar era. An initial year on the JET program morphed into eight years teaching across the archipelago pursued by earthquakes. During this time, he completed an MA in Japanese Language and Society from the University of Sheffield, followed by an extra MA (SOAS) in Japanese Studies. He is particularly interested in visual culture and narratives of gender, alcohol consumption, and identity.

Preface

Forum Mithani and Griseldis Kirsch

The Hepburn system of romanization has been used for Japanese terms, including the names of persons and places. Long vowels are indicated by a macron, except for place names and words that are in everyday use in English (such as Tokyo). The Japanese custom of placing the family name first has been followed for the names of Japanese persons. In the case of citations of works in English by Japanese authors, we have deferred to the romanization style and name order given in the original work.

Unless otherwise noted, translations into English from Japanese and other languages can be assumed to be the authors' own.

Acknowledgements

We would like to express our sincerest gratitude to all the authors who have contributed to this handbook for their tireless patience and dedication in helping to bring this project to fruition during a period of ongoing uncertainty. We appreciate the careful and considered proofreading, editing and formatting undertaken by the publishers, who were generous in their accommodation of our vision for the volume. We would also like to thank the reviewers who gave up their valuable time to read and provide useful comments on our work. Finally, we would not have managed to complete this project without the support and encouragement of family, friends and colleagues.

Introduction

Griseldis Kirsch and Forum Mithani

Long shunned by academic discourse on Japan, Japanese media are at long last seeing the recognition they deserve. As anyone who has travelled to Japan can testify, media are everywhere—from the ubiquitous adverts on trains, to the *tachiyomi* (literally, reading while standing) of manga volumes or magazines in convenience stores, or the inevitable television sets in bars, restaurants or hotels; it is plain to see that Japan is a country saturated with media.

However, as a discipline, media studies is still relatively new. Having been born out of what was then called Communication Studies in the first half of the 20th century, which was initially almost obsessed with assessing the direct effect "mass-mediated" products had on the wider population, media studies as a discipline came to suffer under the perception that they were somehow not worthy of academic attention. Theodor Horkheimer and Max Adorno (1941) in particular, created a dichotomy between "high culture" (anything that was artistic, original and thus pure) versus "low culture" (anything that appealed to "the masses," was produced en masse, and was essentially formulaic), stigmatizing research on anything "popular." Naturally, this also had an impact on how Japanese media came to be studied—or, respectively, not to be studied, in spite of their prevalence and omnipresence in Japan.

When research on Japanese media started, the focus was very much on how it related to the political landscape. Several (anglophone) studies followed in the wake of the 1993 Tsubaki Incident (see page 9), an instance in which the close relationship between the media and the government became particularly visible (Feldman 1993; Krauss 2000; Freeman 2000). In Japan itself, at around the same time, research tended to focus on the representation of gender, or Otherness, in Japanese advertising and television drama, almost existing in separate spheres. What became evident, even then, were two tendencies that continue to dominate academic discourse up to the present day: a focus on case studies, often without looking at the industries that produce them, and a very clear research rationale about identities and discourses (Muramatsu 1979; Gössmann and Muramatsu eds. 1998; Iwao 2000; Iwabuchi 2001, 2002).

In the early 2000s, the popularity of Japanese television drama and, subsequently, the sudden and unexpected popularity of the Korean television drama *Winter Sonata* (*Gyeouryeon-ga*, KBS2 2002) and the resulting fandom around its star, Bae Yong-joon, triggered another wave of interest in the workings of Japanese media. It prompted several publications that dealt with the consumption of content, and the impact of that content on fan behavior across East Asia. (Iwabuchi 2002; Mōri ed. 2004; Chua and Iwabuchi 2008; Hayashi 2005). The focus of these works was very much thematic, again leaving out the industries that shaped and exported or imported these productions, within the region.

As a result, there have been few industry studies, with Jayson Makoto Chun's (2006) volume, *A Nation of A Hundred Million Idiots?*, perhaps being the only one dedicated to Japanese television, and even it only encompasses the formative years up to 1973, offering nothing on recent trends and issues. Similarly, Jeff Kingston's (2017) more recent edited volume *Press Freedom in Contemporary Japan* contains industry-focused papers, but with a narrow emphasis on how the government influences the media. Not unsurprisingly, this book followed the wake of yet another attempt by the Japanese government to change the broadcasting law to exercise control.

However, by the second decade of the 21st century, Japanese media studies had evolved into a rich field, with an increasing number of rising and more established scholars. One of the explicit aims of this volume is to showcase the richness of the field by explicitly including more junior scholars—and thus the future of the discipline—alongside more established ones. Scholars have come to study the intersection of television and film, manga, anime, social media—the approaches are numerous.

Nonetheless, handbooks specifically about Japanese media are still few and far between, and the only media genre that receives significant attention from publishers is Japanese cinema—an approach that overlooks the complex, long-standing relationship between television and cinema and thus risks excluding key insights that could be discovered when they are not looked at in separation from each other. The first handbook—edited by Richard G. Powers, Hidetoshi Katō and Bruce Stronach—was published in 1989 and comprises papers on science fiction, popular architecture, new religions and sport, thus employing a very broad view of "popular culture," very much in line with Horkheimer and Adorno. The review on Amazon advertises the book as follows: "The areas explored are those that have proven to be of durable interest to the Japanese, such as sports, science fiction, and popular music, as well as passing fads and fancies" (Amazon n.d.). In 1995, John Whittier Treat edited *Contemporary Japan and Popular Culture*, which featured papers writing either about case studies, or more generally about the phenomenon of "mass culture." A different approach was taken by Dolores Martinez's edited volume in 1998, *The Worlds of Japanese Popular Culture: Gender, Shifting Boundaries and Global Cultures* which brought together scholars working on sports, anime, magazines and television drama, providing a similar scope to Powers, Katō and Stronach, but more up-to-date insight into Japanese popular culture, with a wider focus than Treat before her. In the year 2000, Timothy J. Craig edited the volume *Japan Pop! Inside the World of Japanese Popular Culture,* with a very similar scope of papers to Martinez's previous book. Since then, countless, more thematic volumes have been compiled and authored which has made the study of Japanese popular culture firmly part of research on Japan.

Most recently, Fabienne Darling-Wolf's (2018) edited volume, the *Routledge Handbook of Japanese Media*, collating twenty-six diverse papers under five different thematic groupings, provides a case-studies-based overview of some aspects of Japanese media, with the notable absence of cinema and popular novels. The *Handbook of East Asian Popular Culture*, edited by Koichi Iwabuchi, Eva Tsai and Chris Berry (2017) comprises papers provided by scholars from East Asia and Europe, looking specifically at transnational flows within the region. While since the advent of the 21st century, East Asian popular culture has indeed become more interconnected, making this collection a valuable addition to the field, to some extent it requires corresponding handbooks looking at national media to be fully contextualized.

Therefore, this handbook aims to close that gap, contextualizing Japanese media within itself, but also within a wider context, of East Asia and its global surroundings, looking at industry constraints as well as content.

What do we mean by Japanese media?

Media is a broad-brush term, often used synonymously with mass media, but in fact referring to any product, printed, filmed or broadcast, that "mediates" a message. In this handbook, we have deliberately opted for a wide definition of the term, using it to mean any product of the creative industries, whether it is a film, television program, magazine or popular novel in order to highlight the full breadth and depth of research on Japanese media.

The wide-ranging array of formats covered by this volume, which encompasses contemporary and classical cinema, television, anime, media mix, popular fiction, advertising, magazines, karaoke and digital media, not only reflects the diversity but also the intertextuality, fluidity and hybridity of media. Manga are adapted into anime (as well as live-action productions) for the small and large screen; novels, such as Kirino Natsuo's *Out* (discussed in Lyle De Souza's chapter in this volume) become the source material for television dramas and feature films; conversely, popular television shows are often novelized. Before even making it on to the screen, novels themselves evolve through a variety of formats, often starting out as a serialized column in a national newspaper, before being collected into hardback *tankōbon*, paperback *bunkobon* and digital editions. As De Souza observes in his chapter in this volume, technological advances have spawned new innovations such as the cell phone novel. Of course, the video games industry has provided the inspiration for some of the most successful media franchises, such as the behemoth that is *Pokémon*. As Rayna Denison observes in her chapter in this volume (112), the complex storyworlds in media mix can be visualized in synchronous adaptations that "burn bright" for a short period of time or diachronic franchises that span decades and multiple media. When fan production and foreign versions are taken into account, the limits of media become unfathomable.

The internet has further expanded the scope and breadth of material to be mined, with online content reworked for various media—see the *Densha otoko* (Train Man) franchise or, more recently, *Tōkyō joshi zukan* (A Tokyo girl's guidebook), which spawned SVOD series and spin-offs. Indeed, SVOD, AVOD and freemium services such as Amazon Prime, Netflix, YouTube, Hulu, TVer, ABEMA and Niconico, have expanded the volume and diversity of content available to Japanese consumers, as well as the ways in which this content is accessed. The number of SVOD paying subscribers reached 44.2 million in Japan in August 2021 (Media Partners Asia 2021), and this growth is set to continue with the recent agreement between BBC Studios and Japanese OTT provider U-NEXT and the expansion of Disney+ services (Veale 2020).

In turn, major streaming services are opening up Japanese content to international audiences with some success—see the popularity of reality show *Terrace House*, screened domestically on Fuji TV and internationally on Netflix. Fans of anime and *dorama* outside Japan will be highly familiar with services such as Crunchyroll, Rakuten Viki and the myriad other platforms for streaming content. Online platforms are also becoming dominant players in film distribution; for example, Japanese feature *37 Seconds* (discussed in Forum Mithani's chapter) received only a limited release internationally—mostly at film festivals—before appearing on Netflix in early 2020, around the same time it was released in cinemas in Japan. As well as buying the rights to screen existing anime, television dramas and films, Netflix and Amazon Prime and others are also producing original Japanese-language content.

Given that the production, distribution and consumption of media and popular culture happens within this complex ecosystem of cross-pollination, no single type of production can be fully understood when viewed in isolation. As Steinberg and Zahlten assert, media should not be understood as an umbrella term comprising individual formats or genres, but as an "emergent system with its own set of dynamics and semiautonomous rules" and thus our focus, as scholars and theoreticians of media, should be trained more on the context and environment in which media are created and operate than on their senders and receivers (Steinberg and Zahlten 2017, 12). In other words, the media is, contrary to how McLuhan put it, not always the message. While it is important to understand media outputs in the context of their production, it is the content that will be consumed—and as such not only provides insight into how Japanese media in its broadest sense function in the third decade of the 21st century, but at the same time also sheds light on societal discourses as shaped by the media.

As Coates and Ben-Ari argue in the introduction to their volume on the de/politicizing effects of Japanese visual media, media products fulfill multiple roles, "whether these be edifying and enriching, preaching and indoctrinating, or providing escapes from people's everyday lives" (2021, 1). They create "multi-sensory experiences," "evoke emotions and sentiments" and "echo, mimic, and reinforce" other forms of cultural production (Coates and Ben-Ari 2021, 1). Media texts offer a lens through which to analyze, interpret and better understand the socio-political history of a nation. Traversing the length of Japan's modern period, from Meiji-era magazine publishing, through postwar cinema to 21st century digital media, the chapters in the present volume touch on topics that include historicity, memory, politicization, disasters, authenticity, dramatization and adaptation, self/censorship, the "hero" figure, the "lost decades" and social disaffection, discourse analysis, gender, sexuality, class, intersectionality, masculinity, disability, localization, trans/nationalism, audiences and users.

Just as new iterations of media open up the potential for multiple narratives and worldviews, the same might be said for academic and social discourses on media. The political implications of media texts are not immutable (Coates and Ben-Ari 2021, 4); they may be subject to repeated reinterpretations that are influenced by (and thus revealing of) the particular socio-political context of a given time. With this in mind, the chapters in this handbook offer new research and perspectives on popular media phenomena, as well as shining a spotlight on texts that are less well known or studied. Drawing on methods and approaches from a range of disciplines, including screen and media studies, anthropology, sociology, history, area studies, audience studies, gender studies and disability studies, the chapters make explicit the interconnections between these areas of research and map out possible trajectories for future inquiry. As such, we envisage the handbook will be of value to both novice scholars and seasoned researchers, working within and/or beyond the Japanese media studies remit.

Structure of the handbook

The chapters in this volume are grouped into five key themes: Reimagining History; Transitions and Transcultural Flows; Franchises and Formats; Gender and Media; and Audiences and Users. While this method of organization better elucidates the intention of this handbook to emphasize the connections between media that transcend simplistic categorizations by genre or format, the thematic systemization chosen is not meant to be definitive or prescriptive. We recognize that interlinks exist between individual chapters in different sections. For example, the themes of displacement and repositioning within the transnational context of East Asia are present in both Julia Stolyar's contribution on Japanese remakes of Korean dramas and Xinyu Promio Wang's study of digital media usage among Chinese migrants. Similarly, Rayna Denison's discussion of early media mix practices overlaps with Hiroyuki Kitaura's re-evaluation of the symbiotic relationship that developed between the film and television industries.

Griseldis Kirsch opens the first section on reimagining Japan's history with her chapter on televisual discourses of Japanese imperialism, considering to what extent the media is shaped by political forces and how this influences its output. As Kirsch observes, politically-driven (from the highest echelons of governance) historical revisionism has colored the lens through which many Japanese learn about and perceive the nation's wartime history. Commemorations that emphasize Japan's status as the victim of two atomic bombs can obscure its role as aggressor and perpetrator of brutal atrocities against its colonial subjects. Kirsch demonstrates how television drama contributes to a "memory industry" that avoids controversial depictions of a complicated history some would rather forget. A pervasive medium that is subject to multiple external pressures from various commercially and politically powerful actors, television must tread a fine line in terms of the messaging it sends out. Kirsch makes sense of the entanglement of complex relationships upon which the structure of Japan's mass media industry is formed, focusing in particular on how political interventions might influence broadcast output and create a climate of self-censorship. Her comparison of dramas broadcast from 2005–2007 and 2015 demonstrates how changes in the way Japan's wartime past is depicted on the small screen reflect an increasingly restrictive atmosphere in terms of what can and cannot be said. Dramas from the earlier period showed more latitude in representing the violence of the imperial era. However, by 2015, as the right-wing LDP administration under Abe Shinzō was taking a firm stance against progressive media outlets, these had given way to images of harmony between Japan and its near neighbors. Such narratives not only feed into contemporary conservative/nationalist revisionist rhetoric, they also shape the ways in which Japanese remember, or imagine, their history.

Continuing this vein of research on dramatizations of historical events, Christopher P. Hood's study focuses on films and television dramas depicting the 1985 JAL air crash disaster. His detailed analysis of five productions reveals the extent to which the "truth" is or can be portrayed on screen, in light of the limitations imposed by the conventions of the disaster genre, as well as the practical and financial considerations of depicting large-scale catastrophes, and the sensitive nature of the subject matter, which involves the suffering of real-life people. Up to now, English-language scholarship on disaster narratives has largely been focused on anglophone productions—primarily Hollywood movies. Hood's examination of the hitherto underexplored Japanese disaster genre brings new insights to the fields of visual media studies and Japanese studies, revealing the shared conventions and local specificities of Japanese productions. Utilizing a framework of conventions established in his previous work, Hood offers detailed assessments of what is represented in each production and what is left out, and how these depictions relate to the known facts of the event. As he notes, even heavily fictionalized portrayals can influence the ways in which people perceive and remember events. Thus, dramatizations as a site of academic inquiry offer the potential to shed light on the processing of moments of historical importance, both on a societal and individual level. Crucially, his chapter provides a template for future research in an area that deserves greater attention.

Another catastrophic event that has provided inspiration for cultural production is the triple disaster of earthquake, tsunami and nuclear meltdown that afflicted the Tōhoku region in March 2011. Hilaria Gössmann's chapter reveals the ways in which television dramas and films have approached a calamity that had (and continues to have) wide-ranging repercussions and is surrounded by fear and controversy. With a specific focus on the most contentious element of the disaster—the meltdown at the Fukushima Daiichi Nuclear Power Plant and its aftermath—Gössmann analyzes the possibilities and limitations of film and television representations of the incident, the characters and attitudes that appear in these media and pays careful attention to the issues that are not addressed. As well as investigating narratives that directly reference nuclear accidents, her examination also considers indirect representations that touch on topics such as grief and "survivor guilt," which affected many in the aftermath of the disaster. Gössmann's study, which incorporates intertextual references to interviews with creatives working in film and television, literature and other media, as well as academic discourse on the topic, reveals the reluctance of the film and television industry to directly address the nuclear accident in dramatic depictions of the disaster. Her careful analysis finds that a few television dramas have made oblique references to the impact of the radiation leak that may be regarded as implicit criticism. Nevertheless, many of the narratives offer happy endings in which the characters overcome grief and adversity, reflecting the wishes of those involved in the productions to offer solace to victims and viewers alike. In relation to films made outside of the major studio system, Gössmann notes a greater willingness to offer a critical, anti-nuclear message. Rather than provide solace to the audience with an uncomplicated, optimistic ending, these films serve as a "dystopian warning" that, Gössmann observes, would have been impossible to air on television, signalling the greater critical potential of the film industry.

Part 2 of the volume, "Transitions and Transcultural Flows" brings together four authors that share an interest in moments of transformation and flux in Japan's socio-cultural history. Irene González-López uses Mary Louise Pratt's (1991) concept of "contact zones" to analyze the representation of the *panpan* in Taniguchi Senkichi's 1953 film *Red-Light Bases*. *Panpan* was a derogatory term used to refer to the female sex-workers that catered to foreign servicemen in Occupation-era Japan. Noting the role of the *panpan* as an "intermediary" between the occupying forces and the Japanese, González-López sees representations of the *panpan* as fertile ground for exploring the power asymmetries between the US and Japan through the lens of gender and sexuality. Building on existing scholarship, she convincingly argues for the film to be viewed as a "cross-temporal contact zone" that reveals the anxieties and experiences of occupation in a nation reckoning with itself in the aftermath of defeat. González-López's careful, intertextual analysis, situated within the socio-political context of the time, offers alternative readings of the film, shedding light on the contradictory perspectives of the *panpan* and the political implications of its handling of a controversial subject. Her detailed visual examination unpacks the use of various cinematic strategies employed in the film to expose the constructed notions of ideal womanhood, female sexuality and the fine line between the "respectable woman" and the "whore." González-López makes a convincing case for reading *Red-Light Bases* as an exposition of the interrelationship between imperialism, patriarchal ideology and the policing of women's bodies. At the same time, her probing reveals that, despite privileging the perspective of women, the film also ultimately validates militarized masculinity. She argues that in doing so, the film reflected the ambiguous position of post-Occupation Japan, offering multiple sites of identification for an audience contending with conflicting feelings and experiences at a time of uncertainty and upheaval. Its optimistic ending also offered a cathartic fantasy of a Japan leaving behind the Occupation and its traumatic past.

Marcos P. Centeno-Martin explores further sites of transcultural and transnational interaction in postwar Japanese cinema in his chapter on the youth star system. Focusing on Nikkatsu's pivot towards youth cinema and *mukokuseki eiga* (films without nationality) from the mid-1950s onwards, his intertextual examination reveals the complex strategies the studio employed to create a new genre influenced by Hollywood films. His chapter questions the concept of a "national cinema" and encourages a critical discourse analysis approach to film scholarship that takes into account multiple contexts and is not restricted by national or textual boundaries. Centeno-Martin reveals that this new, niche cinema targeted at a young audience was driven by demographic changes and followed a precedent set by American studios. He follows the journey of this film genre from its earliest iterations, the *taiyōzoku* (sun-tribe) films, as Nikkatsu pursued a strategy that capitalized on Japanese youth's fascination with the West. Through this new genre of action films, the studio made stars of young actors, including Ishihara Yūjirō, Kobayashi Akira, Akagi Keiichirō and Wada Kōji, who epitomized a new postwar masculinity that blended Japanese and foreign elements of speech, dress, demeanor and values. Centeno-Martin points to the Japanese Western as a genre that was particularly influenced by its US counterpart, exemplifying the ways in which narrative styles and codes of visual representation can transcend not only national borders but also boundaries of cultural and historical contexts. He notes the recycling and reappropriation of cinematic tropes (thus the "lonely wanderer" becomes the "wandering *rōnin*") and demonstrates the process of localization that occurs when these stories migrate from one context to another. He demonstrates how the analysis of such films offer the potential to reveal contemporaneous structures of power and ideological expressions. In the case of youth cinema and the Japanese Western, Centeno-Martin argues that these genres reimagined a new, postwar Japan with stronger political, economic and cultural ties to the US. This symbiosis also extended to the transmedia practices of Japanese stars, which included collaborations with the music industry and appearances on television and radio, a practice that has not only continued but intensified to this day. Furthermore, Centeno-Martin suggests that echoes of the transcultural personas of the youth stars of the postwar era can be found in the popularity of entertainers from multi-cultural and multi-ethnic backgrounds today.

Hiroyuki Kitaura unravels the relationship between the two dominant forms of visual media during the twentieth century, cinema and television. Focusing on the business strategies and technologies employed, he reveals how these competing Japanese industries have managed to coexist through a complex process of negotiation. Cinema audiences reached a record high in 1958, with the six major film companies producing large volumes of output to meet public demand. Yet, within little over a decade, audience numbers had fallen to a quarter of the peak and a number of companies had folded or withdrawn from mainstream film production. Meanwhile, just as cinema was beginning its precipitous decline, the emerging medium of television, boosted by the coverage of events of national importance, was moving rapidly in the opposite direction. Kitaura reveals that the film industry response to this new threat was to bring in a number of countermeasures to distinguish the cinema screen from its rival, including the adoption of color film and the introduction of the widescreen format, as well as preventing broadcasters from using the major studios' talent and content. However, they were unable to stem the growth of the rival medium and soon changed their approach to one of integration. Kitaura's chapter uncovers the mutual benefits each industry enjoyed from their close cooperation, which expanded opportunities for both mediums and established the basis for the current production committee system, which has become almost universal as a means of financing films, spreading both the risk and the rewards. As Kitaura argues, the close partnership between film and television that we see today has evolved through a process of conflict and negotiation. He suggests that in the age in which the internet has emerged as the dominant platform to access visual media, a new path of coexistence may need to be found.

Julia Stolyar brings this section on transitions and transcultural flows up to the present day with her chapter on South Korean-Japanese transnational adaptations. As Stolyar notes, during the late twentieth century, pop cultural exchanges between the two countries eventually overcame the lingering bitterness over their former colonial ties, first surging one way, then, with the advent of the Korean wave, reversing course. Whereas some scholars have situated this development within the context of creating a shared regional identity based on mutual understanding, Stolyar questions this assessment, arguing that the very existence of local remakes appears to challenge such notions. Through Stolyar's examination of the remaking of South Korean television drama *Mawang* (*Maō/The Devil*), we learn that, despite overlap in terms of themes and issues that interest and concern audiences in both countries, the process of adapting a drama for a local audience requires significant alterations that not only fit broadcasting conventions, but can also have implications for the narrative structure and the meanings made by the viewer. The process of relocating the story of *Mawang* to Japan presents, as Stolyar argues, a "complex picture of negotiation of ideas, styles and messages," and in doing so, exposes differences in the levels of trust in the justice system, notions of good/evil and attitudes towards revenge in South Korea and Japan. As such, it pushes back against simplistic conceptions of a "pan-Asian identity." Now that Korean pop culture is making waves on a global scale—see the rise of K-pop icons BTS and the Netflix megahit *Squid Game*—such nuanced readings of non-Anglophone cultural phenomena are needed more than ever.

Separately and together, the three contributions in the third part of this volume, "Franchises and Formats," reveal the ways in which different forms of media are never isolated from each other or their social, cultural, political or economic contexts. Rayna Denison's chapter offers a concise yet thorough overview of the complex, multifarious and diffuse concept of media mix, referencing key literature on the topic, including the work of Marc Steinberg, Henry Jenkins, Mizuki Ito, Anne Allison, Matthew Ogonoski, Bryan Hikari Hartzheim, Ōtsuka Eiji, Azuma Hiroki, Alexander Zahlten, Thomas Lamarre, Jonathan Clements, as well as her own extensive research in this area. As she succinctly describes, media mix encompasses a wide range of movements and practices, across and between texts, boundaries (geographic and otherwise), cultures and languages, infiltrating every part of the media landscape and, arguably, society. Her discussion takes in a number of theories that assist us in understanding the industrial, social and cultural processes responsible for the formation, evolution, participation in and consumption of media mix, including theories of media convergence; product portals; narrative consumption and subcultural databases. As a phenomenon that is constantly evolving to embrace new technologies, creative innovations and changing trends in participation and consumption, the journey of media mix has been accompanied by developments in the way it is (re)conceptualized, theorized and discussed. Denison's detailed evaluation of the academic discourse notes the subtle differences as well as the more significant departures in theoretical and discursive approaches. The second half of the chapter provides some historical context to the development of media mix as a practice as well as concept in Japan, tracing its roots in the cross-media practices of postwar marketing companies, through the media-mix strategies of Kadokawa Publishing, to the role of the *keiretsu* system and other industrial practices of integration and conglomeration, including the production committee system, in facilitating the proliferation of transmedia production. She also notes the pivotal role of the television and gaming industries in the production and consumption of media in Japan and beyond, as well as the shift in focus from discrete media to platforms as hubs for delivering multiple forms of media. As Denison concludes, it is this flexibility and transmutability that forms the crux of what makes and enables media mix to flourish.

Continuing with the theme of manga and anime, Artur Lozano-Méndez and Antonio Loriguillo-López identify a new archetypal protagonist in the genre, the nihilistamina hero/heroine (NH), so-called because of their incessant levels of nihilism and stamina. These characters differ from regular protagonists of the *shōnen* genre in their inability to recover from past trauma, which continues to affect their outlook and sense of self. Nevertheless, these gloomy characters are tasked with performing equally fantastical feats of heroism. As Lozano-Méndez and Loriguillo-López observe, the pessimism and fatalism they exhibit has done little to dampen readers/viewers' enthusiasm, with renowned NH-led titles such as *Neon Genesis Evangelion* and *Attack on Titan* amassing global fandoms. Lozano-Méndez and Loriguillo-López make the case for considering nihilistamina stories (NS) a genre of its own, with distinctive and consistent patterns of narrative modality, characterization and a dark psychological complexity. Their chapter sets out a descriptive framework for the genre, examining the key factors that distinguish the category, including trauma, despondency, sacrifice and bleak endings. They propose a possible explanation for its rise in popularity in a post-capitalist, post-disaster Japan and beyond, linking the phenomenon to increasing levels of anxiety caused by socio-economic instability, which, although exacerbated by the 2008 financial crisis, can be traced even further back to the liberalization of the labor market in the 1990s. As the authors note, it is in the context of the era of precariousness and precariatization that we fully comprehend "the emergence of cynical and (literally) selfless heroes." The NS genre may offer a cathartic outlet for the lost generations, but they note, somewhat ominously, it also prepares an already victimized audience for further trauma and sacrifice. While the NH's unrelenting perseverance against all odds might echo traditional heroes of Japanese history, Lozano-Méndez and Loriguillo-López recognize that such archetypes are not limited to the Japanese context, which may explain the genre's transnational success. As the world contends with multiple challenges with significant economic and socio-political implications, including the COVID-19 pandemic, climate change and the rise of populism and extremist political movements, the NS genre will no doubt continue to grow and evolve to capture and offer relief from the anxieties of the current generation.

Another genre that is reflective of changing circumstances, hopes and anxieties in Japan is the television drama. Elisabeth Scherer's chapter reveals that even a veritable institution such as the *renzoku terebi shōsetsu* (serial televised novel), which is commonly referred to as the *asadora* and has been broadcast on NHK for 60 years, has made adaptations in an attempt to stay relevant to a contemporary, social media-connected audience. Scherer begins by giving us an overview of the format, explaining how its scheduling, female-centered narratives, function as an institution of a collective Japanese memory and role in connecting the local to the national, all contribute to its status as an important fixture in the modern cultural landscape and a vehicle for nation branding. She explains how the series embedded itself within the daily routine and social consciousness of Japan in its heyday, achieving record ratings in the 1980s and producing active fans who discussed the series, emulated the eating habits of the characters and created content and artworks. As Scherer observes, such interactive practices continue today through social media, which has served to further connect the audience in an online community and has become an important tool in the promotion and measurement of the genre's success. Scherer elucidates the *asadora*'s role in (re)producing a national discourse by presenting the country as a harmonious collection of regions, each with its own dialect, specialities, customs and heritage, which nevertheless coalesce to form the "real Japan." She points out that while such idealization of rural Japan belies reality, it has brought significant economic benefits to local communities and increased the visibility of their cultures, which has been particularly important to the areas affected by the triple disaster. However, Scherer argues, while the *asadora* is keen to promote regional diversity, other forms of diversity only receive a superficial treatment, and are often used to further emphasize the national discourse of Japanese unity and uniqueness. Her study, which updates research on the *asadora* to the COVID-19 pandemic era, reemphasizes the importance of the genre as an agent of unity, a producer of collective memory and a site for clarifying the concerns of contemporary Japanese.

Media and popular culture are highly gendered spaces in Japan. As the four papers in the section dedicated to "Gender and Media" demonstrate, they offer multiple sites for (re)producing, (re)articulating and (re)negotiating iterations of femininity and masculinity. One of these sites, as Lyle De Souza recognizes, is the popular fiction novel. Popular fiction writing (*taishū bungaku*) is often considered not serious enough to merit the academic inquiry bestowed upon its literary sibling, *jun bungaku* (lit. pure literature). Yet, the lines between literary and popular fiction have become increasingly ambiguous, as the global acclaim and fandoms of authors such as Murakami Haruki attest. Nevertheless, De Souza takes on the challenge of defining and delineating the category of popular fiction. The first part of his chapter gives an overview of the popular fiction market in Japan, discussing the key genres that make up this category, its formats and offering a brief socio-history, which reveals that, much like the developments in other media forms discussed in this volume, trends in popular fiction have often been driven by technological innovations. The second part of De Souza's chapter focuses on one particular novel, celebrated crime writer Kirino Natsuo's *Out* (1997), that encapsulates many of the key social concerns and public discourses of post-bubble Japan. Utilizing a framework of dualisms, male/female; passivity/violence; freedom/constraint, he analyzes the dynamics of gender, class and ethnicity within the novel, demonstrating the ways in which Kirino's marginalized characters challenge or succumb to hierarchies of power against a backdrop of significant socio-economic change. As De Souza's examination reveals, *Out* not only depicts the ways in which women, ethnic minorities and those in the lower socio-economic stratum are oppressed by these hierarchies, but more importantly, how these circumstances can force them to seek escape. By inverting certain dualisms, hierarchies and dynamics, De Souza argues that Kirino forces the reader to reexamine their own preconceived notions. As he notes, the upending of gender conventions also relates to the world of Japanese literature, where women have recently dominated prestigious awards. The visibility of Japanese women authors has also increased in the international context, with writers such as Kawakami Mieko and Murata Sayaka finding global readerships through translation. Their narratives touch on class, unconventional women, the female body and sex, and have a particular resonance with female readers, demonstrating that the demand (and, thus, the need) for female voices that challenge conventional norms is as robust as ever.

Forum Mithani continues the theme of intersectional feminist inquiry, introducing the category of disability to her examination of contemporary Japanese visual media. Adopting an approach utilized by Rosemary Garland-Thomson and others, Mithani argues that analyzing representations of disability through a feminist lens opens up the potential for revealing new insights and interpretations. In turn, incorporating theories and methods from disability studies into research on gender adds an additional layer of complexity, allowing for more nuanced and inclusive readings that recognize the diverse experiences of women. This is particularly relevant to the Japanese context, where women have conventionally been viewed as a homogenous group, both inside and outside academia. To demonstrate the synergies between feminist studies and disability studies, Mithani applies the theory of the gaze (from feminist film studies) and the concept of "staring" (disability studies) to her examination of the television drama *Perfect World,* showing how it works to reproduce and reinforce both ableist and patriarchal perspectives of disability, gender and male/female relations. However, her analysis of two films featuring disabled protagonists, *Perfect Revolution* and *37 Seconds,* reveals an alternative viewpoint that challenges normative discourses of disabled people as passive, innocent and asexual. Mithani argues that the involvement of disabled creators and actors in the production of these films allows for realistic portrayals that act as a counterpoint to the "inspiration porn" that dominates media representations of disability. Her examination of *Perfect Revolution* reveals the film's critical stance towards the exploitation and objectification of disabled people, while her analysis of *37 Seconds* demonstrates the ways in which representations of disabled women can expose the limitations and expectations placed on all women. Viewed together, both films also reveal that the experiences of disabled people in Japan are by no means uniform, impacted as they are by factors including, but not limited to, gender and visibility.

As James White demonstrates, visual media depictions can have a long-lasting influence on conceptions and articulations of gender. His chapter reveals the impression left by one depiction—Sapporo Beer's 1970 advertising campaign, *"Otoko wa damatte…,"* starring Mifune Toshirō—that continues to resonate in 21st-century Japan as an image of idealized hypermasculinity. He offers a critical discourse analysis of the campaign, including a detailed reading of the gendered images it produced and the layers of context that fed into its construction of masculinity, not least the persona of its star, Mifune. In a departure from previous analyses of gender representation in advertising, White contextualizes his readings with broader discourses from the industry and the public realm to offer a more nuanced examination that recognizes multiple perspectives. His analysis of the ways in which the *"Otoka wa damatte…"* slogan has continually been appropriated, referenced and reused since the original campaign, in a variety of contexts, demonstrates the ongoing relevance of interrogating this type of historical cultural messaging. The chapter highlights the significant role beer, both its consumption and its advertising, played in challenging as well as reaffirming normative models of masculinity and femininity in postwar Japan. White observes that the hypermasculinity projected by the Sapporo Beer and similar campaigns of the time stood in contraposition to the embodiment of masculinity considered to be the dominant (and thus often referred to as hegemonic) model of the time, the salaryman. White argues that linking beer with this image allowed the salaryman to vicariously experience the freedom Mifune embodied through the consumption of beer while preserving the integrity of the salaryman model. His reading also connects the reference to silence in the slogan with militaristic and imperialistic models of masculinity, an association that was not unnoticed at the time. The inclusion of a diachronic discourse analysis of commentary on the campaign is significant not only for what it reveals about contemporaneous social concerns, but also for demonstrating what the evolution of the discourse, including the privileging of certain messages over others, tells us about how a society sees itself and what it wishes to remember or forget.

In the final chapter of this section, Ronald Saladin discusses an alternative discourse of masculinity reproduced in contemporary men's lifestyle magazines. While there is a considerable body of scholarship on Japanese women's magazines, men's magazines remain relatively under-researched, emphasizing the importance of Saladin's study. As he observes, print magazine culture in Japan is highly segmented, catering to a diverse range of readerships, and its enduring appeal is indicative of its reach and influence within Japanese society. The first part of Saladin's chapter offers a historical overview of the development of the modern magazine (*zasshi*) in Japan. One particularly significant development was the genderization of the market, with magazines specifically (and explicitly) targeted at a female readership emerging during this period. As Saladin observes, the subsequent appearance of lifestyle magazines specifically catering to a male readership during the latter half of the 20th century only underlined the degree to which Japanese society itself was gendered. Thus, argues Saladin, magazines offer a unique perspective on the way codes of gender are reproduced, reinforced or renegotiated. A case in point is the development of the men's lifestyle genre, which boomed during the 1990s, at a time when notions of gender and masculinity were being questioned and reconceptualized. Saladin's case study on one title of this era, *BiDaN*, illustrates the changing perceptions regarding manliness, which was no longer limited to the image of the rugged, hypermasculine beer drinker White discusses in his chapter. This new masculinity embraced what was previously considered only of interest to women: fashion and beauty. Nevertheless, Saladin finds, this focus on outward appearance is constructed through a heteronormative lens, reaffirming to some extent the hegemonic masculine ideal. Thus, Saladin sees this apparent "feminization" of men not as an undermining of masculinity, but rather as the emergence of a hybrid masculinity that has expanded to accommodate shifts in attitudes without endangering the existing gender order. As we learn from his chapter, men's lifestyle magazines play a key role in reflecting, shaping, reproducing and reaffirming these social dynamics.

Audiences and users are, of course, crucial to the media ecosystem, not only as the ultimate financiers but also for their active participation in the processes of reception, production and reiteration. As Jennifer Coates observes in the opening chapter to this final section of the collection, academic interest in media usage and its impact on consumers is once again burgeoning. Coates begins by discussing the value of studying audiences of media as a way of uncovering narratives of consumption, diverse audience behaviors and what these tell us about a particular moment in history. In particular, she notes the usefulness of audience studies when evaluating the extent to which censorship and other strategic media-shaping policies are successful. Coates then provides a historical analysis of the development of the field in relation to Japanese screen studies, from its roots in the cinema audience surveys carried out in the early 20th century, through the wartime and Occupation-era surveys carried out for commercial as well as academic purposes, to the late 20th century shift towards studying home viewership and an eventual resurgence of reception studies focusing on postwar cinema audiences, where Coates locates her own area of research. Crucially, she supplements her theoretical and historical overview of the field with findings from her ethnographic study into the memories of Kansai-based cinema goers. The chapter outlines her methodological and analytical approaches, which are drawn from memory studies as well as audience research. Informed by questionnaires, written and electronic communications and interviews with cinema viewers and those connected to the industry, the case study reveals new insights into the memories of cinema-going practices in Occupation-era Japan, including the gender and age profiles of audiences, and how this might have challenged the censorship practices of the time. In doing so, Coates demonstrates the potential for such research to reverberate beyond audience studies, bringing new perspectives to fields such as history, anthropology and gender studies.

Laurence Green continues the theme of probing audience behavior and what this can reveal about wider cultural and social practices in his chapter on karaoke in Japan. Through a discourse analysis of existing scholarship, Green proposes a new approach that views karaoke as a "lubricant or service, enabling an interconnected web of social systems to thrive by virtue of a body of knowledge" and focuses on the value participants gain through their interaction with these systems of practice. His examination takes in the works of a number of scholars that have investigated karaoke engagement both in Japan and further afield, including William H. Kelly, Zhou Xun and Francesca Tarocco, Kevin Brown and Rob Drew. His analysis distills the essential components for a comprehensive understanding of the karaoke "system" in Japan, not only through summarizing key arguments but also by critically engaging with the scholarship. For example, while he concurs with Drew that karaoke offers a space for performing, testing and validating "personal and social identities," Green departs from the view of karaoke as a "short-lived fantasy" to emulate one's idol, seeing it instead as a conduit through which individual performers transpose from the local to the national stage. In other words, by engaging in karaoke in their masses, these individuals become part of the national music scene themselves, an argument that gains more traction when one considers how karaoke bolstered the music industry and shaped its output by creating a demand for songs an ordinary person could sing. Green's suggestion that karaoke "thrives in a nested layering" of manifestations of the self that co-exist both within oneself and the wider social context also offers a new perspective on discussions of authenticity and simulation. Finally, acknowledging that advances in technology have rendered previous attempts to define the nature and scope of the karaoke sphere, Green proposes a "Karaoke 2.0" that would move the conversation beyond discussions focused on the mechanisms of delivery, to the user experience, to how karaoke "seamlessly integrates itself into a person's life, how it might systematically (and continuously) deliver value and drive consumer habits."

Concluding this section, and the volume, on user experiences and behaviors, Xinyu Promio Wang investigates digital media usage among migrants to Japan. As Wang notes, the migrant community in Japan is highly complex and diverse, both in its multitudinous aggregate, citizenship-based forms and on the level of individual, personal experiences, predispositions and motivations. Digital media offers a fruitful site for investigating this complexity and diversity because it not only facilitates a transnational network that connects migrants to their homelands and each other, it also mediates their diasporic experiences and self-identifications. This is particularly the case for Chinese expatriates in Japan who, Wang observes, report significantly higher levels of digital media usage than local citizens or US/UK migrants. Drawing on previous scholarship, Wang argues that studying digital media usage through a transnational lens shifts the focus from an "essentialist notion of homeland, nation, locality, race and ethnicity to a focus on transnationality, imagination, hybridity and heterogeneity that takes shape and is activated through diasporic mobility and connectivity." The findings from Wang's ethnographic study of Chinese migrants exemplifies the benefits of this approach, not only confirming the crucial role technology plays in facilitating their day-to-day lives, but also revealing how these media influence the construction and positioning of their identities vis-à-vis the homeland and the host society. As Wang's research uncovers, access to a diverse range of digital media allows Chinese migrants to question existing narratives and ideologies and renegotiate their identification within Sino-Japanese socio-political dynamics. Furthermore, it lends additional weight to Wang's proposal to move away from definitive understandings of Chinese transnationalism as uniformly exclusionary in ethnic terms to one that recognizes its heterogeneity, acknowledging the importance of context as well as notions of racial community.

The thematic structure of this handbook visualizes these connections and intersections of the media and aims to convey the richness of the field that research on Japanese media has become. It has progressed beyond the observation of "passing fads and fancies" and is now firmly in the territory of theoretically grounded and methodologically sound research.

Bibliography

Amazon, n.d. *Handbook of Japanese Popular Culture.* [online] Available at https://www.amazon.co.uk/Handbook-Japanese-Popular-Culture-Richard/dp/0313239223/ [Accessed 5 November 2021].

Chua, B.-H. and Iwabuchi, K., eds., 2008. *East Asian Pop Culture: Analysing the Korean Wave.* Hong Kong: Hong Kong University Press.

Chun, J. M., 2006. *"A Nation of a Hundred Million Idiots"? A Social History of Japanese Television, 1953–1973.* London: Routledge.

Coates, J. and Ben-Ari, E., 2021. Introduction. In *Japanese Visual Media: Politicizing the Screen.* London: Routledge, 1–12. https://doi.org/10.4324/9781003154259.

Craig, T. J., ed., 2000. *Japan Pop! Inside the World of Japanese Popular Culture.* Armonk, NY: M. E. Sharpe.

Darling-Wolf, F., ed., 2018. *Routledge Handbook of Japanese Media.* Abingdon: Routledge.

Feldman, O., 1993. *Politics and the News Media in Japan.* Ann Arbor: University of Michigan Press.

Freeman, L. A., 2000. *Closing the Shop: Information Cartels and Japanese Mass Media.* Princeton: Princeton University Press.

Hayashi, K., *"Fuyu no sonata" ni hamatta watashitachi. Jun'ai, namida, masukomi… soshite Kankoku* [We fell for Winter Sonata: Pure love, tears mass media and… South Korea]. Tokyo: Bungei Shunjū.

Iwabuchi, K., 2001. *Toransunashonaru Japan. Ajia o tsunagu popyurā bunka* [Transnational Japan: Popular culture uniting Asia]. Tokyo: Iwanami Shoten.

———., 2002. *Recentering Globalization: Popular Culture and Japanese Transnationalism.* Durham: Duke University Press.

Iwabuchi, K., Tsai, E. and Berry, C., eds., 2017. *Routledge Handbook of East Asian Popular Culture.* London: Routledge.

Iwao, S., 2000. *Terebi dorama no messēji: Shakaishinrigakuteki bunseki* [The messages of television drama: A socio-psychological analysis]. Tokyo: Keisō Shobō.

Kingston, J., ed., 2017. *Press Freedom in Contemporary Japan.* London: Routledge.

Krauss, E., 2000. *Broadcasting Politics in Japan: NHK and Television News.* Ithaca: Cornell University Press.

Martinez, D. P., ed., 1998. *The Worlds of Japanese Popular Culture: Gender, Shifting Boundaries and Global Cultures.* Cambridge: Cambridge University Press.

Media Partners Asia, 2021. *Japan Online Video: Consumer Insights & Analytics*. [online] Available at: https://www.media-partners-asia.com/AMPD/Japan2021/PreviewContent.pdf [Accessed 21 October 2021].

Mōri, Y., ed., 2004. *Nisshiki Kanryū: "Fuyu no sonata" to Nikkan taishū bunka no gendai* [Korean Wave Japanese style: "Winter Sonata" and the present situation of Japanese-Korean popular culture]. Tokyo: Serika Shobō.

Muramatsu, Y., 1979. *Terebi dorama no joseigaku* [Feminism and television drama] Tokyo: Sōtakusha.

Muramatsu, Y. and Gössmann, H., eds., 1998. *Media ga tsukuru jendā: Nichidoku no danjo kazokuzō o yomitoku* [Gender as constructed in the media: The image of men, women and family in Japan and Germany]. Tokyo: Shinyōsha.

Powers, R. G., Kato, H. and Stronach, B., 1989. *Handbook of Japanese Popular Culture*. New York: Greenwood.

Steinberg, M. and Zahlten, A., 2017. Introduction. In M. Steinberg and A. Zahlten, eds., *Media Theory in Japan*. Durham: Duke University Press, 1–29. https://doi.org/10.1515/9780822373292.

Treat, J. W., ed., 1995. *Contemporary Japan and Popular Culture*. Richmond: Curzon.

Veale, T., 2020. *BBC Studios Targets Opportunities in the Evolving Japanese Video Market*. [online] Futuresource Consulting. Available at: https://www.futuresource-consulting.com/insights/bbc-studios-targets-opportunities-in-the-evolving-japanese-video-market/?locale=en [Accessed 21 October 2021].

Part 1
Reimagining History

Chapter 1
Imagining Alternative Pasts: Imperial Nostalgia on Japanese Television

Griseldis Kirsch

Japanese victimhood tends to be at the center of commemoration of the Asia-Pacific War on Japanese television, with Japanese imperialism across East Asia being only occasionally represented. During the administration of Prime Minister Abe Shinzō (a known historical revisionist and prominent proponent of tighter media control), several changes in the narrative around Japanese imperialism could be observed on the small screen. Comparing several Japanese television dramas from the mid-2000s (when Abe was not in power) to 2015 (with him firmly in office), this paper will examine how representations of Japanese imperialism changed within that decade.

Introduction: Can television change the past?

The broadcasting of history is a lucrative business. For better or for worse, history and television are almost insolubly tied together. Particularly in countries with a public broadcasting system, and/or educational aims written into the broadcasting laws, television will aim to take the broadcasting of history "seriously." Gary Edgerton (2001, 1, italics in original) asserts that *"television is the principal means by which most people learn about history today."* Nonetheless, whether drama or documentary, television programs tend to put the "story" in history, focusing on narratives, satisfying our thirst for a coherent tale with heroes and villains and a clearly defined plotline. Even documentaries try to woo audiences by telling a gripping tale, to keep the audiences hooked in front of the screen and to remain discernible in the "flow" of televisual images. Because of the narrative structure that most television formats follow, more often than not the lines between fact and fiction can blur and genres converge. Nonetheless, the often-clichéd liveness of television, the sense of being there when "things" happen(ed) allows us to escape to the past, in the same way as Buonanno (2008, 70) establishes for "imaginary tourism;" but in this case, we can time-travel without leaving the security of our homes and the time we live in. Often enough, however, television is not taken as a serious competitor in the selling of history (Anderson 2001, 24), particularly if one looks at fiction, in spite of its pervasiveness and the point that Edgerton makes. And, as

Holdsworth (2008, 139) also argues, DVD sales, online archives and online content providers make the past even more easily available to us.

The narration of televised history is very much a contribution to the imagination of a nation in Benedict Anderson's (1991) sense—it helps to shape a common historical consciousness, a past that we, in the present, can live through together. It has long been established that a common memory, or collective memory, helps to maintain a consciousness of a group (Connerton 1989; Halbwachs 1992; Ricoeur 2009), particularly through common commemorative ceremonies, memorials or, indeed, the media. The media can help keep established narratives alive, but these narratives will always be selective, just as memory is always selective. In that sense, historical dramas and documentaries are but two sides of the same coin, as they will often document—or fictionalize—the same events, contributing to the collective memory of the event. And while this common, and very present, experience of the past might perhaps educate us, it can equally gloss over aspects of the past that would not sell well. The past, after all, needs to be one that we recognise and to which we can relate.

While the above considerations are truisms valid across most of the democratic broadcasting industries in Europe or North America, slightly different tropes apply if we look at East Asia, in particular Japan. With respect to Japan's past as imperial power in the region, the past is not just a selling point, but also a bone of contention, and whatever approach to "unifying the nation" may appear on television, Japan's neighbors will scrutinise it. Although Huyssen (2001, 63) proposes that "the political site of memory practices is still national, not postnational or global," in the day and age of global interconnectedness, collective memory does not stop at borders. If Japan does not "remember correctly" in the eyes of its neighbors, even in television drama, it can easily spark outrage. However, Japan has a tightly regulated broadcasting system, one in which the production of content (fictional or non-fictional) has to follow strict rules and regulations. Japan, too, had its "memory boom" (Seaton 2007), television (and film) bringing us versions of a past, but it takes different shapes than in Europe, and fictional, not factual, formats have taken center stage throughout. *Jidaigeki* (period dramas), for example, started off in cinema and are films or dramas mostly set in a samurai past. When Japanese cinema declined (like its counterparts all over the world), *jidaigeki* moved from the big screens to the small and have been a staple of the broadcasting landscape since the 1960s. The public broadcasting station NHK in particular has high stakes in the market, their *taiga dorama*[1] are highly promoted "media events" (Buonanno 2008; Dayan and Katz 1994) that run over the course of one year. But they will mostly represent a past that is, in Nietzsche's (2009) terms, usable, a past without contest. In other words, a past that does not involve Japan's neighbors or its imperialist desires to a great extent.

Furthermore, Japan has more or less been governed by the same political party since 1955, and not only are the media restricted by broadcasting guidelines (Yamada 2017), media and politics also are in a cosy relationship with one another. While this has always been the case, things changed decisively from 2012 onwards, during Prime Minister Abe Shinzō's second term in office (Fackler 2016).[2] The government has furthermore embarked on a course to "revise" some of the more contentious parts of Japan's past, turning the narrative from conqueror of East Asia to liberator from other imperial powers and benevolent colonial master. Television, as the most ubiquitous and visible medium in Japan is therefore sandwiched between a government intent on revising the past and a restrictive broadcasting system enforced by the same government. While it may thus seem safer not to mention the more contentious bits of Japanese history at all, they do appear on television, albeit to

Handbook of Japanese Media and Popular Culture in Transition

a much smaller extent. As fiction is so important in that respect in Japan, television drama and its focus on stars and the potential for identification that they offer can lure people into an engagement with the past in a way that documentary cannot. They can equally create and uphold narratives (Thornham and Purvis 2005), including those that may perhaps be problematic if discussed in a non-fictional context, as there is controversy over "the facts." As Buonanno (2008, 77, italics in original) points out, "[…] we need to take stories seriously. One reason for doing so is that they provide a stage for social reality and organize and display the dramaturgy through which *society represents itself to itself.*"

Invariably, though, the question of "historical accuracy" pops up, particularly when talking about fiction. But those questions may be for historians to answer (Rosenstone 2018). To some extent that has already happened, as a lot has been written about the significance of collective memory and the media, also in the context of Japan. Most often, the focus is either on the text or on its relationship to actual historical events. Few of these studies, however, have taken into account the constraints set by the industry that produces the texts, the political and legal framework that dictates how content can be produced. Using Japan and its memory of its own imperial past as example, this paper aims to close that gap, by showing that a text exists not just within the context of its society, but also within the context of its creative industries. To do this, I will answer the question: to what extent are the creative industries shaped by political forces, and how does this in turn influence the production of content? Before looking at the Japanese television industry, however, it is necessary to look briefly at the historical background to elucidate why broadcasting "the war" could be problematic in Japan and the wider East Asian context.

Japanese imperialism and the memory of "the war"

For a little less than two-hundred and fifty years, Japan was a comparatively secluded country, trading only with very few other countries. Therefore, it was able to withdraw itself mostly from the world stage. When the maelstrom of global imperialism eventually caught hold of Japan, the nation embarked on a modernization process to catch up with the dominant powers of the day, and thus avoid its own colonization. The key concept, phrased by the most influential political thinker of the time, Fukuzawa Yūkichi, was *datsu-a nyū-ō* (leaving Asia, entering the West); it pointedly explains the aim of Japan to become one of the major powers itself while attempting to leave the supposedly less-developed Asian countries behind.

Japan thus entered the stage as imperial power only relatively late when the world had already been largely carved up. Its eyes, however, were not set on faraway shores, but on its immediate neighbors. Japan considered itself to be "in, but above Asia" (Iwabuchi 2002, 8), superior to the rest of Asia that had not been as successful in avoiding colonization. Japan's first target was China, in the first Sino-Japanese war of 1894–95 which resulted in Taiwan becoming a Japanese colony. Korea was next and became a Japanese colony in 1910. In 1931, Japan established a puppet government in Manchuria (in North-East China) under the leadership of the ousted Chinese emperor Pu-Yi. While the Japanese colonial regime was far from benign—for example, colonial citizens in Taiwan and Korea were forced to take Japanese names and the usage of their native languages became limited—the Japanese government furthermore encouraged its own poorer population to leave the Japanese homeland and settle on the Asian continent (Tamanoi 2008; Young 1998), ensuring a Japanese presence on all levels. The settlement and incorporation of Manchuria into the Japanese Empire was also not without violence, even though it was nominally independent. The incidents in Manchuria led directly to the invasion of China in 1937, another one of Japan's imperialistic targets. While this war tends to be looked at through the lens of the Nanjing Massacre, the events in the then-capital of China during the Japanese invasion in 1937 are but one brutal aspect of a war that was to last eight years and only came to an end when Japan surrendered to the US in 1945. However, not all aspects of that war are equally remembered in Japan. The comfort women (women, mainly, but not solely, from Korea, forced to work as sex slaves for the Japanese Army) and Unit 731 (an army unit testing chemical and biological weapons on Chinese civilians), are aspects of that war that have largely "slipped the mind" of Japanese commemoration in favor of the fight against the US (Buruma 1995).

The USA only entered the fray in 1941 after Japan's attack on Pearl Harbor and only then did the various conflicts across the world become one war fought with various actors on various fronts. For Japan, the USA became the most prominent opponent at that time. The fire-bombing of various major Japanese cities by the US Air Force as well as the two nuclear bombs dropped on Hiroshima and Nagasaki did, arguably, lead to a culture of commemoration focusing on those events, marking Japan as victim rather than perpetrator of the war (Buruma 1995).

This focus on being a victim of the war has led to criticism from other Asian countries that had been at the receiving end of Japanese imperialism, since the fact that Japan colonized East Asia is often left out of such narratives. Textbooks that downplay Japanese actions on the Asian mainland have also led to controversy within East Asia, and the war in Asia and the Pacific in all its complexities is not necessarily taught widely at school, because of Japan's role in starting it. Even more than seventy years after the end of the war, there is still little consensus around the past; in other words, it is not easily usable. In his book on Japanese war memory and media, Philip Seaton (2007, 21–24) establishes that there are five viewpoints from which the war can be seen: progressive and progressive leaning, both accepting that Japan started an unjustifiable war and differing only in that the progressives reject victimhood for the Japanese while progressive-leaning people accept it; conservative, which sees the war as having been justified and Japan becoming its ultimate victim; and nationalist, in which the war was not only justified, but also fought in the right way. The fifth category comprises people who have no interest in, or knowledge of, the topic. That way, it becomes clear that what arouses the least controversy is Japan as victim of the war and this is where the focus is often set in the media.

Yet not even that is easy. As briefly mentioned above, Japan has been governed by the same conservative-nationalist party, the LDP, for most of its postwar history. Many politicians are involved in groups that favor a re-evaluation of Japan's role in the war, ultimately aiming to silence the progressive and progressive-leaning discourses. Abe, Japan's longest serving Prime Minister of the recent past (2012–2020), is one of those historical revisionists. He has been involved in several groups that argue for a reconsideration of Japan's position as "aggressor" in East Asia in the first half of the 20th century to become that of a benefactor to its neighbors, therefore rendering the attacks on its neighbors (and Pearl Harbor) as just and justifiable actions. Historical revisionists such as Abe thus aim to let Japan's history as perpetrator recede to the background, preferring instead to instill "patriotism" by highlighting Japan's achievements (Saaler 2016). Imperialism, particularly if recast as beneficent for the colonized, can fulfill such a purpose and generate a feeling of nostalgia for lost greatness, particularly in the face of a more powerful China in East Asia. As Mariko Asano Tamanoi (2008, 159–60) points out,

> ... the sense of nostalgia does not simply represent the nation's yearning for the landscapes, lifestyles, and spectacles of the lost empire; it also represents the nation's strategy, enabling it to deny the existence of "the rupture in history." And the memory industry, which has replaced the Japanese state, has been playing the major role in assisting the Japanese people to forget the power of their own state, which once dominated ordinary Chinese people in a place where they now entertain themselves.

Television, and particularly television drama, are part of this "memory industry" (Tamanoi 2008, 160), but Japanese television tends to broadcast what can be shown without creating too much controversy, bringing us back to the trope of Japan as victim of nuclear bombings and the wide acceptance of Japanese people as victims of the war. More often than not, the commemoration of the dropping of the nuclear bombs is taken out of context, and the nuclear bombs become some kind of natural disaster (Buruma 1995) that has been unleashed upon Japan. Although, as Seaton (2007, 116) points out for the 1970s to the early 2000s, progressive discourses on Japan's past as colonizer have been broadcast on all channels,[3] since then, substantial changes have happened in the Japanese broadcasting landscape that make this claim no longer valid. In the following, these changes to the Japanese mediascape will be outlined.

Japanese television as aide-mémoire

"Through its repetition and continual re-narrativization of grand historical narratives of, for example, world wars and world cups, television itself is marked by, and generates our obsession with, commemoration and anniversaries" (Holdsworth 2008, 138). Although Amy Holdsworth makes this statement for British television, the same can be said about Japan. In Japan, however, a clear focus on August can equally be observed (Seaton 2007), as not only did the two nuclear attacks happen on the 6th and 9th of August 1945 respectively, Japan also surrendered unconditionally to the USA on 15 August 1945. Furthermore, *obon*, the festival to commemorate the dead, falls during mid-August, and many people take annual leave to visit their family and the family graves. Therefore, the most prominent programs focusing on the war will be promoted as "media events" (Buonanno 2008; Dayan and Katz 1994) around that time. Because documentaries are not a very important format on Japanese television, the media events will most often be television dramas.

One reason for this certainly is that Japanese television is a personality-driven medium as stars take center stage in the promotion of a show. If a new television drama is announced and built up to be the "media event," very rarely, if ever, will the directors or producers be visible. Except for a select few, they tend to hide behind the "big names" they have cast. However, stars in Japan, no matter how famous they are, are contracted employees of their agencies (Aoyagi 2005; Kirsch 2014) and therefore typecasting is a common occurrence, as it would be an economic risk to let actors and actresses go too much against type. For that reason, audiences know exactly what to expect from the dramas. For example, Matsushima

Nanako, the main character in one of the dramas to be discussed, has previously appeared in another drama set during the war and is famous for playing strong women on the small screen. Casting Matsushima will attract a certain fan audience.

This is not limited to fiction; the presence of television stars, or *tarento* in Japanese, is prevalent throughout the medium. Hardly a format works without the participation of *tarento* on screen who, in effect, often replace the audiences. During a variety show, the *tarento* will show their reaction in place of the audiences, with the downside that the reactions to any kind of controversial topic become scripted and enacted, offering an opportunity to silence dissent as the powerful agencies would not want their employees to be involved with anything that could generate controversy (Kirsch 2014).

Therefore, broadcasting a program that is potentially controversial, or goes against established and widely accepted narratives is difficult. Although Japanese television broadcasting has, from its start in 1953, been operating within a dual system of private and public stations, which was set up to guarantee the plurality of opinion, news and narratives do not differ widely across the channels. Most of the broadcasting laws and guidelines were written by the US Occupation Forces in the late 1940s in an attempt to establish a media system that would be free of government control. Initially, they had favored a system solely based on private broadcasting stations, but because the then-state broadcaster NHK had turned into an institution, it could not simply be taken off the air. Instead, the postwar NHK was modelled after the BBC and is financed solely through license fees. It is also the only station that is allowed to broadcast on a nationwide level. Furthermore, the chairman of NHK is appointed by the government, and its budget is set by the Diet, making indirect pressure at least possible (Krauss 2000, 2017).

By contrast, the first private station also went on air in 1953, and subsequently four more followed, making the setup of available channels that have dominated the market up to the present day complete by 1964. As, legally, private stations are regional stations, they need to form conglomerates to ensure nationwide coverage. Even with the digital switchover in 2012, the smallest of these conglomerates have yet to find partners in the most remote regions, so shows need to occasionally travel across conglomerate boundaries in order to be seen by the whole of Japan. Private stations are solely financed through commercials, but any show receives money from sponsors to be produced. As Hilaria Gössmann (1995) has pointed out, not upsetting those sponsors is paramount in the production of content on the private stations, leading to self-censorship in the creation of a show. But that is but one side of the coin. Hirahara (1991) mentions one example of direct influence by sponsors on content in the 1960s. When a television drama was seen to deal too critically with Japan's wartime past and postwar remilitarization, the sole sponsor of the drama withdrew its support, leading to the drama being shelved. More recently, sponsors threatened to withdraw support from a drama, *Ashita mama ga inai* (Abandoned, Nippon TV) in 2014, because its storyline had triggered a wave of complaints (Mainichi Shimbun 2014). But even before that, political influence has led to withdrawal of sponsorship, most notably in 1989 when the then-Minister for Trade and Industry, Kajiyama Seiroku advised the automobile industry to stop funding TV Asahi's flagship news program, *News Station* (Kume 2017). Sponsors, however, are not mentioned in any broadcasting guidelines, neither are the advertising agencies which will provide the station with the sponsors, but they, together with the agencies of the actors, might wield considerable influence over the production of content.

Additionally, all big private television stations are affiliated with newspapers and although cross-ownership laws prohibit ownership greater than one third of the other company (Ministry of Internal Affairs and Communications, n.d.), there are ways to bypass those laws, as the members of a conglomerate can own shares in other companies within the conglomerate. More importantly, newspapers and affiliated television stations tend to cooperate for news programs. Here, another peculiarity of the Japanese media system gains importance, namely the press clubs. Press clubs are informal gatherings of media and politicians (or any other body in need of media coverage). Participation is by invitation only, and it is there that news is shared. Since a violation of the unwritten rules would lead to exclusion from the vital press clubs, few journalists would dare to bite the hand that feeds them. As a result, investigative journalism is not very prevalent in Japan. Risking expulsion from the press clubs is not an easy step to take, so most news programs and newspapers tend to be descriptive rather than analytical, let alone critical. Although in theory, each paper has a political leaning, this leaning is usually only evident in the "Opinions" section and does not always translate to the affiliated television station.

Different rules apply to broadcasting. The broadcasting laws stipulate political neutrality, with controversial topics required to be tackled from as many angles as possible, yet there is no independent watchdog to make sure that the rules are fulfilled.[4] Every private station also has to apply for a renewal of their broadcasting license every five years. The right to grant, renew or indeed withdraw, a broadcasting license lies with the government—the Ministry of the Internal Affairs and Communications to be precise. While usually this is a mere formality, Fackler (2016) reports direct warnings made by government officials ahead of the 2014 election not to violate the broadcasting laws, citing an example that had (almost) been made out of one of the biggest stations in Japan, TV Asahi, in 1993. In that year, the LDP lost the election for the first time since 1955. Although they still were the strongest parliamentary party, they no longer held a majority and hence could not form a government. Instead, a coalition government took over. Shortly after the election, before the new government had been sworn in, the editor-in-chief of the news desk at TV Asahi claimed that the surprising outcome of the election had been due to the influence of the media, in particular his station—which had been very critical of the LDP and had "adapted the broadcasting to definitely destroy the 55-system" (Kume 2017, 260).[5] This conversation was leaked, and the uproar from the LDP was loud; they saw this as a direct violation of the broadcasting law and threatened to block renewal of the station's broadcasting license. A subsequent inquiry saw the editor-in-chief, Tsubaki Sadayoshi, take the blame and resign, and TV Asahi was severely reprimanded. This particular course of events became known as the Tsubaki Incident, but although this was perhaps the most prominent example of media-muzzling, it was not the first exchange of punches between the right-wing LDP and the left-wing Asahi Group, nor was it the last (Kume 2017; Yamaguchi 2017). The media in Japan has thus been operating within a restrictive system that encourages self-censorship. This means they are often at the whim of the prime minister in office at the time and the extent to which they will allow critical questions.

In 2012, with Abe's return to office, this changed decisively. The "battle" between the LDP and the Asahi Group intensified, and in 2014, the LDP embarked on a defamation campaign to discredit some of the reportages on the comfort women issue that only the Asahi Newspaper had ever dared to break, and which had received widespread criticism at the time, and now, particularly from the Japanese right (see, for example, Yamagiwa 2014). In the same year, many news anchors were forced off the air, at NHK, TBS and TV Asahi, seemingly in an attempt to "freshen" their image on screen; the common thread uniting these broadcast journalists was their tendency to ask probing questions. Additionally, the former chairman of NHK is on record stating that NHK should not veer away from government policy, effectively turning the seemingly independent public broadcaster into a state broadcasting station in all but name. In 2016 and 2017, the UN envoy for freedom of speech issued stern warnings to Japan that its media was becoming too tightly regulated. Abe, in particular, has been very vocal in trying to silence his critics. Although the neutrality law still applies, planned legislation would see the law abolished, giving the LDP the opportunity to decide what can be broadcast without having to abide by an already problematic "neutrality" themselves (Kirsch 2016; Yamada 2017).[6]

In a nutshell, when Seaton (2007) states that progressive programs could be observed across the spectrum, this no longer is the case. The LDP has ensured that progressive media have lost market share and therefore broadcasting controversial topics, such as the comfort women or the Nanjing Massacre, is no longer economically viable and potentially dangerous. The fight for the "correct" memory of the war is thus extending into all realms of public society and with the LDP wielding a tight grip on the media, the press clubs can be used as potential leverage. Therefore, when one looks at the topic of war memory from the angle of the industry, it becomes clear why the *taiga dorama* on NHK and the *jidaigeki* on the private stations tend to focus on a non-controversial past. Although it might be easy to say that the tightening of the screws refers solely to "factual" reporting and will not influence fictional content, as Hayden White (1997, 18) reminds us, it is an artificial distinction, and what will influence the production of factual content, also has impact on the creation of fictional content, as it is subject to the same broadcasting law and can equally create controversy, particularly in the age of social media. Production of content is also not outsourced to smaller, independent companies, but happens within the same media conglomerate, reenforcing the point that the one goes hand in hand with the other.

Rewriting the past?

How can this have an impact on content production? We have already established that the focus is on a usable past, and that does not necessarily have to be one that is more recent but is one that is least likely to cause upset with politicians and sponsors alike. While under previous prime ministers, the more "progressive" productions that Seaton (2007) observed seem to have been possible, what does cause upset—and what does not—changed decisively when Abe Shinzō came to power and started his campaign against "progressive" media and began to rewrite the past. As Abe, according to Fackler (2016), did not permit critical questions, the coordinates of the broadcasting landscape changed decisively during his time in office.

The year 2005 marked the start of the memory boom on Japanese television. It was the year of the 60th anniversary of the end of the war—an important date in the Chinese lunar calendar that implies everything has come full circle.[7] It is therefore not entirely unsurprising that the war was commemorated so intensely that year. Starting in May, dramas that represented the war in some form were broadcast, peaking in August when Japan normally commemorates the end of the war in the Pacific. Indeed, among those many dramas, a plethora did deal with the past in a more progressive way. And the memory boom did not stop in that year, but went on until at least 2012, albeit to a lesser extent than in 2005. For example, *Hiroshima Shōwa 20-nen 8-gatsu 6-ka* (Hiroshima 6 August 1945), produced by the television station TBS in 2005 (which is affiliated to another progressive paper, the Mainichi Newspaper) tackled the discrimination and abuse Korean colonial citizens faced in Japan very openly (Kirsch 2012). That all of this was in a narrative on Hiroshima may have made it more palatable for audiences, but it showed that the Empire had a darker side, too.

Similarly, the 2007 biopic *Ri Kōran* (TV Tokyo) also showed the darker side of the Japanese Empire. Ri Kōran was a Japanese actress whose career is intricately interwoven with notions of Empire, as she was a Japanese national who had grown up in Manchuria and was thus fluent in Chinese so she could pose as Chinese during the war. Consequently, she starred as the "hot-headed" Chinese woman to be tamed (High 2003; Kirsch 2015) in many propaganda films. As her life and career are well known in Japan, it would have been difficult not to mention the Empire and Japan's presence in Manchuria. What would, however, not have needed to be mentioned is the killing of Chinese civilians at the hands of Japanese soldiers.[8] Similarly, the drama *Shinjitsu no shuki: BC-kyū senpan Katō Tetsutarō—Watashi wa kai ni naritai* (A True Record: BC Level War Criminal Katō Tetsutarō—I Want to be a Shellfish, Nippon TV 2007) shows explicit killings of a Chinese boy at the hands of Japanese soldiers. Katō, another "real life person" is the author of the very famous short story *Watashi wa kai ni naritai* (I want to be a shellfish) that has since been turned into two films and two television dramas and which tells the story of a common soldier who is falsely tried as a war criminal. When the soldier is hanged for crimes he did not want to commit, he utters the words that if he gets to be reborn, he would like to be a shellfish, at the bottom of the sea, untroubled by any war between humans (Kirsch 2019). So, the Empire has not been absent from the small screen, and, at least for a certain period of time, its representation has crossed political boundaries. TBS and the (Nikkei Newspaper-affiliated) TV Tokyo, the more progressive stations, as well as Nihon TV, which is affiliated to the conservative paper Yomiuri Newspaper, do show cruelty and Japan's imperial enterprise is not as rose-tinted as historical revisionists would want to see it. On the contrary, not much else is actually shown from the Japanese Empire apart from its cruelty. And in *Ri Kōran*, for example, it becomes obvious that it is far from a beneficial enterprise, because it put a strain on colonizer and colonized alike, showing many "imperialists" as broken figures.

Eight years later, in 2015, with Abe firmly in power, several changes could be observed. In 2015, three dramas were broadcast in August, and one drama was rebroadcast. Whatever was shown on television, apart from some fly-on-the wall documentaries and reportages, also tended to focus on the postwar rebuilding efforts, not the events of the war as such. However, two of these three dramas were set in Manchuria, namely *Reddo Kurosu—Onnatachi no akagami* (Red Cross—Call-up Orders for Women) and *Tsuma to tonda tokkōhei* (The Kamikaze Pilot who Flew with His Wife), made by TBS and TV Asahi respectively, two supposedly progressive stations affiliated with progressive papers, and in the case of TV Asahi, also at loggerheads with Abe's administration.[9]

In order to understand the significance of these dramas, not just in their industry context, but in their historical one as well, it is necessary to quickly outline the guiding principle under which Manchuria was to function. The most important one is that of *gozoku kyōwa*—the harmony of the five "races": the Japanese, the Han Chinese, the Manchurians, the Mongols and the Koreans. The Japanese were to guide the others, but the overall aim was "racial harmony." While nothing of that harmony is shown in the previous dramas—on the contrary, the Empire is mainly full of violence—the slogan of *gozoku kyōwa* becomes visualized in the 2015 representations. *Red Cross*, for example, tells the story of a family of Japanese farmers living in rural Manchuria in close contact with their Chinese neighbors. They celebrate together and, all in all, few prejudices exist between them. In one particular scene during such a celebration, the setting is in very warm colors, suggesting "harmony" even on a visual level. The fighting that takes place around them is blamed on criminals—turning the first years of the war in East Asia into no war at all, therefore also referring to the parlance of the time, when these Chinese guerrilla forces were called "bandits" by the Japanese (Yamaguchi and Fujiwara 1987). Only with the fighting in China in 1937 is this idyll shattered and the family torn apart, but the time in Manchuria shines in glorious nostalgia of times when the Japanese still ruled the Asian mainland. No atrocities whatsoever are being shown, unlike in any of the previous dramas, and the colonial enterprise is represented as very successful, also in integrating the Japanese with their Chinese neighbors. The enemy that tears the idyll apart is the Soviet Union in their advance in 1945, not the Japanese or the Chinese.

Similar tropes appear in *Tsuma*. Again, the harmony of the five races is visualized, this time even by putting the slogan on screen with the help of flags and signs advertising it. In this drama, the focus is on a small military community in rural Manchuria in the final months of the war. Manchuria becomes the land of milk and honey, as the Japanese population in the homeland is at the brink of starvation. The female Japanese main character (who has fled to Manchuria where her husband is stationed with a kamikaze training unit) is overwhelmed by the affluence in the colony. Again, the peace and harmony of the five races is disturbed by the advancing Soviet Army and some Chinese troublemakers who resist this principle. As in *Red Cross*, the experience of the Japanese Empire is rendered harmless. It is without violence on the side of the Japanese and the crimes are always perpetrated by others. There is no space for mentioning Unit 731, comfort women or arbitrary killings. Just by watching these dramas, it becomes inconceivable that a nation as benevolent as Japan would have ever instigated the Nanjing Massacre; Japan solely appears as benefactor and in both instances, the "war" is turned into a misunderstanding of the true intentions of the Japanese by some Chinese, a representation much more in line with what historical revisionists in Japan argue for than the previous representations of violence and arbitrary behavior. Contemporary friction between Japan and China is glossed over by the rose-tinted version of the past, when it is precisely that past that causes the friction in the present. The representations of the Empire therefore follow Rosaldo's argument about colonial nostalgia, "people mourn the passing of what they themselves have transformed" (Rosaldo 1989, 108).

Conclusion: Memory alterations

Memories can change. We change them for ourselves when we are not comfortable with them, but we can equally also change them for our society, as Halbwachs (1992) has argued. And we can also choose to forget. But both acts, remembering and forgetting, are ultimately about the present, and, as Lyotard (1984, 22) put it, "[t]he narratives' reference may seem to belong to the past, but in reality, it is always contemporaneous with the act of recitation." In the case of Japan, the way in which the contemporaneity of the past manifests itself becomes highly visible. A simple change in the political administration can influence the coordinates in which content is being produced and historical memory is televised. At the beginning of the memory boom, mainly between the years 2005 and 2007, some very progressive dramas acknowledged Japanese aggression, however subtly, and the Empire was not a source of nostalgia. Ten years later, and with a historical revisionist in power and the media in a stranglehold, televised narratives begin to change. Notably, although the summer of 2015 was another round anniversary, only very few dramas were broadcast and only by the private stations affiliated to more progressive papers (and having aired more progressive content in the past). Other than that, many shorter features focused on the rebuilding in the immediate postwar period, indicating that it is time to move on (while we seemingly never move on from the *taiga* dramas and *jidaigeki*). The two dramas in question were both set in Manchuria, but there is no mention of other Japanese colonies, let alone of expansion and they very much fall under the "rose-tinted nostalgia" that Tamanoi (2008) has observed. No criticism is voiced and everything that stands in the way of inner-regional cooperation is but a misunderstanding from the others, as they appear as having never quite understood what Japan had intended to do in colonizing them. Therefore, Japan is completely absolved from any crimes in the creation of its Empire. In a way, both dramas are closer to the propaganda films on the Empire prevalent in the 1940s (Chang 2015; Kirsch 2015) than to the historical discourse on it. Therefore, "[t]he constant danger of confusing remembering and imagining, resulting from memories becoming images in this way, affects the goal of faithfulness corresponding to the truth claim of memory" (Ricoeur 2009, Kindle loc 134–35).

When indeed it is impossible to show the events of the war in all their facets, it seems as if producers (or any other actors in the Japanese creative industries) try to avoid the topic altogether. It appears to be a safer bet to not broadcast anything controversial at all—in other words self-censoring of content—than to stir up controversy. This avoidance of controversy adds another layer to reasons for the demise of the memory boom. It did not just come to an end because it had simply worn out; political considerations also played a part. An approach that looks only at the content of the dramas themselves and assesses them for their historical value (which in itself is highly problematic) will only ever reveal that dramas often sacrifice accuracy for dramaturgy. Ignoring the industry and its political constraints does not permit us to see what has driven the changes that have become so visible throughout the past decade. A mildly self-critical version of the past possible in 2005 has been replaced by a white-washed version of the same past from 2015 onward. This version is one that is less likely to cause friction with the political powers and may not necessarily even be what audiences want to see, given that there is no evidence to suggest that the attitude towards the war within Japanese society at large has shifted. Because of political constraints, the production of content has become much more of a one-way route than it has been in the past, where what was produced and broadcast was much more in line with the prevalent discourses within Japan. The media are catering to the political establishment, having evidently been shocked by various attempts to silence dissent.

Therefore, returning to the provocative question posed at the beginning of this chapter concerning whether television can change the past (discounting alternate histories à la *Man in the High Castle* or *SS-GB*), television has the potential to at least change the narratives about the past. Memories can be altered to suit the present-day political discourses and something contentious can easily be turned into something pleasant. The memory industry is very much an industry in which various actors shape what can be consumed, and thus remembered, and what cannot be consumed, and thus forgotten, with an eye on the political powers and the content they supposedly like to see. It is within those hierarchies of power that content is shaped, thereby enabling television to be used as a tool to rewrite the memory of the war more decisively than ever before.

Notes

[1] According to information provided in the NHK Museum of Broadcasting (visited on 4 November 2017), *taiga dorama* (literally, big river dramas) were created in 1963 in order not to lose out against the *jidaigeki* on the big screen.

[2] Abe Shinzō's first term in office stretched only over one year in 2006–2007. He resigned for health-related reasons. He was re-elected in December 2012 and resigned for health reasons in August 2020.

[3] For a detailed discussion on several case studies, see Sakurai (2005) and the papers in Takai, ed. (2011).

[4] The BPO, the Broadcasting Ethics & Program Improvement Organization, comes closest to an independent watchdog, however, it consists of members of the industry and is thus mainly about self-control (BPO, 2021). Nonetheless, it is also seen to be in danger of falling under government control (Monthly Takarajima 2015).

[5] The 1955 System (*1955 seido*) refers to the dominance the LDP has had over Japanese politics since 1955, when the LDP was formed after the merger of two strong political parties. This merger weakened opposition parties, leaving them practically unable to form a government since (with the exceptions of 1993–1995 and 2009–2012).

[6] The changes to the broadcasting law have yet to be executed and the neutrality clause (Article 4 of the broadcasting law) still applies (Ministry of Internal Affairs and Communications, n.d.).

[7] The Chinese lunar calendar was used in Japan until the end of the 19th century and still has some influence on Japanese numerology. Sixty marks the number in which all twelve animal signs have been paired up with all elements once and a new cycle begins. The sixtieth birthday for that reason tends to be celebrated more than others.

[8] The autobiography of Ri Kōran mentions several atrocities that the Japanese Army committed during the time (Yamaguchi and Fujiwara 1987).

[9] The third drama was *Ichiban densha ga hashitta* (The first train is running) and was broadcast by NHK. They "played it safe" by telling the story of how quickly after the bombing, the trams in Hiroshima started operations again.

Bibliography

Anderson, B., 1991. *Imagined Communities: Reflections on the Origin and Spread of Nationalism* (Revised and extended edition). London: Verso.

Anderson, S., 2001. History TV and Popular Memory. In G.R. Edgerton and P.C. Rollins, eds., *Television Histories: Shaping Collective Memory in the Media Age*. Lexington: The University Press of Kentucky, 19–36.

Aoyagi, H., 2005. *Islands of Eight Million Smiles: Idol Performance and Symbolic Production in Contemporary Japan*. Cambridge: Harvard University Press.

BPO (Broadcasting Ethics & Program Improvement Organization), 2021. About BPO. Available at: https://www.bpo.gr.jp/?page_id=1092 [Accessed 26 October 2021].

Buonanno, M., 2008. *The Age of Television: Experiences and Theories*. Translated by Jennifer Radice. Bristol: Intellect Books.

Buruma, I., 1995. *The Wages of Guilt: Memories of War in Japan and Germany*. London: Vintage.

Chang, C-N., 2015. Introduction: Yamaguchi Yoshiko in Wartime East Asia: Transnational Stardom and Its Predicaments. In Y. Yamaguchi and S. Fujiwara, *Fragrant Orchid: The Story of My Early Life* (Kindle edition). Translated by Chia-Ning Chang. Honolulu: University of Hawai'i Press, Kindle loc 185–967.

Connerton, P., 1989. *How Societies Remember*. Cambridge: Cambridge University Press.

Dayan, D. and Katz, E., 1994. *Media Events: The Live Broadcasting of History*. Cambridge: Harvard University Press.

Edgerton, G. R., 2001. Introduction: Television as Historian: A Different Kind of History Altogether. In G.R. Edgerton and P.C. Rollins, eds., *Television Histories: Shaping Collective Memory in the Media Age*. Lexington: The University Press of Kentucky, 1–16.

Fackler, M., 2016. *Abe seiken ni hirefusu nihon no media. Taming the Watchdogs: Political Pressure and Self-Censorship in Abe's Japan.* Tokyo: Futabasha.

Gössmann, H., 1995. Zwischen Fremdeinfluß und Selbstzensur. Literatur und Massenmedien im Japan der Gegenwart [Between external influence and self-censorship. Literature and mass media in contemporary Japan]. In W. Schaumann, ed., *Gewollt oder geworden? Planung, Zufall, natürliche Entwicklung in Japan. Referate des 4. Japanologentages der OAG in Tokyo 17./18. März 1994* [Intended or unintended? Planning, coincidence and natural development in Japan. Papers of the 4th Japanese Studies conference of the OAG (East Asia Society) in Tokyo, 17/18 March 1994]. Munich: Iudicium, 67–82.

Halbwachs, M., 1992. *On Collective Memory.* Translated by Lewis A. Coser. Chicago: The University of Chicago Press.

High, P. B., 2003. *The Imperial Screen: Japanese Film Culture in the Fifteen Years' War, 1931–1945.* Madison: University of Wisconsin Press.

Hirahara, H., 1991. Television Drama in the Thirties of the Shōwa Era (1955–1965). In M. Sata and H. Hirahara, eds., *A History of Japanese Television Drama: Modern Japan and the Japanese.* Tokyo: The Japan Association of Broadcasting Art, 19–71.

Hiroshima Shōwa 20-nen 8-gatsu 6-ka [Hiroshima 6 August 1945], 2005. TBS.

Holdsworth, A., 2008. "Television Resurrections": Television and Memory. *Cinema Journal* 45(3), 137–44.

Huyssen, A., 2001. Present Pasts: Media, Politics, Amnesia. In A. Appadurai, ed., *Globalization.* Durham: Duke University Press, 57–77.

Iwabuchi, K., 2002. *Recentering Globalization. Popular Culture and Japanese Transnationalism.* Durham: Duke University Press.

Kirsch, G., 2012. Memory and Myth: The Bombings of Dresden and Hiroshima in German and Japanese TV Drama. *Contemporary Japan,* (24)1, 51–70.

———., 2014. Next-door Divas: Japanese Tarento, Television and Consumption. *Journal of Japanese and Korean Cinema,* (6)1, 74–88.

———., 2015. *Contemporary Sino-Japanese Relations on Screen: A History, 1989–2005.* London: Bloomsbury.

———., 2016. Controlling the Media in Japan. Ballots & Bullet: School of Politics & International Relations, University of Nottingham. Available at: http://nottspolitics.org/2016/07/11/controlling-the-media-in-japan/ [Accessed 26 October 2021].

———., 2019. Recreating Memory? The Drama Watashi wa Kai ni Naritai and Its Remakes. In B. Guarné, A. Lozano-Méndez and D. Martinez, eds., *Persistently Postwar: Media and the Politics of Memory in Japan.* Oxford: Berghahn Books, 85–102.

Krauss, E., 2000. *Broadcasting Politics in Japan: NHK and Television News.* Ithaca: Cornell University Press.

———, 2017. NHK: The Changing and Unchanged Politics of Semi-Independence. In J. Kingston, ed., *Press Freedom in Contemporary Japan.* London: Routledge, 64–75.

Kume, H., 2017. *Kume Hiroshi desu: Nyūsu sutēshon wa za besuto ten datta* [My name is Kume Hiroshi: News Station was the best ten]. Tokyo: Sekaibunka Kureatibu.

Lyotard, J., 1984. *The Postmodern Condition: A Report on Knowledge.* Translated by Geoff Bennington and Brian Massumi. Manchester: Manchester University Press.

Ministry of Internal Affairs and Communication (Sōmushō), n.d., *The Broadcast Act.* Available at: https://www.soumu.go.jp/main_sosiki/joho_tsusin/eng/Resources/laws/pdf/090204_5.pdf [Accessed 27 October 2021].

Nietzsche, F., 2009. *Vom Nutzen und Nachtheil [sic!] der Historie für das Leben* [On the Use and Abuse of History for Life]. Stuttgart: Philipp Reclam.

Mainichi Shimbun, 2014. NTV Drama Controversy Represents Conflict between Delicate Issue and Freedom of Expression. *Mainichi Shimbun* (English edition), 8 November. Available at: https://web.archive.org/web/20141107153734/http://mainichi.jp/english/english/perspectives/news/20140206p2a00m0na010000c.html [Accessed 26 October 2021].

Reddo Kurosu—Onnatachi no akagami [Red Cross—call-up orders for women], 2015. TBS.

Ricoeur, P., 2009. *Memory, History, Forgetting* (Kindle edition). Translated by Katherine Blamey and Charles Pellauer. Chicago: University of Chicago Press.

Ri Kōran, 2007. TV Tokyo.

Rosaldo, R., 1989. Imperialist Nostalgia. *Representations* 26, 107–22.

Rosenstone, R. A., 2018. *History on Film/Film on History.* Abingdon: Routledge.

Saaler, S., 2016. Nationalism and History in Contemporary Japan. *The Asia-Pacific Journal: Japan Focus* 14 (20:7). Available at: https://apjjf.org/2016/20/Saaler.html [Accessed 25 October 2021].

Sakurai, H., 2005. *Terebi wa sensō o dō egaitekita ka* [How has television portrayed war?]. Tokyo: Iwanami Shoten.

Seaton, P. A., 2007. *Japan's Contested War Memories: The 'Memory Rifts' in Historical Consciousness of World War II*. London: Routledge.

Shinjitsu no shuki: BCkyū senpan Katō Tetsutarō—Watashi wa kai ni naritai [A true record: BC level war criminal Katō Tetsutarō—I want to be a shellfish], 2007. Nippon TV.

SS-GB, 2017. BBC.

Takai, M., 2011. *"Hansen" to "kōsen" no popyurā karuchā: Media, gendā, tsūrizumu* [Pacifism and militarism in popular culture: Media, gender, tourism]. Kyoto: Jinbun Shoin.

Tamanoi, M. A., 2008. *Memory Maps: The State and Manchuria in Postwar Japan*. Honolulu: University of Hawai'i Press.

Takarajima, 2015. *Terebi no rinri chekku kikan "BPO" wa seifu shihaika ni: Abe Seiken ni yoru "kane to atsuryoku" no terebi kanzen chōkyō* [BPO (the Broadcasting Ethics & Program Improvement Organization), the mechanism to check the ethics of television is under control of the government: The full taming of television through money and pressure from the Abe government]. *Monthly Takarajima*, June, 12–15.

The Man in the High Castle, 2015–2019. Amazon Prime.

Thornham, S. and Purvis T., 2005. *Television Drama: Theories and Identities*. Houndmills: Macmillan.

Tsuma to tonda tokkōhei [The kamikaze pilot who flew with his wife], 2015. TV Asahi.

White, H., 1997. The Modernist Event. In V. Sobchak, ed., *The Persistence of History: Cinema, Television and the Modern Event*. London: Routledge, 17–38.

Yamada, K., 2017 [2016]. *Hōsōhō to kenryoku* [The broadcasting law and power]. Tokyo: Tabata Shōten.

Yamagiwa, S., 2014. *Subete wa asahi shinbun kara hajimatta "ianfu mondai"* [The "Comfort Women Problem" all started with the Asahi Shimbun]. Tokyo: Wac.

Yamaguchi, T., 2017. Press Freedom under Fire: "Comfort women," the Asahi Affair and Uemura Takashi. In J. Kingston, ed., *Press Freedom in Contemporary Japan*. London: Routledge, 135–151.

Yamaguchi, Y. and Fujiwara S., 1987. *Ri Kōran: Watakushi no hansei* [Ri Kōran: My half-life]. Tokyo: Shinchōsha.

Young, L. 1998. *Japan's Total Empire: Manchuria and the Culture of Wartime Imperialism*. Berkeley: University of California Press.

Chapter 2
Truth and Limitations: Japanese Media and Disasters

Christopher P. Hood

Japan has a long history of disaster narratives, and this chapter considers five related to a single historical event, the 1985 JAL flight JL123 crash, which remains the world's deadliest single plane crash. The chapter reviews relevant literature in relation to how dramatizations portray "the truth" while seemingly needing to fit with disaster narrative conventions. The chapter analyzes the way in which five dramatizations handle aspects of the JL123 crash and its aftermath. While the focus is on the JL123 crash, the methods used in this chapter could be applied to other events in the same way.

Introduction

Just as "fake news" has been discussed in relation to reporting, so it is pertinent to think about dramatizations and the degree to which they present "the truth" about events. This chapter addresses this topic by considering the media representation of a single event that occurred in 1985 in Japan. On 12 August 1985, JAL flight JL123 crashed in Ueno-mura, north-west of Tokyo. The crash remains the world's deadliest single plane crash, with an official death toll of 520. Miraculously, four survivors were found when search and rescue teams reached the site the next morning. Naturally, news media covered the aftermath of the crash in the days and weeks that followed, but there have also been books, documentaries and dramatizations over the years. The scale and other aspects of the crash have ensured that significant interest remains in the disaster.

By focusing on the dramatizations relating to the JL123 crash, this study allows for a detailed analysis of disaster narratives. Japan has a long tradition of disaster movies, with the *Godzilla* franchise being the most well-known. To frame the study, the chapter begins with a review of the relevant literature to understand the role of dramatizations in portraying "the truth" together with their need to fit with conventions that disaster narratives include. The rest of the chapter analyzes the way in which five dramatizations handle aspects of the JL123 crash and its aftermath.[1] The five dramatizations analyzed are: *Kuraimāzu hai* (Climber's High, Wakaizumi Hisaaki 2005, a two-part dramatization on NHK television), *Kuraimāzu hai* (Climber's High, Harada Masato 2008, feature film), *Shizumanu taiyō* (The Unbroken/ The Sun Which Doesn't Set, Wakamatsu Setsurō 2009, feature film), *One no kanata ni* (Inseparable Souls: Fathers, Sons and The Crash of JAL123/Beyond The Ridge, Wakamatsu Setsurō 2012, a two-part dramatization on satellite channel WOWOW), and *Shizumanu taiyō* (The Sun Which Doesn't Set, Mizutani Toshiyuki and Suzuki Kōsuke 2016, a 20-part dramatization on WOWOW).

The research includes details from interviews with Yokoyama Hideo (author of *Kuraimāzu hai*, the novel), Wakaizumi Hisaaki (director of *Kuraimāzu hai* (2005)), Harada Masato (director of *Kuraimāzu hai* (2008)), Kubo Rikei (producer of *Kuraimāzu hai* (2008)), Kadota Ryūshō (author of *One no kanata ni*), Okano Makiko (producer of *One no kanata ni*) and Sheldon Hall (Sheffield Hallam University lecturer and film critic). Interviews were also held with a number of people related to the crash itself, including Miyajima Kuniko, Peter Mathews and Kawahara Shinobu. All interviews were semi-structured and conducted according to the appropriate research ethics.

This study is significant because it highlights the various limitations that exist in how dramatizations may portray, and so influence public understanding of, an actual event and particularly the "truth" about that event. While the focus is on the JL123 crash, the methods used in this chapter could be applied to other events in the same way.

Media, truth, influence and conventions

Toplin (2002, 9) points out that "[e]nthusiasts of history communicate a sense of frustration and disgust when assessing Hollywood's treatment of the past." He further goes on to argue that "[d]etractors claim that the attention to entertainment strategies proves that filmmakers are not really interested in producing 'true' pictures of the past [...] The result is Hollywood-style entertainment, but not sophisticated history" (Toplin 2002, 16). Does this even matter? The answer to this may depend on the viewer. As Hall (2014, 8) notes about the movie *Zulu* (Cy Endfield 1964), when he refers to "disparities between film and history, no automatic critic is implied. *Zulu* is a drama, not a documentary, and deserves fair consideration in its own terms," a view that he reiterated during an interview with me in 2018.

Historical narratives are those that may be "based around a real event" or "based on a true story" and, while they may not inherently be concerned with only portraying the truth, there are likely to be limitations to what can be changed (Hood 2020, 183). A movie which is merely "inspired by real events" does not face the same limitations, as can be seen with the movie *Aftermath* (Elliott Lester 2017), for example, which, although inspired by events surrounding the aftermath of an actual accident, changed a range of details such as the location of the crash from Germany to the United States (Hood 2020, 187, 195). However, dramatizations do not necessarily clarify the basis for how the narrative is related to an actual event, and so it will be left to the viewer to determine. This issue became the focus of the UK's Culture Secretary, who suggested that the Netflix series *The Crown* (Peter Morgan 2020 (Series 4)) should make it clear that it was a work of fiction at the beginning of each program, to avoid a situation whereby "a generation of viewers who did not live through these events [...] mistake fiction for fact" (BBC News online 2020). Despite such concerns, it should be noted that, even in works of seemingly pure fiction, elements of truth can be found. These are what the author of *Kuraimāzu hai* (2006), Yokoyama Hideo, describes as "pillars of truth" as will be discussed further below. An example of this is when the character Quint in *Jaws* (Steven Spielberg 1975) discusses the sinking of the *USS Indianapolis* and its role in delivering the atomic bomb, to be dropped on Hiroshima, to Tinian Island.

While there may be an inherent understanding that dramatizations are not documentaries, this does not mean that they are devoid of influence when it comes to how people remember and understand historical events. Nye (1966, 145) points out that both works on history and literature can seek understandings of the reality of the past. By extension, therefore, so do those who consume such works. However, although "[t]he reader agrees to what critics have called a 'willing suspension of disbelief'" (Nye 1966, 149) in the case of novels, perhaps the same is not true for those outputs that deal with actual events or people. It is for this reason that Belin (1996) argues that the "entertainment industry leaders have a moral obligation to avoid major distortion of the facts in films." Connor (1988, 1201) went further in discussing influence by stating that "even well-educated Americans are learning most of their history from film and television." Toplin (1996, 1) concurs with Connor by arguing that Hollywood "can make a significant impact upon the public's thinking about the past. Historical dramas reach millions of viewers. Often they stimulate wide-ranging debates about their interpretations and lead to the publication of articles and books about the issues they address." However, this assessment overlooks the fact that there is likely to be a huge disparity between how many consume the dramatization and how many read the articles and books related to the dramatization's interpretation. Therein lies one crux of the problem: it is very difficult to measure what the impact of such dramatizations are. Reach and influence are not the same thing, just as the sales of a newspaper is not the same as readership, for example (Hood 2012, 148).

Two studies that have attempted to look at the influence of movies, specifically in relation to how people perceive risk and how they respond to a disaster, which is pertinent to this chapter, are Quarantelli (1985) and Mitchell et al. (2000). Quarantelli (1985, 41) concludes that "disaster movies either perpetuate the wrong ideas according to scientific studies or present empirically wrong facts." Mitchell et al. (2000, 400) also found that "[d]isaster films often do not reflect reality. The physical characteristics of hazards are frequently distorted to the point that any real behavior based upon these facts could lead to serious personal injury or death." In other words, most people appear to be able to suspend disbelief and understand that they cannot do in real life what they see in the movies.

In relation to disaster movies, it is important to emphasize that, generally, viewers are not likely to want to view a movie merely for the spectacle of the disaster itself. What are needed are hooks. Toplin (2002, 15) suggests, however, that in the case of historical dramatizations, it is "a particularly challenging effort to establish an emotional 'hook' that draws in the audience." He (2002, 17) goes on to point out that "[t]o make history understandable and exciting, filmmakers have to narrow the scope of their portrayals. Usually they dramatize only a few events, cover a narrow space of time, and give detailed attention to the thoughts and actions of only a few key people." When we consider one of the most successful movies of all time, itself a disaster movie based on a real event, *Titanic* (James Cameron 1997) (Box Office Mojo 2020), it is unlikely that most people would go to watch the movie for the sinking itself. Just as *A Night To Remember* (Roy Baker 1958) had successfully placed a fictional story within the framework of a factual event, and so helped to cement the story of the sinking of the *Titanic* into popular cultural memory 44 years after the disaster (Lennon and Foley 2004, 8), so did Cameron's *Titanic* for another generation.

If the disaster itself is not the hook, how are we to know what the hooks are? The answer to that is likely to be found in the trailer for the dramatization. The trailer's primary role is to encourage people to go to view the output, and therefore it needs to set out what the hooks are. In the case of *Titanic*, rather than merely being about a ship sinking, we discover that the movie involves a love story, a possible crime and friction between social classes, for example.

Regardless of what moral obligations movie makers may have in relation to portraying accuracy, there are certain conventions appropriate to the genre that they will follow. While I have pointed out elsewhere that there is not, at least according to IMDb, a specific "disaster" movie genre (Hood 2020), the study identifies 17 conventions that are found in disaster movies, as summarized in Table 2.1. For the sake of this study, which is only concerned with Japanese disaster movies, one would only expect to find the conventions in Groups A and C as set out in the table.

Table 2.1 Conventions in Disaster Movies

Group	Convention
A	1. Pillars of truth
	2. Mood of dread/threat
	3. Primarily impacts nationality of narrative makers
	4. Image of disaster
	5. Dominance of male characters
	6. Mini-victories
	7. Family
	8. Suffering protagonist
	9. Cross section of society represented
	10. Savagery but optimism
	11. Death of main character
	12. No distancing in time (may not apply to historical narratives)
B	13. Conflict between characters, but unite against disaster
	14. Panic
	15. Isolation
C	16. Show dead bodies
	17. Contemporary significance

Based upon Table 2 in Hood 2020: 196. Conventions in Group A were found in at least 60 percent of both English-language and Japanese-language disaster movies; those in Group B were found in at least 60 percent of English-language movies, but less than 60 percent of Japanese-language ones; those in Group C were found in less than 60 percent of English-language movies but at least 60 percent of Japanese-language ones.

Hooks, conventions and the "truth" in the JL123 dramatizations

Having established the framework, the chapter now turns to analyzing the dramatizations in relation to the hooks, the conventions of disaster narratives and considering what is presented in relation to the "truth."

The obvious starting point is the plane crash itself. The trailers of all five refer to the crash site being Osutakayama (Mt. Osutaka). However, this reveals an issue with accuracy, as, although the crash site is commonly referred to as being on Osutaka, and the crash site is officially *Osutaka no one* (literally "the ridge on Osutaka"), it is actually on another mountain, Mount Takamagahara. The misuse of the crash site name seems to stem from what the site was announced as being by the best-selling newspaper, *Yomiuri Shimbun*, and its linked television station on 13 August 1985 after several hours of confusion and 18 different locations being suggested as the correct location (Hood 2012, 60). In essence, there is a form of the "Galapagos effect" or "echo chambers" taking place whereby two, or more, positions exist in parallel, seemingly choosing to ignore evidence from other sources. That the dramatizations do this is important to note as it underlines the fact that their default position is not to perform a documentary role and the preference is to use nomenclature with which most viewers would be familiar.

The way in which the five dramatizations handle the crash is quite different. *Kuraimāzu hai* (both adaptations) and *One no kanata ni* cover it from the first news breaking of the plane's disappearance. Both versions of *Shizumanu taiyō*, on the other hand, provide the build-up to the take-off and the scenes in the plane itself, as will be discussed further below. The crash is not shown, with the 2009 version cleverly interlacing sounds of the plane crashing with a scene in which the protagonist, Onchi, is hunting in Africa. Onchi shoots and kills an elephant; the dead jumbo collapsing to the ground with the sound of the plane, a jumbo jet, crashing.

Both versions of *Shizumanu taiyō* and *Kuraimāzu hai* (2008) have a re-creation of the crash site. Although there is a degree of accuracy in these, there are also some important differences. First, while in reality, most of the "J" of "JAL" was missing from the only large piece of wreckage that remained, *Kuraimāzu hai* (2008) includes the whole "J." In the case of *Shizumanu taiyō*, the letters are now "NAL." as the airline name has been changed to "National Airlines," and all letters are visible. Although *Kuraimāzu hai* (2005) and *One no kanata ni* do not have re-creations of the crash site, they do include actual news footage of the crash site from 1985, as is also done in the other dramatizations. The crash site becomes the focal point of one of the key scenes in both versions of *Kuraimāzu hai*, with the 2005 NHK version using archive footage as a backdrop. This was done because a re-creation of the crash site would have been prohibitively expensive (Wakaizumi interview 2010). In the scene, which is also in the 2008 version but handled differently, an eye-witness account of the crash site written by one of the reporters, Sayama, is recited. Yokoyama (interview 2009) describes this as the article that he wishes he could have written in 1985; it took him 17 years to get to a point where he could write it. However, as it reads more like a piece of poetry than a standard newspaper article, it is unlikely it would have been published.

In terms of the cause of the crash, *Kuraimāzu hai* largely presents a version based on the official investigation. However, the 2008 movie also includes a scene, not in the original novel on which it is based, where a reporter talks to a member of the local search and rescue team and is told that they were following orders, that they knew where the crash site was, and that they could have arrived there earlier and saved more people. The movie finishes with text pointing out that while the official report concluded that the plane had probably experienced rapid depressurization following a failure in the rear bulkhead, which had not been correctly repaired by Boeing after a previous accident, there are those who question the official report and continue to seek a reinvestigation. Harada (interview 2011) said that he felt obligated to include this having discussed the crash with many people and having read books about the crash which brought the official narrative into question. *Shizumanu taiyō* (both adaptations), on the other hand, includes nothing equivalent to this, which is somewhat surprising given that the novel *Shizumanu taiyō* raises the question of whether the plane was struck by a missile (Yamazaki 2001, 153–56), for example, for which there is some corroborating evidence (Hood 2012).

One consistency between the five narratives is that all not only cover the time around the crash, but also extend over wider time periods. However, of the five dramatizations, the NHK version of *Kuraimāzu hai* is the only one that includes dates based on the Imperial reign (the Shōwa period in the case of the crash), reflecting that the anticipated main target audience would be those over 60 who are most accustomed to using this system (Wakaizumi interview 2009). While for many viewers the use of these dates will be sufficient to stir up certain memories about what they were doing at the time of the crash, there are many others who would have been too young to remember or were born subsequent to the crash. For those who do remember 1985, the dramatizations provide a range of other visual clues to help connect with the events of that year. The most notable of these is the heavy usage of Hanshin Tigers memorabilia in many of the dramatizations. Over half of the victims came from the Kansai area (Hood 2012, 45), where the Hanshin Tigers baseball team is based, and the president of the team was one of those who died in the crash. Following the crash many people supported the Tigers to win their first-ever championship, which they achieved, as a way of supporting the team, families and region as it recovered from the crash (Hood 2012, 236). However, in terms of overall accuracy, there is an issue with the depiction of one of the victims, based upon Miyajima Ken (discussed further below) who was actually a Kintetsu Buffalos fan (Miyajima interview 2009) and not a Hanshin Tigers fan as shown in the 2009 version of *Shizumanu taiyō*.

Throughout the dramatizations, a variety of techniques are used to aid viewers not only "suspend disbelief" but to believe that the dramatizations are factually accurate. This accuracy not only relates to events themselves, but also more universal aspects such as how people behave. These moments of accuracy are what Yokoyama (interview 2009) calls "pillars of truth," and he argues that these "pillars" enable people to "flip" the more unbelievable moments in between and find the whole output believable. As noted above, both versions of *Kuraimāzu hai* use actual television footage from 1985 to make the content seem credible, as well as using the actual name JAL (as *One no kanata ni* does). Furthermore, the NHK dramatization, which is generally faithful to the original novel, includes a narration with photographs from 1985 explaining more details about the crash (similar text is in the novel also), and footage from the anniversary in 2005 to provide background factual information to viewers.

Although all five narratives involve the plane crash in some form, they also feature many other locations and the degree to which these are accurate also impacts the believability of the narrative. Both versions of *Shizumanu taiyō* and *One no kanata ni* recreate the scenes in Fujioka where families waited for news and the identification of remains was performed. Looking at photographs of these sites in 1985, there is no doubt that the re-creations look authentic, although one should note that most viewers would probably be unaware of the authenticity. In the case of *Kuraimāzu hai*, perhaps the most noticeable difference between the two versions can be found in the offices of the newspaper company. While some (e.g., *Kinema Junpō* 2008, 36) criticized the 2008 version for looking too much like the *Daily Planet* in *Superman* (Richard Donner 1978), the director (Harada interview 2011) suggests that it was authentic and the NHK version was pandering too much to what people's expectations would be, rather than accuracy.

As noted above, both versions of *Kuraimāzu hai* and *One no kanata ni* maintained the real name of JAL. In the case of NHK, it was the first time that a real company's name was used in an NHK television drama and was something that led to a lot of deliberation before being agreed (Wakaizumi interview 2010). However, it meant that NHK had to be careful to keep the focus of the 1985 part of the story on the week around the time of the crash, with text at the start of both parts making this clear rather than discussing the crash investigation too much (Wakaizumi interview 2010). *Shizumanu taiyō*, like the novel itself, used the name National Airlines (NAL) instead of JAL, and Prime Minister Nakasone's name is changed to Tonegawa, a river in Nakasone's home prefecture, Gunma. In the case of *Shizumanu taiyō*, the visual nature of dramatizations meant that one issue that had to be addressed was the logo of the airline. While both versions came up with differing solutions, both managed to provide a hint to the original JAL *tsurumaru* logo of a red circle, based upon the Japanese flag, with a stylized crane. In the case of the movie, the red circle was largely kept by using a crescent moon inside which there was a single cherry blossom (*sakura*), a potent symbol of Japan (Hood 2015, 104–5). In the WOWOW TV version, the logo is a red circle in which there is a stylized picture of a mountain based on Mount Fuji, another of Japan's well-known symbols.

In addition to the change of the company name, *Shizumanu taiyō* also changes the names of families. This also happens in the case of *One no kanata ni*. For those wanting to consider the historical authenticity of the dramatizations, the change is notable. Further, it stands out in the case of *Shizumanu taiyō* due to the inclusion of Miyajima Ken, mentioned earlier, and his mother, Miyajima Kuniko, in the story. Mrs Miyajima became the head of the 8/12 *Renrakukai*, the association for the families of the JL123 crash. While the novel contains the real names of Miyajima and other families, after some late pressure from the publisher despite the original draft having pseudonyms and Miyajima agreeing, with some regret now (Miyajima interview 2009), to the change, the dramatizations do not. The change is somewhat ironic given that, in the 2008 version of *Kuraimāzu hai*, Miyajima Ken's name appears when Yūki looks at the passenger manifest, whereas this is not in the original novel.

One of the "hooks" that appears in most of the trailers is that of the "suffering protagonist." This concept is found in many Japanese movies and is based on the tradition of there being a "tragic hero" (Standish 2007). The key aspect of the suffering protagonist is that, despite everything that is thrown at them, they keep going and do not quit. Yūki in *Kuraimāzu hai* frequently finds his position undermined or decisions overruled. In the novel and the NHK version, despite some outbursts, he continues his work. Only in the movie version, which was intended to have a more international release (Harada interview 2011), do we see him resign from the company. Similar to Yūki, Onchi in *Shizumanu taiyō* does not quit NAL despite numerous overseas postings (the real person upon which the character was based actually had such postings (Ogura 1999)), much to the confusion of some foreign viewers (e.g., HamsapSukebe 2016). *One no kanata ni* is different from the other stories in that the suffering protagonists are families who lost loved ones in the plane crash and so the "suffering" is tied in with their bereavement process.

Given that all of the stories have a hook that relates to suffering and a dark story related to a plane crash, it may raise the question why people would want to watch them, particularly as they are clearly not the thriller or action type movies that often typify disaster movies

(Hood 2020, 195). In relation to this, Okano (interview 2019) points to the concept of *tōijō* put forward by Kuramoto (2013). Kuramoto argues that Japanese dramatizations are like a Japanese sweet, *tōijō*, a sugar-coated pill. As argued elsewhere (Hood 2020, 192), the analogy may not work as neatly as suggested, but the underlying concept—that many Japanese people are prepared to watch dramas that have traumatic parts and not necessarily a happy ending—remains valid. Perhaps this acceptance comes from the concepts of *wabi-sabi* and *mono-no-aware* that are key within Japanese culture and that reflect an acceptance of the transience of things and the inevitability of death, for example (Hood 2015, 104). While there may be an acceptance of the transience of things in Japan, "untimely deaths" (van Bremen 2005, 26) are still shocking and the five dramatizations studied here, in their own ways, point to the poor support given to people suffering from trauma.

A hook that comes out in many of the trailers is that of "conflict," further supporting the suffering protagonist convention. However, my study on disaster narratives found that this convention was in the group that was expected to be found more in English-language narratives than Japanese ones (Hood 2020, 191). But what exactly is the disaster and when does it end? In the case of *Kuraimāzu hai*, the disaster includes longer-term issues relating to the impact upon families and the need to find the cause of the crash, for example. In relation to this, the protagonist Yūki has many conflicts with colleagues over the choice of headlines and stories, and there is conflict between different parts of the newspaper, including physical fights, but ultimately not only do the reporters unite, but a degree of unity sweeps across most of the newspaper company after issues come to a head. Only in the 2008 version does conflict remain between Yūki and the company president, leading to Yūki's resignation.

Within *Shizumanu taiyō*, due to the protagonist's involvement in a union and the confrontation that this causes with management, the themes of conflict and unity are central to the overall story, and it could be argued that the disaster is not so much the plane crash but the disastrous company management throughout the whole period covered by the narrative. Although there is some unity between the protagonist and management after the crash and a new chairman is brought in, which aids with how the company deals with the families after the crash and with the company's corruption, the ousting of that chairman means that the conflict returns once again. *One no kanata ni* focuses on three families and various details in the years prior to the crash, as well as the response to the crash itself. In the case of two families this reveals friction and conflict within the families prior to the crash. After the crash, there are responses which lead to conflicts, but ultimately there is not only unity and peace in the present, but aspects which show how the key characters come to an understanding of the tragic events.

With their re-creations of the scenes inside the plane, both versions of *Shizumanu taiyō* clearly provide a hook about one aspect of the story and disaster and one of the key conventions of disaster movies: there being a mood of dread/threat. In terms of accuracy, there are elements of the re-creations which do not fit with what is known about the conditions inside JL123, and of course there is also much which will never be known, but it does also accurately point out that the cockpit crew did not don oxygen masks, which may be significant in relation to finding out what really caused the crash (Hood 2012, 203–4). During the re-creation of the scene inside the plane, both dramatizations show the passengers panicking. Although this is unsurprising, there are two things to note about this. First, the convention of "panic" is in the group of conventions that tend to be more prevalent in English-language narratives than Japanese ones, and this convention does not appear in the other JL123-related narratives. Second, based on information taken from notes (*isho*) written by some of those on board (discussed below) and statements given by one of the survivors (Yoshioka 1986, 72), there may have been very little panic during the fateful 32 minutes. Also, in relation to the convention of mood of dread/threat, both versions of *Shizumanu taiyō* and *One no kanata ni* show rows of coffins, further underlining the traumatic issues that the narratives handle. Although most of the scenes in Fujioka look authentic, some re-creations show the coffins being on stands, while photographs taken by Peter Mathews, whose son, Kimble, died in the crash, clearly show that the coffins were on the ground (see Hood 2012, 100 and Hood 2018, 107–9). The fact that the coffins are on stands makes them more visible and would have made the filming of some scenes easier in terms of positioning of the camera. Although less obvious from the trailers, both versions of *Kuraimāzu hai* also contain the convention of mood of dread/threat, although it is exercised more in relation to the contemporary story of Yūki climbing Mount Tanigawa many years after the JL123 crash, where he slips.

In all five dramatizations there is a dominance of male characters. Although there are some female characters, the protagonists are male and the subtitle of *One no kanata ni* has a focus on the "fathers and sons." However, the 2008 version of *Kuraimāzu hai* makes a significant change in comparison to the original novel and NHK version to address some of the gender imbalance. In the movie, one of the key characters is Tamaki. In the original novel Tamaki is male; although he is not included in the NHK version, in the film version, Tamaki is female and is the one who uncovers the scoop about the cause of the crash. At one point the film makers had even considered merging the Tamaki and Sayama (the main reporter) characters, but decided it would be a step too far to have the main reporter being female and Yokoyama would probably not allow it (Harada interview 2011). The change was made in consideration of what a current audience may like to see, rather than being faithful to the novel or what would have been probable in 1985 when the Equal Employment Opportunity Law was only just coming into force (Harada interview 2011). When it comes to female characters and accuracy, it would be amiss not to mention at this point that all four of the survivors of the JL123 crash were female (see below). Also, it should be noted that women played a key role in the bereavement and support activities, as *Shizumanu taiyō* portrays.

One way or another, "family" features in all the trailers and becomes one of the hooks. While the NHK version is perhaps the most subtle in this regard, the others, particularly *One no kanata ni* are more obviously about the impact of the disaster on families. The convention of families being impacted by disasters is prevalent in most disaster movies, so it is of no surprise to find it in narratives about a real plane crash that included 92 child victims, 189 mothers being left behind and 7 cases where the mother was pregnant at the time of the crash (8/12 Renrakukai 2005, 4). In the cases of *Kuraimāzu hai* and *Shizumanu taiyō*, the family issues are not merely limited to the bereaved, but also center around the protagonists. In both versions of *Kuraimāzu hai*, as in the novel, Yūki has a difficult relationship with his son, but the film version does not show his wife (who is only briefly referred to) or daughter (who is not even referred to) but does include a scene at the end, not in the original novel, where Yūki not only leaves Gunma Prefecture, but Japan altogether to visit his son and family in New Zealand. Onchi in *Shizumanu taiyō*, on the other hand, has to deal with the issues of his various postings overseas and how that impacts his family and also how his union activities impact his daughter, in particular. That he is also overseas when his mother is taken ill, and subsequently dies as he is returning to Japan, raises other issues related to families and death and ties in with the issues faced by the families caught up in the plane disaster.

All five of the JL123-related narratives only focus on a few key people. What is interesting is the relative overlap that we see of certain families in these narratives and elsewhere, such as in documentaries and in the media. Given that the crash impacted over 400 families (8/12 Renrakukai 2005, 4), there should not be a need to have such restrictions. Perhaps due to the familiarity of certain families, there is a desire for production companies to focus on the same families. It could also be that only these families are prepared to have their story told. When considering the bereaved families shown in the dramatizations, there is only one shown in *Kuraimāzu hai* and no name is included, although the movie version also makes passing reference to Miyajima Ken and alters the story about Yūki and his son to make an element of the story, that of Yūki's son traveling by himself on a plane, comparable to Ken's experience of flying by himself for the first time. As noted above, Miyajima Ken and his family also appear in *Shizumanu taiyō*, but unlike the novel, the name has been changed (different names in the two versions). Mrs. Miyajima is probably the most recognizable and well-known of the bereaved families related to JL123 and is also involved in activities to improve support for families of other disasters (Miyajima interviews 2009, 2017) as well as being in the news and documentaries. That her name is not used in *Shizumanu taiyō* is perhaps a little odd in this respect, though many viewers would soon make the link between the character on screen and the real person.

Like *Shizumanu taiyō*, *One no kanata ni* shifts from using real names. Furthermore, three families who appear in the original book are not featured at all in the dramatization due to issues that occurred after its publication (Kadota interview 2018). According to the producer of *One no kanata ni*, the names of the families were changed, even though real names had been in the media, as there was concern about any negative impact on their day-to-day life (Okano interview 2019). In terms of the three families that were included, they allow the narrative to focus on particular themes and issues which are pertinent in Japanese society. In the case of the Ogura family (real name Maeda), the mother and sister were killed in the crash. The main focus is on the son (real name Shintarō, changed to Kōtarō) and the idea of *amaenbō* (spoiled child) and how he handles the crash. His father does not handle the crash well, takes to drinking a lot and eventually dies. The son goes on to university where he meets a girl whom he marries (*kokoro no sae*, support of the heart). In the case of the Uesugi (real name Taniguchi) family, the story focuses on how the son adores his father (*akogare*) and then goes on, despite his young age, to try to protect his mother, drawing on his, and his father's, scouting traditions. This story also allows for inclusion of one of the *isho* (see below). The third family is the Minegishi (real name Kawahara), with the focus being on the severe education (*genkakuna kyōiku*) imparted by the father, the resistance (*hanpatsu*) that one son in particular feels towards his father, but how the son ultimately wants to become a dentist like his father. Meanwhile, the story also shows the mother watching over (*mimamoru*) her sons. The dramatization does not include the daughter at all, which was ironic for me, given that I know her, and this connection was one of the reasons I started my research about the JL123 crash. Following this particular family also allows for inclusion of a story of continuity and circularity, for not only do the sons go on to become dentists, but one of their sons says he wants to become a dentist too in a scene similar to one played out between his father and grandfather earlier in the dramatization. All these families have often featured in newspaper articles and/or documentaries about the crash.

That the dramatizations *Shizumanu taiyō* and *One no kanata ni* followed a number of families meant that they could include a cross section of society, although, as I have noted elsewhere (Hood 2020, 185, 189–90), part of the issue here is how one defines a "cross section of society." The degree to which all areas of society, such as racial minorities, sexual minorities and those with disabilities, are shown in any disaster movie, especially Japanese ones, is questionable. One minority that does not get included are foreigners—although there were 22 non-Japanese passengers on JL123 (Hood 2012, 45)—keeping with the disaster narrative convention focusing primarily on the nationality of the narrative makers (Hood 2020).

As noted above, Japanese dramatizations do not necessarily have a happy ending. In the case of the JL123-related dramatizations, there is very little optimism throughout *Kuraimāzu hai* and, even with the inserted New Zealand scene in the movie, there is very little in the way of a feel-good ending. The ending of *Shizumanu taiyō* is more up-beat, even though it comes when Onchi has seemingly been defeated and been posted to Africa once again—the difference is that this time he wants to go—and has taken to shooting animals with a camera rather than a rifle. The families in *One no kanata ni* have much more obviously positive endings as alluded to above. However, if one is to speak of optimistic and positive stories relating to JL123, there is one glaring absence from many of the dramatizations, other than passing mentions, and virtually all of the trailers (and so not seen as worthy of being hooks for the narrative itself): the four survivors. In the case of *Kuraimāzu hai*, the novel and NHK version only make a brief reference to the survivors, showing iconic television footage of one of the survivors, Kawakami Keiko, being winched from the site. No attempt is made by any of the journalists to interview any of the survivors in the dramatizations. The movie, despite recreating the crash site, does not attempt to recreate the iconic scene. In the case of *One no kanata ni*, the original book has a chapter (the prologue) about the SDF soldier who winched up Kawakami and includes a photograph of the scene. In the revised edition after the dramatization, the chapter is now the first chapter of the book, but the photograph is not included and there is no inclusion of this storyline, other than in passing, in the dramatization itself. When asked why this story was not included, both Kadota (interview 2018) and Okano (interview 2019) say that there was nothing new to add to documentaries about the crash. The dramatizations of *Shizumanu taiyō*, however, do include the survivors in some form. In the case of the movie version we see a survivor's hand move, but it, like the *Kuraimāzu hai* movie, backs away from recreating the sight of a survivor being winched away. In the case of the 2016 television version, we do not see survivors being found at the crash site, but, like the novel itself, it contains one of the survivors, an off-duty flight attendant, Ochiai Yumi, who was on the flight, giving an interview, which appeared in the media—the contents of which were largely discredited by Ochiai in a subsequent interview (Yoshioka 1986). It would appear that, in comparison to Hollywood dramatizations, Japanese dramatizations are less concerned with survivors and more on the grim reality of disasters (Hood 2020).

One of the hooks that comes up in trailers, and also features heavily in each of the dramatizations, are the *isho* written by some of the passengers. In total six notes written by passengers and one by a crew member were found (Hood 2012). These *isho* are poignant as they clearly reveal the suffering and issues facing the stricken crew and passengers. *Kuraimāzu hai* and the movie version of *Shizumanu taiyō* include the longest and most well-known of the passenger *isho*—written by Kawaguchi Hirotsugu. In the case of the movie version of *Shizumanu taiyō* we even see the *isho* being written inside the plane, as well as being discovered by the son and read out again at a later point (with the names changed). In *One no kanata ni* the focus on the Uesugi family allows for inclusion of Taniguchi Masakazu's *isho* (with the name changed). As discussed elsewhere (Hood 2012, 104–5), the *isho* are one of the factors for which the crash is best known, so it would have been surprising for one not to be included.

Let us conclude this section by briefly discussing the other conventions of disaster movies in relation to the five dramatizations, but which were not hooks in the trailers. First, all five dramatizations include images of dead bodies at some point and also, as is particularly the case with *Kuraimāzu hai*, discussion of what was seen at the crash site. Both *Shizumanu taiyō* and *One no kanata ni* also show dead bodies and, particularly in the case of the latter, body parts as the two Minegishi brothers become involved in trying to identify remains using dental records and such like. In real life not only did they do this, but they would also later be involved in this process for the Hanshin Earthquake in 1995 and the Fukuchiyama Line derailment in 2005 (Kawahara interview 2009).

In the case of the NHK version of *Kuraimāzu hai* the closest to the death of a main character there is, is in relation to Yūki's friend, Anzai, with whom Yūki was meant to climb Mount Tanigawa in August 1985, and Yūki climbing the Tanigawa with Anzai's surviving son in memory of this. In addition to this storyline, the movie version has an additional scene in which one of the reporters, Kanzawa, suffers greatly from the trauma of visiting the crash site and is subsequently killed after running in front of a car. This storyline was suggested by the actor as he thought Kanzawa wanted to be released from the trauma he was suffering (Harada interview 2011). In both versions of *Shizumanu taiyō* Onchi's mother dies. In the case of *One no kanata ni*, as well as the family members who die in the crash, one of the widowers dies.

In all five of the dramatizations, there are "mini victories" where a protagonist manages to achieve a particular goal. However, in keeping with the overall themes of the suffering protagonist many of these victories may be undone, as is particularly apparent in the dramatizations of *Kuraimāzu hai*. When it comes to the convention of "isolation," this only appears in the two versions of *Shizumanu taiyō* when Onchi goes alone on some of his foreign postings. Even though, as discussed above, Yūki is essentially fixed to Gunma, he is not totally isolated, even within the newspaper where he has conflicts, as he has people, most notably Sayama. Similarly, those in *One no kanata ni* tend to be surrounded by people who provide support.

The final issue to discuss is whether there is contemporary significance. At one level, due to the inclusion of universal issues or morals, it could be argued that almost any story has contemporary significance. However, if we take a much narrower view and consider the contemporary significance in relation to the disaster itself, then *Kuraimāzu hai*, due to its main focus on the single week of reporting of the crash in 1985 has no contemporary significance, although the movie does end, as discussed above, with the fact that some are still calling for a reinvestigation. In terms of *Shizumanu taiyō*, an implication of the dramatizations is that the crash was related to poor management within the company. In that respect, the timing of the movie had additional contemporary significance as its release coincided with JAL going into administration. While initial media stories about JAL's woes focused purely on the financial aspect, when the publicity for *Shizumanu taiyō* began, articles referring to safety being a concern within JAL also began to appear. In relation to *One no kanata ni*, Okano (interview 2019) points out that they chose this story as they wanted to make a connection to the Great East Japan Disaster of March 2011, but in 2012 it was too soon to do one explicitly on that event and so chose another story with similar themes.

Conclusions

This chapter has considered the way in which Japanese disaster dramatizations portray the "truth" about actual events. To do this, the chapter focused on five narratives that relate to a single event, the crash of JAL flight JL123. It has pointed out that there are a number of factors that frame what a narrative can show. There are some practical limitations, such as the budget and length of the production. Further, there are certain conventions that tend to be a feature of a genre, which influence the way in which a narrative is constructed. There are also issues with the degree to which the "truth" is known.

Dramatizations are not documentaries, which are expected to be truthful. In fact, this assumed truthfulness of documentaries may be misplaced. For example, in relation to the JL123 crash, in one documentary (Cineflix 2005) one of the NTSB investigators says that he was at the crash site as flowers were dropped from helicopters to the crash site by families of victims. Such a thing could not have happened as the site was cleared that day. I subsequently learned from someone involved with the documentary in an anonymous interview that the investigator had been asked to say those things to make the story seem more dramatic. Dramatizations, on the other hand, much more explicitly have to play a balancing act between having an engaging narrative, while also ensuring that it is believable, even if not "truthful." In relation to truthfulness, accuracy and credibility, the concept of "pillars of truth," as put forward by Yokoyama, the author of a novel upon which two of the narratives that are analyzed in this study are based, is particularly pertinent. As noted, Yokoyama stresses that these pillars, which help readers/viewers to "flip"' the parts in between so that the relatively unbelievable parts are not an issue, are not merely about the "truth" of what actually happened in 1985 but are related to universal truths concerning human behavior. Consequently, what we find in the dramatizations is an assortment of aspects which appear to accurately reflect what happened in 1985, but other parts which are less accurate in terms of the crash and its aftermath itself, but which are in some way accurate in reflecting how people behave, interspersed with elements that are more fictional. Sorting through which is which requires significant time and is beyond what the typical viewer would do. That there are question marks still about the cause of the crash itself, for example, further points to the problems of not only comparing a dramatization with an actual event, but also highlights the way in which narratives could have the power to influence or even distort the debate on such issues.

The influence of the media cannot be ignored, and it is probable that dramatizations will have an impact on the public knowledge of the event. The degree to which this can be measured was beyond the scope of this study. Although I have come across some who were not aware that *Shizumanu taiyō*, for example, was based on a real event, I have also come across others who were inspired to learn more about what actually happened to JL123 after seeing one of the dramatizations, and so went on to read not only the novel upon which the dramatization was based, which contains more detail than a dramatization can show, but also more factual books. Given the level of interest in the JL123 crash, it is likely that we will see further dramatizations related to the crash in the future and these will further cement JL123's place in social memory in the same way that happened for the sinking of the *Titanic*. Further, although there have already been two versions of *Kuraimāzu hai* and *Shizumanu taiyō*, given the propensity for remakes in Japan, further remakes of these narratives could happen, opening up the possibility for additional analysis of how and why the contents of different narratives based on the same original book come about.

Will these dramatizations help us uncover the truth about what happened in 1985 or are they helping to distort the reality of events? Would a distortion aid or hinder responses to future disasters? The purpose of these narratives is largely to entertain and make money, but they clearly have influence and so we ignore their contents at our peril.

Notes

[1] This study does not include the movie *Osutakayama* (Watanabe Fumiki 2005) as it has not had widespread circulation.

Videography

Aftermath, 2017. [Film]. Directed by Elliott Lester. Santa Monica: Lionsgate Premiere.
Kuraimāzu hai [Climber's High], 2005. [TV program]. Directed by Wakaizumi Hisaaki. Tokyo: NHK.
Kuraimāzu hai [Climber's High], 2008. [Film]. Directed by Harada Masato. Tokyo: Tōei.
A Night to Remember, 1958. [Film]. Directed by Roy Baker. London: The Rank Organization.
One no kanata ni [Inseparable Souls: Fathers, Sons and The Crash of JAL123/Beyond The Ridge], 2012. [TV series]. Directed by Wakamatsu Setsurō. Tokyo: WOWOW.
Shizumanu taiyō [The Unbroken/The Sun Which Doesn't Set], 2009. [Film]. Directed by Wakamatsu Setsurō. Tokyo: Tōhō.
Shizumanu taiyō [The Sun Which Doesn't Set], 2016. [TV series]. Directed by Mizutani Toshiyuki and Suzuki Kōsuke. Tokyo: WOWOW.
Superman, 1978. [Film]. Directed by Richard Donner. Los Angeles: Columbia/EMI/Warner.
Titanic, 1997. [Film]. Directed by James Cameron. Los Angeles: Paramount Pictures/20th Century Fox.
Zulu, 1964. [Film]. Directed by Cy Enfield. Los Angeles: Paramount Pictures.

Bibliography

8/12 Renrakukai, 2005. *Akanegumo sōshūhen—Nikkōki Osutakayama tsuiraku jiko izoku no 20 nen* [Compilation of Akanegumo—The 20 years of the JAL Mount Osutaka crash bereaved]. Tokyo: Honnoizumisha.
BBC News Online, 2020. *The Crown should carry fiction warning, says culture secretary*. [online] Available at: https://www.bbc.co.uk/news/entertainment-arts-55122965 [Accessed 29 November 2020].
Belin, D.J., 1996. History According to Hollywood. *Wall Street Journal*, 13 February, 14.
Box Office Mojo, 2020. *All Time Box Office: Worldwide Grosses*. IMDbpro. [online] Available at: http://www.boxofficemojo.com/alltime/world/ [Accessed 17 November 2020].
Cineflix. 2005. "Out of Control," Episode 3, Season 3 of the series *Mayday*. Directed by Douglas Williams.
Connor, J.E., 1988. History in Images/Images in History: Reflections on the Impact of Film and Television Study for an Understanding of the Past. *American Historical Review*, 93(5), 1200–09.
Hall, S., 2014. *Zulu: With Some Guts Behind It*. Sheffield: Tomahawk Press.
HamsapSukebe. 2016. Shizumanu Taiyo Eps 1-8. [blog] July 13. Available at: http://hamsapsukebe.blogspot.co.uk/2016/07/shizumanu-taiyo-eps-1-8.html [Accessed 1 July 2017].
Hood, C.P., 2012. *Dealing with Disaster in Japan: Responses to the Flight JL123 Crash*. Abingdon: Routledge.
———., 2015. *Japan: The Basics*. Abingdon: Routledge.
———., 2018, *Osutaka: A Chronicle of Loss in the World's Largest Single Plane Crash*, Second Edition. Caradoc Books. https://caradocbooks.wordpress.com/2018/03/26/osutaka-a-chronicle-of-loss-in-the-worlds-largest-single-plane-crash-2/
———., 2020. Disaster Narrative by Design: Is Japan Different? *International Journal of Mass Emergencies and Disasters*, 38(2), 176–200.
Kinema Junpō, 2008. No 1512, Tokyo: Kinema Junpō.

Kuramoto, S., 2013. *Kiki kaki Kuramoto Sō dorama jinsei* [Account of what one hears—Kuramoto Sō, drama and human life]. Sapporo: Hokkaidō Shimbunsha.

Lennon, J. and Foley, M., 2004. *Dark Tourism*. London: Thomson Learning.

Mitchell, J.T., Thomas, D.S.K., Hill, A.A., and Cutter, S.L., 2000. Catastrophe in Reel Life versus Real Life: Perpetuating Disaster Myth through Hollywood Films. *International Journal of Mass Emergencies and Disasters*, 18(3), 383–402.

Nye, R.B., 1966. History and Literature: Branches of the Same Tree. In R.H. Bremner, ed., *Essays on History and Literature*. Columbus: Ohio State University Press.

Ogura, H., 1999. *Watashino ayundekita michi* [The path I walked]. [online] Available at: http://minseikoma bahongo.web.fc2.com/kikaku/99ogura.html [Accessed 8 May 2020].

Quarantelli, E.L., 1985. Realities and Mythologies in Disaster Films. *Communications*, 11(1), 31–44.

Standish, I., 2007. *Myth and Masculinity in the Japanese Cinema: Towards a Political Reading of the Tragic Hero*. London: Routledge.

Toplin, R.B., 1996. *History By Hollywood: The Use and Abuse of the American Past*. Chicago: University of Illinois Press.

———., 2002. *In Defense of Hollywood: Reel History*. Kansas: University Press of Kansas.

van Bremen, J., 2005. Monuments for the Untimely Dead or the Objectification of Social Memory in Japan. In T.Y. Hui, J. van Bremen and E. Ben-Ari, eds., *Perspectives on Social Memory in Japan*. Folkestone: Global Oriental, 23–43.

Yamazaki, T., 2001. *Shizumanu taiyō* [The Sun Which Doesn't Set] (5 volumes). Tokyo: Shinchōsha.

Yokoyama, H., 2006. *Kuraimāzu hai* [Climber's high]. Tokyo: Bungei Shunjū.

Yoshioka, S., 1986. *Tsuiraku no natsu—Nikkō 123bin jiko zenkiroku* [The summer of the crash—a complete record of the JAL123 accident]. Tokyo: Shinchōsha.

Chapter 3
Solace or Criticism? The Representation of the Fukushima Nuclear Disaster in Television Dramas and Films

Hilaria Gössmann

This chapter examines television dramas and films that tackle the triple disaster of March 11, 2011. It focuses on the possibilities and limitations of these fictional genres with regard to taking a critical stance. The first section addresses television dramas that either avoid mentioning the nuclear disaster or lack any criticism about how it was handled. This is in contrast with two films that describe a fictional nuclear disaster that occurs after Fukushima. Both films convey the message that Japan has learned nothing from the Fukushima catastrophe, since the fictional disaster is handled in the same problematic way.

Introduction

The triple disaster of the earthquake, tsunami and nuclear catastrophe that struck Japan on 11 March 2011—often referred to as 3.11—became the topic of many different genres in media and popular culture.[1] Several documentaries were produced soon after the disaster, the majority of which "are critical of the government and nuclear industry to a greater or lesser extent" (Fujiki 2017, 93). In terms of popular culture, manga (Japanese comics) were probably the first to deal with the disaster. However, manga artists have obviously been afraid "that bringing up the topic of Fukushima in the mainly entertainment-oriented form of manga might further traumatize the people who lived or still live in the region afflicted by the disaster" (Maser 2015, 560). Creators in different genres might have had similar concerns. Although it is characteristic of Japanese television dramas to tackle current social problems, very few dramas dealing with the 3.11 catastrophe have been produced. Furthermore, most of these dramas focus on the flood disaster, avoiding mention of the nuclear accident and contamination. Producers may have worried that it would be difficult to find sponsors for dramas addressing the nuclear disaster due to opposition from the "nuclear village" (*gen-shiryoku mura*)—"the institutional and individual pro-nuclear advocates who comprise the utilities, nuclear vendors, bureaucracy, Diet (Japan's parliament), financial sector, media and academia" (Kingston 2012).

While creators may have generally avoided tackling this difficult subject, some television and film productions have addressed issues related to 3.11, either directly or indirectly. This chapter analyzes some of these examples, with the aim of answering the following questions:

- What are the possibilities and limitations of dramas and films as entertainment genres with regards to depicting the nuclear accident?
- When describing the nuclear accident, what kind of people appear and what kind of attitudes do they have?
- What is missing or not addressed in these depictions?

The analysis reveals that, on the one hand, in dramas aired on the mass media format of television, there has been a tendency to avoid depicting the nuclear disaster and any criticism of the way it was handled. On the other hand, movies tackling the subject have offered greater potential for criticism.

Indirect representations of disaster: *Kaseifu no Mita*

Some months after 3.11, television dramas often portrayed people who had lost their family or loved ones or even a pet, but in the end succeeded in overcoming their grief and sorrow. This indirect way of dealing with a catastrophe that had caused the deaths of so many people might have been regarded as some sort of solace to those viewers who had lost relatives and loved ones in the disaster. The most famous example of this kind of drama is *Kaseifu no Mita* (I'm Mita, Your Housekeeper), broadcast from October to December 2011 on NTV. Its average audience rating of 25 percent was the highest for any television drama broadcast in 2011. The final episode achieved an audience share of 40 percent.[2]

The main character of the drama, Mita Akari, lost her husband and son in a fire. As she is the only one in her family who did not die, she is suffering from "survivor guilt," a type of trauma that typically manifests following an accident or catastrophe that results in a large loss of life. Sufferers feel extremely guilty for being the only ones who survived. As a result, Mita has lost all her will and motivation for life. She starts working as a housekeeper for a family of four children who have lost their mother. Because they have experienced similar pain, they have a mutual understanding of each others' grief. Ultimately, by helping each other, protagonist Mita and all the members of the family are able to recover. Thus, it could be argued that the drama had the potential to comfort many people with similar experiences.

Television dramas dealing directly with 3.11

As mentioned above, television dramas depicting 3.11 have tended to focus on the tsunami, leaving out the nuclear disaster. In 2013, the "morning television novel" (*asa no terebi renzoku shōsetsu* or *asadora* for short), *Ama-chan*,[3] named after its protagonist, was aired by public broadcaster NHK. As Scherer observes elsewhere in this volume, the motivation to set the series in a fictitious town in Tōhoku was likely a desire to support the region where the disaster happened, since the morning serials often encourage tourism. The tsunami disaster was not the main topic, given that it was only depicted in the last episodes of the series, and the nuclear accident is not mentioned at all. A characteristic of the morning series is that it tries to be rather optimistic, which might be the reason why in *Ama-chan*, none of the characters are killed by the tsunami. However, the morning television novel *Hanbun, aoi* (Half Blue Sky), which was broadcast by NHK from April to September 2018 and set in Tokyo, ends with the triple disaster and the subsequent death in the tsunami of the heroine's friend, who lives in Tōhoku. Nevertheless, this serial also makes no mention of the nuclear catastrophe. Although people in Tokyo, in particular parents with young children, also worried about radioactivity after the disaster, this is not addressed at all by any of the characters in the drama.

References to the nuclear disaster and its consequences are omitted in many television dramas. Even renowned screenwriter Yamada Taichi, who often incorporates various social issues into his television dramas, avoided addressing the events in his work in the direct aftermath. He explained his perspective in an essay:

> *After the earthquake catastrophe that was so terrible, and the nuclear power plant accident, I did not know what to do. I did not know how to write a drama. Following such a terrible disaster, it might be possible to impress people with heroic stories in a documentary. However, in the case of drama, which is fictional, a simple story would make no sense.* (Yamada 2015, 308)

Nevertheless, he eventually wrote the scripts for three dramas addressing 3.11. In the first one, *Kiruto no ie* (House of Quilt), aired by NHK in two parts on 28 January and 4 February 2012, the disaster is not the main topic. Yamada decided not to depict the victims living in the region. Instead, the drama focuses on a young couple that has moved to Tokyo from Tōhoku, where they experienced the tsunami disaster.

Three years after the disaster, Yamada Taichi travelled to the region and talked to survivors of the disaster. He then wrote the script for *Toki wa tachidomaranai* (Time Doesn't Stand Still), broadcast by commercial station TV Asahi on 20 July 2014. Here, Yamada focuses on the contrasting situations of two families. One family have been fishermen for generations, while the father of the other family is a banker. The son of the fisherman family was the fiancé of the banker's daughter. However, he and many members of his family died in the tsunami, while the young woman's entire family was saved because their house is on top of a hill. The website for the drama described it as "A touching drama that not only provides solace, but also delivers the light of hope" (TV Asahi 2014). As in the case of *Kiruto no ie*, the nuclear accident is not mentioned at all.

In the next drama Yamada Taichi wrote, the focus is also on the psychological consequences of the disaster. *Gonenme no hitori* (Alone for Five Years) was aired by TV Asahi on 19 November 2016 and achieved relatively high ratings of 11.4 percent. The main character is a veterinarian from the Tōhoku region who lost his entire family in the tsunami. He is played by the internationally renowned actor Watanabe Ken, who has appeared in both Japanese and Hollywood movies. One could say he was predestined for this role because of his volunteer work in Tōhoku (Masangkay 2021).

In the drama, the veterinarian is depicted as suffering from survivor guilt because he was not at home when the tsunami hit the coast. First, he tries to overcome his sorrow by working hard, but then realizes that he needs to be hospitalized for treatment. When he is discharged from the hospital, an acquaintance invites him to live in Tokyo to recover. He starts working in a small bakery. However, it is obvious that he still suffers from the trauma and has nightmares. One night he hallucinates a cow coming directly towards him though a thick fog. This scene perhaps hints at the trauma he is suffering because, as a veterinarian, he had to kill cows that were contaminated by radiation. However, this is the only scene in which the nuclear accident is referenced, albeit very indirectly.

The protagonist is able to gradually recover from his trauma thanks to his communication with a young girl who reminds him a lot of his own daughter, who was only 14 when she died. Since he deeply regrets that he rarely spent time with his daughter, he is very eager to talk to the teenage girl. When she learns from the owner of the bakery that he is hiding the fact that he lost his whole family in the tsunami, she encourages him to speak openly about it. Eventually, he is able to weep for the first time. While discussing the scene, Yamada noted that although five years had passed since the catastrophe, there were surely victims who were not yet able to really cry. He wanted Watanabe to weep on behalf of all those people (Orion News 2016).

The drama has a positive ending: the veterinarian decides to go back to his home town and starts working in his own profession again. The last scene shows him with a newborn calf and mother cow, after he has helped her give birth. The drama communicates to viewers the message that although five years have passed, for many victims, time is indeed standing still, as they cannot talk about their grief and thus cannot accept their loss. It demonstrates the power of the television drama genre to give valuable insight into the psyche of people and thus enable the viewers to empathize with them, which was undoubtedly the main goal of the scriptwriter.

The television drama, *Kizuna. Hashire, kiseki no kouma* (Bonds. Run, Miraculous Foal), based on the novel *Kizuna. Aru jinba no monogatari* (Bonds. A Story of Men and Horses), by Shimada Akihiro, was aired on NHK in two parts on 23 and 24 March 2017. The drama shows how a family in the town of Sōma in northeast Japan experienced the tsunami disaster and the aftermath. The father, played by the famous actor Yakushō Kōji, feels guilty because his son died while helping their horse give birth to a foal. Again, the topos of "survivor guilt" is addressed in this drama. Because it had been his son's dream to raise the foal as a race-horse, the father and his daughter do their best to realize that dream. That this now becomes their own dream helps both overcome their grief, because they can now look forward to the future instead of dwelling on the past.

Towards the end of part II of the drama, when the horse is one year old, they look for a farm where the horse can be trained for racing. However, they are refused over fears the horse might have been contaminated by radiation, even though it has already been tested. Finally, they decide to buy land from an acquaintance to use as an exercise area for the horse. However, this plan also fails when the government turns the land into a temporary storage area for vinyl bags filled with radioactive waste. Thus, all the obstacles that the father and daughter confront are due to the nuclear accident. Furthermore, the drama shows that animals, as well as human beings, can be discriminated against because of radiation. Nevertheless, as is the case with all the other television dramas about 3.11, there is a happy ending when, in the last scene, the horse runs in his first race.

A rare drama about the nuclear catastrophe

On 11 March 2015, the fourth anniversary of the Great East Japan Earthquake, a television drama that directly depicted the nuclear accident was aired for the first time. It was broadcast on commercial channel TV Tokyo, and 10 days later on Fukushima Television, and the following year, it was rebroadcast on BS Japan. The drama *Furagāru to inu no Choko* (The Hula Girl and Dog Choko) is based on the non-fiction children's book *Furagāru to inu no Choko: Higashi nihon daishinsai de hisaishita inu no monogatari* (The Hula Girl and Dog Choko: The story of a dog who became a victim of the Great East Japan Earthquake disaster) by Haraikawa Manabu, published the year after the earthquake.[4] Both the children's story and the television drama based on it reflect the true stories of the hula girls (dancers performing the Hawaiian hula dance on stage) at the Spa Resort Hawaiians leisure resort in Iwaki City, Fukushima Prefecture. A documentary film about the efforts of the hula girls to help the region recover after the disaster was screened throughout Japan in 2012 and was also released on DVD.

Although the television drama tells the story of a hula girl and her family who live near the nuclear power plant and are evacuated after the accident, the nuclear accident is completely omitted in the description published on the broadcaster's website (see TV Tokyo 2016). This stands in contrast to the website of the publisher of the children's book, which states: "The Fukushima nuclear power plant has exploded and large quantities of dangerous radioactive particles have been emitted" (Hāto Shuppan 2012). This is even more explicit than the language used in the children's book itself: "Radiation has been released; it is said to have a negative effect on humans, animals, plants, and vegetables" (Haraikawa 2012, 70).

The actress Takimoto Miori, who plays the lead role of the hula girl, expressed her feelings about the drama: "Honestly, I was so anxious that when those who actually suffered from the disaster watch the drama, they would remember that time, and feel pain. I wanted to give a more positive message beyond that" (Spa Resort Hawaiians Kōshiki Blog 2015). Dancer Omori Rie, whose story is told in the drama, reiterated these thoughts: "When people in Fukushima watch the drama [...] I don't think they will feel sad, but hopeful instead" (Spa Resort Hawaiians Kōshiki Blog 2015). Clearly, the actress, and most likely the production team, intended the drama to offer comfort to the audience.

Against this background, an analysis of the way in which the drama addresses the issue of the nuclear accident provides useful insight. The home of the protagonist of the drama, hula girl Sae, is in Futaba, where the nuclear power plant is located. The sign at the entrance to Futaba conveys a positive impression of the nuclear power plant: "Nuclear power—energy for a bright future" (Furagāru to inu no Choko 2015). In a scene of reminiscence, Sae says the following when the nuclear power plant can be seen quite close by: "The Fukushima Daiichi Nuclear Power Plant is located in Futaba, where I grew up, and we have lived with it" (Furagāru to inu no Choko 2015). After the earthquake, when Sae's family hear the evacuation warning, they do not realize that it could be related to a nuclear accident. They leave their dog at home, assuming they will be able to return the next day. The scene demonstrates that people living near the nuclear power plant believed it was safe, in what is referred to as *anzen shinwa* (myth of safety)..

One of the rare scenes in the drama that is directly related to the nuclear contamination shows the evacuated residents receiving instructions on returning home temporarily to

Handbook of Japanese Media and Popular Culture in Transition

collect some of their belongings. They are told that they are not allowed to take their pets out of the evacuated zone because they may have been contaminated by radiation. One of the evacuated men argues that they could decontaminate the cats and dogs, but the only answer he gets is: "For us, your health is the highest priority right now" (Furagāru to inu no Choko 2015). The authorities just keep repeating "Please cooperate." At the end of the scene, Sae's father complains that he has left all their property without knowing when he can return, and he is not even allowed to bring their dog back. Others protest loudly that they want their pets back, that they are part of their families. The victims are shown as being frustrated and angry which could be interpreted as criticism of the state and the nuclear power company's response to the victims. However, it is the only scene that portrays such criticism.

When Sae and her father are allowed to return home for just two hours, they give their dog Choko a large amount of food and water and remove the chain that is connected to the kennel, but are not able to take him with them. When they leave by car, the dog chases behind them and Sae weeps. This is shown in a long shot that seems designed to evoke an emotional response in the viewers too.

There is another interesting scene in which the issue of radioactive contamination is directly mentioned. After the disaster, the Spa Resort Hawaiians has to close, and the hula girls go on a nationwide tour to dance and promote the resort in order to invite people to visit the Spa Hawaiians again. They also hand out vegetables from Fukushima to passers-by, provoking negative reactions from some who say: "I don't want any. They are surely covered with radiation" (Furagāru to inu no Choko 2015).

The young couple refusing the vegetables here are depicted in quite a negative light. In the way they act and the words they use, they are conveyed as discriminating against the people from Fukushima. Another group of three young people appears to be a bit more cautious in the way they communicate that they do not approve of the hula girls giving away the vegetables. One man who is offered a tomato says: "I think you should stop doing this" (Furagāru to inu no Choko 2015).[5]

Nevertheless, the producers of the drama fail to use this scene as an opportunity to depict in more detail who, why and how the action of giving away the vegetables would be problematic. The scene could also have been used to provide valuable information about radioactivity. Or they could have tried to show the diversity of attitudes and ways of coping in the aftermath of the nuclear accident, for example by depicting parents worried about the health of small children and trying to learn about the dangers of radiation. Here the limitations of television become apparent. The creators' intention was obviously to use such scenes to criticize "harmful rumors" (*fūhyō higai*). The fact that it can indeed be dangerous to eat food contaminated by radioactive materials, especially for small children, is completely ignored, as is the case in almost all the programs that were aired on television after the disaster. At the end of the scene, Sae says that she knows that people are worried whether food from Fukushima is safe and pleads: "But please don't hate Fukushima. Don't think like that" (Furagāru to inu no Choko 2015). This is, of course, also an appeal to the audience.

In the drama, the Spa Resort Hawaiians resort serves as a microcosm symbolizing the whole region. As such, the reopening of the resort at the end of the drama embodies the revival of the disaster region. The hula dancers have written their own lyrics. In one of the very long scenes in the drama before it ends, the hula girls sing and dance to their own song, "Aina [homeland] Fukushima." The positive message of the song, asserting that they will make smiles bloom again in their homeland, is further strengthened by the protagonist's narration: "Four years after the earthquake, still overflowing with smiles" (Furagāru to inu no Choko 2015). The radioactivity problem is not addressed at all. The same is true for the abovementioned documentary film about the hula girls' campaign for the Spa Resort Hawaiians, which describes the post-disaster recovery efforts. This was criticized by Müller, who argues that the film seems to send the message that radioactivity disappears through smiling (2012, 228). The same might be said about the ending of *The Hula Girl and the Dog Choko*. However, as the linguistic analysis by Akiko Hayashi (2021) shows, the lyrics also imply that the situation is severe and there actually might be no reason for being optimistic.

What are the possibilities and limitations of the drama? It can be greatly appreciated, because beyond the main topic—Sae's grief that her dog is still in the evacuated zone—the drama tackles various issues that the survivors of the disaster face. Without doubt, this is one of the valuable possibilities of the genre, which can contribute to preserving the memory of the victims' suffering. Sae's best friend, who is also in the hula dance troupe, has lost many of her relatives and, like many survivors, suffers from survivor guilt; as a result, she is no longer able to continue dancing. However, when the hula dance troupe performs at the shelter where she lives, she is able to mentally recover and joins the group again. One of the senior dancers, who had wanted to leave the dance troupe to get married, suffers when her fiancé's family, who live in Tokyo, oppose their marriage because they are afraid she might be contaminated by radiation. Much like the survivors of the atomic bombs that were dropped at Hiroshima and Nagasaki in 1945, women from Fukushima often met discrimination because of the assumption that they would not be able to have healthy children (Makino 2021). Nevertheless, all these problems are resolved. On the day of the Spa Resort Hawaiians reopening, the dancer's fiancé is in the audience during the show and holds up a sign toward his fiancée on stage, on which he has written in big letters "Let's stay together forever," (Furagāru to inu no Choko 2015). Of course, a happy end for the dog Choko is also obligatory. The final scenes show how the dog is saved by volunteers and protagonist Sae is reunited with him.

Clearly, the aim of this drama is to comfort the audience, and thus anything that might hurt the feelings of the victims is avoided. Therefore, the limitation of the drama lies in that it does not deal with the dangers of nuclear power and conceals the fact that the problem of radioactive contamination has not been solved. This might have been self-constraint on the part of the show's creators, because it would have been impossible to find sponsors for a drama that is critical about nuclear energy.

Films after 3.11 depicting fictional nuclear disasters

Among the fictional films about the triple disaster that have been produced so far, very few focus on the nuclear accident. The danger of nuclear energy was clearly regarded as equally problematic within the film industry, and considered to be a topic that the big production companies would reject. Furthermore, filmmakers, similarly to producers of television dramas, might have been afraid to hurt the feelings of those who experienced 3.11. This could be one reason why in the two films that will be analyzed here, the setting is a fictional nuclear disaster that happens in Japan after 3.11.

Prominent filmmaker Sono Sion said in an interview that he had hoped that major film production companies like Tōhō would make a movie on this topic, because it would cause a lot of people to think about the matter (Iwata-Weickgenannt 2017, 111). Sono, who had already touched on the 3.11 tsunami disaster in *Himizu* (2011), released *Kibō no kuni* (The Land of Hope)[6] just one year after the disaster. The film was produced with funding from the UK, Taiwan and Germany (Iwata-Weickgenannt 2017, 112). It has been described as the first fictional movie based on the Fukushima nuclear accident; however, this movie, which depicts a nuclear accident in the near future, is set in a fictional prefecture called Nagashima, a name that of course simultaneously represents Hiroshima and Nagasaki, where the atomic bombs were dropped, as well as Fukushima. Thus, Sono links nuclear power to the atomic bomb and the Second World War. This analogy is reinforced in the film through the use of the term "invisible war" to describe the battle against radioactivity.

The main characters in *Kibō no kuni* are the Ono family: the father Yasuhiko, a dairy farmer, and his wife, who suffers from dementia, along with their son and his wife. After the nuclear accident, the border of the mandatory evacuation zone is built right through the middle of the Ono family's garden. The neighbors in the house next-door are evacuated, while the Ono family is ordered to stay. Watching this scene, you get the impression that the director intended to criticize, through the use of sarcasm, the idea of formally defining an area to be evacuated, for example, a 20-km range, without considering that radioactivity knows no borders. Nevertheless, this was based on fact: when Sono travelled to Fukushima Prefecture to scout for locations for his film, he actually met a family whose garden was demarcated in this way using "KEEP OUT" tape (Sono 2012).

The main character, Yasuhiko, understands very well the dangers of radioactivity. When the earthquake strikes, he immediately worries about the nuclear power plant, which is located 20 km away. In his warehouse, he looks for a geiger counter that he bought at the time of the Chernobyl nuclear accident and gives his daughter-in-law several books on the dangers of radioactivity that he bought when the Fukushima nuclear accident happened. The books shown in this scene were actually published around 2011. These critical books are obviously presented as an important alternative to the mass media approach, which is continually assuring the public that there is no danger of radioactivity. This is expressed in scenes where television programs tell housewives that they have nothing to worry about.

Yasuhiko decides to stay at home because evacuation would be difficult for his wife, who has dementia. However, he tells his son and daughter-in-law to evacuate voluntarily. After they move to another town, the daughter-in-law becomes pregnant and from then on, she is extremely afraid of being exposed to radiation. When she goes outside, she wears protective clothing resembling an astronaut's spacesuit, and she and her husband are laughed at and criticized.

When the evacuation area is extended to include the Ono family's house, they are ordered to evacuate, but Yasuhiko refuses to leave. He first sets his neighbor's dog free and then kills all his cows by shooting them. Finally, he kisses his wife and asks her whether they should die together. It is clear that she understands him and agrees, so he shoots her and himself. This is reminiscent of the double suicides by lovers that are often depicted in premodern Japanese literature, although the older age of the couple might be quite unusual.

Without being aware of their deaths, the son and his wife take the car and drive far away. When they take a rest at a beautiful beach, only the husband hears the alarm of their geiger counter go off. When the wife realizes that her husband seems to be worried, she says, "If we love each other, we will be fine" (Kibō no kuni 2012). How should one interpret both this conclusion as well as the word "hope" in the movie title? It might be considered ironic, or perhaps a way to avoid evoking feelings that are too dark. Of course, this is not exactly the happy ending that is presented in the television dramas, because the message clearly conveyed is that there is no escape from radioactivity anywhere.

Although the film sharply criticizes nuclear power plants and the mass media, its gender representation is very conventional, which can be seen as a limitation of the critical potential of the film. The pregnant young woman is depicted as hysterical, which can be viewed as an "uncritical reproduction of topoi such as 'female hysteria'" (Iwata-Weickgenannt 2017, 114). It is very common for Japanese mass media (especially those with a male readership or audience) to discredit women who worry about radioactivity by labelling them hysterical (see Yazawa 2012, 63). Iwata-Weickgenannt sees the reason for "Sono's reliance on a clear affirmation of traditional gender roles" in that it "makes his anti-nuclear criticism more socially acceptable" (2017, 114).

In 2013, the year after *Kibō no kuni* came out, the film *Asahi no ataru ie* (The House of (the) Rising Sun), directed by Ōta Takafumi, was released. The two movies have several similarities, since *Asahi no ataru ie* also depicts a fictional nuclear accident. The accident happens some years after Fukushima at the fictional Yamaoka nuclear power plant, a name that obviously references the real Hamaoka nuclear power plant in Shizuoka Prefecture.

The main characters in the film are a family of four—a father, mother, and two daughters, one attending college and one at junior high school. The father runs a strawberry farm, and the mother is a housewife. The mother's brother, who lives in Okinawa, also appears. One of the oldest daughter's friends is an anti-nuclear activist. He has an important role in the film, and is played by Ishida Issei, who published an autobiographical essay titled *No genpatsu, one love* (No nuclear power plants, one love) (Ishida 2012). In the film his nickname is "nuclear power plant brother" (Asahi no ataru ie 2013), but in fact, the term "anti-nuclear power plant brother" would be more appropriate He distributes leaflets promoting anti-nuclear rallies using the language "Don't Forget 3.11," thus directly mentioning Fukushima. He repeatedly teaches the dangers of nuclear power to the family and, of course, to the movie audience as well.

When the earthquake happens, the oldest daughter is attending a university lecture. After the earthquake, a friend sitting next to her remembers Fukushima and says, "Maybe there will be another nuclear accident?", but the students are not really worried (Asahi no ataru ie 2013). Rather, they wonder if their favorite band will play at a relief concert in their area if a nuclear accident occurs, as had happened in Fukushima. The goal of this scene seems to be to show the audience the kind of problematic, easygoing attitude some young people tend to have.

After the accident, the anti-nuclear activist comes to the family's house to explain the dangers of the Fukushima accident and the current situation and urges them to evacuate immediately. However, the family stays at home until the evacuation is ordered. As in the Hula Girl drama, the residents clearly assume they will be able to return the next day. However, they eventually wait six months, and only the adults are allowed to return home for just two hours. This scene is very different from the one in the television drama, because thieves had broken into the family's house in the intervening period and destroyed everything. The younger daughter, who was not allowed to join them, is worried about the beloved dog in the neighboring house, who had been left in the zone. Therefore, she hides in the trunk of her parents' car and searches in vain for the dog, thus staying in the zone until her parents find her later that night.

When the family is finally allowed to return to their own house, only the father moves back home in order to try to decontaminate the house, while the mother and two daughters remain in their temporary housing. The younger daughter becomes ill and has to be hospitalized, but the doctor explains that she is not sick from radiation exposure, but because of stress, which could be interpreted as an indication of the psychological effects of the disaster and radiation leak. The uncle comes from Okinawa to see her and invites the family to live with him in Okinawa, but the father refuses because he cannot leave his hometown. Eventually, the younger daughter is hospitalized in a distant town, and the family moves to an apartment near the hospital.

The mother of the nuclear power activist leaves her temporary housing and returns home. However, her dog is missing and she is told that she cannot eat the vegetables in her garden. Finally, she commits suicide after writing "I hate nuclear power" on the wall of her house (Asahi no ataru ie 2013). Later, her son participates in an anti-nuclear demonstration in Tokyo, holding a picture of his mother. This is the only scene depicting an anti-nuclear demonstration in either of the two fictional films discussed in this chapter and helps to convey at least a little hope, although the film has a very sad ending.

How are nuclear power and radioactivity represented in *Asahi no ataru ie*? While the film *Kibō no kuni* does not present any images of the nuclear power plant, in this movie, it is shown from a distance. The mother is the person most worried about the nuclear power plant. She uses almost all of the subsidies she receives from the power company to buy geiger counters. However, there is no depiction of the female hysteria found in *Kibō no kuni*. Of all the dramas and films examined here, the mother in *Asahi no ataru ie* is the only woman who protests against the way the people in charge handle the radioactivity problem. At an assembly, the people who were evacuated are informed that they will soon be allowed to return to their houses, with decontamination measures to start after they are back home. During the meeting, she is the first to suddenly stand up and demand that they finish the decontamination process before the families return home. Following her lead, almost all the other women at the assembly also stand up, one after the other. Finally, the anti-nuclear activist and another young male friend of his are the only men who join in the protest, which, nevertheless, is not successful. This scene emphasizes that it is women who are mostly concerned about radioactivity, as was actually the case in Japan.

As in *Kibō no kuni*, *Asahi no ataru ie* also repeatedly criticizes the mass media, especially television. This is very evident when the oldest daughter says in a voice over: "While television was telling us we were safe, the radiation had already leaked out" (Asahi no ataru ie 2013). In a symbolic scene, the television screen is shown, with a man criticizing the "false rumors that children in Fukushima have been having nosebleeds," while the younger daughter actually sits in front of the television with her nose bleeding. Thus, the scene conveys the gap between the media messaging and the actual situation in the affected area. The anti-nuclear activist also addresses media issues, asserting that the media do not want to criticize the nuclear power plant because the electricity company pays advertising fees to television stations and newspapers.

In addition, the anti-nuclear power message of *Asahi no ataru ie* is emphasized by Yamamoto Tarō's appearance as the uncle living in Okinawa. Yamamoto was originally an actor, but stopped receiving job offers after he started his anti-nuclear activities and became a politician. In an interview, he explained why he was interested in appearing in the film:

When I read the script, I thought that all the people who have not been able to get the real facts because of the biased mass media, such as television and newspapers, which worry about sponsors, might be able to experience the misery of the nuclear accident through this film. I thought that because I am actively against nuclear power plants in my personal life, it would not be necessary to be active as an actor in a film, but I talked with the director and read the script and that changed my mind. (Asahi no ataru ie. Kōshiki hōmupēji 2013)

Conclusion

Both television dramas and films have demonstrated the potential to portray the triple disaster from the victim's point of view. "Survivor guilt" has been a particularly common topos, even in television dramas. Giving an insight into the psychological aspects and showing different ways of dealing with them, as well as the possibility of subsequent recovery from trauma, are without doubt some of the positive messages that dramas and films have to offer. Some even use the genres to convey inner feelings directly through narration, as is the case in *Furagāru to inu no Choko* and *Asahi no ataru ie*.

In terms of the characters who appear, it is common to all the television dramas that not even one person takes a critical stance. This aligns with the messaging in the mainstream Japanese mass media at that time, and reveals the limitation of dramas broadcast on television. In the film *Kibō no kuni*, however, the main character Yasuhiko is very critical of nuclear energy and explicitly tells his son and daughter-in-law that they should not believe what the government and mass media say. However, only *Asahi no ataru ie* features an anti-nuclear activist.

Most of the dramas and films analyzed here have a tendency to depict conservative gender roles. In *Furagāru to inu no Choko*, among the group of evacuated people, it is predominantly men who protest against the order to not take pets out of the evacuated zone. In *Kibō no kuni* and *Asahi no ataru ie*, the gender roles are also very conventional. However, in contrast to *Kibō no kuni*, *Asahi no ataru ie* does not depict "female hysteria." Furthermore, the mother in the latter film not only acts on an individual level, but at least in one scene, she openly protests against allowing the families to return to their homes before decontamination has been undertaken.

While the television dramas focus on cheering up and comforting the audience, the two films, on the contrary, emphasize the dangers of radiation. Unlike the television dramas, the films provide important information about the perils and the problematic way the mass media "inform," indicating sharp criticism of the media. By depicting nuclear accidents in the near future, these two films show that the lessons from Fukushima are not being understood by many people. Such a dystopian warning surely would not have been feasible in dramas aired on television. Iwata-Weickgenannt's (2017, 113) assessment that "*Land of Hope's* setting in the not-too-distant post-'Fukushima' future further encourages a reading of the film as an indictment of an industry, a government, and a society that apparently learned nothing from the most serious nuclear disaster since Chernobyl" also applies to *Asahi no ataru ie*.

Notes

1 For an analysis of the representation of 3.11 in different genres in media and popular culture, see e.g., Gebhardt and Yuki (2014), Gebhardt and Richter (2013), Geilhorn and Iwata-Weickgenannt (2017), Gössmann (2021).

2 The drama received several awards, including the "Best Drama Award." For an analysis of this drama series, see Usami et al. (2016).

3 Almost all dramas mentioned in this chapter are available on DVD.

4 For an analysis of this children's book, see Gössmann (2019) and Hayashi (2021). The drama is the only one mentioned in this chapter that was not released on DVD.

5 See Hayashi (2021) for an analysis of these scenes.

6 See Iwata-Weickgenannt (2017) for an in-depth analysis of the film.

Videography

Asahi no ataru ie [The House of (the) Rising Sun], 2013. [Film] Directed by Ōta Y. Japan: Shibuya Production.
Furagāru to inu no Choko [The Hula Girl and Dog Choko], 2015. [TV program] TV Tokyo, 11 March 2015.
Kibō no kuni [The Land of Hope], 2012. [Film] Directed by Sono Sion. Japan: Third Window Films.

Bibliography

Asahi no ataru ie. Kōshiki hōmupēji, 2013. *Yamamoto Tarō intabyū* [Interview with Yamamoto Tarō]. [online] Available at: http://asahinoataruie.jp/yamamoto.html [Accessed 12 July 2021].

Fujiki, H., 2017. Problematizing Life: Documentary Films on the 3.11 Nuclear Catastrophe. In B. Geilhorn and K. Iwata-Weickgenannt, eds., *Fukushima and the Arts. Negotiating Nuclear Disaster*. London: Routledge, 90–109.

Gebhardt, L. and Richter, S., eds., 2013. *Lesebuch Fukushima. Übersetzungen, Kommentare, Essays* [Fukushima reader: translations, comments, essays]. Berlin: EB-Verlag.

Gebhardt, L. and Yuki, M., eds., 2014. *Literature and Art after "Fukushima": Four Approaches*. Berlin: EB-Verlag.

Geilhorn, B. and Iwata-Weickgenannt, K., eds., 2017. *Fukushima and the Arts. Negotiating Disaster*. London: Routledge.

Gössmann, H., 2019. Der Hund, der in Fukushima blieb. Die Atomkatastrophe im dokumentarischen Kinderbuch *Furagāru to inu no Choko* [The dog that stayed in Fukushima: depiction of the nuclear disaster in the nonfiction children's book *Hula Girl and Dog Choko*]. In L. Gebhardt and M. Kinski, eds., *Nukleare Narrationen. Kinder im Atomzeitalter. Berichte, Befunde, Bilder* [Nuclear narrations: children in the nuclear age—reports, findings, images]. Berlin: EB Verlag, 185–95.

————., ed., 2021. *Dokumentation, Trostspende oder Anklage? Die Atomkatastrophe von Fukushima in japanischen Medien, Populärkultur und Literatur* [Documentation, solace or accusation? The depiction of the Fukushima nuclear disaster in Japanese media, popular culture and literature]. Schriften der Gesellschaft für Japanforschung [Publications of the Japan research association], vol. 4. Available at: https://www.gjf.de/netzpublikationen.htm [Accessed 12 July 2021].

Haraikawa, M., 2012. *Furagāru to inu no Choko. Higashi nihon daishinsai de hisai shita inu no monogatari* [The Hula Girl and Dog Choko. The story of a dog that became a victim of the Great East Japan Earthquake]. Tokyo: Hāto Shuppan.

Hāto Shuppan, 2012. *Furagāru to inu no Choko. Higashi nihon daishinsai de hisai shita inu no monogatari* [The Hula Girl and Dog Choko. The story of a dog that became a victim of the Great East Japan Earthquake]. [online] Available at: http://www.810.co.jp/hon/ISBN978-4-89295-912-7.html [Accessed 12 July 2021].

Hayashi, A., 2021. Die Dreifach-Katastrophe im Kinderbuch und im Fernsehdrama *Furagāru to inu no Choko* [The triple disaster in the children's book and the television drama *Hula Girl and Dog Choko*]. In H. Gössmann, ed., *Dokumentation, Trostspende oder Anklage? Die Atomkatastrophe von Fukushima in japanischen Medien, Populärkultur und Literatur* [Documentation, solace or accusation? The depiction of the Fukushima nuclear disaster in Japanese media, popular culture and literature]. Schriften der Gesellschaft für Japanforschung, vol. 4. Available at: https://www.gjf.de/netzpublikationen.htm [Accessed 12 July 2021].

Ishida, I., 2012. *No genpatsu, one love!* [No nukes, one love]. Tokyo: Seishisha.

Iwata-Weickgenannt, K., 2017. Gendering "Fukushima": Resistance, Self-Responsibility and Female Hysteria in Sono Sion's Land of Hope. In B. Geilhorn and K. Iwata-Weickgenannt, eds., *Fukushima and the Arts. Negotiating Nuclear Disaster.* London: Routledge, 110–26.

Kingston, J., 2012. Japan's Nuclear Village. *The Asia-Pacific-Journal: Japan Focus,* 10 (37/1). [online] Available at: https://apjjf.org/2012/10/37/Jeff-Kingston/3822/article.html [Accessed 12 July 2021].

Makino, H., 2021. Testimonies Reveal Discrimination, Oppression of Fukushima Women after Nuclear Crisis. *Mainichi Daily News* [online]. 10 March. Available at: https://mainichi.jp/english/articles/20210310/p2a/00m/0na/030000c [Accessed 1 October 2021].

Masangkay, M., 2021. Feature: Actor Ken Watanabe's Encounters with 3.11 Victims a "Lifetime's Work." Kyodo News, [online] 4 March. Available at: https://english.kyodonews.net/news/2021/03/0d8cc741e88f-feature-actor-ken-watanabes-encounters-with-311-victims-a-lifetimes-work.html [Accessed 25 September 2021].

Maser, V., 2015. Nuclear Disasters and the Political Possibilities of Shōjo (Girls') Manga (Comics): A Case Study of Works by Yamagishi Ryōko and Hagio Moto. *The Journal of Popular Culture,* 48(3), 558–71.

Müller, J. C., 2013. Der japanische Film nach "Fukushima" [Japanese cinema after "Fukushima"]. In L. Gebhardt and S. Richter, eds., *Lesebuch Fukushima. Übersetzungen, Kommentare, Essays* [Fukushima reader: translations, comments, essays]. Berlin: EB-Verlag, 220–32.

Oricon News, 2016. Watanabe Ken: Dorama no chikara o kanjita. Yamada Taichi no kyakuhon de shinsai no "sono go" o egaku [Watanabe Ken: I felt the power of dramas. A script by Yamada Taichi depicting the time after the disaster]. *Oricon News* [online]. Available at: https://www.oricon.co.jp/news/2081643/full/ [Accessed 12 July 2021].

Sono, S., 2012. *Kibō no kuni* [Land of Hope]. *Making of.* DVD.

Spa Resort Hawaiians kōshiki blog, 2015. *Dorama supesharu "Furagāru to inu no Choko" shuzaikai nite* [At the press conference of the drama special "The Hula Girl and Dog Choko"]. [online] Available at: http://blog.hawaiians.co.jp/archives/51579284.html [Accessed July 12, 2021].

TV Asahi, 2014. *Yamada Taichi dorama supesharu. Toki wa tachidomaranai* [Yamada Taichi drama special: Time doesn't stand still]. [online] Available at: https://web.archive.org/web/20140203124229/http://www.tv-asahi.co.jp/tokitachi/ [Accessed 12 July 2021].

TV Tokyo, 2015. *Dorama shupesharu. Furagāru to inu no Choko* [Drama special: The Hula Girl and Dog Choko]. [online] Available at: https://www.tv-Tokyo.co.jp/hula_choco/index.html [Accessed 12 July 2021].

Usami, T., Hayashi, A. and Gössmann, H., 2016. Terebi dorama gakusaiteki bunseki no kokoromi: "Kaseifu no Mita" o rei ni [Interdisciplinary analysis of a television drama: "The Housekeeper Mita" as a case study]. Chūō Daigaku Bungakubu, ed., *Kiyō gengo, bungaku, bunka,* 117, 119–48.

Yamada, T., 2015. *Sono toki ano toki no ima: shiki terebi dorama 50 nen* [Past and present: my memory of 50 years of television drama]. Tokyo: Kawade Shobō Shinsha.

Yazawa, M., 2012. "Umu sei" to genpatsu. Tsushima Yūko o tegakari ni [The gender that gives birth and nuclear power plants. With reference to Tsushima Yūko]. In Shin feminizumu hihyō no kai, ed., *San ten ichi ichi ikō no feminizumu: Datsu genpatsu to atarashii sekai e* [Feminism after "3.11 Fukushima": Towards a nuclear power phase-out and a new world]. Tokyo: Ochanomizu Shobō, 57–68.

Part 2
Transitions and Transcultural Flows

Chapter 4
Red-Light Bases (1953):
A Cross-Temporal Contact Zone

Irene González-López

This chapter examines the gender politics at play in the cinematic imagination of post-Occupation Japan through the analysis of the controversial film Akasen kichi (Red-Light Bases, Taniguchi Senkichi, 1953). To this end, it focuses on the film's depiction of the panpan sex worker and the returned soldier—arguably the most symbolic figures of early postwar Japan—and their interactions with other members of the community in a town marked by the presence of an American military base. It argues that, while Taniguchi's film critically depicts the complex power dynamics at play in this sexual "contact zone," it also works to disavow Japanese men's responsibility for the war by translocating their moral accountability and trauma onto "fallen" women and the Occupation.

Introduction

In a 1990 keynote address, Mary Louise Pratt introduced the concept of "contact zones," which she defined as "social spaces where cultures meet, clash, and grapple with each other, often in contexts of highly asymmetrical relations of power, such as colonialism, slavery, or their aftermaths" (Pratt 1991, 34). Since then, the term has been adopted and developed across the humanities, and especially in postcolonial studies, feminist theory and critical race theory. The notion of a contact zone encourages thinking beyond the dichotomy of vanquisher versus victim and rejecting the image of a community as a homogeneous entity. It calls attention to multi-directional and multi-layered discourses that co-exist in tension with each other. A contact zone is a creative space in flux where instances of bilingualism, miscomprehension, parody, denunciation and appropriation take place under vernacular and imposed forms of expression as well as under new hybrid forms of communication (Pratt 1991, 1992).

For its potential to unearth disregarded voices and to problematize what may appear as absolute positions of domination and subordination, Pratt's concept has been applied to the study of interactions of Japanese subjects, as both colonizers and colonized (Ballantyne and Burton 2005; Tanaka and Funayama 2011; Kramm 2017). In his study of prostitution under the Allied Occupation of Japan (1945–1952), Robert Kramm emphasizes both conflict and cooperation *between* and *among* Japanese and American institutions and individuals when he argues that prostitution and its regulation constituted a contact zone "for both occupiers and occupied to negotiate, reproduce, but occasionally also undermine the asymmetric power relations between and among them" (2017, 22–23). Tanaka Masakazu (2012) analyzes the social perception of *panpan* as "intermediaries" (borrowing an expression of Ōe Kenzaburō) who could be both "cooperator and part of the resistance." *Panpan* was the derogatory expression commonly used in the postwar era to refer to streetwalkers and was usually—although not entirely accurately—identified with those soliciting foreign servicemen. Tanaka posits occupied Japan as a "sexual contact zone" where notions of gender and sexuality are utilized to comment on the power asymmetries between the US and Japan. Social anxiety was projected on the *panpan* and complicated by the social, financial and personal interactions between *panpan*, the rest of the local community and the settled foreigners.

Japan officially regained its sovereignty on 28 April 1952 (Okinawa not until 1972). The following year saw an explosion of books and films critically reflecting on the Occupation and the impact of the remaining US military installations in Japan. Among the seven films developed in 1953 depicting base cultures, *Akasen kichi* (Red-Light Bases), directed by Taniguchi Senkichi, attracted great controversy because it was the only one produced by a major studio. Taniguchi's film revolves around two of the most symbolic figures of early postwar imagination—the *panpan* and the returned soldier—and exemplifies the dynamics at play in the contact zone.

Nakamura Hideyuki (2014) analyzes the political controversy around the release of *Akasen kichi*, which he reappraises for its articulation of the postwar theme of identity crisis. Saitō Ayako (2018) compares the representation of *panpan* in Taniguchi's film with that of *Yoru no onnatachi* (Women of the Night, Mizoguchi Kenji, 1948) to discuss the connections between the Occupation, censorship and sexuality. Examining the films' narratives and their use of real and fictional spaces, Saitō investigates what the films reveal of the perception and imagining of the body politics of occupied and post-occupied Japan. In dialogue with Nakamura's and Saitō's work, I seek to explore the political implications of the narrative and creative choices made in *Akasen kichi* in depicting such a controversial and timely subject. Viewing the film through the lens of the contact zone, I analyze the representation of the *panpan* and the returned soldier through their interactions with other members of the community. Finally, I propose to read the base theme in Taniguchi's film as a cross-temporal contact zone that speaks more of the past experience of national occupation than it does of the contemporaneous context of base towns in 1953.

Prostitution and the base towns

In 1953, more than 700 US military bases extended over 245,000 acres of Japanese land and continued to expand (Kovner 2012, 9). Japan's logistic support to the US army during the Korean War (1950–1953) and other regional conflicts during the Cold War, provoked a social backlash but also a boost to the national economy. Japan became the "Rest and Recreation" destination for international forces (Rowley 2002, 45) and the number of prostitutes in proximity to bases rose. Many of these prostitutes had previously worked in the Recreation and Amusement Association (RAA)—the private organization established at the Japanese government's request to provide prostitutes and other entertainment for the Occupation Forces upon their arrival, which closed down in March 1946 (Fujime 1997; Kramm 2017).

Soon after abolishing state-regulated prostitution, in December 1946 General Douglas MacArthur, Supreme Commander for the Allied Powers (SCAP), declared prostitution legal in delineated red-light districts in each city. A survey conducted in 1948 showed that, while most people disapproved of illegal streetwalkers or *panpan*, they held ambiguous judgments about brothels because they fulfilled a "social necessity" (*Kokuritsu yoron chōsajo* 1951, 5). The early 1950s witnessed a reinvigorated campaign for the ban of prostitution in the name of human rights, public morality and democracy. In the journal *Fujin kōron* (Women's review), the primary voice of the abolitionist movement, articles justifying prostitution almost faded away. Prostitutes were rendered "different from Japanese women," "depraved," "crazy" and "aggressive" (e.g., *Fujin kōron* 1950a, 99–103, 1950b, 34). The prostitute embodied all the decadence that the postwar democratic society aimed to overcome, and the fiercest criticism targeted the *panpan*. In May 1952, the journal published a letter by Uemura Tamaki, a major figure in the anti-prostitution movement, to the wife of General Matthew Bunker Ridgway, MacArthur's successor during the last year of the Occupation. Uemura decried that Japanese children "play *panpan*" by mimicking the vulgarities of prostitutes and GIs while using indecent slang mixed with English (1952, 39). From the "universal stance of motherhood," she claimed to feel sorry for the mothers of the GIs and ashamed that these "parasites" were perverting decorous American boys (1952, 40). Blame fell exclusively on the *panpan*, a smart approach that allowed Uemura to criticize prostitution and its connection to the Occupation while avoiding SCAP censorship. Just a few months later, an editorial published after Japan had regained its sovereignty explicitly assigned responsibility to the US forces in the matter:

> As long as foreign soldiers do not leave our land, these grotesque women born from the blood of war will not decrease, and we have to admit that there is even the possibility that they will spread even further. (Fujin kōron 1952, 27)

The anti-prostitution movement made children and motherhood the core of their campaign, which generated synergies with parent-teacher associations and the anti-base movement (which was evolving from dispersed local disputes into a nationwide crusade) (Shimizu et al. 1953; Kovner 2012, 74–98, Bardsley 2014; Kusunoki 2016). The presence of streetwalkers, they argued, infringed upon the right of children to be raised in an environment free from "sexual sights and sounds" (Sanders 2012, 427). The fact that many *panpan* were also mothers was systematically ignored, and the existence of other kinds of prostitution—brothels and streetwalkers catering to Japanese men, for example—was generally disavowed when speaking about base towns. *Fujin kōron* depicted "mixed-race children" (*konketsuji*) as the ultimate victims, and articles on the subject appeared almost invariably next to articles on prostitution around military bases, although even Uemura acknowledged that the percentage of mixed-race children born of *panpan* was actually quite low (1953, 44).

After Japan regained its sovereignty, prostitution in the proximities of US military installations also became the subject of an array of literature that often followed a clear political agenda (e.g., Mizuno 1953; Hiroike 1953 [reprinted in Molasky 2015]; Shimizu et al. 1953; Nishida 1953; Kanzaki 1974). Some non-fictional accounts were carefully edited to project a certain image and others were manufactured (Molasky 1999, 123). In these texts the *panpan* is frequently "otherized," eroticized and ultimately blamed for her inescapable, tragic fate.

Some *panpan* novellas, like Hiroike Akiko's *Onrii-tachi* (The Only Ones, 1953), offered a more sympathetic view of these women's agency and revealed a wider web of discrimination and exploitation (on the depiction of *panpan* in literature after 1952 see Molasky 1999; Tanaka 2012). As Nakamura notes, while several fictional and non-fictional publications were adapted for the cinema in 1953 by independent production companies that were often labelled anti-American and pro-communist, *Akasen kichi* became the target of the most vociferous criticism from American journalists because it was the first "base film" produced by a major studio, Tōhō (2014, 93–95).

Against this historical context and burgeoning media production, *Akasen kichi* was due to be released on 30 September 1953. However, after a private preview screening, American journalists based in Japan vehemently accused the film of being anti-American, triggering a public debate that led to the cancellation of the film's release (for an analysis of the film's production and reception see Nakamura 2014, 89–104). When the film eventually reached the screens in December, Tōhō utilized the political controversy as a promotional strategy but the film's reception was somewhat lukewarm. Some noted the film had missed the momentum of the "base films'" (*kichi mono būmu*), others found it not critical enough of the base problem, and others rendered it as mere sexploitation or political sensationalism (Togawa 1954; Anderson and Richie [1959] 1982, 219–20; Nakamura 2014, 92–98).

If one were to examine only the first ten minutes of the film, the accusations of anti-Americanism would not seem far-fetched. The opening credits begin with the film's title superimposed in white and run over the images of wood-block prints of Mount Fuji (Hokusai's *Thirty-six Views of Mount Fuji* series, c.1830–1832). The dramatic orchestral score is overlaid with the sounds of a military band. As Nakamura and Saitō note, the metaphor is self-explanatory; Japan is under siege, transformed into a prostitution market by the presence of the American bases. After ten years away, Kawanabe Kōichi (Mikuni Rentarō), dressed in the distinct fashion of repatriates from Manchuria, rides a bus under the judgemental eyes of other passengers. He is returning to his hometown at the foot of Mount Fuji, which has been drastically transformed by the establishment of an American military base. On the bus he meets Julie, whom he mistakes for a respectable lady from a well-off neighborhood to the amusement of other passengers who, unlike Kōichi, read the visual codes that identify her as *panpan*. After Kōichi steps off the bus, a pastoral landscape overseen by a grand zelkova tree accompanies his voice-over, in which he describes dreaming of the tree every night in Manchuria because, for him, underneath it are his "father, mother, siblings." The camera cuts to a close-up of the treetop as the dramatic military-like music score returns and then tilts down to reveal the tree behind a barbed wired fence. Bewildered, Kōichi walks along the fence. In the background, two GIs play catch ball while another one talks to a Japanese woman on this side of the fence. Two signs appear on screen: the first, written in English and Japanese, warns against trespassing and the second, in Japanese only, warns women against being in the surroundings after 5 p.m.—implying it is ultimately women's responsibility to protect their bodies and reputations. The camera closes in on this sign as Kōichi exits the frame. The symbol of his home has been shuttered, occupied by foreign troops who idly spend their time, catch ball and flirting being presented as equitable pastimes. The association between the base and the corruption of Japanese women's chastity is visually and audibly reinforced in the scene.

Akasen kichi is set in the surroundings of the East Fuji Maneuver Area (Shizuoka Prefecture), an actual US military training ground that had previously belonged to the Japanese imperial army (nowadays operated by the Japan Ground Self-Defense Force). This fact added to the sense of realism of the film, while probably setting off the alarms of American observers. The second sequence of the film introduces the base town in a documentary style, shot on location near the base in what is now the city of Gotemba. GIs move around loudly on streets full of bars with signs written in English. As Kōichi asks around trying to locate his family, he realizes that many people are new to the town, lured by the job opportunities brought about by the base. It is noteworthy that the two mixed-race children featured in the sequence appear under the care of men. An old man, for example, is registering a mixed-race girl as his daughter; she is in fact his granddaughter, but the father is unknown and the mother absent. In a close-up the girl looks out of the frame paying attention to how the adults speak about her. The abandoned child is linked to the figure of the missing mother implying that women, whether due to work or lack of responsibility, are not fulfilling their expected duty as mothers. Yet, from a different perspective, it hints at women as breadwinners outside the domestic realm and the inversion of traditional gender roles. The base's negative influence on children is underscored throughout the film by showing, for instance, children witnessing the embrace of *panpan* and GIs or playing with bullets.

This opening evokes critical independent productions of 1953 in its filming style and its relatively bold depictions (it was still rare to see American GIs and mixed-race children in Japanese cinema) that highlighted local and transnational socio-economic dynamics. The film also includes references to contemporaneous discourses and media texts. For instance, Nakamura (2014, 107–8) explains that the appearance, location and problems of Toshio's school, constantly disrupted by the noise of bombs and the presence of *panpan*, closely resemble that of the actual Fujioka school, located near the East Fuji Maneuver Area and discussed in the popular book *Kichi nihon* (Fortress Japan, Shimizu et al. 1953) as an example of the base town's threats against children. Intertextual references and the general media context arguably influenced the viewers' expectations towards and understandings of *Akasen kichi* and hampered other potential readings that this chapter seeks to unpack. After the first ten minutes, the film leaves aside the documentary-like depiction of the town to focus on the melodrama that unravels among specific characters in the contact zone.

The *panpan*, an extraordinary intermediary

In the early 1950s there were between 50,000 and 100,000 *panpan* in Japan (Fujime 1997; Sanders 2012). Their earnings usually ranged between 20,000 and 50,000 yen per month; at least three times that of a factory worker (Minami 1949, 80; Rowley 2002, 42–43; Kovner 2012, 81). As shown in the film, most *panpan* worked independently, but some had a pimp—in *Akasen kichi* Harue, Kōichi's first love, works under his brother, Ken'ichi. A substantial number of *panpan* had middle-class backgrounds and some left their standard jobs to enter the trade (Sanders 2012, 419–20)—the character of Julie worked in a pharmaceutical company until one year prior to the start of the story. The reasons for becoming a *panpan* were varied and often complex, including economic need, seeking a new life, having engaged in a relationship with a GI, experiencing rape and being deceived by a pimp (Minami 1949, 74–76; Sanders 2012, 419–20). According to a 1955 survey by the Women and Minors Bureau (Ministry of Labor), in comparison to brothel workers, panpan carried fewer debts, preferred to work alone and fewer wished to marry; those working near military bases tended to be the most independent (Kovner 2012, 81).

The different subplots involving Kōichi's family members illustrate how the base town's economy, both officially and underground, depended heavily on the servicemen and the prostitutes and mistresses that followed them. His family's land was expropriated for the sake of the base and, to make ends meet, they rent Kōichi's old room for 10,000 yen a month to Julie, a *gāru-san*—the more polite way of referring to *panpan* in the base towns (from the English "girl"). Sugio (Kaneko Nobuo), the second brother, is a town clerk who deals with, among other tasks, the registration of mixed-race children with unknown paternity. Sugio turns a blind eye to the third brother, Ken'ichi (Hieno Akira), who is a drug dealer and pimp of Japanese women to American GIs. Sugio's wife, Tokiko (Hirose Yoshiko), works at a souvenir shop, in one scene communicating with a GI in English while he replies in Japanese calling her by her name. Kōichi has two younger sisters; the eldest, Shizuko (Kawaai Tamae), works at the base, and Fumiko (Aoyama Kyōko) is a schoolgirl who is friends with a GI and his American wife. The youngest of all, Toshio (Itō Takashi), is intrigued by the scenes of "fraternization" that the base town offers.

Due to their purchasing power, *panpan* were pivotal agents in the local economy, profiting bars and restaurants, landlords, hairdressers and other businesses; yet they were ostracized. They were admired and envied by some for their looks, luxury goods and independence, but despised by many for their occupation and appearance. Members of "legitimate" society often carved narratives of the *panpan* so as to define themselves in contraposition to them (Tanaka 2012). Men, especially veterans and the unemployed, condemned them as an oblique way of criticizing the US servicemen (Kovner 2012, 82); but presumably many of the same men also paid for sex. Due to her essential yet controversial role in the community, the *panpan* became a contact zone between the domestic and the foreign, a recipient of conflicting feelings and attitudes often tainted by moral duplicity and economic necessity.

Julie's adoption of an English name follows a common practice among panpan soliciting foreigners. In discussing *panpan* novellas, Michael Molasky notes that often the reader never finds out the women's original names, "as if their Japanese identity had been erased the moment they first had sex with an American soldier" (1999, 150). In *Akasen kichi*, Kōichi is the only one who asks Julie her real name, just to then encourage her to return to her "Japanese identity," which he equates to her quitting prostitution. But before his moralizing speech, Julie, smiling, speaks her name, Yukiko. This moment, which also creates a sense of intimacy between Julie and Kōichi, functions to assert her agency and the possibility of shifting from one identity to the other while revealing the performative aspect of names and languages in the contact zone. The character of Julie is presented as a liminal entity also through the star persona of Negishi Akemi. Born in 1934, Negishi was quite tall compared to the average Japanese woman and had a voluptuous body, which led her to be identified as *nikutai-ha*, literally "flesh school," which in this case referred to a new conception of beauty associated with the imagined western body (Saitō 2018, 65). Her body granted her an aura of not being "typically" Japanese, and thus her casting in Taniguchi's film suggests the identification of *panpan* as an "other." Moreover, Negishi had only recently debuted in June 1953 in the US-Japanese co-production *Anatahan* (Josef von Sternberg 1953), where she played an attractive woman stranded on an abandoned island with twelve men who strive to conquer her. Therefore, Negishi's star persona, which evoked the aesthetic *Zeitgeist* of the postwar era and was associated with the US and a dangerous sexuality, fed into the image of the *panpan*.

A promotional piece for *Akasen kichi* published in the film journal *Kinema junpō* (1953), features a low angle photograph of Negishi seductively pulling her skirt up to her thighs as she aggressively looks straight into the camera (resembling Kyō Machiko as another iconic *femme fatale* in the poster of *Mesu inu* (Bitch, Kimura Keigo, 1951)). In contrast, Kōichi appears in a smaller photograph, smiling and surrounded by people of the village, underscoring her position as a dangerous, ostracized "other."

Julie's ambiguous identity and agency are charted through her relationships with others. During the twenty-four hours recounted in the film, her relationship with Kōichi evolves from friendly conversation to confrontation, seduction (on Julie's part), humiliation and reunion. By shifting between different power positions and ideological discourses, Julie becomes an intermediary for and catalyst of Kōichi's experience of homecoming. In the early bus scene mentioned above, Julie exhibits a proud attitude against the hostile gaze of the villagers, while Kōichi feels overwhelmed by their mocking glances. When Kōichi initiates conversation with her, she is the only one who emotionally engages with his longed-for return, making him feel at ease. Later on, Kōichi learns of her trade and criticizes her lack of morality, claiming he kept strong throughout the war by living up to the memory of his family. Julie does not buckle: "Why do you turn a blind eye to geisha and brothel prostitutes, and make only us the enemy?" "If the customer is Japanese you don't make such a fuss" "Thanks to whom do you think that young women around here are safe?" "Where the army goes, screwing follows...The same goes for the Japanese army.... You gave it more dignified names like 'comfort women' (*ianfu*), but wasn't that much worse than the *panpan*?" (*Akasen kichi*, 1953). As Saitō rightly notes (2018, 69), Julie's words are some of the most critical on the relationship between the military and the exploitation of sexuality to have featured in Japanese cinema by 1953. Julie not only attacks the moral duplicity of men, but also stresses the continuity from prewar systems of sexual exploitation and the structural connection between militarism and sex across national borders. Against typical portrayals of *panpan* in popular culture, she does not frame herself as a victim, neither does she seek to justify herself.

Julie's relationship with her patron Bob (played by Bob Booth) is also ambiguous. She is his "only" (*onrii*), meaning he pays for her and she does not date anyone else. However, in their daily interaction, Julie seems to dominate; for instance, he gives her all his salary from which she allows him spending money—a common financial arrangement in marriages in Japan. When Kōichi confronts her for playing around with Bob in front of the child Toshio, Bob runs around shirtless, helplessly trying to escape from Julie, his clumsy body and flabby stomach exposed. In reaction to Kōichi's recriminatory looks, Julie snaps at him and he retreats after his mother pleads not to upset their essential source of income. Bob, who barely speaks Japanese, asks Julie what the fuss is about, demonstrating that Julie's power as intermediary partially comes from her mastery of both languages. Yet, it is hard to believe that Bob would not be able to figure out the tense situation based on body language and the overall political, racialized and gendered context. As Julie and Bob retreat to her room, she sits upright on a chair while he sits on the floor at her feet, underscoring her dominance over him. Bob is presented as a playful, harmless young man that could hardly be taken for the embodiment of an aggressive, occupying power; rather he appears as another intermediary caught in a web of intricate power relations.

The most meaningful relationship for Julie is her friendship with Shizuko, Kōichi's sister. In the evening, when the family is celebrating Kōichi's return, Shizuko steps out to offer Julie some *sekihan*—rice with red beans. Julie, with her back to the camera, is looking at herself in the mirror when Shizuko appears behind her in the mirror's reflection. Both are in high spirits: Shizuko will soon marry a schoolteacher and Bob has proposed to Julie. As they chat, laugh and share food, the camera moves dynamically in relatively long takes, mostly following Julie but also showing how comfortable Shizuko feels in Julie's space. This camera work underscores their relaxed intimacy and contrasts with that employed in scenes featuring Kōichi and Julie, where fixed camera shots and short takes abound. Following a conventional strategy to oppose the "pure" Japanese woman to the westernized "fallen" woman, Shizuko wears a *yukata* (summer kimono) and Julie provocative western clothes. Yet this is the only relationship where there are no domination/subjugation dynamics at play; it is a friendship based on equality and, as we will see, on similarities that unite them in spite of their differences. The scene is interrupted when Shizuko's grandfather suddenly yells at her to return to the house as the frame is divided in two; in the foreground to the left both women laugh and in the background to the right the rest of the family sit in the room across the courtyard.

Soon after, Julie finds Shizuko in her room but the mood is completely different. Her fiancé's family has cancelled the engagement because of Shizuko's job in the base and the presence of a *panpan* in their house. Neighbors will talk; Shizuko's chastity will be called into question because, word has it, there is not a single maiden woman working in the base; ultimately the marriage will fail. Shizuko is devastated, drunk and seeks the comfort of her friend. She asks Julie to introduce her to a GI so she too can become an "only," but Julie tries to persuade her against the idea. It is not as enjoyable as it may look and "there is no return ticket" from this way of life, she claims. Shizuko moves to the mirror and, while putting on Julie's makeup, asks anxiously, "Am I pretty? A woman will be alright if she's pretty, right?" (Akasen kichi, 1953). As Julie approaches Shizuko from behind, the composition of the previous mirror shot is replicated but this time the women's positions are inverted. The next shot finds Julie (left) behind Shizuko (right) and the camera revolves around them to fix on the mirror where, in the reflection, Shizuko now appears on the left and Julie on the right.

Mirror games and reflections, divided frame compositions, repetition with variation, exchange of positions; all are cinematic strategies that convey duplicity, ambiguity and complexity. Following the second mirror scene, the two women dance to loud jazzy music, holding hands, laughing, and looking into each other's eyes, emphasizing their friendship. As they turn around dancing, their positions are constantly interchanged. Despite their distinct looks, these women are similar and their different fates, the film suggests, may just be a matter of fortune. In an analysis of Mizoguchi's *Women of the Night*, Kim Bokyoung argues that the idea of "crossing" from the position of respectable woman to that of prostitute is represented in the film through the motif of railroads and the sound of trains. According to Kim, these instances of "crossing" work to dramatize and condemn the manufactured and mythicized dichotomy of "*madonna*/whore" (2014, 57–70). In a similar fashion, Taniguchi's film utilizes cinematography and *mise-en-scène* to highlight the ambiguous line that separates women's life choices in times of adversity and, consequently, to humanize and de-otherize Julie. Additionally, this sequence exposes the constructed notion of female sexuality that hovers over women and irremediably marks their value and status in society. When Shizuko asks "Am I pretty?" she could be preoccupied with her chances of finding either another prospective husband or a GI patron. The rationale behind both positions stems from the same foundations of patriarchal ideology; something Kōichi fails to comprehend.

While Kōichi was away, Harue quit working at the local school and became a "butterfly" (*batafurai*)—a *panpan* catering to an unlimited number of men—and has an Afro-Asian son. When Harue must face Kōichi, she hides behind a bush shaking in uncertainty. She finally resolves to thrust her chest out and walk towards Julie's room swinging her hips and handbag carelessly. Harue performs as she believes Kōichi expects a "butterfly" and drug addict to behave; but in this way she also avoids explaining to him a much more complicated reality. The camera's long take remains focused on Harue, leaving Kōichi out of frame. When the reverse shot comes, it is not Kōichi but Julie who appears, crying bitterly. Nakamura, who argues that the entire story is told from the perspective of Kōichi, stresses this exceptional *mise-en-scène* that prevents the spectator from seeing and identifying with the protagonist's reaction to the most crucial episode in the film where his sense of identity is on the verge of collapse. According to Nakamura, "by shifting the focus of identification to Harue, Kōichi's experience is no longer portrayed as exclusively his own, but as belonging to the entire Japanese nation" evoking in the spectators "a sense of collective empathy" (2014, 115). Saitō, on the other hand, underscores that the crisis of identity is a masculine one and reads the scene as leaving Kōichi aside to convey the women's point of view. By showing to us Harue's and Julie's tears, which remain unseen by Kōichi, the film is positioning itself on their side (2018, 69–70). Following Saitō's interpretation, I argue that the cinematography here encourages us to concentrate not on Kōichi's feelings but on Harue's performance, on her effort to utilize and explain her body following the stereotypes of the *panpan*. Julie's tears could be a projection of Kōichi's feelings (projecting masculine loss onto female emotionality); they could be out of guilt because she has helped shatter his romantic fantasy; and yet, they could be tears shed for Harue, in solidarity with her, because Julie reads through Harue's performance. Kōichi who has, up to that moment, continuously enquired about Harue, never speaks of her again. He rejects her because he does not question the codes that Harue has performed for him. But simultaneously, by hiding Kōichi's breakdown, the film protects the traumatized masculine identity that he stands for and disavows its fragility.

After the encounter with Harue, Julie, in seeming contradiction with her previous subversive words, desperately begs Kōichi to take her with him implying that the only way out of prostitution is through marriage or men's protection. Nakamura notes that in the first draft of the film's script Julie neither apologizes nor seeks Kōichi's support (2014, 116). This conservative turn in the final version of the film also runs against the findings of the survey on *panpan*'s lifestyles in the base towns mentioned above. Despite the highly publicized gender reforms of the Occupation, women were far from enjoying equal rights and opportunities in both the domestic and professional spheres. For women, marriage was not necessarily an escape from exploitation, nor, as Julie stresses in the film, would it necessarily erase the stigma of prostitution. Saitō argues that while this scene appears to advance the domestic ideology that advocated the disciplining of women's sexuality as part of the socio-economic progress of postwar Japan, it also works to dramatize Julie's desperation in the face of the stigma she carries and thus, implicitly, criticizes the community's moral duplicity towards the military base (2018, 71).

The stories of Julie, Shizuko and Harue exemplify the female body as contact zone. As in other contexts of imperialism, under the Allied Occupation women's bodies were a source of anxiety that needed to be disciplined and surveilled, because their management was deemed crucial to preserving the social order and political stability (Enloe 1988; Ballantyne and Burton 2005; Kramm 2017). Imperialism is grounded on the ideology of militarized masculinity, which exacerbates patriarchy and polarizes gender roles (Enloe 1988), but women as individuals are also active agents in the contention over the meanings of their bodies. In occupied Japan as in the base town, women performed their understanding of the new order and sought to intervene through how they presented, used and spoke of their bodies. *Akasen kichi* exposes the intimate connection between colonialism and sexuality and in doing so, addresses the unresolved trauma of the Allied Occupation, implicitly questioning whether it is actually over. This idea could feed into the postwar narrative of victimization, but the film also poignantly questions whether the dynamics between militarism and sex under the Occupation are essentially different from those of prewar, imperial Japan. When Julie claims that what angers Japanese men is that *panpan* cater to foreigners, and when she mockingly tells Kōichi that had Japan won the war he could have had "their" women (which could refer to both American and Asian women), she gets to the crux of the issue. While Julie's words lay bare the contradictions of Kōichi's discourse of morality, the subplots of Shizuko and Harue further underscore the patriarchal construction of "woman" that undergirds and amplifies the connection between occupation and sexuality. Heteropatriarchal ideology operates interwoven with hierarchies of class and race, transforming the female body into a contact zone of intersectionality.

Where does the returned soldier return to?

In 1953 the first groups of official repatriates from China and the Soviet Union (since 1948 and 1950 respectively) arrived in Japan (Watt 2009, 136; Igarashi 2016, 1–2). During this year, over 20,000 civilians and soldiers were repatriated, and their return awoke memories of war and created a media frenzy.

Yoshikuni Igarashi (2016) argues that by 1953 the media were presenting an image of the repatriated that conformed to carefully crafted narratives on the war and Japan's successful postwar recovery. Avoiding associating the returned soldiers with responsibility for the war, they were rendered victims of circumstance who should endeavor to adapt to a country that was no longer afflicted by defeat. The media described the veterans as "outdated," unfamiliar with the new democratic and prosperous Japan, but their integration into the domestic sphere would naturally re-establish their role in the family and bring stability to all (Igarashi 2016, 2–9). What happens when the returned soldier does not come back to this imagined, reinvented and homogeneous Japan, but to a base town, as if time travelling to an era—the Occupation—he had not experienced together with his compatriots? Like the returned soldiers, the base towns constituted a traumatizing reminder of defeat and the human cost of economic recovery that threatened the validity of the media's positive discourse. *Akasen kichi* offers an opportunity to explore the representation of the returned soldier and the Japan he returns to against the dominant narratives circulated by the government and the media. Nakamura contends that the film depicts Kōichi's identity as "uncertain" and that, by simultaneously encouraging and hampering our identification with him, it engages affectively with the subject of identity crisis (2014, 109). Drawing on Igarashi's work, I see the uncertainty of identity that Nakamura discusses as stemming from the contradictions that arise from the film's disavowal of Kōichi's problematic past as imperial soldier and from the media's narrative of postwar Japan.

Upon his return, Kōichi must renegotiate his role and status in the domestic and social spheres. He soon learns that his father died in his absence and, as the eldest son, he attempts to act as the new head of the household. It is in this way that he refers to himself (*kono ie no shujin*) when thugs try to raid the house to search for Ken'ichi's drugs, only for Kōichi to beat them before throwing them out of the house. This exhibition of physical prowess and authority suggests a confident masculinity that is at odds with other aspects of his character. For instance, Kōichi does not have a job and has no prospects of getting one in town, according to Sugio. He has also lost his own physical space in the house; "A *panpan* has occupied his room" (Akasen kichi, 1953), Tokiko notes using the Japanese expression for military occupation (*senryō*). In his confrontations with Julie, Kōichi's failure to assert authority becomes apparent. When Julie and Shizuko are dancing, Kōichi bursts into the room and turns off the music but Julie defiantly turns it back on. In the end, while the women continue to dance in the background to the left, he stands alone in the foreground and calls for his mother to resolve the situation. Kōichi is isolated from the women's bonding; he cannot reach out emotionally to his sister and neither can he restore order as the head of the household would be expected to do.

Unlike Kōichi, Shizuko and other female characters in the film do not have problems being friends with Julie, or at least avoid openly judging her. Likewise, women are at ease interacting with GIs (Shizuko is satisfied working at the base and Tokiko selling souvenirs to American soldiers, Fumiko is friends with a GI, and all speak fondly of Bob). However, every time a GI approaches Kōichi, he freezes and, unable to speak, casts his eyes downwards in a mixture of frustration and contempt. This contrast suggests that, although Kōichi claims to despise Julie on moral grounds, his anxiety is essentially connected to a masculinity that he feels is threatened. However, this dissatisfaction is not shared by other male characters— except his grandfather, who could be read as embodying tradition. The problem, therefore, does not lie with masculinity alone. Instead, and in accordance with Igarashi's (2016) reading of media narratives, it is depicted as Kōichi's personal problem. The rest of society has already come to terms with the past and aims to make the most of the new *status quo*. It may be a utilitarian society, but it is no longer afflicted by the trauma of defeat; the post-Occupation masculinity has finally freed itself from anxiety.

However, neither does Kōichi conform to stereotypes of prewar masculinity as violent and authoritarian. He is instead connected to tropes of purity or innocence and Japanese cultural traditions, and depicted as being highly moral. For instance, upon hearing about his father's death, Kōichi sits in the foreground, his back to his mother, and discreetly sheds some tears. The singing of a swallow catches his attention and he stands up, tenderly smiling as he follows the bird flying around the room. Later on, as he leaves the house, he puts on *geta* (Japanese wooden clogs)—for the first time in ten years—and stands there, in front of his mother, turning around looking at his feet like an excited child. There is never a mention of his experiences at the warfront, let alone of sexual practices in the army. In his arguments with Julie, he presents himself as having always adhered to virtuous ideals and avoided sexual decadence. For Kōichi, his and Japan's current problems are rooted in the presence of the US military, detached from the war and placed in opposition to his fragmented, idealized memory of prewar life.

Igarashi argues that, despite the media's intention, images of the late returned soldiers worked at times as a "haunting presence of the past" which "represented a state of homelessness, an anxious transitional status in the postwar period" (Igarashi 2016, 9). The character of

Kōichi embodies a sense of homelessness and uncertain liminality, which translates into his failure to efficiently interact in the contact zone (in contrast to Julie). However, by disavowing his experiences and memories of war, Kōichi also evokes an idealized, perhaps lost, Japan of virtue, which is reified in the image of Mount Fuji, as established in the film's opening. When Toshio is sent out to play until Bob leaves the house (to prevent him from witnessing Julie and Bob embracing), Kōichi, unable to confront Julie, walks away with the child. In the next shot, both brothers look up, Toshio still with tears in his eyes, and the reverse shot reveals in a low angle the majestic Mount Fuji bathed in the sunset light. The scene links Mount Fuji to Kōichi's aspirations for a "true" Japan as the solution to the current menace to children's wellbeing in base towns. Mount Fuji appears once again in the final scene where Kōichi and Julie, now transformed into Yukiko, meet again on a bus, to his surprise. Both are heading for Tokyo in search of a new life. Yukiko praises the beauty of Fuji and claims, "I was here for half a year, but I never paid any attention to it" (Akasen kichi, 1953). This line feeds into the image of Mount Fuji as national allegory implying that Julie, in becoming a *panpan*, had forgotten and neglected her Japanese "essence." The film ends on a long shot seeing off the bus that advances in the direction of Mount Fuji—the idealized Japan that the nation can still become.

Julie functions as an extraordinary intermediary for other characters to confront and navigate the base town's economy. In the case of Kōichi, it is Julie who first welcomes him into town, who challenges his authority as the returned head of the household and who prompts him to face Harue. Conversely, meeting Kōichi provokes Julie to change her life. We are led to sympathize with Kōichi's feeling of alienation, his nostalgia for the prewar era and his high moral standards, and simultaneously with Julie's determination, adaptability, self-awareness, power and fears. Saitō argues that by shifting the site of identification and empathy from Kōichi in the first half of the film to Julie in the second, the narrative portrays them as complementing each other (2018, 72). This connection is emphasized by the editing of the scene of the night before their departure, when Julie and Kōichi are shown in cross-cutting, each in a different space, coping with sorrow and reflecting on their future (Saitō 2018, 74). The opening scene already underscored this correlation by identifying them as outsiders to the community, while the development of their personal struggles reveals inconsistencies in their attitudes and arguments. The two characters function together as a site of identification that would allow audiences to negotiate their own contradictory experiences, feelings and attitudes towards the *panpan*, the US presence and the constructed notion of "postwar Japan."

Conclusion: The need to move on

Kōichi's friend recommends he forget all his beautiful memories because "all those beautiful things no longer exist in this town" (Akasen kichi, 1953). The gender politics of *Akasen kichi* are worth reconsideration through the lens of breaking with the national past. I suggest that the figure of the returned soldier was used in combination with the *panpan* as a means to avoid engaging with the men's responsibility for the war by translocating their moral accountability and trauma onto "fallen" women and the Occupation.

In his analysis of *Kimi no na wa* (What is Your Name?, 1953–54), the extremely popular film series featuring veterans, prostitutes and mixed-race children, Igarashi argues that the film "reverses the causal relations between the defeat and subsequent social confusion" and postulates the disciplining of female sexuality as the necessary means to recovering social order (Igarashi 2000, 111). Indeed, in *Kimi no nawa* all the female characters are victimized and those who escape the sex trade do so under the protection and guidance of men. The presence of notoriously strong female leads prevents *Akasen kichi* from adhering completely to this conservative premise; yet it is not free from ideological contradictions. The film's ending is ambiguous but a successful romance is hinted at in the last scene, where the noise of bombs exploding prevents Kōichi from arguing with Julie, and his angry face turns to humorous capitulation. Julie's reintegration into society relies on the premise that she is a "good" *panpan*. In contrast to Harue, who is a "butterfly," Julie is an "only," allegedly closer to a mistress than to a prostitute, and seeks to change her life. As Saitō argues, Julie symbolically adheres to the division between normative women and *panpan* by relegating herself to indoor spaces and the night-time without intruding on the intimate space of Kōichi's family, while as Yukiko she appears outdoors and during the daytime (2018, 72). I would argue that her favorable depiction is primarily contingent on the fact that she is free from the ultimate evidence of miscegenation: mixed-race children. This explains why Harue, the actual love interest of Kōichi, disappears from the film after her Afro-Asian son is exposed. Her child stands as indelible evidence of defeat and occupation that is unforgettable and hence renders impossible her reintegration into the post-Occupation Japan that seeks to forget its past.

Saitō argues that, despite unresolved contradictions in the film that seem to adhere to the domestic ideology of the 1950s in Japan (such as Julie's suddenly begging to become Kōichi's partner), the film positions itself on the side of women to de-otherize Julie as a member of the community despite discrimination (2018, 73–76). However, I would suggest that although the plot offers poignant criticism of the correlation between gender politics and the contact zone, the narrative seeks closure for the benefit of a national image intrinsically linked to masculinity and its militarized past; and this bears witness to the ambiguous and tangled position in which Japan found itself in 1953. On the one hand, I have argued that through Julie, Shizuko and Harue the film critically represents the female body as a contact zone. Despite the three women's self-awareness of the gender economies, roles and stigmas that entrap them, the resolution of their stories—Julie following Kōichi, Shizuko's fate negotiated between the men of two families and Harue condemned to oblivion—seems to render unavoidable their capitulation to heteropatriarchal hierarchies. On the other hand, GIs, like Bob, are generally depicted in a positive light. When a teenage girl appears riding the back of a scooter driven by a GI as she screams and beats his back, Kōichi and we as spectators are impelled to interpret it as a reference to sexual violence. However, it turns out the girl is Fumiko and the GI a good friend of hers who is very polite towards Kōichi and his sisters. One could contend that, nevertheless, the connection between servicemen and sexual violence has already been imprinted in the spectator's mind (as the American journalists did at the time; see Nakamura 2014, 110). Shizuko claims, "If only all GIs were such good guys" (Akasen kichi, 1953), implying he is an exception to the disruption and fear caused by the troops. However, these are very mild references considering the 1950s records of violence and criminal acts in base towns committed by servicemen, who enjoyed a privileged legal status, and which fuelled the anti-base movement (Kovner 2012, 130–32, 150; Wright 2015, 68–71, 86–88). Moreover, taking into account that Kōichi, a returned soldier, is also portrayed as virtuous and courageous (albeit intransigent and "outdated"), it follows that militarized masculinity is depicted in a tamed manner but that its underlying ideology is ultimately validated. Kōichi, who rejects Harue and preaches to Julie while avoiding reflecting on his own past, is presented as embodying the moral standard to which women must endeavor to return. In other words, to protect the returned soldier (and by extension Japanese men) and to disavow Japan's imperial past, the hierarchies and practices of militarized masculinity, as continued by the US forces, cannot be fully contested when depicting a base town that bears witness to this continuity—transferred from one national army to the other. This comes at the expense of women.

Finally, I wish to reconsider *Akasen kichi* not as a "base film," but as a film about overcoming the recently ended Occupation. The dénouement was criticized by film critic Togawa Naoki for forcing onto the story a far-fetched happy ending considered unsatisfactory for what one would expect from a "base film" (1954, 64). The humorous reunion that foresees a romance between Julie and Kōichi in Tokyo comes across as a *deus ex machina* plot device that suddenly resolves the bitter confrontation that had built up until then. But, more importantly, the protagonists' departure fails to provide any solution to or meaningful comment on the troubled situation of the base town. This ending renders the base towns doomed to political, moral and health decay and the only way for the protagonists to improve their lives is to leave it behind. One can only imagine how spectators personally involved with base towns would feel watching this. However, if one interprets the film's base town as a cross-temporal contact zone standing in for the Occupation, the film offers a much more optimistic reading. The protagonists succeed in leaving behind the Occupation (symbolized by the base town) to advance towards a better, freed Japan (symbolized by Mount Fuji). Under this interpretation, the ending conforms to the Japanese media's narrative of national reconstruction and contemporaneous films advocating to forget. The *panpan* and the returned soldier function together as a site of identification that can accommodate ideological contentions and contradictions as well as ambiguous practices characteristic of a contact zone. The base town serves as the scenario of a conflicted yet cathartic fantasy through which audiences could embrace the official, auspicious narrative of a Japan that had freed itself from its traumatic past.

Videography

Akasen kichi [Red-Light Bases], 1953. [Film]. Directed by Taniguchi Senkichi. Tokyo: Tōhō.
Anatahan, 1953. [Film]. Directed by Josef von Sternberg. Tokyo: Tōhō.
Kimi no na wa [What is Your Name?], 1953-1954. [Film series]. Directed by Ōba Hideo. Tokyo: Shōchiku.
Mesu inu [Bitch], 1951. [Film]. Directed by Kimura Keigo. Tokyo: Daiei.
Yoru no onnatachi [Women of the Night], 1948. [Film]. Directed by Mizoguchi Kenji. Tokyo: Shōchiku.

Bibliography

Anderson, J. L., and Richie, D., [1959] 1982. *The Japanese Film: Art and Industry*. Expanded ed. Princeton, N.J: Princeton University Press.
Ballantyne, T. and Burton, A., eds., 2005. *Bodies in Contact: Rethinking Colonial Encounters in World History*. Durham: Duke University Press.
Bardsley, J., 2014. *Women and Democracy in Cold War Japan*. London: Bloomsbury.
Enloe, C. H., 1988. *Does Khaki Become You? The Militarization of Women's Lives*. London: Pandora.
Fujime, Y., 1997. *Sei no rekishigaku* [The historiography of sex]. Tokyo: Fuji Shuppan.
Fujin kōron, 1950a. Josei ofurimitto [Women off-limits]. *Fujin kōron*, August, 99–103.
———., 1950b. Tōkyō no 25 ji [Tokyo's 25th hour]. *Fujin kōron*, November, 30–39.
———., 1952. Panpan to bōeki [Panpan and international trade]. *Fujin kōron*, October, 27.

Igarashi, Y., 2000. *Bodies of Memory: Narratives of War in Postwar Japanese Culture, 1945–1970*. Princeton, N.J: Princeton University Press.

———., 2016. *Homecomings. The Belated Return of Japan's Lost Soldiers*. New York: Columbia University Press.

Kanzaki, K., 1974. *Baishun: ketteiban Kanzaki repōto* [Prostitution: Kanzaki's definite report]. Tokyo: Gendaishi Shuppankai.

Kim, B., 2014. *Sengo minshushugi to josei eiga: Amerika senryōki no Mizoguchi to "josei kaihō"* [Postwar democracy and women's film: The Mizoguchi of the American Occupation and "women's liberation"]. PhD dissertation. University of Tsukuba.

Kinema junpō, 1953. Akasen kichi [Red-Light Bases]. Early September, n.p.

Kokuritsu yoron chōsajo, 1951. *The Japanese People Look at Prostitution*. Tokyo: National Public Opinion Research Institute.

Kovner, S., 2012. *Occupying Power: Sex Workers and Servicemen in Postwar Japan*. Stanford: Stanford University Press.

Kramm, R., 2017. *Sanitized Sex: Regulating Prostitution, Venereal Disease, and Intimacy in Occupied Japan, 1945-1952*. Oakland: University of California Press.

Kusunoki, A., 2016. Consensus Building on Use of Military Bases in Mainland Japan: US-Japan Relations in the 1950s. *The Japanese Journal of American Studies*, 27, 145–66.

Minami, H., 1949. Zadankai panpan no sekai [Roundtable discussion: the world of panpan]. *Kaizō*, December, 74–87.

Mizuno, H., ed., 1953. *Nihon no teisō: Gaikokuhei ni okasareta joseitachi no shuki* [Chastity of Japan: the memoirs of women raped by foreign soldiers]. Tokyo: Sōjusha.

Molasky, M. S., 1999. *The American Occupation of Japan and Okinawa: Literature and Memory*. London: Routledge.

———., ed., 2015. *Gaishō panpan & onrii* [Streetwalkers, panpan and "only"]. Tokyo: Kōseisha.

Nakamura, H., 2014. *Haisha no miburi: posuto senryōki no nihon eiga* [Gestures of the defeated: Japanese films in the post-occupation period]. Tokyo: Iwanami Shoten.

Nishida, M., 1953. *Kichi no onna: tokushu josei no jittai* [Women of the military bases: the reality of "differentiated" women]. Tokyo: Kawade Shobō.

Pratt, M. L., 1991. Arts of the Contact Zone. *Profession*, 1991, 33–40.

———., 1992. *Imperial Eyes: Travel Writing and Transculturation*. London: Routledge.

Rowley, G. G., 2002. Prostitutes against the Prostitution Prevention Act of 1956. *U.S.-Japan Women's Journal, English Supplement*, 23, 39–56.

Saitō, A., 2018. Senryōki kara posuto senryōki eiga ni okeru "panpan" hyōshō ga toikakeru mono: "Yoru no onna" kara "kichi no onna" he [Enquiring the representation of *panpan* from occupation films to post-occupation films: from "women of the night" to "women of the bases"]. In H. Tsuboi, ed., *Haisen to senryō* [Defeat and occupation]. Kyoto: Rinsen Shoten, 33–88.

Sanders, H., 2012. Panpan: Streetwalking in Occupied Japan. *Pacific Historical Review* 81(3), 404–31.

Shimizu, K., Inomata, K., and Kimura, K., 1953. *Kichi nihon: ushinawareiku sokoku no sugata* [Fortress Japan: the disappearing face of our nation]. Tokyo: Wakōsha.

Tanaka, M., 2012. The Sexual Contact Zone in Occupied Japan: Discourses on Japanese Prostitutes or Panpan for U.S. Military Servicemen. *Intersections: Gender and Sexuality in Asia and the Pacific*, 31. Available at: http://intersections.anu.edu.au/issue31/tanaka.htm [Accessed 6 January 2020].

Tanaka, M. and Funayama, T., eds., 2011. *Kontakuto zōn no jinbungaku 1* [Humanities studies of contact zone 1]. Kyoto: Kōyō Shobo.

Togawa, N., 1954. Akasen kichi [Red–Light Bases]. *Kinema junpō*, late January, 64-65.

Uemura, T., 1952. Panpan ni atarashii michi wo hiraku tame ni wa [In order to open a new life to panpan]. *Fujin kōron*, May, 36–40.

———., 1953. Baishōfu no inai sekai wo [For a world without prostitution]. *Fujin kōron*, April, 44–47.

Watt, L., 2009. *When Empire Comes Home: Repatriation and Reintegration in Postwar Japan*. Cambridge, MA: Harvard University Asia Center.

Wright, D., 2015. *The Sunagawa Struggle: A Century of Anti-Base Protest in a Tokyo Suburb*. PhD dissertation. University of California Santa Cruz.

Chapter 5
Creating the Youth Star System in Japan: Transnational and Transmedia Phenomena

Marcos P. Centeno-Martin

This chapter examines the transnational and transmedia strategies that were implemented by the Japanese film industry to create the early youth icons of late 1950s and early 1960s. They illustrate how the very term "Japanese cinema" is increasingly outdated and needs to be revisited. Thus, the main objective is to problematize the paradigm of "national cinema" not only through its national affiliation, but also its form as media, and in relation to the historical context in which it is defined. The analysis focuses on two case studies: Ishihara Yūjirō as the protagonist of taiyōzoku films and Kobayashi Akira as the hero of the Wataridori series of "Japanese westerns," a genre of "film without nationality" (mukokuseki eiga). The chapter contextualizes these Japanese films within the global flow of images, trends and media languages. Additionally, it demonstrates how the Cold War created not only a political and economic context but also a cultural environment that conditioned these transcultural and transmedia interactions.

Introduction: Transnational transmediality: The end of "Japanese Cinema"?

Western literature devoted to Japanese cinema proliferated in the 1970s, and in the following decades, scholars engaged in projects examining the apparent singularities of this film culture, seeking to demonstrate how it provided an alternative to the dominant modes of representation that had been developed in the West (Bordwell and Thomson 1976; Burch 1979). These approaches often regarded Japanese films as products of the Japanese aesthetic and philosophical tradition. I have explored elsewhere how this limited understanding of Japanese cinema as a film culture confined to its national borders was sparked by specific films that were exported to European film festivals from the 1950s onwards (Centeno-Martin 2019). A group of *jidaigeki* (period dramas) starting with Kurosawa Akira's *Rashōmon*, and followed by the films of Mizoguchi Kenji, Kinugawa Teinosuke, Imai Tadashi and Takizawa Eisuke, played a key role in fostering this early understanding of Japanese cinema. They triggered the so-called "kimono effect" (Weinrichter 2002): the astonishment of western audiences at the exoticism projected in these films featuring characters wearing the kimono.

However, this "discovery" of Japanese cinema was misleading for several reasons. First, it neglected the complexity of these films' transcultural interactions. For example, it is well known today that Kurosawa Akira was greatly inspired by moral and philosophical conflicts depicted in foreign literature (from William Shakespeare to Leo Tolstoy). Second, audiences and scholars in the West only had access to a small selection of films that had been carefully selected for foreign consumption (Giuglaris and Giuglaris 1957, 32).

The rich transnational intertextuality existing in the Japanese film industry of the time was obscured by the selection of these *jidaigeki* films for export. Indeed, the most popular genre in 1950s Japan was in fact *gendaigeki* (contemporary dramas) (*Eiga Nenkan* 1963, 36). Within this category, Japanese film studios created a "youth cinema" (*seishun eiga*), largely shaped by the American popular culture of the time. Beginning with the release of the *taiyōzoku* (literally "Tribe of the Sun") films, produced by Nikkatsu, which stopped producing *jidaigeki* in 1958, youth cinema came to dominate the industry. The company initiated a ground-breaking strategy aimed at the younger audience by featuring transcultural heroes in a genre of *mukokuseki eiga* (films without nationality). One style of film that epitomized this was the "Japanese Western" which, like the *taiyōzoku*, mirrored a number of Hollywood genre codes. This chapter examines the transnational and transmedia strategies that were implemented to create the persona of these youth icons. The analysis is also designed to cast light on the complexity of this phenomenon that extends beyond Japan and the cinematic medium itself. Thus, the goal of this case study is to help the reader problematize the "national cinema" framework and propose updated methodologies to assess films in relation to their social, cultural, political and economic contexts.

The demographic factor and a new "teenage cinema"

The changes that took place in the Japanese film industry from the late 1950s onwards have been assessed in economic terms (the high economic growth) and political terms (the postwar democracy, the protests against the US-Japan Security Treaty, the tensions within the left, etc.). However, the cinematic changes of the time were to a great extent due to demographic factors. The *dankai no sedai* (baby boom generation), those who were born after the end of World War II, became an unseen social force that prompted economic, cultural and political changes.[1] They were the teenage audience that filled cinemas, eager to see the youth icons created by American and Japanese film studios towards the end of the 1950s. This generation also became the students who led the protests in the 1960s, the audience of the New Wave cinema and occasionally even the directors of this film movement.

American studios had discovered this new teenage market with *The Wild One* (László Benedek, 1953), starring Marlon Brando, and *Rebel Without a Cause* (Nicholas Ray, 1956), starring James Dean. Simultaneously, Daiei studios pioneered a series of films aimed at teenagers (*jūdai*) from 1953: *Jūdai no seiten* (Teen Sex Manual, Shima Koji, 1953), *Jūdai no yūwaku* (Teenage Seduction, Hisamatsu Seiji, 1953), *Jūdai no himitsu* (Teenage Secret, Nakai Shigeo, 1954), *Jūdai no hankō* (Teenage Crime, Tanaka Shigeo, 1955) and *Sabakareru jūdai* (Judged Teens, Saeki Kōzō, 1956). For the first time, Japanese studios were not producing films for the wider audience but for a specific niche market. This resulted in a "teenage cinema" that was driven by demographic changes and revolved around the generation gap. These demographic tensions materialized on the big screen through the *taiyōzoku* phenomenon, which was triggered by a group of films adapted from the novels of Ishihara Shintarō and released in the summer of 1956. The first one, *Taiyō no kisetsu* (Season of the Sun, Furukawa Takumi), was released in May 1956 and a second adaptation, *Kurutta kajitsu* (Crazed Fruit, Nakahira Kō), which was released in July, made Ishihara Shintarō's younger brother, Ishihara Yūjirō, an icon of Japanese popular culture from the late 1950s onwards. Both films present a group of unworried youngsters from well-off families who spend their summer in resorts, normally in upmarket areas along the Shōnan coast, practicing water skiing, sailing, boxing or chasing girls in nightclubs. In June, Daiei tried to profit from the success of this film by adapting another Ishihara novel, *Shokei no heya* (Punishment Room, Ichikawa Kon). In August, Nikkatsu released *Gyakkōsen* (Backlight, Furukawa Takumi), which was an adaptation from a novel written by female author of youth literature, Iwahashi Kunie; and in September, Tōhō produced *Nisshoku no natsu* (Summer in Eclipse, Horikawa Hiromichi) starring Ishihara Shintarō himself, whose westernized look caused a great impact, particularly his hairstyle, which came to be known as the *Shintarō-gari* (the Shintarō cut) (Ishihara 1956, 280–93). An article in the *Sunday Mainichi* (1956, 3) titled "Hawaiian T-shirts have become a uniform" reveals that even in chic districts like Ginza, *taiyōzoku* beach fashion had become omnipresent.

This small group of films made youth a mark of identity for Nikkatsu. However, while uninhibited attitudes presented by the *taiyōzoku* characters projected a freedom (in many cases a sexual freedom) that attracted the youth audience (Uryu 1958), the open depiction of violence and carnal desires was scandalous to older generations and sparked intense discussion in the press. News of juvenile vandalism associated with *taiyōzoku* proliferated and the term "decadent youth" (*dekadan no seishun*) became recurrent.[2] The press also published articles on young groups intimidating swimmers with the *taiyōzoku* look—Hawaiian T-shirts and the "Shintaro cut" hairstyle. The scandal spread across the country, reaching the Japanese government on 15 August 1956, when Prime Minister Hatoyama Ichirō organized a meeting to discuss the issue. Two days later, Nikkatsu's president Hori Kyūsaku promised to cease production of *taiyōzoku* films. A planned adaptation of Ishihara's novel *Haiiro no kyōshitsu* (The Grey Classroom) was cancelled.

A youth star system for the new *mukokuseki eiga*

The *taiyōzoku* became mainstream as quickly as it went out of fashion. In the early 1960s, the Japanese press suggested that the *taiyōzoku* had completely vanished.[3] Only a decade later, the majority of young people not only seemed to have stopped being influenced by this trend but "even rejected it" (Kawade Shobō Shinsha 1979, 216–17). However, the sudden disappearance of the *taiyōzoku* phenomenon did not mean the end of youth cinema. From that point on, Nikkatsu tried to avoid controversy around nihilism and sexual licentiousness and replaced the *taiyōzoku* genre with a series of "films without nationality" creating cinematic hybrids between Hollywood and the Japanese film industry. This trend first materialized in the so-called *Nikkatsu akushon* (Nikkatsu action)—also called *mukokuseki akushon eiga* (action films without nationality)—a genre of gangster films starring a group of young heroes. Nikkatsu created a star system based on male youth icons that was marketed as the "First Diamond Line," which consisted of actors Ishihara Yūjirō, Kobayashi Akira, Akagi Keiichirō and Wada Kōji.[4]

The Americanized look of Nikkatsu films, far from disappearing, intensified in subsequent productions. The studio clearly capitalized on the fascination developed by many Japanese viewers for the US, which has been discussed on several occasions (Kitamura 2011, 33; Hirano 1992). However, its close connection to historical developments also played a role. Despite being the oldest of the big studios in Japan, founded in 1912, Nikkatsu ceded its filming facilities to Daiei during World War II. During the postwar period, its activities had been restricted to the management of film theaters and the distribution of foreign films. The company quickly prospered due to the warm reception of Hollywood films among Japanese audiences (Kitamura 2011, 33) and its executives were undoubtedly familiar with the latest cinematic trends coming from overseas. Interestingly, when Nikkatsu resumed production in 1954, its films invariably adapted codes of representation from the Hollywood films it had been distributing and exhibiting. The impact of American iconography must have been particularly intense between 1952 and 1957, when the distribution of foreign films increased from 63 to 118 (*Eiga nenkan* 1963, 35). Even the company president, Hori Kyūsaku, stated that Nikkatsu's new production facility was an American style studio inspired by Warner Bros (Kitamura 2011, 33).

As a consequence, it is not surprising to see that this youth cinema gave rise to hybrids between tradition and foreign fashions. But how did this phenomenon of cultural hybridization take place? One can witness a singular process of mimesis, by which the characters created by the Japanese film industry increasingly resembled those of American productions, which were being simultaneously screened on cinemas. They featured fearless, cunning and intelligent heroes of foreign appearance, who were successful with women, which sublimated the wishes of many young viewers. This strategy was hugely successful and Nikkatsu increased its production from 11 films in 1954 to 101 in 1960 (Jiji tsūshinsha 1963, 41).

Since the premiere of *Kurutta kajitsu*, Ishihara Yūjirō had become the leading figure of the youth star system created by Nikkatsu. His look, attitude, speech and lifestyle, on and off screen, represented a surprising and controversial generational change. Yūjirō also stood out for his long legs, and other physical attributes, such as his puffy cheeks and deep voice. His physique was not especially attractive and was significantly different from the long tradition of the *bidanshi* (handsome young man) in Kabuki theater, embodied by actors such as Nakamura Kinnosuke and Ōkawa Hashizō (Toida 1958, 50–53). Initially, Japanese critics even pointed out his height would be a problem for the shot scale (Raine 2000, 203). Raine links these physical changes to the social context, as improvements in the Japanese diet as a result of economic growth would have introduced changes in the physiognomy of young Japanese (2000, 205). For Uryu (1958), Yūjirō's popularity is a consequence of cultural changes related to a new postwar masculinity; his easy-going attitude and carefree, wandering lifestyle sublimated everyday frustrations. Moreover, his sunglasses, baggy pants and Hawaiian T-shirts made him an idol for many Japanese teenagers (Nathan 2001, 108) who looked suspiciously foreign (Schilling 2007, 30). His success on the big screen also became the iconic symbol of a new era. It has even been claimed that the "postwar period ended with the appearance of Yūjirō in Japanese cinema" (Kawade Shobō Shinsha 1980, 230). His *taiyōzoku* characters driving convertible cars and living in expensive mansions were far from the social reality of the audiences, but they nurtured the aspirations of the baby boom generation.

Across the twelve films in which Yūjirō appeared between 1956 and 1958 (*Kinema junpō* 1958, 101) his "bad boy" role gradually softened. As his image became less threatening it also became less transnational. Yūjirō claimed that this character was closer to his real personality, as he was a traditional man who loved his mother and enjoyed folk music (Ishihara Y. 1989, 184). Nevertheless, he continued to speak in a way that sounded foreign. Yūjirō used a number of foreign words and neologisms in films as well as in the media, which were written in *katakana* when published in popular magazines (Ishihara 1958, 248). This was not a completely new cinematic phenomenon but rather a revival of previous attitudes of Westernization that had been synonymous with modernity in the prewar period. As Barnett (2020) shows, both "Modern Boy" and "Modern Girl" stereotypes in the 1920s and 1930s had popularized western-style clothes as well as loan-words in films and printed media.

Kobayashi Akira was the other leading figure of the Diamond Line until his departure from Nikkatsu in 1963. He was discovered by Imamura Shōhei, who was an assistant director at the time, during one of Nikkatsu's campaigns for "new faces" (*nyū feisu*) carried out to find young talents. Kobayashi debuted in a student role in *Ueru tamashii* (Hungry Spirit, Kawashima Yūzō, 1956). However, the first appearance for which he is often remembered is his portrayal of a mobster-turned-bartender in *Sabita naifu* (Rusty Knife, Masuda Toshio, 1958) co-starring Ishihara Yūjirō. From the following year, he embodied the role of a "mobile hero," starting with *Nangoku tosa o ato ni shite* (Leaving Tosa of the South, Saitō Buichi, 1959) and continuing with the series *Wataridori* (The Wanderer, 1959–1962), *Nagaremono* (Drifter, 1960–1961), *Ginza senpūji* (Ginza Whirling Boy, 1959–1963) and *Abarenbō* (Roughneck, 1960–1963). In total, Kobayashi appeared in 47 films in only three years between 1959 and 1962 (Kitamura 2011, 36). At the time, Kobayashi was included in another campaign to promote the "Three Bad Boys" of Nikkatsu, alongside Kawachi Tamio and Sawamoto Tadao (Watanabe 1978). As a result, he was nicknamed "[Dyna]Mite Guy" for his roles as a "lone thug" who embodied individual freedom, inspired by American films and legitimized during the Occupation period.

Akagi Keiichirō was known as Nikkatsu's *daisan no otoko* (third man) after Kobayashi and Ishihara Yūjirō. He had been recruited in 1958 during the fourth Nikkatsu campaign to search for "new faces;" he subsequently became another transnational youth icon for *mukokuseki akushon eiga*, starring in ten films in 1959, mostly as an assassin or thug.[5] Authors of the time noted that Akagi had an exotic "foreign look" and popular culture magazines referred to him as a new postwar archetype (Nozawa 1997, 42–62), which helped to bring Nikkatsu youth cinema closer to Hollywood stars. He was nicknamed "Tony" since his appearance in *Shimizu no abarenbō* (Roughnecks from Shimizu, Matsuo Akinori, 1959)—his roughish expression, robust constitution and tangled hairstyle—resembled that of Tony Curtis. Akagi deliberately sought this exotic resemblance and he acknowledged his admiration for the appearance of foreigners (Eiga arubamu 1961, 74) and American popular music (Watanabe 1977, 37–38).

His popularity rocketed in 1960 after appearing in the four-part series *Kenjū buraichō* (Tales of a Gunman, Noguchi Hiroshi, 1959–1960) and his persona became strongly associated with his protagonist role here, particularly as a result of the first film, *Nukiuchi no Ryū* (Ryuji the Gun Slinger, Noguchi Hiroshi, 1960). Akagi received the prize for "Best New Actor" awarded by the Japan Film Producers Association (Nihon eigaka kyōkai shinjinshō) in January 1961, one month before his death as a consequence of a car accident while filming *Gekiryū ni ikiru otoko* (A Torrent of Life) which was finally renamed for its release in 1967 as *Akagi Keiichirō wa ikite iru gekiryū ni ikiru otoko* (Akagi Keiichirō is Alive: A Torrent of Life, Yoshida Kenji, 1967). After that, Akagi came to be known as the "Japanese James Dean" for the similarities in their deaths but also in their acting styles (Schilling 2007, 49), exemplifying the continuous parallels between Japanese and American stars that the Japanese audience would establish in this period.

Nikkatsu continued with this successful tendency of creating transnational youth stars with Wada Kōji, who was fifteen years old when he debuted in *Mugon no rantō* (The Silent Drunkard, Nishikawa Katsumi, 1959). Wada's success in *Suttobi kozō* (Kid in a Hurry, Nishikawa Katsumi,

1960), the first film of the *Kozō* (Young Boys) series, marks a shift in Nikkatsu towards a new kind of production defined as "action comedy" (*akushon komedi*) (Suenaga, 89). Towards the end of the 1960s, Nikkatsu strengthened the foreign look of its youth brand by including Joe Shishido as the fifth man of a "New Diamond Line."[6] Shishido came to be known as *Ēsu no Jō* (Joe the Ace) and his roles were used to complement those of Kobayashi and Akagi under a similar Westernized look. His characters as "hitman Joe" (*koroshiya Jō*) echoed other actors of American B movies such as Timothy Carey, Lee Marvin and Henry Silva (Todoroki 2002, 16).

Shin Tōhō Studios tried to copy Nikkatsu's commercial strategy by creating another juvenile star system marketed as the "Handsome Tower" brand. However, it was not as successful as the "Diamond Line" and the company went bankrupt in 1961. By the early sixties, the second Golden Age of Japanese cinema had ended due to the competition brought by television. Nikkatsu attempted to renew its youth star system by giving roles to emerging actors such as Watari Tetsuya, Takahashi Hideki, Fuji Tatsuya and Kawachi Tamio (Schilling 2007, 19). However, the popularity of the *mukokuseki eiga* came to an end around 1963.

Mukokuseki eiga: The case of the Japanese Western

The "Japanese Western" (*wasei uesutan*) was the most recognisable genre of *mukokuseki eiga* produced at the turn of the decade, particularly as a consequence of Kobayashi's role as protagonist of the successful *Wataridori* series. These films project a singular transcultural merger that transfers American national stereotypes and imaginaries, such as the cowboy, the "Indians" and the conquest of the Far West, to a fictionalized Japan. Thus, Kobayashi ultimately embodies the Japanese version of the "lonely wanderer" by incorporating iconic elements such as his fringe, leather jacket, horse and whip. References to the American Western were also strengthened by Kobayashi's acting; he acknowledged mimicking the gestures of Hollywood stars by practicing the way Alan Ladd handled pistols and John Wayne the rifle (Nishikawa 2004, 152).

The Japanese Western brought fresh air to film production of the late-1950s by keeping a suggestive exoticism while also departing from previous representations of traditional Japan in *jidaigeki* that had prevailed in the nationalist propaganda films made during the years of the "dark valley" (1937–1945). However, it has not been emphasized enough that this concept of "stateless films" is misleading. While these films did not aim to represent faithfully any country, they did contain a direct cultural affiliation to the US, its myths and iconographies. Therefore, the Japanese Western illustrates well the extraordinary fluidity and malleability of film genres, showing how codes of representation may migrate across different contexts and historical periods, and are constantly re-appropriated, adapted and renewed. The *Wataridori* series showcases the weight of Hollywood as a global hegemonic force. There are other examples in which studios and filmmakers have adapted American Western conventions, from the "spaghetti Western" in Italy and "*chorizo* Western" in Spain to other African (Burns 2002) and Indian (Teo 2011, 425) experiences. This circulation of genre codes between the late 1950s and early 1960s was not new, but a revival of earlier transcultural experiences. Satō (1975) claims that the hybridity of the western genre and samurai films dates back to the influence that the "good bad man" roles played by William S. Hart had on Japan from the 1910s. Tropes like the "lonely wanderer" had been recycled, for example in the *matatabi mono* ("wanderer gambler") stories written by Hasegawa Shin and adapted for the big screen, creating Japanese heroes such as the "wandering rōnin" and yakuza of the 1920s and 1930s, as Exley (2018) has also noted. These free and individualistic heroes who were not loyal to any master and would only sacrifice themselves for the helpless and the poor, rather than for the country or its elites, fuelled the stories created by anarchists and left-wing directors until they disappeared from the screen with the rise of militarism in the early 1930s. These heroes were featured on the big screen at least until the release of *Koina no Ginpei: Yuki no wataridori* (Koina no Ginpei: Migratory Snowbird, Miyata Tomikazu, 1931), also written by Hasegawa.

The restoration of relations with the US after Japan's surrender in 1945 created a more favorable context for reviving this kind of transcultural flow. Yomota (2000, 138) also notes that during this period cinema became the ideal medium to restore the cultural pride that the Japanese had long lost in the international arena. The international recognition of Japanese film culture started with the western "discovery" of Kurosawa Akira's *jidaigeki* films (Centeno-Martin 2019; Weinrichter 2002), which, ironically, had been created through elements taken from the Hollywood tradition, particularly John Ford's Western films. Examples can be seen in the Far West duels to the death taking place in the square of a border village in *Yōjinbō* (Yojimbo, Kurosawa, 1961). In this film, the US gunman archetype is replaced by an early-Meiji-period *rōnin*, which in turn, is transformed back into a cowboy in the Spaghetti Western remake *A Fistful of Dollars* (Sergio Leone, 1964). Similarly, the gunmen-inspired *rōnin* of Kurosawa's *Shichi nin no samurai* (Seven Samurai 1954) revert back to Far West gunmen in John Sturges' remake *The Magnificent Seven* (1960).

Both Kurosawa's *rōnin* and Saitō's wanderer renewed postwar Japanese cinema by combining Japanese *matatabi mono* tropes and the US cowboy stereotypes. However, unlike the exotic appeal of legendary Japan found in Kurosawa's *jidaigeki*, Saitō's *Wataridori* series reproduces Far West iconography more overtly. The apparently "Japanese" look of Kurosawa's films contributed to his international success, triggering a "kimono effect" among European audiences (Weinrichter 2002), while Saitō's "western exoticism" explained the success of the *Wataridori* series at the domestic box-office. The fifth film, *Daisōgen no wataridori* (Plains Wanderer, Saitō Takeichi, 1960), illustrates well the predominance of Hollywood elements. The film is shot in Hokkaido, whose natural beauty mirrors the wide landscapes of the "Far West" even if, ironically, Hollywood filmed many of these locations in Almería, Southern Spain in the 1950s and 1960s. This exemplifies how the western creates an autonomous set of genre codes grounded on a self-referential universe. However, the Japanese Western does implement some local adaptations. The recurrent trope of the native Americans who inhabit this "wild landscape" are replaced by the Ainu people in *Daisōgen no wataridori*. In addition, Kitamura (2011, 138) notes that the climactic scene in which the villain Kōdō is killed during a shoot-out by Kobayashi Akira´s rival, Masa (Joe Shishido), is a reference to *Rio Bravo* (Howard Hawks 1959), released the year before, in which a boy tosses a gun to John Wayne to kill the villain. Also, the sequence featuring Kobayashi's departure on horseback as a weeping boy shouts "brother!" (*oniichan!*) echoes a scene from *Shane* (George Stevens 1954) in which a young boy cries the name of the protagonist, portrayed by Alan Ladd, as he leaves the community (Kitamura 201, 139). Furthermore, Satō (1995, 292) observes that Kobayashi's engagement in protecting Setona (Shiraki Mari) and her Ainu village reproduces the "good bad man" encounter with the innocent heroine and the weak, which materializes the heterosexual integration of codes taken from William S. Hart's prewar westerns.

This is not the first film using remote regions in rural Japan to present an exotic "other."[7] However, *Daisōgen no wataridori* uses the Ainu people to project the primitivism that was needed to build the idea of a "Far West" in Hokkaido. Unlike many US westerns of the time, these indigenous people are not represented as the antagonists of the hero but as innocent people who must be protected. Even the heroine Junko (Asaoka Ruriko), a folk-art researcher who runs an Ainu arts and crafts store, allies Kobayashi to support the Ainu community. The film does not deal with contemporary issues of poverty and social exclusion suffered by the Ainu and instead retains an exotic portrayal—the paternalist images of the Ainu as pure, innocent and primitive were also being created by tourist agencies of the time (Centeno-Martin 2017). However, the fact that an airport is to be built on Ainu land in *Plains Wanderer* anticipates narratives of the Ainu being forced to leave their land that were popularized by Tezuka Osamu in his manga *Shumari* (1974–1976)[8] and later by postcolonial scholarship, which has revisited the modernization of Hokkaido as a military settlement and violent colonization (Mason and Lee 2012).

These elements from the American Western are combined with other tropes from the aforementioned wanderer *matatabi* tradition in Japan, making this "Japanese Western" a more complex phenomenon than just a mere reproduction of Hollywood patterns. For example, Kobayashi appears in a scene with a boy, Nobuo (Egi Toshio), who appears in the previous film in the series, *Akai yūhi no wataridori* (Rambler in the Sunset, Saitō Buichi, 1960). It is quickly established that their mission is to find the boy's mother, who happens to be the villain's lover, Kazue (Minamida Yoko). The trope of the child is repeatedly found in the *matatabi* narrative structure and is used again in the eighth film of the *Wataridori* series, *Wataridori kita e kaeru* (Wanderer Returns North, Saitō Buichi, 1961), in which Kobayashi tries to unite a boy with his sick mother. Kobayashi eventually saves the Ainu village, but the boy's mother is badly injured in the crossfire. Thus, the hero inflicts pain on the very community he is trying to save and, as Kitamura (2011) has noted, this tension between the hero and the community is a common trope in lone ranger and yakuza stories, in which the hero eventually has to leave town.

Projecting the mentality of a nation

The elements described in the section above show how these *mukokuseki eiga* articulate their own self-referential universe which does not necessarily have parallels in reality. For example, while Kobayashi crosses Hokkaido on a horse and encounters the Ainu in traditional garments, Hokkaido people did not use horses to travel, nor did the Ainu people live in *cise* (Ainu traditional houses) or hunt with bows and arrows as is depicted in *Daisōgen no wataridori*. Moreover, the reference to the famous *iyomante rimse* (Ainu bear ceremony), which in reality was no longer being performed in the 1960s,[9] presents the Ainu dancing around a bonfire, echoing iconographies from cultural representations of American natives but with no references to the actual ceremony.[10] In fact, the Ainu are not even played by Ainu actors. Consequently, *Daisōgen no wataridori* does not represent any specific place or time but merely the exoticism of an imagined land in which cultural references to the US and Japan are interwoven. Nevertheless, can these films tell us anything about the moment in which they were made? Can fiction films like *Daisōgen no wataridori* be used as an object of any social, cultural or historical enquiry?

Images are rarely free from subjectivities of any kind. In that sense, they might be a valid testimony of the aspirations, hopes and anxieties of the society that has produced them. Kracauer opened up the discussion on how films may project the mentality of a nation in his seminal work *From Caligari to Hitler* (1947). This approach was revisited by historians and sociologists from 1970s onwards, with some assessing the validity of studying how films project the fantasies of a society (Ferro 1977) and how they echo a collective psychology, as after all, images are just "ideological expressions of the time" (Sorlin 1977, 42). Films can never guarantee any faithful representation of reality, as they are always subject to a set of choices and interpretations, but they may also reproduce structures of power—an approach developed by a wide range of Marxist and structuralist authors (Louis Althusser, Jacques Lacan, Max Horkheimer, Theodor Adorno, Stephen Prince), in which culture and ideology are unavoidably intertwined. In this sense, the representation of fantasies related to wider geopolitical tensions and international affiliations should be a valid field of perusal in a film analysis.

This avenue for research would allow scholars to explore the relationship between the Cold War and Hollywood films set in Ancient Rome, as well as Soviet films on Russian medieval heroes. Film theorists may find in the historical context a fruitful field to examine the parameters that condition films' aesthetics and narratives. Similarly, these *mukokuseki eiga* between the late 1950s and early 1960s may also be interrogated within the cultural context of the Cold War.[11]

After its surrender in World War II, Japan fell into the American sphere of influence, and was included in the "Economic Recovery in Occupied Areas (EROA)" established in 1948, which operated like a Marshall Plan in Asia to counterbalance the "Pan-Asiatic movement" under Soviet and Chinese leaders (Schaller 1982). While Japan attended the 1955 Bandung Conference that sparked the Non-Aligned Movement, the Kishi Nobusuke administration (1957–1960) marked a shift in Japanese foreign policy. Kishi, who had been imprisoned as a suspected Class A war criminal for his brutal rule of the puppet state of Manchukuo, was released in 1948 and, alongside other wartime bureaucrats, engaged in a more active anticommunist policy in the Cold War. This aligned with the US policy in Asia aimed at making Japan an industrial hub that would contain the expansion of communism on the continent (Schaller 1982, 393). Under the Kennedy administration (1961–1963), the economic ties between the US and Japan strengthened even further as a way of securing American military bases. The exoticism portrayed by the *Wataridori* series was a way of re-imagining the nation in relation to the new role that Japan had in Asia. Indeed, these *mukokuseki eiga* were not a realistic portrayal of Japan. Even the previous *taiyōzoku* films featured youngsters driving convertible cars and navigating on sailing boats that were not attainable for the majority of the Japanese population at the time. However, these films made suggestive references to the new imaginary status of Japan under the American sphere of influence.

Taiyōzoku films and the *Wataridori* series presented a fantasized Japan that was visually close to American popular culture. This illustrates a process in which Japanese society becomes not only politically and economically linked to the US but also closer at a psychological and subjective level. This process prompted the production of images that enabled the audience to imagine a Japan that increasingly resembled America. For Kitamura (2011, 38–40), this is a process of back and forth as *Daisōgen no wataridori* would also present a nostalgia for a past homeland (*furusato*) since it articulates a strong contrast between the innocent rural and the evil urban life. The abuses against the Ainu are embodied by Kōdō, the entrepreneurial Tokyoite who aims to build an airport for tourists on the site of an Ainu village, which may be framed within concerns of the time about the exploitation of the Ainu in the strategies to promote tourism in Hokkaido. This tension between the Ainu and other Japanese in the film could also be criticism of industrial capitalism and the socio-economic conditions of the postwar era. Furthermore, this trope of evil villains from Tokyo exploiting the rural can be found in other Japanese Westerns such as *Akai kōya* (The Crimson Plains, Noguchi Hiroshi, 1961), *Hayauchi yarō* (Quick Draw Joe, Nomura Takashi, 1961) and *Mekishiko mushuku* (Mexico Wanderer, Kurahara Koreyoshi, 1962) (Kitamura 2011). However, this criticism is ambivalent. For example, the fact that Junko is a Japanese seller of Ainu arts and crafts in *Daisōgen no wataridori* is never problematized.

The ethnic and misleading look of the Ainu in *Daisōgen no wataridori* may indeed project a nostalgia for a pre-industrial Japan. However, the film is not set in any specific historical period; while urban areas in Hokkaido featuring cars and airplanes seem to refer to contemporary Japan, characters are presented in the fashion of the 19th-century American Far West, including jeans, handkerchiefs around the neck and Texan hats—as noted above, Kobayashi even travels by horse. This cinematic phenomenon may be explained by "internal exoticism" (Yano 2010, 18) or a "paradox of transnationalism" that helps to solidify ironical national delineations (Kitamura 2011). It can be argued that filmmakers were able to represent a Japan that resembled the US not only because of the strong influence of American popular culture during the postwar period but also because the Cold War nurtured a process of cultural identification and assimilation in the collective psychology of the Japanese audience.

Transnational transmediality

The phenomenon of these transnational youth icons exemplifies not only how Japanese cinema expanded beyond its national borders but also how it expanded beyond the cinematic medium itself. The film industry of this period created intense synergies with the entertainment industry and the personas of Ishihara Yūjirō, Kobayashi Akira and other youth icons were created through multiple appearances on the radio, magazines, photo-novels and television, as well as on the big screen. They would not only participate in the media as film actors but were also commercially exploited as singers.

The media made Yūjirō the first multifaceted star, depicting him as a sportsman and musician as well as actor. He was often featured participating in yacht races in the press between 1959 and 1963, including in the magazine *Sports Nippon* (Raine 2000, 211). Yūjirō also became a radio presenter and had his own culture program, "Ishihara Yūjirō Hour." from 1957 to 1959 and participated in the radio drama *Kaikyō o koetekita otoko* (The Boy who Crossed the Strait, NHK Radio, 1957). In addition, audiences started to see him on the television program *Daiyaru 110 ban* (Dial Number 110, Nihon TV, 1958). However, it was in the music industry that he was most successful. Films would regularly include scenes of Yūjirō performing songs that later would be broadcast on radio and released as LPs. Although for Yūjirō music was just a secondary dedication, he released four albums, eighteen LPs, and forty-three singles in his first two years as an actor.[12] In these early years, Yūjirō also participated as a singer in musicals such as *Jazu musume tanjō* (Birth of a Jazz Girl, Sunohara Masahisa, 1957) and *Subarashiki dansei* (Wonderful Guy, Inoue Umeji, 1958) as well as in television shows such as *Kōhaku uta gassen* (Song Battle, NHK, 1957 New Year's Eve) and the *Misora Hibari Show* in 1958 (Takayanagi 2000, 100–1). In his music performances, Yūjirō alternated songs from American popular culture—like jazz songs played with a guitar, piano and drums—with more local genres such as *kayōkyoku* (Japanese pop music) and particularly his famous *enka* (Japanese ballad).

His transmedia performances were also transnational. His first song was an *enka* played with a ukulele for the film *Kurutta kajitsu* in the summer of 1956 which sold 730,000 LPs. This mirrored the Hollywood release, a few months earlier, of *Rock Around the Clock* (Fred F. Sears 1956), featuring Bill Haley and his Comets, which was produced in order to capitalize on the success of the song of the same name, whose popularity had been prompted by the film *Blackboard Jungle* (Richard Brooks, 1955) the year before. In addition, Elvis Presley started his film career in November 1956 with *Love Me Tender* (Robert D. Webb, 1956) and Gene Vincent with *The Girl Can't Help It* (Frank Tashlin, 1956) in December, singing the song "Be-Bop-A-Lula," which became a great success. The Japanese press even referred to Elvis Presley, Gene Vincent and Bill Haley as "*taiyōzoku* singers," which illustrates how these transmedia phenomena became increasingly transcultural as well.[13]

These transmedia strategies, including the strong alliances with the music industry, were also used to commercially exploit Kobayashi Akira, Akagi Keiichirō and Wada Kōji. They all adopted this dual dimension of "actor-singer." Kobayashi performed songs on screen in the successful *Onna o wasurero* (Forget about Women, Masuda Toshio, 1959) and *Arashi o yobu yūjō* (The Friendship that Started a Storm, Inoue Umetsugu, 1959), which depicts the jazz world. Likewise, the premieres of the *Wataridori* (1959–1962), *Nagaremono*, (1960–1961) and *Abarenbō* (1960–1963) series were scheduled simultaneously with the release of their soundtracks.[14] Many of these songs, which had the same titles as the films in which they were featured, became great hits, such as the *okesa* song,[15] *Umi kara kita nagaremono* (The Drifter Returns from the Sea), *Wataridori itsu mata kaeru* (Return of the Vagabond), the *enka Gitā o motta wataridori* (The Rambling Guitarist), *Ginza senpūji* (Ginza Whirling Boy) and the twist song *Yume ga ippai abarenbō* (A Rampage Full of Dreams). The entertainment industry also played a significant role in boosting the popularity of Kobayashi after he married Misora Hibari, the most popular singer and actress in Japan at the time.[16]

Akagi Keiichirō sang his first songs *Kuroi kiri no machi* (Black Fog Town) and *Kyō kagiri no koi* (Only Today's Love) in *Kenjū buraichō Nukiuchi no Ryū*, the first film in the *Kenjū buraichō* series. These songs were released in March 1960, a month after the premiere.[17] Akagi had a contract with the record label Polydor Records and by the time of his death in 1961, he had appeared in 13 films and released 25 songs, 18 of which were included in the films' soundtracks.[18] Finally, Wada Kōji's films often included musical performances. He becomes the drummer of a jazz club in the *Kozō* series. *Junjō gurentai* (Innocent Fools), the theme song for the *Gurentai* series, became widely known, although Wada's place in the music industry did not achieve a popularity comparable to the aforementioned stars.

From that point, the film industry entered a new period of competition with television that brought the "Second Golden Age" of Japanese cinema to an end. Although Nikkatsu kept releasing films with a certain westernized air, the *mukokuseki eiga* genre began to decline from 1963 (Schilling 2007, 5). However, the transnational and transmedia dimension of Japanese film stars, far from vanishing, has continued to evolve and adopt a variety of forms right up to the present day. Assessing these links between Japanese films in relation to the record industry and media culture, which Thomas Elsasser (2004, 117) termed "media interference," is an approach increasingly adopted by scholars. Raine (2020a) has investigated other interactions between cinema and popular culture in the same period through the *kayō eiga* (popular song film) developed by Toho studios in the 1950s, which explains the creation of a female stardom led by Misora Hibari. Kanno (2020) has explored the more recent case of Miwa Akihiro, a transgender star and singer whose popularity spread through films, television shows, radio and theater.

The appeal of the transcultural transmediality that could be found in Ishihara, Akagi and others intensified over the years. It is evidenced by the proliferation of new stars in the contemporary entertainment industry who not only have a "foreign look" but also have transcultural and multi-ethnic backgrounds such as the singer-actor Shirota Yū and the singer-actress Maria Mori as well as more recently Crystal Kay Williams, Mizuhara Kiko, Sawajiri Erika and Itō Yuna. These media phenomena may indeed reflect an increasing diversity in Japanese society. Cultural hybridity, such as the combination of jazz and *enka* ballads performed by youth icons, also existed in the high economic growth era and was part of everyday life. However, it must be remembered that rather than offering a realistic social portrayal, Nikkatsu films of the time sought escapist depictions of an exotic, while in a way also familiar, Japan.

Conclusion

The transnational nature of the early youth star system in Japan through the *taiyōzoku* and Japanese Western films casts light on the complexity of Japanese cinema as a multidimensional phenomenon. This analysis has illustrated the extraordinary exposition of Japanese films in the global flow of images, trends and media languages as well as the sensitivity of Japanese filmmakers to foreign ideas and practices. Yamamoto (1983) pioneered this analytical approach by interrogating the impact of foreign influence on Japanese cinema. This perspective enriched the work of other scholars in the following years, and the transnational nature of some of these youth icons has been commented on previously (Raine 2000; Schiller 2007; Centeno-Martin 2016). However, the analysis provided in this chapter problematizes the paradigm of "national cinema" not only through its national affiliation, but also its form as media. This implies that the very term "Japanese cinema" is increasingly outdated and needs to be revisited.

Therefore, my conclusion is twofold: on the one hand, the *mukokuseki eiga* from the late 1950s highlight precisely the limitations of the "national" in film analysis. This is not new; in fact, what Raine (2020) refers to as "global simultaneity and cultural permeability" can be found in Japanese cinema since its inception (see Miyao 2020). It continued to be transnational during the Japanese empire and wartime period (Taylor-Jones 2019; Centeno-Martin 2020; Yan 2020) and during the Cold War (DeBoer 2020), until it became part of the global culture from the 1980s onwards through its global fandom (Dew 2007; Allison 2006; Denison 2008). But the case studies introduced here demonstrate how the Cold War created not only a political and economic context but also a cultural environment that conditioned these transcultural interactions.

The construction of the youth star system helps to understand the extraordinary fluidity of the cinematic "medium," providing relevant examples of "media interference." This "interference" was not new either as it can be traced back to, for example, the interactions between cinema and radio, the record industry, print media and theater of the 1930s (Elsasser 2004; Barnett 2020; Fujiki 2021). However, this *kontentsu* (industrial collaboration) is particularly significant in the media environment of the late 1950s and early 1960s, during which the emergence of television intensified these interactions.[19]

While Japanese cinema was being discovered in the West from the 1950s onwards through films portraying an exotic Japan, the *taiyōzoku* and Japanese Western films examined here reveal a different kind of film, made for the domestic market and projecting another kind of exoticism, based on American iconographies. They demonstrate how the Japanese film industry has constantly been evolving and also call into question the very concept of "Japanese cinema" that western authors were simultaneously trying to construct. These *mukokuseki eiga* evidence a complex transnational and transmedia phenomenon that helps to situate Japanese cinema in the global media culture. Thus, this analysis calls into question essentialist views of Japanese cinema and proposes alternative approaches that are not restricted to national and media boundaries.

Notes

[1] Births peaked in 1949 at 2.69 million. See: National Institute of Population and Social Security Research (2010)

[2] See news on *"Taiyōzoku* youngsters" published in *Asahi Shinbun* between July and August 1956.

[3] Asahi Graph (1994, 45).

[4] Ishihara Yūjirō broke his leg in January 1960 and Akagi died in February of the same year. As a consequence, Nikkatsu created a "Second Diamond Line" that year giving more leading roles to Joe Shishido (Shishido Jō) and Nitani Hideaki.

[5] For a list of all the films in which Akagi participated see *Kindai eiga* (1967, 138).

[6] According to Shishido, due to the fact that Wada Koji was too weak (Todoroki 2002, 15).

[7] See how rural settings were depicted as an exotic "foreign country" (ikoku) in the *bunka eiga* (documentary films) from the 1920s in Fujii (2018).

[8] For more on the influence that the imaginary exploitation of Hokkaido portrayed in Tezuka's *Shumari* had on later Japanese Westerns, see Exley (2018, 153).

[9] There were some attempts to revive it in the 1970s. See Centeno-Martin (2017).

[10] One can compare it with the prewar documentaries shot by Gordon Munro featuring the bear ceremony (Centeno-Martin 2018).

[11] Raine (2020b) has embarked on this proposal with his analysis of links between the Cold War and the cinematic phenomena of the time.

[12] Although these songs were originally by Teichiku Entertainment, given the success of his musical career, Yūjirō created his own record company, Ishihara Ongaku Shuppansha, in 1966, and another one, Ishihara Music, in 1977. Since then, there have been countless compilations of his songs, including "Ishihara Yūjirō Hitto Shū" which counts 39 editions.

[13] See the press articles published in the Summer of 1956, "Taiyōzoku kashū no tōyō" [The appearance of taiyōzoku singers], *Asahi Shinbun*, 13 July 1956; "Amerika taiyōzoku wo kiru" [Cutting the American taiyōzoku], *Asahi Shinbun*, 28 August 1956.

[14] These LPs were commercialized by Nippon Columbia from 1958 to 1964 and Nippon Crown between 1964 and 1980.

[15] Traditional song from Sado island, Niigata Prefecture.

[16] See details in Kobayashi's autobiography (Kobayashi 2001).

[17] *Fukushima Minpō* (1960).

[18] For a complete list of Akagi's songs see Matsuzaka (1968: 45).

[19] Rayna Denison (2020) examines the concept of *kontentsu* (the industrial collaboration) through the relationship between manga, film and television in postwar Japan.

Videography

Akagi Keiichirō wa ikiteiru gekiryū ni ikiru otoko [Akagi Keiichirō is Alive: A Torrent of Life], 1967. [Film]. Directed by Yoshida Kenji. Tokyo: Nikkatsu.
Akai kōya [The Crimson Plains], 1961. [Film]. Directed by Noguchi Hiroshi. Tokyo: Nikkatsu.

Akai yūhi no wataridori [Rambler in the Sunset], 1960. [Film]. Directed by Saitō Buichi. Tokyo:Nikkatsu.

Arashi o yobu yūjō [The Friendship that Started a Storm], 1959. [Film]. Directed by Inoue Umetsugu. Tokyo: Nikkatsu.

Blackboard Jungle, 1955. [Film]. Directed by Richard Brooks. Beverly Hills: MGM/Loew's Inc.

Daisōgen no wataridori [Plains Wanderer], 1960. [Film]. Directed by Saitō Takeichi. Tokyo: Nikkatsu.

A Fistful of Dollars, 1964. [Film]. Directed by Sergio Leone. Rome: Jolly Film

The Girl Can't Help It, 1956. [Film]. Directed by Frank Tashlin. Los Angeles: 20th Century Fox.

Gyakkōsen [Backlight], 1956. [Film]. Direced by Furukawa Takumi. Tokyo: Nikkatsu.

Hayauchi yarō [Quick Draw Joe], 1961. [Film]. Directed by Nomura Takashi. Tokyo: Nikkatsu.

Jazu musume tanjō [Birth of a Jazz Girl], 1957. [Film]. Directed by Sunohara Masahisa. Tokyo: Nikkatsu.

Jūdai no hankō [Teenage Crime], 1955. [Film]. Directed by Tanaka Shigeo. Tokyo: Daiei.

Jūdai no himitsu [Teenage Secret], 1954. [Film]. Directed by Nakai Shigeo. Tokyo: Daiei.

Jūdai no seiten [Teenage Sex Manual], 1953. [Film]. Directed by Shima Kōji. Tokyo: Daiei.

Jūdai no yūwaku [Teenage Seduction], 1953. [Film]. Directed by Hisamatsu Seiji. Tokyo: Daiei.

Koina no Ginpei: Yuki no wataridori [Koina no Ginpei: Migratory Snowbird], 1931. [Film]. Directed by Miyata Tomikazu. Tokyo: Shinkō Kinema.

Kurutta kajitsu [Crazed Fruit], 1956. [Film]. Directed by Nakahira Kō. Tokyo: Nikkatsu.

Love Me Tender, 1956. [Film]. Directed by Robert D. Webb. Los Angeles: 20th Century Fox.

Mekishiko mushuku [Mexico Wanderer], 1962. [Film]. Directed by Kurahara Koreyoshi. Tokyo: Nikkatsu.

Mugon no rantō [The Silent Drunkard], 1959. [Film]. Directed by Nishikawa Katsumi. Tokyo: Nikkatsu.

Nangoku tosa o ato ni shite [Leaving Tosa of the South], 1959. [Film]. Directed by Saitō Buichi. Tokyo: Nikkatsu.

Nisshoku no natsu [Summer in Eclipse], 1956. [Film]. Directed by Horikawa Hiromichi. Tokyo: Tōhō.

Nukiuchi no Ryū [Ryuji the Gun Slinger], 1960. [Film]. Directed by Noguchi Hiroshi. Tokyo: Nikkatsu.

Onna o wasurero [Forget about Women], 1959. [Film]. Directed by Masuda Toshio. Tokyo: Nikkatsu.

Rashōmon, 1950. [Film]. Directed by Kurosawa Akira. Tokyo: Daiei.

Rebel Without a Cause, 1956. [Film]. Directed by Nicholas Ray. Burbank: Warner Bros.

Rio Bravo, 1959. [Film]. Directed by Howard Hawks. Burbank: Warner Bros.

Rock Around the Clock, 1956. [Film]. Directed by Fred F. Sears. Culver City: Columbia Pictures.

Sabakareru jūdai [Judged Teens], 1956. [Film]. Directed by Saeki Kōzō. Tokyo: Daiei.

Sabita naifu [Rusty Knife], 1958. [Film]. Directed by Masuda Toshio. Tokyo: Nikkatsu.

Shane, 1954. [Film]. Directed by George Stevens. Los Angeles: Paramount Pictures.

Shichi nin no samurai [Seven Samurai], 1954. [Film]. Directed by Kurosawa Akira. Tokyo: Tōhō.

Shimizu no abarenbō [Roughnecks from Shimizu], 1959. [Film]. Directed by Matsuo Akinori. Tokyo: Nikkatsu.

Shokei no heya [Punishment Room], 1956. [Film]. Directed by Ichikawa Kon. Tokyo: Daiei.

Subarashiki dansei [Wonderful Guy], 1958. [Film]. Directed by Inoue Umeji. Tokyo: Nikkatsu.

Suttobi kozō [Kid in a Hurry], 1960. [Film]. Directed by Nishikawa Katsumi. Tokyo: Nikkatsu.

Taiyō no kisetsu [Season of the Sun], 1956. [Film]. Directed by Furukawa Takumi. Tokyo: Nikkatsu.

Ueru tamashii [Hungry Spirit], 1956. [Film]. Directed by Kawashima Yūzō. Tokyo: Nikkatsu.

Wataridori kita e kaeru [Wanderer Returns North], 1961. [Film]. Directed by Saitō Buichi. Tokyo: Nikkatsu.

The Wild One, 1953. [Film]. Directed by László Benedek. Culver City: Columbia Pictures.

Yōjinbō [Yojimbo], 1961. [Film]. Directed by Kurosawa Akira. Tokyo: Tōhō.

Bibliography

Allison, A., 2006. The Japan Fad in Global Youth Culture and Millennial Capitalism. In F. Lunning, ed., *Emerging Worlds of Anime and Manga*. Minneapolis: University of Minnesota Press, 11–22.

Asahi Graph. 1994. Taiyōzoku. *Asahi Graph*, 8 July, 45.

Asahi Shinbun, 1956a. Taiyōzoku kashū no tōyō [The appearance of taiyōzoku singers]. *Asahi Shinbun*, 13 July.

———., 1956b. Amerika taiyōzoku wo kiru [Cutting the American taiyōzoku]. *Asahi Shinbun*, 28 August.

Barnett, L., 2020. The Modern Boy and the Screen: Media Representation of Young Urban Men Wearing Western Style Clothing in 1920s and 1930s Japan. In M. Centeno-Martin and N. Morita, eds., *Japan Beyond its Borders: Transnational Approaches to Film and Media*. Tokyo: Seibunsha, 67–84

Burns, J., 2002. John Wayne on the Zambezi: Cinema, Empire, and the American Western in British Central Africa. *The International Journal of African Historical Studies*, 35 (1), 103–17.

Centeno-Martin, M., 2016. Transcultural Corporeity in *Taiyozoku* Youth Cinema. In A. Becker and K. Adachi-Rabe, eds., *Körperinszenierungen im japanischen Film*. Darmstadt: Büchner-Verlag, 143–60.

———., 2017. The Fight for the Self-Representation: Ainu Imaginary, Ethnicity and Assimilation. *Aphaville. Journal of Film and Screen Media*, 13, 69–89.

———., 2018. Contextualising N. G. Munro's Filming of the Ainu Bear Ceremony. *Japan Society Proceedings*, 154, 90–106.

———., 2019. The Misleading Discovery of Japanese "National Cinema." *Japanese Transnational Cinema, Arts*, 7(4), 87, 7–20.

———., 2020. Re-editing the War in Asia. Japanese Newsreels in Spain (1931-1945). *L´Atalante. Revista de Estudios Cinematográficos*, 29, 101–19.

DeBoer, S., 2020. Japanese Cinema and its Postcolonial Histories. In H. Fujiki and A. Phillips, eds., *The Japanese Cinema Book*. London: BFI, Bloomsbury.

Denison, R., 2008. The Global Markets for *Anime*: Miyazaki Hayao's *Spirited Away* (2001). In A. Phillips and J. Stringer, eds., *Japanese Cinema: Texts and Contexts*. London: Routledge.

———., 2020. Transmedial Relations Manga at the Movies. In H. Fujiki and A. Phillips, eds., *The Japanese Cinema Book*. London: BFI, Bloomsbury.

Dew, O., 2007. Asia Extreme: Japanese Cinema and British Hype. *New Cinemas*, 5 (1), 53–73.

Eiga arubamu, 1961. *Eiga arubamu 12. Akagi Keiichirō zensakuhinshū* [Film album 12. The complete works of Akagi Keiichirō]. Tokyo: Handobukkusha.

Elsaesser, T. 2004. The New Film History as Media Archaeology. *Cinemas: Journal of Film Studies*, 14 (2–3), 75–117.

Exley, C., 2018. No Land's Man: On Remaking the Last Western in Japan and the Politics of Revision. *Journal of Japanese and Korean Cinema*, 10 (2), 147–62.

Ferro, M., 1977. *Cinéma et Histoire, Le Cinéma agent et source de l'Histoire*. París: Editions Denoël (English trans. 1988. *Cinema and History*. Detroit: Wayne State University Press).

Fujii, J., 2020. Yanagita Kunio and the Culture Film: Discovering Everydayness and Creating/Imagining a National Community, 1935–1945. In M. Centeno-Martin and M. Raine, eds., *Developments in the Japanese Documentary Mode. Arts*. Basel: MDPI, 17–32.

Fujiki, H., 2020. Spectatorship: The Spectator as Subject and Agent. In H. Fujiki and A. Phillips, eds., *The Japanese Cinema Book*. London: BFI, Bloomsbury.

Fukushima Minpō, Fukushima: Fukushima Minpōsha, 4-4-1960.

Giuglaris, S. and Giuglaris, M., 1957. *Le cinema Japonais* [Japanese cinema]. Paris: du Cerf.

Hirano, K. 1992. *Mr. Smith Goes to Tokyo: Japanese Cinema Under the American Occupation, 1945–52*. Washington, D.C.: Smithsonian Institute.

Ishihara, S., 1956. Boku no satsueijo nikki. Sutā shōbai yameraremai [My filming diary: can't stop business with stars]. *Bungei Shunjū*, 10, 280–93.

Ishihara, Y., 1989. *Waga seishun monogatgari* [Our youth story]. Tokyo: Magajin Hausu.

———., 1958. Ashita wa ashita no kaze ga fuku [Tomorrow is another day]. *Bungei Shunjū*, 04-1958, 248.

Jiji Tsūshinsha, ed., 1963. *Eiga nenkan 1963nen han* [Film Yearbook 1963]. Tokyo: Jiji Tsūshinsha.

Kanno, Y., 2020. Queer Resonance: The Stardom of Miwa Akihiro. In H. Fujiki and A. Phillips, eds., *The Japanese Cinema Book*. London: BFI, Bloomsbury.

Kawade Shobō Shinsha, ed., 1979. *Waga no sedai. Shōwa jūdai umare* [Our generation: born in 1926–1936]. Tokyo: Kawade Shobō Shinsha.

———., ed., 1980. *Waga sedai shōwa hachinen umare* [Our generation: born in 1933]. Tokyo: Kawade Shobō Shinsha.

Kindai eiga. 1967. Gekiryū ni ikiru otoko: Akagi Keiichirō wa ikiteiru tokushūgō [A man who lives in a torrent: living Akagi Keiichirō Special Issue]. *Kindai eiga*, 11, 138.

Kinema junpō, 213, 9-1958, 101.

Kitamura, H., 2011. Shoot-Out in Hokkaido: The "Wanderer" (Wataridori) Series and the Politics of Transnationality. In P. Gates and L. Funnell, eds., *Transnational Asian Identities in Pan-Pacific Cinemas*. London: Routledge, 30–45.

Kobayashi, A., 2001. *Sasurai*. Tokyo: Shinchōsha.

Kracauer, S., 1947. *From Caligari to Hitler: a Psychological History of the German Film*. Princeton: Princeton University Press.

Mason, M. and Helen, J. S. L., 2012. *Reading Colonial Japan: Text, Context, and Critique*. Palo Alto: Stanford University Press.

Matsuzaka, N., 1968. *Toni no omoide: maboroshi no sutā Akagi Keiichirō* [Memories of Tony: Akagi Keiichirō, a ghost star]. Tokyo: Kyōrakusha.

Miyao, D., 2020. *Japonisme and the Birth of Cinema*. Durham: Duke University Press.

Nathan, J., 2001. Profiles. Tokyo Story. Shintarō Ishihara's Flamboyant Nationalism Appeals to Many Japanese Voters who are Looking for a Change in Government. *The New Yorker*, 9 April, 108.

National Institute of Population and Social Security Research, 2010. Table 5. Vital Statistics. *National Institute of Population and Social Security Research* [online]. Available at: http://www.ipss.go.jp/p-info/e/S_D_I /Indip.asp#t_5 [Accessed on 14 October 2021].

Nishikawa, H., 2004. Kobayashi Akira densetsu [Akira Kobayashi legend]. *Kinema junpō*, 14-5, 152.

Nozawa, K., 1997. *Akagi Keiichirō: "hikari to kage" nijūssai no fināre* [Akagi Keiichiro: "light and shadow" 21-year-old end]. Tokyo: Seisei Shuppan. 42–62.

Ōi, C., 1968. *Photo Story. Akagi Keiichirō wa ikiteiru* [Akagi Keiichiro is a life]. Tokyo: Nikkatsugeinō.

Raine, M., 2000. Ishihara Yūjirō: Youth, Celebrity, and the Male Body in late-1950s Japan. In D. Washburn and C. Cavanaugh, eds., *World and Image in Japanese Cinema*. Cambridge: Cambridge University Press, 202–25

———., 2020a. The musical Heibon and the popular song film. In H. Fujiki and A. Phillips, eds., *The Japanese Cinema Book*. London: BFI, Bloomsbury, 116–17.

———., 2020b. The Cold War as Media Environment in 1960s Japanese Cinema. In P. Fu and M-F. Yip, eds., *The Cold War and Asian Cinemas*. London: Routledge, 119–38.

Satō, T., 1975. *Hasegawa Shin ron* [Hasegawa Shin's theory]. Tōkyō: Chūō Kōronsha

———., 1995. *Nihon eiga shi* [History of Japanese cinema]. Tokyo: Iwanami Shoten.

Schaller, M., 1982. Securing the Great Crescent: Occupied Japan and the Origins of Containment in Southeast Asia. *The Journal of American History*, 69 (2), 392–414.

Schilling, M., 2007. *No Borders, No Limits: Nikkatsu Action Cinema*. Godalming: FAB.

Sorlin, P., 1977. *Sociologie du cinéma, Ouverture pour l'histoire de demain* [Sociology of cinema: introduction for tomorrow's history]. Paris: Aubier-Montaigne.

Stringer, J., 2008. The Original and the Copy: Nakata Hideo's *Ring* (1989). In A. Phillips and J. Stringer, eds., *Japanese Cinema: Texts and Contexts*. London: Routledge.

Sunday Mainichi, 1956. Taiyōzoku seifuku haiken [Hawaiian T-shirts have become a uniform]. *Sunday Mainichi*, 26 August.

Suenaga, S., 2006. *Denkō sekka no otoko: Akagi Keiichirō to Nikkatsu action eiga* [Lightning man: Akagi Keiichiro and Nikkatsu action film]. Tokyo: Gomashobō.

Takayanagi, R. 2000. *Ishihara yūjirō uta densetsu: Otozukuri no genba kara* [The legend of Yujiro Ishihara's song: from the creation of sound]. Tokyo: Shakai Shisōsha.

Taylor-Jones, K. 2019. *Divine Work, Japanese Colonial Cinema and its Legacy*. London: Bloomsbury Academic.

Teo, S., 2011 Film and Globalization: from Hollywood to Bollywood. In B. Turner and R. Holton, eds., *The Routledge International Handbook of Globalization Studies*. London: Routledge.

Todokori, Y., 2002. Front Interview. Shishido Joe. *Kinema junpō*, 10, 15.

Toida, M., 1958. Eiga engiron 5. Ishihara Yūjirō no baai [Theory of film acting: The case of Ishihara Yujiro]. *Eiga geijutsu*, 6(6), 50–53.

Uryu, T., 1958. Yūjirō eiga no honshitsu [The essence of Yujiro's films]. *Kinema junpō*, 24, 9.

Watanabe, K., 1977. *Kaettekita umi ōji* [A returned prince of the sea]. Tokyo: Byakuyashobō.

Watanabe, T., 1978. Fujimi no hīrō ni idomu Kobayashi Akira no intabyū [Interview with Kobayashi Akira who challenges the immortal hero]. *Kinema junpō*, 15-04.

Weinrichter, A., 2002. *Pantalla Amarilla: el cine japonés* [Yellow screen: Japanese cinema]. Las Palmas de Gran Canaria: Festival Internacional de Cine.

Yan, N., 2020. Empire Cinematic Dualities. In H. Fujiki and A. Phillips, eds., *The Japanese Cinema Book*. London: BFI, Bloomsbury.

Yano, C.R., 2010. *Tears of Longing Nostalgia and the Nation in Japanese Popular Song*. Cambridge, MA: Harvard Univ. Press.

Yomota, I., 2000. *Nihon eigashi 100 nen* [Japanese film history 100 years]. Tokyo: Shūeisha.

Chapter 6
Film and Television: Looking Beyond a Historic Rivalry

Hiroyuki Kitaura

Abstract

This chapter covers the historical development of film and television, the representative visual media of the 20th century, in Japan. Films were first imported and screened in Japan at the end of the 19th century, with domestic production starting soon after. The first cinema specializing in film exhibition was built in the Asakusa district of Tokyo in 1903. Following this, the number of cinemas increased to reflect the growing demand for films, and this in turn led to a string of film studios being created mainly in Tokyo and Kyoto from 1908 onwards.

From these beginnings, the Japanese film industry found its greatest success in the 1950s. In keeping with Japan's postwar recovery, the number of movie-goers rapidly increased every year. At its peak, each person in Japan went to the movies at least once a month, on average, and movies became deeply entrenched in people's lives. Six major film companies—Nikkatsu, Toho, Toei, Shochiku, Daiei and Shintoho—released new films every week. Each had its own directors and actors who were bound by contract and could not work for other companies. In 1958, film audiences reached a peak of 1.12 billion, but this turned out to be the last year of growth, and five years later, in 1963, the number had dropped sharply to less than half, at 510 million. Television broadcasting, which began in 1953 and rapidly permeated society, was seen as the problem, and indeed, the spread of television and the consequent decline in movie theater attendance gathered momentum.

In this chapter, I consider the history of Japanese film and television from the 1950s onwards, in terms of the interaction between the two media. In particular, I take a closer look at how an existing media industry, film, was forced to respond to the rise of an emerging one in television. Then, I clarify how the two representative visual media of the 20th century have continued to coexist to the present day.

Chapter 6
映画とテレビ: その歴史的相克を越えて

北浦 寛之 *Hiroyuki Kitaura*

　20世紀の代表的映像メディアである映画とテレビの日本での歴史的展開を本章では取り上げる。草創期には活動写真と呼ばれていた映画は、19世紀末に輸入され、製作も程なくしておこなわれるようになると、世紀をまたいで1903年に初の常設映画館が東京・浅草に開館し、産業基盤が出来上がっていく。1908年には、映画館の増加を受けて、製作を充実させるべく初の映画撮影所が東京・目黒に開設する。すぐに西の京都にも撮影所が建設され、以後、日本映画は東京と京都を中心に生み出されながら人気を獲得し、大衆娯楽としての地位を確立していく。いわんや、唯一の映像メディアであった映画の存在感は戦後になってからも続き、日本の主権が回復した1950年代には、国民の圧倒的な支持を得るようになる。この年代を通して、観客数が増加し続け、58年には、歴代最高の11億2700万人に到達する。この観客数を、当時の日本の人口9100万人で割ると、計算上、月に一度は国民各自が映画館に足を運んでいたことになるほどであった。

　だが、こうした日本映画黄金期の1950年代は、他方で、新しい映像メディアであるテレビの登場とその成長を刻印する時代でもあった。テレビは1953年の本放送開始から、受像機の価格低下や、電波の受信エリアの拡大などを実現させながら、大衆に浸透していった。そして、この新たな映像メディアの台頭が、それまでは唯一の映像メディアであった映画を慌てさせることになるのである。

　ここでは、日本の映画とテレビの歴史的関係を紐解いていく。とりわけ、既存メディアであった映画産業側の視点から、新興メディアとして台頭してきたテレビとどう向き合ってきたかについて、ビジネス戦略や技術的対応という点に注目しながら見ていきたい。そして、その20世紀を代表する二つの映像メディアが、折衝を繰り広げながら、いかにして現在まで共存するに至っているのかを明らかにしていく。

映画産業のテレビ対抗措置

映画の技術的革新

　1950年代に映画の観客数が急増し、58年には歴代最高の数を記録した。こうした状況にあって、映画館の数も増え、映画を供給する側の松竹、東宝、東映、大映、日活、新東宝の大手映画会社6社は、大量に映画を製作し、市場に流通させ、そして大量消費を実現した。だが、そうした状況は、翌59年から観客数が減少へと転じることで変調をきたす。1960年代は、50年代と打って変わって、観客数の減少に歯止めが利かなくなり、60年には延べ10億人超だった観客数が、わずか3年で半数に、70年を迎えるとき

には4分の1になってしまう。映画会社の経営も傾き、1961年に新東宝が倒産すると、71年には日活が一般劇映画から撤退して成人映画専門の会社となり、大映も同じ年に倒産して表舞台から姿を消す。こうして日本の映画産業は好景気から10年余りで一気の転落を見たのである。

　他方で、新興のメディアとして1953年に誕生したテレビは、当時好景気に沸いていた映画の背後で着実に浸透していき、59年の皇太子・明仁親王と美智子妃のご成婚パレードがあった年に一気に普及する。多くの国民がテレビ中継でパレードを見ることを望み、1958年4月に100万だったテレビ登録世帯数が、パレード一週間前の59年4月3日に200万に倍増し、さらに同年10月になると300万に達するのである[1]。実に映画界においては、その1959年から観客数の減少が始まるのであり、こうした時期的な重なりから、映画の斜陽は、テレビの普及によるものだと見なされてきた。

　例えば、日本映画界の状況をとりまとめた1962年の『映画産業白書』には、次のように産業の問題が述べられている。

> 戦後順調に増加し続けてきた映画観客数は、テレビ等の影響によって昭和33年［1958］をピークとして著しく減少しはじめ、昨年はピーク時に対して76％に減少した。37年［1962］に入ってからもその傾向は著しく、1～6月で前年よりもさらに22％減少し、映画産業に深刻な問題を投げかけており、一部には映画産業の斜陽化の声さえある[2]。

　1950年代とは打って変わっての60年代以降顕著になっていく観客数の減少について、ここで、はっきりと「テレビ」という名前を出して影響を指摘しているのがわかる。

　このテレビに対して、1950年代に黄金期を迎えていた映画会社は、すでに当時から対抗措置を講じていた。例えば映画会社は、テレビとの違いを打ち出すべく、1957年より従来のスクリーンを拡大させたワイドスクリーン映画を導入し、なかでもその代表的規格となったスコープ映画の製作を推進した。スコープ映画は、そもそもアメリカの20世紀FOX社が、1953年の『聖衣』（ヘンリー・コスター監督）で初めて試みた大型映画シネマスコープと同様の規格であり、「シネマスコープ（シネスコ）」がFOX社の商標名であったことから、日本では各映画会社の名前を冠した「スコープ」映画として普及していった。

　このワイドスクリーンのスコープ映画は、アナモフィック・レンズという特殊なレンズを撮影ならびに上映の際に使って、拡大映像を生み出す。キャメラに同レンズを取り付けて撮影すると、映像が圧縮してフィルムに焼き付けられ、次に、そのレンズを映写機に装着して映写することで、圧縮された映像が復元され、上映される仕組みになっている。そうして映し出された映像は、従来のスタンダードな縦横比1:1.37（サイレント時代は縦横比1:1.33であったが、トーキー以降同サイズが標準化した）の画面を横に大きく拡大させ、縦横比1:2.35（初期には、縦横比1:2.55など、しばしば他の比率で製作されることがあった）の画面を構成し、テレビの小さな画面では味わえない興奮を観客に伝えるとされたのである。

　テレビとの差異化を目指して、同時期にはカラー映画の推進も期待された。テレビは当時白黒の映像であったため、カラー映画がテレビに対抗する技術革新として注目された。1958年の『映画産業白書』を見ても、「天然色映画の製作は、最近テレビ等の進出に対する対抗策の一つ」[3]、「わが国における大型化の将来の見通しとしては、それが最も有力なテレビ対策の一つ」というように[4]、テレビという新たなメディアに対抗する上で、映画のカラー化、大型化が求められていたことがわかる。

　とはいえ、映画のカラー化には課題もあった。カラー映画の製作は、1951年の松竹作品『カルメン故郷に帰る』（木下惠介監督）から本格的に始まり、53年の大映作品『地獄門』（衣笠貞之助監督）がその鮮やかな色彩の魅力もあってカンヌ映画祭でグランプリを受賞するなど、57年から製作されたワイドスクーン映画よりも先行して実績を上げていた。ただ、57年の時点でカラー映画の平均製作費が5261万円、白黒映画のそれが2923万円であったことから、前者は後者の1.8倍の製作費を必要とし、映画の

Table 6.1 カラー映画とワイドスクリーン映画の本数の推移

年	カラー映画の本数 (割合%)	ワイドスクリーン映面の本数 (割合%)
1951	1 (0.5)	—
1952	1 (0.4)	—
1953	3 (1.0)	—
1954	5 (1.4)	—
1955	11 (2.6)	—
1956	32 (6.2)	—
1957	85 (19.2)	72 (16.3)
1958	150 (29.8)	379 (75.3)
1959	167 (33 9)	485 (98.4)
1960	239 (43.7)	545 (99.6)
1961	251 (46.9)	529 (98.9)

(通商産業省企業局商務課編『映画産業白書 1958年版』と通商産業省企業局商務課編『映画産業白書 1962年版』より作成)

カラー化には相当な費用が掛かっていたのである。他方でワイドスクリーン映画は、専用の機械設備さえ整えば、毎回の製作費については最初期の1957年頃で、従来のスタンダード映画より15％から20％増だと言われていた[5]。それゆえ、普及率にも違いが見られる（Table 6.1）。カラー映画が1951年の製作開始から10年かけても全体の5割に満たない中、ワイドスクリーン映画は57年の導入からわずか3年で、10割近い製作比率を占めるようになっていた。こうしてコスト面を考慮に入れると、ワイドスクリーン映画は最初期の頃でもカラー映画に比べて生産しやすい、テレビに対抗するのに最有力の商品であったとみなすことができる。

テレビ産業への強硬策

　映画会社はより直接的にテレビへの対抗策を打ち出してみせる。大手6社はテレビ対策研究委員会を設け、1956年7月のその席上で「テレビに対して積極的に協力しない」という文句で申し合わせをおこなう[6]。それにより、映画会社は実質的に専属の俳優やスタッフがテレビで仕事できないような制限を設けるのである。

　新しく誕生したテレビ産業は、映画人の協力を仰ぎながら映像製作のノウハウを蓄積していった。1953年のテレビ本放送開始前からすでに、テレビ・ドラマの製作に従事することになった者たちは、映画界から監督の山本嘉次郎、キャメラマンの三浦光男、唐沢弘光、美術の松山崇などキャリアのある一流の映画人たちを講師として招いて、勉強会を開催するなど、映画界との人的交流をおこなっていた。とはいえ、テレビ放送が始まると、映画人たちはテレビの世界に興味を持つ者もいたが、一般的にはテレビのことを見下す傾向にあった。前節でも見たように、技術的に映画はテレビより先進であったし、またさらに先を行く革新を遂げようとしていた。

　当初、テレビは盛り場や駅頭など、人が多く集まる場所に設置され、普及は限定的であった。国民に幅広く普及するにはテレビの値段は、あまりに高価だったのである。1953年のテレビ放送開始時に、標準の14型テレビが17万5千円～18万円で販売され、一般のサラリーマンの月収が手取りで1万5千円～6千円の時代に、テレビは高価なものであり、大衆にとって遠い存在であった。それでも、最初の民間放送局としてその年に誕生した日本テレビ（NTV）は、広告収入によって運営する必要があり、そのためにテレビを普及させることが求められた。それゆえ、このテレビ局はテレビの魅力を国民に浸透さ

せるため、多くの人が行き交う盛り場や駅頭などにテレビを設置したのである。そうして設置されたテレビは、街頭テレビと言われ、草創期のテレビ放送に関する記述で必ず言及される現象である[7]。そして、NTVのこの試みは成功する。個人的に所有できずとも、テレビの前には多くの人だかりができ、とりわけプロレスなどスポーツ中継が人気を博した。そのように人が集まる光景は、現在、人々が国際的なスポーツ・イベントなどをパブリック・ビューイングという形態で観戦し楽しむ様子を思い浮かべると、想像しやすいのではないだろうか。

こうしてテレビの魅力をすでに知っていた人たちが、その後テレビの価格低下や視聴エリアの拡大といった個人での入手可能な要件が満たされていくことで、実際に購買へと展開する。その状況に、前節で見たような、皇太子のご成婚パレードという国家イベントが拍車をかけて、一気の普及へとつながったのである。

こうしたテレビ消費の拡大に対して、テレビを見下しながらも、その勢いに脅威を覚えた映画会社が、自社の俳優やスタッフにテレビで仕事をさせない圧力をかけていった。さらに映画会社はそうした人的流出だけでなく、コンテンツの流れもストップさせる。すなわち、大手6社は、テレビ局に自社作品を提供することも止める。各社は当初、テレビに劇映画を提供していた。だが、映画の提供料金の値上げに絡む交渉の決裂から[8]、まずは1956年10月に日活を除いた東映、松竹、東宝、大映、新東宝の5社が、テレビ局に自社作品の提供を停止した。さらに1958年には日活も加わり、大手映画会社の作品はここで完全にテレビでは放映されなくなり、独立プロか海外の映画だけに放映作品が限定される。

そのため映画番組の不在を補うように、また映画依存から脱却するように、各テレビ局は自らの力でドラマを製作していくことを推進する。あるいは、海外のテレビ向けフィルム映画、いわゆるテレビ映画を求めるようになる。とりわけ、アメリカ製の西部劇・アクションものが好評で、『モーガン警部』『ララミー牧場』『ローハイド』『アンタッチャブル』などが、大手劇映画の提供停止期間中に放送されて、高視聴率を叩き出した。例えば、『ララミー牧場』の最高視聴率の回は、放送局の日本教育テレビ(現・テレビ朝日)のネットワークにおいて、1960年、61年の年間視聴率1位を獲得し(それぞれ37.0%、43.7%)、『ローハイド』のそれも同様に、同局の62年の視聴率で、年間1位となった(41.3%)[9]。大手映画会社から劇映画が提供されなくとも、そうしたコンテンツの存在が、視聴者を満足させたのである。

こうした状況も関係してか、映画会社による提供禁止措置は1964年で終了する。同年7月から外国映画の輸入自由化によって大量のテレビ映画と劇映画の輸入が予想される事態を迎え、大手映画会社は自社作品の商品価値を考慮しながら、ついに、10月に劇映画の提供を再開するのである。最初の停止措置から8年が経過していたが、その間には、映画の興行収入がテレビ放送事業者の収入に抜かれるなど、力関係が逆転してしまっていた。この点も、テレビへの強硬措置の見直しにつながったと考えられる[10]。

接近する映画とテレビ

東映の成長とテレビ事業への参入

このように、成長を見せるテレビ産業に対して、1950年代から映画会社は対抗的な姿勢で臨んでいた。ただ、その一方で、ライバルのテレビを利用して増収を図ろうとする動きも、映画業界内に存在した。その先鋒にいた会社が、東映である。

東映は1951年に誕生した会社で、大手6社の中ではもっとも後発でありながら、わずか5年後の56年には、配給収入でトップに立つ。この会社はその後60年代にかけて、業界首位の座を維持し続けるのであり、この時代の日本映画界においてもっとも重要な会社であったと言える。戦後の映画界で新参の会社であった東映は、既存の会社を追い抜くために、従来の制度や慣習を変革しながら急成長を遂げて

いった。そのもっとも顕著な動きが、新作2本立て全プロ配給である。従来、映画館での上映というのは、一度の入場料金で2本の映画を見せる2本立て興行が採用されており、館は複数の映画会社と契約して、各社の映画を併せて上映することをおこなっていた。だが東映はその2本立てプログラムをすべて自社作品で埋めようと、1954年1月から通常の長編劇映画に加え、中編作品も同時に配給するようになる。これが先述の「新作2本立て全プロ配給」というわけだ。他の映画会社も、遅れて2本立て配給を開始したが、東映の勢いに呑み込まれた形で、後手の対応を強いられてしまう。結果、2本立てプログラムをすべて東映作品に切り替える映画館が続出し、東映市場が飛躍的に拡大するのである。

　東映が主導権を握って他の映画会社をリードしていく光景は、テレビ事業参入に対しても見られた。前述のように大手映画会社が、劇映画のテレビへの提供停止を表明した1956年に、東映は郵政省にテレビ免許申請書を提出し、テレビ局の運営を目指すのである。いわば、テレビへの対抗と、テレビへの接近という、アンビバレントな態度を示していた東映だが、その当時、社長の大川博は、劇映画の放映禁止措置については映画館主の希望だと断りを入れながら、テレビ会社設立を含む経営戦略について次のように語った。

> 私が今回テレビ会社を設立しようとする目的は、もっと大きな観点からなのである。テレビの番組を見ても判るように、80％は娯楽演芸で占められている。云いかえれば80％の分野は、映画にも置きかえられるものだと云えるのだ。映画、テレビ、ラジオの一元的な経営は、将来もっとも有望なものだと私は思う。社会一般へのサービスとして最適のものだろう。こんな意味合いから、さきに発起人会を作りテレビ会社設立の申請をした。[中略]映画会社が、テレビをやるとなれば、まず企画、俳優、それにスタジオと共用出来るし、従来の生の芝居を全部フィルム化して放送するなど、コストを安くする方法をとるつもりだ。そうすれば、スポンサーの利用度も高くなるだろうし、テレビの普及にも寄与するところ大であると考えている。[11]

　大川は経営の展望として「映画、テレビ、ラジオの一元的な経営」を掲げ、映画会社がテレビ局経営に関わる意義を強調している。当時、ここまでテレビ経営について積極的な発言をした映画会社の経営者はおらず、せいぜいテレビの宣伝利用が語られるだけだった[12]。対して東映の大川は、「テレビ攻勢に対抗して、映画が生きて行こうとする道」は、この「映画、テレビ、ラジオの一元化経営にある」とまで言い切り[13]、テレビ局の経営をとても重要視している。

　それでも、東映の2本立て配給に続く攻勢として、テレビ事業への参入は、他社にとって脅威となり、翌57年に松竹、東宝、大映、日活、新東宝とすべての大手映画会社がテレビ免許の申請をおこなうに至った。映画会社がテレビという新興のメディアに脅威と興味を公けに示して見せたのは、映画大国のアメリカ・ハリウッドでも同様で、メジャー映画会社がテレビ事業への参入を試みていた。パラマウントが参入にもっとも積極的な会社で、テレビ局を所有し放送事業を展開しようと1920年代後半にはその準備を開始した。だが、連邦通信委員会は反トラスト法を理由に、パラマウントなどメジャー各社によるテレビ局の免許申請をすべて却下した[14]。

　日本の場合、映画会社のテレビ局申請については、アメリカのように完全に却下されることはなく、統合調整が進められた後、一定の成果を見る。東映は、旺文社と日本短波放送と各1億8000万円を出資して、1957年に日本教育テレビ（NET）を設立し、59年2月に開局する。NET設立までには、日活と新東宝が申請したテレビ局は、すでに東映側に吸収されていて、東映は他の申請者たちを取り込みながら勢力を増していったのである。一方で、このグループに属さない松竹・東宝・大映は文化放送とニッポン放送と共にフジテレビに出資し、NET開局から1ヶ月後の1959年3月に開局する。ただ、文化放送・ニッポン放送がそれぞれ4割出資したのに対し、松竹・東宝・大映は残りの2割を3等分するかたちで各4000

万円の出資にとどまる。それは、東映の出資額と比べても大きな開きがあり、やはり、東映がいかにテレビを含めた「一元的経営」に本気だったかが理解できる。事実、大川博は東映の社長を務めながらNET設立時に会長に就任する。さらに、開局から無配が続く状況で、大川は1960年11月にNET社長に就任。彼は経営現場の陣頭指揮を執って、立て直しを図ったのである[15]。

融合する映画・テレビ技術

東映の経営戦略にあった映画とテレビの一元的思考は、映像テクノロジーの領域においても、実践されることになる。それは、テレビ電波を利用して送られてきた映像をスクリーンに映写する装置で、アイドホールやアイドフォアなどと呼ばれた。この電波利用型のスクリーン映写だが、そのメリットとして、大きく2点あると考えられていた[16]。

第一に、フィルムでの撮影・上映などにかかる莫大なコストの削減が果たせること。例えば、映画を全国で上映する際には、フィルムを相当数プリントして、順番に配給していく必要があるが、そのプリント代を削減でき、またプリントの運送料や管理代なども不要になる。くわえて、受容の面から言っても、フィルムだと各映画館で一度に共有されるプリント数に限界があり、すべての映画館でいっせいに特定のフィルムを鑑賞できるわけではない。それに対して、テレビのように電波で映像が配信されれば、原理的には、いっせいに鑑賞することが可能になる。

このテレビの原理的特性と絡む特徴として、第二の利点が挙げられる。それは、テレビの生中継のように、同時的に特定の映像を視聴できること。映画では、通常撮影から公開まで相応の時間差が生じるが、テレビの電波はそうした映画の本質的課題を乗り越えることができる。いま起こっている出来事などを、即座に別の場所で映し出すことが可能であり、アイドホールは、こうしたテレビ的特徴を、テレビ技術を取り入れることで、発揮することができるというわけだ。

東映はこの新しい上映形態にいち早く目をつけ、1957年頃より研究を開始した[17]。1958年9月からは日本ビクターと提携して、技術的な実験を重ねていく[18]。他の映画会社も、関心を示していた。そこで東映は、実用化に向けてより積極的な動きを見せる。1961年7月に白黒で公開の実演会がおこなわれると、翌62年2月にはカラーで開催され、どちらも成功を収めたのである[19]。

このまま実用化へ向けて突き進むかに見えた矢先の1962年、東映大川博社長はアメリカ視察から帰国後に、次のような発言を残す。「アイドホールは、カラー3000万円、白黒2000万円と価格がそうとう高い。1台500万円ぐらいで出来ないと商品化はむずかしい」と、コスト的な問題が実用化の壁になっていることが語られるのである[20]。実は、ハリウッドでも、前述のように、とりわけパラマウントが、同様の規格、シアター・テレビジョンの実用化を目指すものの、費用対効果で成果を上げられず、すでに撤退した経緯がある[21]。こうして大川はアメリカ視察について触れながら、アイドホール実用化への消極的な思いを語っていたのである。そして、1965年には、大川は採算面の理由から、アイドホールからの撤退を表明し、映画界全体としても、この新しい上映形態への関心は、一気に退潮していく[22]。

映画会社のテレビ映画製作

映画とテレビの技術的融合は未遂に終わったが、映画会社は、他にも並行して、テレビ事業の可能性を探っていた。その中で、もっとも大々的に展開された事業が、主に16ミリフィルムで撮られるテレビ向けの映画（テレビ映画）であった。このテレビ映画事業にも、東映が積極的に関与していく。1958年7月、この会社は、テレビ・プロダクションを設立し、自社の撮影所でテレビ映画の製作を開始する。大映・松竹・東宝といった他の映画会社も同時期に子会社や傍系会社を通してテレビ映画の製作に乗り出してはいた。だが、東映の場合は、テレビ映画のために東京撮影所にステージ二棟を新設、「テレビ映画製作に必要な、専用の設備機構を持った我が国最初にして唯一のスタジオ」と言われるほどの施設を用意

し[23]、テレビ映画製作にかける真剣度は他と大きく異なっていた。1960年代になり、全般的にテレビ映画製作が本格化していくが、それでも東映以外の会社はステージの新設はおろか、撮影では既設のステージもろくに使わせず、ロケとロケセットで間に合わせるというのが普通であった。依然として、東映と他の大手とのテレビ映画に対する決定的な態度の違いが確認できる[24]。

東映は「一元的経営」の実践として、傘下にあるNETで、製作したテレビ映画を開局時から順次放映していった。ただ、大映・松竹・東宝といったフジテレビに出資している映画会社も、同局での放映を見込んでテレビ映画を作ってはいたのだが、東映の経営戦略にはさらに続きがあった。東映は、1959年5月から、30分のテレビ映画2話分をまとめて50分程度の中編劇映画にし、メインの長編映画に添える作品として劇場に配給するようになったのである。そしてついには、東映は、テレビ映画の配給を含む新たな配給系統を担当する第二東映という会社を作り、東映作品の流通量を増やすことで、市場の拡大を目論んだ。

けれども、元々テレビ用に作った番組までも、劇場で流してしまうこの会社のやり方には、大衆はなびかなかった。一方では、スコープ映画を製作し、大型画面を生かしてテレビには真似できない映像を追求しようとする試みがなされていたにもかかわらず、テレビと変わらぬ映像を劇場に提供していった東映のこの試みは、矛盾を含んでいた。前述の通り、1957年より日本映画はワイドスクリーン時代に突入していたが、それでも、こうした東映の体質に象徴されるように、真の意味で良質な映画を届けようという意欲は、映画界全体で見ても、不十分なものであった。世間では、業界は映画の質より量を求めていると映り、非難の声が高くなっていった[25]。結局、そうした世論に対応できないまま、東映の第二配給系統である第二東映は1961年に解消してしまう。

テレビ映画の意義

テレビ映画の劇場への転用は失敗に終わったが、それでも、東映をはじめ各映画会社ともテレビ映画の製作を、1960年代に入って活発におこなっていく。そのことをテレビ産業側から、確認しておきたい。

今では信じられないことだが、1953年にテレビ放送が開始された当初から、大部分のテレビ・ドラマは生放送で提供されていた。東映がテレビ映画の製作に着手した1958年でさえ、ドラマの主流は生放送という状況だった。というのも、フィルム作品の製作費が30分で50万円から80万円だったのに対して、生ドラマは最高でも40万円と考えられていて、フィルムの半分ほどのコストで製作できたのである[26]。

こうした製作形態が大きく変化するのが、1960年代半ば以降である Table 6.2 は、1963年10月と67年10月のゴールデン・タイムにおけるドラマ番組の形態を比較したものであるが、これを見ると、1963年には、外国のテレビ映画、スタジオ・ドラマが隆盛であり、4年後の67年になると、今度は国産テレビ映画の本数・時間数が他を圧倒しているのがわかる。実は、この変化の背景には、テレビ局側の事情が関係していた。

1960年代初頭に、テレビ放送は、時間が拡大され、全日放送へと切り替わる。それに伴い、テレビ局は番組数の増産が必要となった。そして、その際テレビ局は、内部で設備投資やスタッフを増員しつつ、増産に対応するのではなく、「合理化」として外部に活路を見出す。TBSの企画担当だった岩崎嘉一は、「民放では設備投資にも限界がある。それにやたら人間をふやせない、企業として成立させるためには、マンモス化よりもまず、合理化が必要だった。その合理化の一環として、テレビ映画の外部発注が行なわれた」と、製作上の「合理化」が「外部発注」だったと語っている[27]。こうして「外部発注」に向かう機運の中で、テレビ映画を求める動きが加速していったのである。

また、外国のテレビ映画の値上げも、テレビ局が国産テレビ映画に関心を向ける要因となった。1964年7月1日から実施されたテレビ映画の貿易自由化により、これまでのテレビ映画の輸入基準単価1本

Table 6.2 ドラマ形態の量的変化

時間帯	外国 映画(本)		国産 映画		スタジオ・ドラマ	
	～30分	～60分	～30分	～60分	～30分	～60分
1963年10月のドラマ番組本数						
19時～	17	2	5	0	9	0
合計時間	10時間半		2時間半		4時間半	
20時～						
	11時間		3時間		6時間	
21時～						
	8時間半		2時間半		12時間半	
22時～						
	5時間		3時間		7時間	
1967年10月のドラマ番組本数						
19時～	6	2	20	0	3	0
	5時間		10時間		1時間	
20時～	0	2	0	14	0	7
	2時間		14時間		7時間	
21時～	4	4	6	9	9	5
	6時間		11時間45分		9時間15分	
22時～	0	2	2	2	1	6
	2時間		2時間45分		6時間15分	

（日本放送協会総合放送文化研究所編『放送学研究28』より作成）※ひとつの連続ドラマで1本という計算。1963年は NTV、TBS、フジテレビ、NETの4局合計、67年は東京12chを加えた5局の合計を表す。

あたり2500ドル以下という制限が撤廃される[28]。それに伴いアメリカ側が一方的な値上げをおこなって、1時間もの1本あたり4000ドルを要求することもあったと言われている[29]。こうして、テレビ局にとっても、外国テレビ映画や自社製作のスタジオ・ドラマの代わりに国産テレビ映画を求める需要が高まっていった。

さらに表2を見ると、国内のドラマ番組の放送時間自体が拡大していることもわかり、1967年の特に20時以降では、60分もの国産テレビ映画が主流になっていることが把握できる。実は、この60分のテレビ映画製作こそが、大手映画会社が得意とした分野であった。30分程度の番組もゴールデン・タイムに限らず多数あったが、それらはもっぱら、映画会社ではないテレビ映画専門の小規模プロダクションにて、低予算で作られていた。だが、60分のワイド番組となると、やはり十分な製作環境と資本力を有する大手映画会社の領域であり、長時間ドラマの製作において、大手映画会社の製作能力は大いに役立てられていった。

他方で、映画会社の側からいえば、テレビ映画の製作は、映画事業の歪みをいくらか緩和してくれるものでもあった。前述のとおり、1950年代から製作現場では量産体制が敷かれていたが、60年代に入ると景気の傾きで、映画が以前より作れなくなっていく。それにより、映画製作において余剰人員が発生するようになった。そうして、仕事を失った多くの者の受け皿として、テレビ映画の製作が機能し始めたのである。好景気の1950年代には、映画会社は専属の俳優・スタッフがテレビの仕事に携わることを妨げていたが、60年代になると、テレビとの連携も活発化し、さらに映画の仕事も少なくなってきたことで、製作の人員をテレビ事業に充てることも増えていった。以前なら、映画館でしか見ることができなかったスターたちが、お茶の間でテレビ画面を通して見ることができる、そういう時代になっていったのである。

Handbook of Japanese Media and Popular Culture in Transition

1960年代半ば以降、各映画会社とも本業の映画部門の不振を、テレビ事業の他、ボーリング場やホテル経営などさまざまな事業で埋め合わせようとするのだが、70年代以降になると、テレビの仕事へと収斂していく。映画館に掛けられる「映画」は観客動員に左右されるいわゆる水物事業である一方、テレビ向けに作られる「テレビ映画」は安定的な収入が見込める。その安定性が映画会社にとって魅力であった[30]。

　1980年代以降になると、テレビ・ドラマの主流が、フィルム作品からVTR作品へとシフトしていく。テレビ映画は、こうして別のものに取って代わられたが、歴史的に見れば映画産業とテレビ産業が提携する契機となった重要な事業であったことがわかるだろう。映画とテレビの対立的構図は、映画会社のテレビ映画製作の本格化で大きく塗り替えられていくことになったのである。

現代の映画とテレビ

テレビ局の映画事業参入

　映画会社は、テレビの成長に歯向かうだけでなく、テレビ技術の利用やテレビ事業の可能性を模索しながら突き進んできた。他方で、テレビ局もまた、「映画」事業への関心を示すようになる。それが顕著になるのが1980年代である。すでに、その頃には大手映画会社はかつての勢いをすっかり失ってしまっていた。自社単独での製作本数を大幅に減らし、他社と共同か、あるいは他から買い取って配給するような形態を各社とも採用していた。1970年代半ばには、映画作りと無縁であったはずの、角川書店が映画事業に乗り出し、自社の書籍を原作にした映画で、書籍の売上げを伸ばそうと図った。「読んでから見るか　見てから読むか」という惹句のもと、角川のメディアミックス商法は大旋風を巻き起こした。テレビCMを大々的に流し、製作費よりも宣伝費にお金を費やしたと言われるほど、徹底した商業主義的戦略で次々にヒット作が出現した。角川は映画宣伝の重要性を証明した。だが皮肉にも、角川が宣伝で活用したテレビが、角川に代わって存在感を示すようになる。

　フジテレビが製作に参加した1983年公開の『南極物語』（蔵原惟繕監督）が、当時の日本映画最高の配収59億円を記録する。この成功もあって、以後テレビ局の映画製作が相次いだ。豊富な資金力に、宣伝で期待されるテレビのメディアとしての力によって、テレビ局の映画事業はやはりスケールの大きさを見せつけるものとなった。

おわりに: 映画とテレビの共存

　現代ではもはや日本の商業映画は、テレビとの関係なくして成立しえない。商業映画の製作では、「製作委員会方式」と呼ばれる共同出資型の製作システムがもっぱら採用され、その委員会には、映画会社とともに、いずれかのテレビ局が毎回のように参加し、映画作りに関わっている。他に、広告会社、出版社、芸能プロダクション、ソフト関連会社などが委員会に名を連ねることが多い。各社は莫大なコストを要する映画製作に共同出資することでリスクの分散を図り、さらにはテレビ放映やDVD、書籍の販売、キャラクター版権などの副次的利益を目当てに参加する。映画会社は映画の配給・興行で大きく貢献することを期待され、テレビ局はやはり変わらずの宣伝力を期待されている。

　また、人気のマンガ／コミックスの劇場アニメ化、あるいは実写映画化が盛んだが、映画とテレビの間で、そうしたコンテンツの利用／再利用がしばしばおこなわれている点も見逃せない。結果的に映画とテレビ間でコンテンツの共有がおこなわれているわけだ。

　例えば、世界的にも人気のマンガ『名探偵コナン』（1994年〜）は、テレビで1996年から現在まで放送されていて、人気の高さを証明している。くわえて、1997年から、2020年を除き、毎年劇場版アニメが公

開されている。そして、テレビアニメを放送している、日本テレビ／読売テレビは、その劇場版アニメの製作委員会に毎回参加し、配給を担当する映画会社の東宝などと、コナンの映画化を実現させている。劇場版コナンは当然のように毎回ヒットし[31]、一定の期間を経て、日本テレビ・読売テレビ系列で放送され、同系列局に利益をもたらす。映画とテレビは、すっかりビジネス・パートナーと言える関係である。

　ただこうした現在の映画とテレビの状況を見ながらも、忘れてはならないのは、過去には衝突や模索を経て、こんにちの協力関係が築かれてきたということである。今では、映画、テレビに限らず、インターネットなどを介した映像コンテンツが盛んに流通しているが、そうした様々な映像のメディアやプラットフォームもまた、衝突や模索を経て、新たな共存の道を探していくことになるのかもしれない。

Note: This chapter is a condensed and revised version of my earlier book publication『テレビ成長期の日本映画——メディア間交渉のなかのドラマ』to which I have added substantial new material.

Notes

1　志賀信夫『昭和テレビ放送史　上』(早川書房、1990)、220頁。

2　通商産業省企業局商務課編『映画産業白書　1962年版——わが国映画産業の現状と諸問題』尚文堂、146頁。

3　通商産業省企業局商務課編『映画産業白書　1958年版』大蔵省印刷局、10頁。

4　同上、12頁。

5　常石史子「シネマスコープの時代(上)：草創期」、『NFCニューズレター』2001年8-9月号、8頁。

6　『映画年鑑　1958年版』時事通信社、441頁。

7　「日本でのテレビ放送史の多くは、街頭テレビに関する記述とともに始まる」とも言われている(飯田豊『テレビが見世物だったころ——初期テレビジョンの考古学』[青弓社、2016年]、344頁)。

8　『映画年鑑　1957年版』時事通信社、375頁。

9　全国朝日放送株式会社総務局社史編纂部編『テレビ朝日社史——ファミリー視聴の25年』(全国朝日放送、1984年)、366頁。

10　古田尚輝『「鉄腕アトム」の時代——映像産業の攻防』(世界思想社、2009年)、112–121頁。

11　大川博「テレビ・二本立・直営館」、『合同通信映画特信版』1956年7月8日、2–3頁。

12　『映画年鑑　1957年版』、375頁。

13　大川、前掲、3頁。

14　アメリカのメジャー各社のテレビ局運営の試みと、その挫折についての詳細は、White, Timothy R. "Hollywood's Attempt at Appropriating Television: The Case of Paramount Pictures." In Tino Balio, ed.,. *Hollywood in the Age of Television* (Boston: Unwin Hyman, 1990), pp. 145–49頁を参照。

15　瓜生忠夫「テレビ映画と映画産業(上)」、『調査情報』1964年7月号、8頁。

16　『朝日新聞』1961年1月3日。

17　「東宝もアイドフォアを来年夏から実施」、『映画時報』1961年5月号、32頁。

18　東映十年史編纂委員会編『東映十年史——1951年–1961年』(東映株式会社、1962年)、193頁。

19　「カラー・アイドホールの公開実験成功」、『映画時報』1962年3月号、28–29頁。

20　大川博「アイドホールより有料テレビ」、『映画ジャーナル』1962年7月号、35頁。

21　ハリウッドのメジャー各社はシアター・テレビジョン計画の失敗で、その関心は有料テレビ事業に移った。パラマウントがこれにも積極的で、1955年より各社のテレビ局へのフィルム売却は始まっていたにもかかわらず、パラマウントだけが有料テレビのために58年まで映画を放出しなかった。しかし、同社は1959年よりカナダで有料テレビ事業を展開したものの、これも上手くいかず、多額の負債を出して65年に撤退する。結局、映画会社のテレビ事業はどれも成就しなかった。こうしたテレビ事業参画の動きに関しては、White, pp. 149–162に詳しい。

22　大川博「努力すればよくなる年」、『合同通信映画特信版』1965年1月24日、5頁。

23　野坂和馬「テレビ映画／プロダクションとして」、『テレビドラマ』1962年6月号、22頁。

24　瓜生、前掲、8頁。

25 映画産業の斜陽が顕著になった1963年に、映画興行者139人を対象に実施された雑誌のアンケートでは、興行の不振の原因を「映画の質の低下」だとする回答が「テレビ」に次いで占めていた（「興行者におたずねします質問・10」、『合同通信映画特信版』1963年1月6日、30頁）。

26 塩沢茂「テレビ映画論」、『キネマ旬報』1958年5月下旬号、122頁。

27 「ブラウン管の主導権を握るもの<<座談会・現場からの発言>>」、『シナリオ』1967年5月号、44頁。

28 『映画年鑑　1965年版』時事通信社、78頁。

29 同上、273頁。

30 川野泰彦「映画の脇役・大手五社のテレビ室」、『シナリオ』1967年5月号、26‐27頁。

31 例えば、2017年から2019年までの3年間のコナン映画の興行収入を順にあげておくと、68.9億円、91.8億円、93.7億円であり、日本映画の年間興行収入ランキングにおいて、17年が年間1位で、他が2位という好成績であった。

【参考文献】

飯田豊『テレビが見世物だったころ——初期テレビジョンの考古学』（青弓社、2016年）

北浦寛之『テレビ成長期の日本映画——メディア間交渉のなかのドラマ』（名古屋大学出版会、2018年）

佐藤忠男『日本映画史<2>』（岩波書店、1995年）

———．『日本映画史<3>』（岩波書店、1995年）

志賀信夫『昭和テレビ放送史<上>』（早川書房、1990年）

———．『昭和テレビ放送史<下>』（早川書房、1990年）

田中純一郎『日本映画発達史<3>』（中央公論社、1976年）

———．『日本映画発達史<4>』（中央公論社、1976年）

———．『日本映画発達史<5>』（中央公論社、1976年）

古田尚輝『「鉄腕アトム」の時代——映像産業の攻防』（世界思想社、2009年）

四方田犬彦『日本映画史100年』（集英社、2000年）

Chapter 7
Remaking Revenge: Transnational Television Drama Flows and the Remaking of the Korean Drama *Mawang* in Japan

Julia Stolyar

This chapter explores the transnational television drama flows between South Korea and Japan in the 2000s, a new phenomenon which diversified media flows in the region. It uses one of the first Japanese remakes of a Korean drama, The Devil, to explore the ways in which Japan negotiates the topic of the drama—revenge—to highlight its local traditions of representations, views, and values. This process of negotiation in a transnational remake highlights how Japan sees itself vis-à-vis its not-so-proximate neighbor.

Introduction: Transnational television drama flows between Japan and South Korea

The last three decades have seen the rise of transnational cultural flows within the East Asian region. Popular culture, in the forms of animation, film, fashion and music, primarily from Japan, were at the forefront of that flow, fostering a process of "regionalization," the creation of shared regional references and likings among those who consume Japanese content in other Asian countries (Iwabuchi 2002; Otmazgin 2014). Japanese popular culture had won attention and audiences with anime and manga since the 1960s, but in the 1980s and 1990s another medium came to the fore: Japanese television dramas. "Trendy dramas," as they were called, which present the lives, strives and loves of Japanese youth in the stylish setting of urban Japan (mainly Tokyo), won the hearts of Asian audiences, particularly in Taiwan and South Korea. Japanese trendy dramas tapped into the growing affluence of the region and presented a pan-Asian youth culture. This youth culture was supported by Japanese fashion magazines and other Japanese products such as electronics that made it to the East and West at the same time (Iwabuchi 2002).

However, not everyone welcomed Japanese popular culture with open arms. South Korea, whose culture was heavily oppressed during the Japanese occupation (Caprio 2011), had banned Japanese culture since its liberation from Japanese rule in 1945, thus prohibiting the broadcasting of Japanese dramas on Korean television. This is not to say that Japanese trendy dramas did not find their way into South Korea. With the democratization of South Korea at the end of the 1980s and the rapid opening of South Korea to the world, many products and innovations entered the country, including Japanese dramas and music, mostly due to the advancement of technology and the use of VCRs for recording and copying televisual texts. These cassettes made their way into South Korea with the flow of business people between the two countries who brought back pirated copies of popular Japanese dramas, bypassing the restrictions and gaining audiences for these Japanese dramas, fashion and style (Otmazgin 2014). The ban was gradually lifted during the presidency of Kim Dae-jung (1998–2003), enabling Japanese film, music and television dramas to officially enter the Korean market and be broadcast, although still not on the main terrestrial nationwide channels (Kyodo 2003; Suzuki 2004).

Original products were not the only way Japanese television dramas entered the Korean television mediascape. Another way was unofficial remakes of Japanese television dramas by Korean channels (Lee 2001). Striking similarities in characters and plotlines between some Korean dramas and Japanese dramas produced in the 1990s, however, alerted Japanese broadcasters to the possibility of copyright infringement, with one drama even taken off air for this reason (Lee 2004). Those similarities also point to an important aspect of remakes: Korean remakes were a way to mask Japanese influence. The Korean television industry appreciated the skill and know-how of their Japanese counterparts, but for the public, the images on television were Korean actors, Korean settings and Korean myths. The Korean television industry of the 1990s was trying to quickly bridge the gap that was left after 30 years of military rule, during which the media, including television dramas, were heavily censored. Looking for successful examples, Japan stood out as a country that was able to mix not only the old with the new but also the East and the West (Lee 2001). This, however, had to be done carefully. The ban on broadcasting Japanese content was still in place, the ghosts of the Japanese occupation still haunted South Korea, and so acknowledging the Japanese source materials could have caused an outcry from the public and accusations of another form of Japanese imperialism.

The 2000s, however, saw the reverse, or at least the diversification of this cultural flow from Japan to South Korea. The gradual expansion of Korean television in general, and Korean television dramas in particular, gave rise to what became known as the "Korean Wave" or Hallyu, the success of Korean television dramas outside South Korea. First successful in China in the late 1990s (Huat and Iwabuchi 2008), attracting attention and gaining fans, it was the success of the Korean drama *Gyeouryeon-ga* (Winter Sonata, KBS2, 2002) in Japan in 2003 that gave rise to the "Korean Wave" or *kanryū* in Japan. The fandom of the drama and its star Bae Yong-joon caught the attention of the press when a few hundred fans, mostly middle-aged women, went to Haneda airport in Tokyo to welcome him to Japan (The Japan Times 2005). The phenomenon of Japanese fans of Korean dramas and by extension Korean culture became a fascination for academics and the general public alike. Fans of Korean dramas and music became interested in Korean language, history, culture and cuisine. Many participated in "drama tours" of famous locations in South Korea where successful dramas were filmed (Creighton 2016).

The success of *Gyeouryeon-ga* and subsequent broadcasting of other Korean dramas in Japan led to the founding of Japanese magazines covering the developments and latest news in the Korean pop industry. For example, *It's Koreal* and, *Kankoku terebi dorama gaido* (Korean television drama guide),[1] published since 2007, cater to the growing fandom of Korean pop culture who are eager to follow the latest developments of the industry and the projects of their favorite actors and actresses (for example, see Iwami 2007). Other magazines dedicated more generally to the entertainment industry and television such as the *Shūkan asahi* (Weekly Asahi), *Shūkan josei* (Shukan Josei, lit. "weekly women") and television guides such as *Za terebijon* (The Television) also devoted spreads and articles to promote Korean dramas on Japanese television and supply the fandom with the latest gossip from South Korea. Such magazines not only run articles about the dramas but also include extensive interviews with the stars (for examples, see Hanana 2008; Takahashi 2009).

The success of Korean dramas and the creation of a fandom surrounding Korean dramas and culture in Japan led to high hopes for the promotion of mutual understanding and reconciliation. On the face of it, this sharing of stories is creating a regional, pan-Asian identity (Iwabuchi 2002), one which is based on the shared values of the region, promoting mutual understanding and presenting common points of reference. The fans of Korean dramas in Japan speak about their newly discovered interest in the pop culture of a country that they previously associated with the history of war (Hirata 2008; Mori 2008; Yang 2012). Within this reversal of flow, the rise in the profile of South Korea in Japan and the increase in the quality and variety of the Korean dramas led to another phenomenon starting in the middle of the first decade of the 21st century: Japanese remakes of Korean dramas. Although their number is not vast compared to locally originated productions, this trend is consistent and growing, with three new remakes being broadcast during the summer of 2019 alone.[2] This new trend raises a number of questions. If something is familiar enough to be understood, why is there a need to make a local version? What is there that requires adaptation to local contexts and what can this process of adaptation tell us about the construction of Japanese identity vis-à-vis the influx of Korean media content?

To answer these questions, the focus of this chapter is the Korean original drama *Mawang* (KBS2, 2007) and its Japanese remake, *Maō* (TBS, 2008a); both titles translate into English as "The Devil." At a basic level, the story underpinning these dramas discusses revenge, an individual's wish for justice where none could be found through legal channels, a concept that is shared across times and cultures. However, differences in television industries (broadcasting patterns, funding, casting), and representation conventions (what and how topics are represented), render the original text different enough from the local culture to merit a remake. The process of remake sharpens definitions of local identity through the encounter of the "other," in this case, South Korea, presenting a form of local resistance to foreign content, preserving the myths of "Japaneseness" as distinct even from its East Asian neighbor, thus challenging notions of pan-Asian identity and regionalization. Before discussing the case study, a brief review of the conventions around the representation of revenge in each television culture is given to establish the context in which the Japanese remake is produced and the conventions it aims to fit. An analysis of the representation of the two main characters will follow to highlight how the decisions in the remake (what to leave, what to cut and what to change) lead to a construction of revenge that fits the local convention, negotiating and masking the foreign Korean representation and its values to strengthen local ideas and representations.

Revenge plots in South Korea and Japan:
The remakeability of *Mawang*

Revenge and justice are two intertwined ideas. "Revenge is an action taken in direct response to a perceived wrongdoing that is intended to damage, injure, or punish the responsible party... [It] is most often used as a way for the *victims themselves* (italics in the original) to restore justice, when group authorities have failed to address their concerns" (Okimoto and Wenzel 2008, 304). Justice is a level of "equilibrium between victim and victimizer" (Jacoby 1983, 332). Revenge is therefore the way by which victims can reach this "state of equilibrium" and it can take many forms and have different levels of disruptive effect (Okimoto and Wenzel 2008, 304). However, as Bohm and Kaplan (2011) point out, revenge might become a "spiral," a cycle in which each side "perceives wrongdoings" and wishes to exact revenge. As such, revenge is socially dangerous as it operates outside the law and can lead to a cycle of individuals taking the law into their own hands and destabilizing the social order.

Revenge is a powerful motivator and thus a fruitful topic for works of fiction, be they plays, films or television dramas, with both South Korea and Japan exploring it extensively on screen. Such films as Park Chan-wook's renowned revenge trilogy, *Boksuneun naui geot* (Sympathy for Mr Vengeance, 2002), *Oldeuboi* (Oldboy, 2003), *Chinjeolhan geumjassi* (Lady Vengeance, 2005) and Kim Jee-woon's *Akmareul boatda* (I Saw the Devil, 2010), as well as television dramas such as *Buhwal* (Resurrection, KBS2, 2005), *Gaewa neukdaeui Sigan* (Time between Dog and Wolf, MBC, 2007), *Eden-ui dong-jjok* (East of Eden, MBC, 2008), *Namja iyagi* (A Man's Story, KBS, 2009), *Miseu Ripeuli* (Miss Ripley, MBC, 2011) and *Sesang eodiedo eobneun ehakan namja* (The Innocent Man, KBS2, 2012) highlight a fascination with the idea of revenge in Korean cinema and television. Japanese television is also no stranger to the topic. Such dramas as *Ryūsei no kizuna* (Ties of Shooting Stars, TBS, 2008b), *Tokyo DOGS* (Fuji TV, 2009), *Rakkī Sebun* (Lucky Seven, Fuji TV, 2012), and *Uroborosu* (Ouroboros, TBS, 2015) all have revenge as their central plot and motivator. The story of *Mawang* (KBS2, 2007) therefore appealed to the production team of the Japanese version, as they mentioned in an interview I conducted with them during my fieldwork in Japan in July 2019. The producers stated that they chose the drama due to its story, its style and its interesting exploration of the human soul and condition and wished to expose the topic to a wider audience.[3] Korean dramas, although enjoyed by a dedicated number of fans, are still a niche market in Japan, being mostly broadcast on cable and satellite channels that have much smaller audiences than commercial terrestrial channels. A remake thus enables the transition of a Korean drama into a Japanese one, expanding the audience along the way.

Despite the familiarity with the topic of revenge and personal vendettas as a basis for stories and dramas in both Japan and South Korea, the conventions that are constructed around representation of revenge on television are significantly different. In Korean film and television dramas, the focus is on the victim-turned-avenger, and the plot follows their journey from the initial trauma, through the act of revenge, to the disastrous end such as in *Oldeuboi, Gaewa neukdaeui sigan*, and *Sesang eodiedo eobneun chakan namja*. The focus is not necessarily on how the protagonist exacts their revenge but rather the emotional and psychological implications of such a violent endeavor. An inevitable parallel is created gradually between the criminal and the avenger, where both lose their humanity and become "the devil" or the monster. As Kelly Jeong points out, revenge plots "start with reclaiming and restoring […] and end with losing the stable self" (Jeong 2012, 170). The protagonist starts with the wish to "get even" but becomes just as bad as the original victimizer. The police and any other law enforcement and judicial systems are either absent from the story or presented as "ineffectual bureaucrats" and their representation is either minimal or ironic (Jeong 2012, 177). This representation legitimizes the revenge. Since the justice system is not able to give justice to the victim, either because of incompetence, corruption, or because the crime or grievance is outside the limits of what the law defines as crime, the victim has no choice but to pursue justice on their own in the form of revenge.

Contrary to the representation and treatment of revenge on Korean television, revenge in Japanese dramas is carried out through and within the limits of the law and any personal revenge or vendettas outside those limits are simply additional crimes and should be punished as such. In both *Tokyo DOGS* and *Lucky Seven*, the child of the murdered victim grows up to seek revenge by joining the police or becoming a private detective. Both avengers operate within the boundaries of their position and the limits of the law. They eventually bring the criminal to justice by arresting him and making him stand trial. Even when the avengers are not law enforcement but just the victims' children, as is the case in *Ryūsei no kizuna*, the aim is to find the murderer and the evidence and then hand him over to the authorities. Although each episode starts with a voice over: "when we grow up, the three of us will find the killer, and we will kill him" (TBS 2008b), when they indeed catch the criminal and have the evidence, they hand him over to the police, executing their revenge by punishing him through the appropriate mechanisms and institutions. The fact that they do not stoop to the same level of murderous revenge as the murderer is their revenge and their victory. *Ouroboros* is somewhat an exception to that rule. The heroes are two children who join forces to find the murderer of their orphanage teacher. One becomes a policeman and the other becomes a gangster, and in the process of their search, they kill other criminals. However, the inevitable tragic ending resulting in their deaths after they have exacted revenge, solidifies the view of personal vendettas as a negative influence on society that should not be pursued.

This difference in the ways in which revenge is represented on Korean and Japanese television points to a difference in local attitudes towards revenge and the justice system. Under Park Chung-hee's military rule (1961–1979), the Korean justice system operated under strict supervision from the government, which damaged its ability to protect individuals (Kim 2015, 604). This has left a residue of mistrust; according to a study conducted by the OECD, only 27 percent of Koreans trust the justice system (OECD 2015). In Korean dramas, revenge is represented as an inevitable course of action to characters who seek justice and cannot get it through official channels, presenting the justice system as corrupt, easily manipulated if one has the money and connections, and thus unable to give justice to the simple people. Characters are presented as those who find themselves in circumstances not of their own doing and see it as inevitable to seek revenge even at the price of their own life (although the avenger does not always die).

By contrast, in the Japanese justice system prosecutors only bring a case to court when they are certain they will get a conviction; consequently, Japan has a record 99 percent conviction rate. This remarkable success rate has its caveats, with a few wrongful convictions making the news and bringing attention to some of the weaknesses in the system (Kingston 2011). Despite this media coverage and the ensuing debate, Japan still enjoys a high level of trust—65 percent according to the OECD study cited above (OECD, 2015)—and prosecutors are respected members of society (Kingston 2011; Fujita et al. 2016). This may explain why in

Handbook of Japanese Media and Popular Culture in Transition

Japanese dramas depicting revenge, the avengers are presented as good and relatable only as long as they do not exact revenge themselves. In *Rakkī Sebun*, *Ryūsei no kizuna* and *Tokyo DOGS*, the avengers collect evidence but hand the culprit to the police, letting the justice system do its job. In effect, the image portrayed is one of a system perhaps short of resources, time or manpower to do work properly, but if the work is done, the system will take care of the rest.

This presents two themes: one is the reliability of the justice system and the other is the usability and social acceptance of revenge. Fujita et al (2016), argue that trust in the justice system leads to the acceptance of its rulings. It therefore stands to reason that in a society where there is little trust in the justice system such as in Korea, there is more social acceptance of revenge, as this will be seen as an avenue for justice that bypasses a flawed system. Indeed, as I demonstrate in this chapter, Korean television, with its particular representation of revenge and avengers reproduces that view. In Japan, where the justice system and its professionals enjoy public trust, an attempt to seek justice outside of official channels is seen as undermining the system and disruptive. I also explore how those perceptions affect the representation of the main characters and the topic of revenge in the transition between the original Korean drama and the Japanese remake. My analysis of the differences between the two versions is divided into three topics: the definition within the drama of good and bad behavior, the focus on the past vs. focus on the present, and finally the question of choice and responsibility. Through this analysis, I propose to answer the question "who is the devil?" in the world of each drama, and thus demonstrate how revenge is constructed and whether, despite the commonality of revenge as a topic, the social legitimacy of revenge is accepted in each context.

Mawang—Maō: Who is the Devil?

In his youth, Kang Oh-soo was a bully who was responsible for the death of a classmate. However, with the help of his rich and influential father, the case was ruled as self-defense and he walked free. Putting his past behind him and wishing to be a better person, he became a policeman in the homicide section of the Seoul Police Department. One day, a mysterious parcel arrives with a Tarot card drawn by a young woman, So Hae-in, and strange coincidences around him and his family and friends begin to occur, suggesting that his past has come to haunt him. People connected to him, to the past incident and to a mysterious lawyer, Oh Seung-ha, are killed or injured. While Kang, the policeman is trying to find out who the kingpin is and how to stop the murders, a psychological battle begins between him and Oh, the lawyer.

Good-bad divide

Even before the first episode of the remake was broadcast, the posters of the Japanese remake circulated in Japanese television magazines promoting the drama among the new dramas of the summer of 2008 (Kanno 2008a). Comparison of the posters presents a distinctive view of the attitudes towards the characters and the information they give to the viewers about which character is good and which one is bad. The drama attracted attention mainly due to its stars: Ōno Satoshi and Ikuta Tōma, both familiar faces on Japanese television. For Ōno, who was the leader of the popular boyband *Arashi*, this was his debut in a leading role. For his co-star,

Ikuta Tōma, who was known for his role in *Hanazakari no kimitachi e* (Hana Kimi, Fuji TV, 2007), his role in *Maō* represented a departure from his previous comic performances and a transition into more serious character portrayal. Japanese actors and television and media personae (*tarento*) are a significant draw for viewers and are essential to the publicity of any new drama (Lukács 2010). Both Ōno and Ikuta featured in a number of magazine articles, and the drama received significant attention before and during its broadcast (Kanno 2008b; Negishi 2008; Ōno and Ikuta 2008). However, most of the attention was given to the stars of the show and not to the discussions around the remake, or comparison with the original Korean version. This is not to say that the fact there *was* an original version was ignored or hidden. An extensive interview over five pages with the star Joo Ji Hoon, who played the lawyer in the Korean production, was published in Japanese in the magazine *It's Koreal* in 2007, exploring his persona and his role in the drama as well as an overview of the original version itself (Iwami 2007). However, much of the discourse around the remake treated it as any other Japanese drama, focusing on the Japanese actors and performances and including a number of interviews with the stars (Hanana 2008; Hiyama 2008; Horie 2008; Negishi 2008). One reviewer mentioned the inadequacy, in his opinion, of Ōno Satoshi's acting, writing that "if that is the level of the Japanese remake," then "they should have broadcast the original" (Hiyama 2008). Although this comment touches upon the fact that the drama is a remake, which signals that its origins were known to some viewers, it is unclear whether the reviewer had seen the original and preferred it, since he did not actively compare the two versions. His disappointment in the outcome may be related to the general perception of remakes as inferior to the originals or the feeling that Ōno fell short of the devilish mastermind his character is supposed to be.

The posters of the dramas play on different forms of suspense, building different expectations for the audience and give different foreknowledge to the viewers. In the Korean poster, three main characters are presented standing or sitting in a triangular composition, looking at the camera. The two male figures sit on chairs in front of each other in the foreground but do not look at each other, and the woman is standing in the background positioned right between them but also looking at the camera and not at the men. The colors are dark grey and blue, creating intrigue and a menacing atmosphere to the overall image. The information given is not extensive in terms of expectation of the plot. The poster discloses the three main characters, the color scheme hints that it is a serious drama (i.e., not a comedy), and that perhaps some form of love triangle is involved, judging from the position of the figures relative to each other. The Japanese poster, on the other hand, gives a lot more information regarding the characters and the plot: there are only two figures, the men. The composition of the image puts one of them above the other, and there is a significant difference in size: the lawyer is the bigger image, hovering over the policeman, looking down at him and spanning the width of the poster, taking up the entire upper part of the image. The lawyer's hands are around the little figure of the policeman, closing in on him from above. The policeman's figure is at the bottom of the image, looking beyond the frame but not at the lawyer or the camera. The poster gives a clear idea of the relations between the characters and the potential plot direction as well as the moral division between the characters: the lawyer is menacing and violent, catching an unsuspecting small (even helpless?) victim.

The Korean drama plays with the binary of good and evil that divides the lawyer and the policeman throughout the drama. As suggested by the poster, there is no clear answer to the question of who the devil is; with each new piece of information the characters and the viewers discover the answer shifts slightly between the policeman and the lawyer. By the end of episode one the viewers get a sense of the animosity between the lawyer and the policeman due to the use of close-ups and tense music, however, the full story and the reason for the animosity is still unknown. Moral judgement of the characters remains ambivalent, as various visual representations play with this ambiguity and prevent any clear-cut conclusion.

The end of episode one presents the lawyer and the policeman on a split screen against a red- and blue-colored background. Similar to the Yin-Yang symbolism of the Korean flag, red and blue are opposite colors with red representing life, good, positivity, while blue represents death, evil and negativity (Ministry of Interior and Safety n.d.). In this scene, the background of the lawyer is red, and the background of the policeman is blue, signifying that the "good guy" is the lawyer and the "bad guy" is the policeman. However, the beginning of episode two presents them in another scene with the color scheme reversed: the lawyer is on a blue background and the policeman on red. This inversion of colors creates an inversion in the good-bad division, making the policeman the "good guy" and the lawyer the "bad guy." This inversion complicates the binary of good and evil and presents it not as something that is intrinsically part of a character but rather as something that shifts and changes depending on the actions and motives of the characters. This ambivalence is kept throughout the series with every new development and piece of information shifting the image of the lawyer and the policeman eventually showing both as complex humans who have done both good and bad deeds and are unable to move on from their mutual trauma.

The Japanese drama, on the other hand, is more consistent in presenting a clear-cut divide between the lawyer and the policeman. It starts with an image of a devil: red, angry-faced, with evil-looking eyes and horns. The female voiceover, which we later discover to be a woman at a churchyard, tells the story of the angel-turned-devil Lucifer, to a group of children. They are surprised that this evil-looking picture was once called an angel. She turns the page in the book to reveal a white, winged, beautiful figure—a typical "angelic" picture and the children are excited. As the conversation goes on, the picture dissolves into the character of the lawyer. This sets the tone of revenge and anger and creates the expectation that something serious is to happen from the beginning.

This tone is kept throughout the drama with the image of the devil superimposed on the face of the lawyer at the beginning of every episode, presenting a clear view of who the evil character is. This is strengthened through the plot as well. In the first episode, the lawyer, who usually comes to the defense of the weak and the less fortunate, is nicknamed "the angel" by the press. When he hears this from the reporters following him after another victorious trial, he feels uncomfortable, suggesting that he knows that the plan of revenge he is about to execute is evil, or at least something that will be perceived as such, and not a way to achieve justice. This reference to the lawyer as an "angel" happens only in the beginning, befitting the first episode and the story of Lucifer as the angel-turned-devil, but does not repeat itself throughout the drama, therefore stressing the "turned-devil" nature of his character. Following the opening scene of the drama discussed above, each subsequent episode starts with the image of the devil dissolving into the face of the lawyer. It imprints the identification of the one with the other, leaving no place for alternative interpretations. Although the plot does add information about the motivation of the lawyer's revenge, there is no sympathy towards him, and he is presented solely as evil with the overall division of good and bad staying intact. The lawyer is the fallen angel, and despite his angelic origins, i.e., his previous good nature or even his help for the weak, he is now the devil and should be judged and viewed accordingly.

This characterization of the lawyer as ambiguous and relatable in the Korean version versus the bad character who behaves in an unacceptable manner in the Japanese version presents the different attitudes towards revenge and justice in both versions. The ambiguity of the characters in the Korean drama presents revenge as a potential course of action, perhaps even an understandable one. However, in the Japanese remake, by stressing the evil character of the lawyer and disregarding his angelic origins, his revenge is delegitimized. The next section will show how the use of scenes set in the past, as well as their absence from the Japanese adaptation, present and strengthen those disparate views on the legitimacy of revenge.

Past-present divide

The legitimacy of revenge is also created by the temporal focus of the drama. In the Korean drama, the past is significant and the emphasis is created and constructed through several methods, the main one being the number of scenes taking place in the past, presented through flashbacks, which give additional information about the characters' inner mindset, motivation and aims. Most of those scenes are cut from the remake, keeping the focus predominantly on present events. It is important to note here that the decision to cut scenes is not only artistic. Korean drama series are typically longer than Japanese ones; the original version of the *The Devil* consists of 20 one-hour-long episodes while the Japanese adaptation ran to only eleven 50-minute ones. This difference in length necessitates adjustments in the plot to accommodate for the shorter broadcasting time. However, those decisions highlight what is important, and therefore demonstrate the local convention and signal local values. Among the scenes that were cut are development of secondary characters, but it is the omission of scenes related to the main characters that makes the most difference.

The scenes omitted from the life of the lawyer in the remake detail his difficulties as a teenager who lost his eldest brother and his mother in short succession and had to survive on his own, as well as the fact that he put himself thought law school and became a successful lawyer. It presents a character that is determined, focused, but also isolated from society. Showing the lawyer's struggles and his longing for his family and sense of belonging justifies his wish for revenge and presents it as an inevitable course of action; the presentation of the past is therefore a justification for the present. By cutting those past scenes, the Japanese version omits the extensive explanation and justification for revenge. Past hardships are of no significance to the present actions of the lawyer and thus there is no justification for revenge. Reducing the reference and representation of the troubled past of the lawyer focuses the plot on his present behavior, and stresses the view that a troubled past or childhood trauma are no excuse for behaving badly in the present and that under no circumstances is revenge an acceptable course of action.

The scenes from the policeman's past in the Korean version, present him as a troubled youth who goes too far (killing a schoolmate) but understands the consequences and is willing to bear the punishment of both the law and society. The adults around him, however, are presented as corrupt or helpless. They are preoccupied with their social standing at the expense of supporting him. His high school teacher did not believe that the killing was an accident. His father used his money and connections to argue self-defense and have the case

Handbook of Japanese Media and Popular Culture in Transition

dismissed in court. These scenes in the Korean original present a picture of a misguided youth who lacks the support of wise adults but knows when he is wrong. He has a row with his father about the father's plan to argue self-defense in court and argues with him about not going to prison and wishes to ask the family of the dead boy for forgiveness. Omitting these scenes from the remake presents a character that lacks the same level of depth. However, the omission of those past troubles focuses the representation and construction of the character on the present, in which he is a law abiding, even if somewhat unconventional policeman who leads an honest life. Although this does not excuse his past actions, the focus on his good present highlights the evil deeds of the lawyer, stressing that revenge is wrong. This does not mean that the past killing is condoned or forgiven, as the tragic death of both characters at the end of the drama shows, but by omitting these past scenes the drama suggests that whatever was done in the past, the future can be better if one chooses wisely and behaves well.

Choice and responsibility

The question of choice and responsibility is a significant one to the general exploration of "who is the devil?" This is in effect a question of agency, a question of whether an individual has a choice in his destiny despite adverse conditions or external constraints and thus showing what is the preferred course of action that will be beneficial for both the individual and society. The perceptions surrounding choice and responsibility are constructed through two mechanisms: the past/present focus discussed in the previous section and a book reference that sets the tone for the drama.

In the first episode, the lawyer visits a library and is looking at or reading a specific book. The title of the book hints at the overall attitude of the lawyer to his life, to the policeman and to revenge, and provides a reference point to the question of good-evil. Although the scene appears in both the original and the remake, the books are different. In the Korean version it is M. Scott Peck's (1983) *People of the Lie*. In it, Peck argues that evil people are evil not because of choice or intrinsic evil, but because they are unaware that what they do is bad. Once this lack of awareness is rectified, they have the chance of becoming good. This presents a forgiving view of evil. It is unintentional and can be amended and dealt with. Referring to the characters in the drama, the lawyer who sees himself in the role of a teacher, sets out, through his revenge, to educate the policeman and reform him, assuming that the policeman is not aware of his sins. However, the drama is not specific, and as the previous section on good-evil showed, plays around with who the good or evil character is, presenting both as complex and ambivalent individuals. Thus, the same ignorance the book ascribes to evil can be applied to the lawyer himself, with his righteous focus on revenge blinding him from seeing his own evil. This eventually presents the lawyer as someone who does not have a choice simply because he is unaware that there are choices to be made, and so only partly responsible for his evil and its effects. The book in the Japanese version is *Faust* by Goethe, first published in 1790, the story of a person selling his soul to the devil in exchange for knowledge and power. Combined with the image of the devil superimposed on the face of the lawyer as discussed previously, the book reference hints that the lawyer sold his soul to the devil in exchange for the power to exact his revenge. This suggests that the lawyer is responsible for his actions, aware of his evil and is making a conscious choice to pursue revenge despite knowing it is wrong. The different books symbolize divergent views on the question of choice and responsibility. While the Korean version presents revenge as an act of ignorance, reducing some of the responsibility of the avenger for the harm he causes and thus making it forgivable, the Japanese version puts the responsibility directly and solely on the lawyer for choosing this path. It is his choice to become evil, to pursue revenge, to cause the ruin and death of several people, and so he bears full responsibility for his actions. He has chosen evil and so cannot be excused or forgiven.

This difference between the level of leniency and understanding toward revenge in the Korean version and a clear representation of choice and responsibility and good/evil in the Japanese remake is strengthened by the past/present focus discussed previously. By presenting the lawyer's past struggles, the drama not only justifies his pursuit of revenge by explaining his motivation, but also limits the potential for choice and responsibility in choosing a path of action. Revenge is therefore the fault of those who evaded justice, in this case the policeman and his family, removing the responsibility for the revenge and its consequences from the lawyer. The past therefore strengthens the perception of revenge as inevitable and understandable. Omitting many of those past scenes from the Japanese remake and emphasizing the present, focuses the attention on the choice and therefore the responsibility of the lawyer for his revenge. His past is no excuse for operating outside the law and thus revenge has no justification even if justice was not meted out in the past.

This fits within each of the conventions explored prior and within the general trust put in the justice systems in both countries. The Korean representation of revenge is upheld by presenting the lawyer as finding himself in a situation in which he sees revenge as the only possible course of action open to him, after the system failed him. Despite its role, the system did not uphold fairness regarding his brother's death with the policeman's father, a wealthy businessman, used his connections and money to present the case in court as self-defense, effectively putting the blame on the innocent victim and absolving his son from the manslaughter charges, despite Oh-soo's wishes to receive punishment and atone for his crime. The difference in position, financial ability and connection has corrupted the system and prevented justice from being served, leaving the road open for personal revenge to achieve this state of equilibrium between the victim's only remaining next of kin and the victimizer. The failure of the justice system is not only a failure of the system due to its structure, but a failure caused by the system to uphold its own rules. A quote from the Korean constitution, mentioned in the first episode, states that all citizens are equal before the law regardless of social position and status, age, sex or religion. However, in the case of Oh Seung-ha's brother, the law was not applied equally. Although he himself, as a lawyer, is now part of the system and can use his knowledge to go through the proper channels and procedures, he decides to pursue his own plan for revenge because he knows how easily the system is manipulated. This lack of trust functions as a justification for revenge, both in the social context, which accounts for the popularity of revenge plots in Korean television, and in this specific drama.

Conclusion

The choice to remake *Mawang* points to the relatability and remake-ability of the topic of revenge and the appreciation within the Japanese television industry for Korean content. The rise in transnational cultural flows, firstly between Japan and South Korea and then diversified and reversed from South Korea to Japan, was seen as a process of creating a pan-Asian identity and regionalization. In the case of South Korea and Japan, it was viewed as a positive development, with the potential to improve relations between the two countries and foster mutual familiarity and understanding.

Nevertheless, the existence of transnational remakes also appears to challenge notions of mutual understanding between Japan and South Korea and a pan-Asian identity. The process of remaking also signals that familiarity with the topic is not enough. It highlights that although the countries are close and share some traditions and ideas, they are not identical and there is a need for adaptation to local conventions, values and modes of behavior. Television in Japan is seen as a way to learn about society (Gössmann 2000), and thus, regardless of genre, keeps a level of realism even if it is the type of realism that merely adheres to the laws of the world (Fiske 2010). As such, the Japanese representation of revenge and its legitimacy fits the educational role of television, to teach the viewers how the world works and, moreover, where the boundaries of acceptable behavior lie. Thus, the Japanese remake morphs the original Korean version to fit not only Japanese television broadcasting needs such as number of episodes and their length, but also the common form of representation which highlights local perceptions about revenge and its potential disruptive power. Revenge is only acceptable within the limits of the law.

Although the beginning and the ending of the dramas are similar, the different methods and decisions in creating the characters of the policeman and the lawyer have influenced the final message of the drama, making it more culturally specific. The focus of the Korean version is on the inner world of the characters, exploring the effects of revenge on the identity, morality and even psychology of the executer and the victim. The Japanese version, on the other hand, focuses on the action and events of the revenge. While the Korean drama allows for the opportunity to empathize with both characters, and presents revenge as an understandable, even if not desirable, course of action; the Japanese version makes a very clear statement that revenge should not be pursued under any circumstances.

These differences in representation of revenge and its legitimacy are all constructed through the two main characters, the lawyer who exacts revenge, and the policeman who suffers from it. Three methods are employed in representing revenge: good-bad division between the characters, the inclusion or reduction of scenes from the past and the representation of choice and responsibility. The first one is the construction of the main characters as good, evil or ambivalent. The Korean original presents both characters as complex making their actions understandable if not excusable. This is aided by the inclusion in the Korean original of numerous scenes from their past, deepening their reasoning, aims and motivations.

The effect of presenting the past also aids the exploration of responsibility and choice. The Korean scenes set in the past put the blame for the events on the evasion of justice through official and legal channels by using the policeman's father's connections and money, leaving revenge as an understandable and inevitable course of action for the poor lawyer if he wishes to have justice, that "state of equilibrium between victim and victimizer" (Jacoby 1983, 332). Revenge is therefore an acceptable course of action especially for the less privileged, even if the price to pay is high. By not including these expositional scenes, the Japanese drama focuses on the present choices of the characters, presenting a view that the past is no longer significant and cannot and should not be used as an excuse to break the law in the present. Thus, the main message of the drama becomes "no matter what happened in the past, it is what you do now that matters." This is supported by the representation of the lawyer as "evil" and the policeman as "good." Despite the crime in the policeman's past, it is his law-abiding present that is more important; thus revenge is presented as a disaster rather than a punishment for not paying one's dues to the social order through the court system.

As the case of *Mawang/Maō* exemplifies, the practice of remaking presents a complex picture of negotiation of ideas, styles, and messages in the original and remade televisual texts. The trend of remaking Korean dramas for Japanese television hints at an increasing appreciation of the Korean industry among its Japanese counterparts, admitting, in a way to its quality and attraction. However, a remake, by its nature, naturalizes the original story into the local culture to fit its structure, conventions, traditions and values, thus obscuring the original from view and preventing the possibility of a conversation between the cultures. By remaking a drama, the Japanese industry highlights, whether intentionally or unintentionally, what it considers to be part of Japanese identity sharpened by the encounter with Korean content. More than a conscious decision to mold the representation, there is a sense that "we do not see this that way" and "we do not behave that way" when it comes to the representation of revenge, referring to the view of television as a medium that is designed to represent and foster desirable behavior. The Korean original continues the convention of seeing revenge as a possible course of action, and even an inevitable one for those without means that seek justice and cannot get it through official judicial systems, presenting the process as understandable even if destructive to the avenger in the end. The Japanese remake, however, discourages the legitimacy of revenge through visual means that present the lawyer as the "bad guy," focusing on his present deeds and omitting his troubled past, and putting all the responsibility for his actions on him, fitting it into the representation conventions of Japanese television dramas. The changes imposed on the text render it different enough from its original source to make it familiar to the local audiences and obscure the original from view. The fact that remakes are becoming more common puts into question the extent to which popular culture and television dramas can promote mutual understanding and reconciliation between the countries.

Notes

1 Some of the issues of those magazines were found during my fieldwork in Japan in July-August 2019 in the Oya Soichi Library and the National Diet Library. The earliest edition of *It's Koreal* is 2007, and *Kankoku terebi dorama gaido* is 2009. There are, of course, Japanese magazines that cover Korean dramas broadcast in Japan, but 2008–2009 was the first time when magazines were dedicated to covering exclusively Korean pop culture topics and news. This attests to the growing popularity of Korean pop culture in Japan.

2 This is based on my fieldwork in Japan, when Fuji TV, NTV, and TV Asahi produced and broadcast remakes of Korean dramas during their summer season.

3 Interview conducted in person on 1 August 2019 at the offices of TBS, the production and broadcasting station.

Videography

Akmareul boatda [I Saw the Devil], 2010. [Film] Directed by Kim, J. South Korea: Peppermint & Company.

Boksuneun naui geot [Sympathy for Mr. Vengeance], 2002. [Film] Directed by Park, C. South Korea: Im Jin-gyu.

Buhwal [Resurrection], 2005. [TV series] KBS2.

Chinjeolhan geumjassi [Lady Vengeance], 2005. [Film] Directed by Park, C. South Korea: Jo Yeong-wook and Lee Tae-hun.

Eden-ui dong-jjok [East of Eden], 2008. [TV series], MBC.
Gaewa neukdaeui sigan [Time Between Dog and Wolf], 2007. [TV series], MBC.
Gyeouryeon-ga [Winter Sonata], 2002. [TV series] KBS2.
Hanazakari no kimitachi e [Hana Kimi], 2007. [TV series], Fuji TV.
Maō [The Devil], 2008. [TV series] TBS.
Mawang [The Devil], 2007. [TV series] KBS2.
Miseu Ripeuli [Miss Ripley], 2011. [TV series], MBC.
Namja iyagi [A Man's Story], 2009. [TV series] KBS.
Oldeuboi [Oldboy], 2003. [Film] Directed by Park, C. South Korea: Lim Seung-yong.
Rakkī Sebun [Lucky Seven], 2012. [TV series] Fuji TV.
Ryūsei no kizuna [Ties of Shooting Stars], 2008. [TV series] TBS.
Sesang eodiedo eobneun chakan namja [The Innocent Man, 2012. [TV series] KBS2.
Tokyo DOGS, 2009. [TV series], Fuji TV.
Uroborosu [Ouroboros], 2015. [TV series] TBS.

Bibliography

Bohm, T. and Kaplan, S., 2011. *Revenge: On the Dynamics of a Frightening Urge and Its Taming.* London: Routledge.

Caprio, M.E., 2011. *Japanese Assimilation Policies in Colonial Korea, 1910–1945.* Seattle: University of Washington Press.

Chua, B.-H. and Iwabuchi, K., eds., 2008. *East Asian Pop Culture: Analysing the Korean Wave.* Hong Kong: Hong Kong University Press.

Creighton, M., 2016. Through the Korean Wave Looking Glass: Gender, Consumerism, Transnationalism, Tourism Reflecting Japan-Korea Relations in Global East Asia. *The Asia-Pacific Journal: Japan Focus,* 14. Available at: https://apjjf.org/2016/07/Creighton.html [Accessed 3 October 2021].

Fiske, J., 2010 *Television Culture* 2nd ed. London: Routledge.

Fujita, M., Hayashi, N., and Hotto, S., 2016. *Trust in the Justice System: Internet Survey after Introducing Mixed Tribunal System in Japan.* SSRN Scholarly Paper ID 2769587, Social Science Research Network, Rochester, New York

Gössmann, H., 2000. New Role Models for Men and Women? Gender in Japanese TV Dramas. In T.J. Craig, ed., *Japan Pop!: Inside the World of Japanese Popular Culture.* Armonk, NY: M.E. Sharpe, 207–21.

Hanana, Y., 2008. Ono Satoshi Ikuta Toma ikemen kurabu [Ono Satoshi and Ikuta Toma handsome club]. *JJ,* September, 216–217.

Hirata, Y., 2008. Touring "Dramatic Korea": Japanese Women as Viewers of Hanryu Dramas and Tourists on Hanryu Tours. In B.-H. Chua and K. Iwabuchi, eds., *East Asian Pop Culture: Analysing the Korean Wave.* Hong Kong: Hong Kong University Press. 142–55

Hiyama, T., 2008. Rimeiku suru yori sono mama nagaseba? [Why not broadcast it as it is, rather than remake?). *Shukan Gendai,* August, no. 298, 73.

Horie, J., 2008. Ōno Satoshi Ikuta Toma. *Nikkei Za Terebijon,* August, 27–29.

Iwabuchi, K., 2002. *Recentering Globalization: Popular Culture and Japanese Transnationalism.* Durham: Duke University Press.

Iwami, M., 2007. Ju Ji-hoon tto donna hito desuka [What kind of person is Ju Ji-hoon?]. *It's Korea!* July, no. 7, 52–56.

Jacoby, S., 1983. *Wild Justice: The Evolution of Revenge.* London: Harper Perennial.

Jeong, K.Y., 2012. Towards Humanity and Redemption: The World of Park Chan-wook's Revenge Film Trilogy. *Journal of Japanese and Korean Cinema,* 4 (2), 169–83.

Kanno, M., 2008. Natsu no shin dorama shuyaku fēsu messēji [Summer new drama leading actor face message]. *Za Terebijon,* 10, 17.

Kim, M., 2015. Travails of Judges: Courts and Constitutional Authoritarianism in South Korea. *The American Journal of Comparative Law,* 63(3), 601–54.

Kingston, J., 2011. Justice on Trial: Japanese Prosecutors Under Fire. *The Asia Pacific Journal,* Vol. 9, issue 10, no. 1, 1–23.

Lee, D-H, 2001. The Cultural Formation of Korean Trendy Dramas: Transnational Program Adaptation and Cultural Identity. *Korean Journal of Journalism and Communication. Special English Edition*, 491–509.

Lee, D-H, 2004. Cultural Contact with Japanese TV Dramas; Modes of Reception and Narrative Transparency. In K. Iwabuchi, ed., *Feeling Asian Modernities Transnational Consumption of Japanese TV Dramas*. Hong Kong: Hong Kong University Press, 251–74.

Lukács, G., 2010. *Scripted Affects, Branded Selves: Television, Subjectivity, and Capitalism in 1990s Japan*. Durham: Duke University Press.

Ministry of Interior and Safety, n.d. The National Flag—Taegeukgi [online]. Available at: https://www.mois .go.kr/eng/sub/a03/nationalSymbol/screen.do [Accessed 14 September 2021].

Mori, Y., 2008. Winter Sonata and Cultural Practices of Active Fans in Japan: Considering Middle-Aged Women as Cultural Agents. In B.-H. Chua and K. Iwabuchi, eds., *East Asian Pop Culture: Analysing the Korean Wave*. Hong Kong: Hong Kong University Press.

Negishi, S., 2008. TV Special Ono Satoshi and Ikuta Toma. *Oricon Style*, 21 July, 50–52.

OECD, 2015. *Public Governance: A matter of trust*. Available at: https://www.oecd.org/governance/public -governance-a-matter-of-trust.htm [Accessed 23 October 2021].

Okimoto, T.G. and Wenzel, M., 2008. The Symbolic Meaning of Transgressions: Towards a Unifying Framework of Justice Restoration. *Justice*, 25, 291–326.

Otmazgin, N., 2014. *Regionalizing Culture: The Political Economy of Japanese Popular Culture in Asia*. Honolulu: University of Hawai'i Press.

Peck, M.S., 1983. *People of the Lie: The Hope for Healing Human Evil*. New York: Touchstone.

Takahashi, N., 2009. "Kain to Aberu" no Sekai [The world of "Cain and Abel"]. *Kankoku TV doramagaido*, 22, 12–13.

The Japan Times, 2005. Despite Secrecy, "Yon-sama" Met by 600 Fans. *The Japan Times* [online]. Available at: https://www.japantimes.co.jp/news/2005/08/30/national/despite-secrecy-yon-sama-met-by-600-fans/# .XeKCi-j7TIU [Accessed 30 November 2019].

Yang, J., 2012. The Korean Wave (Hallyu) in East Asia: A Comparison of Chinese, Japanese, and Taiwanese Audiences Who Watch Korean TV Dramas. *Development and Society*, 41(1) (June), 103–47.

Part 3
Franchises and Formats

Chapter 8
Media Mix: Theorizing and Historicizing Japanese Franchising

Rayna Denison

The media mix has become Japan's answer to contemporary global media franchising practices. The logics of media mix travel through Japan's media culture creating chains of production that reach from manga into the worlds of film, television and videogames. This chapter explores the development of media mix and the diverse transmedia worlds created under its auspices, while considering the industrial structures that have underpinned it. In doing so, the chapter argues for a reconsideration of the scope and reach of media mix, contending that media mix now accounts for not just major franchises, but also everything from art cinema to theater.

Introduction

Media mix is everywhere that Japanese media flows. It can be found in the movement of a character across texts, in the movements of texts between cultures and languages and in a plethora of reimaginings, adaptations and franchising practices. You can hold its results in your hand (as a toy, via a video game controller), you can watch it (as an anime, a live action film, a theatrical performance), you can read it (as a manga, a light novel), and you can participate in it (as a player, a creator, a cosplayer). It is also more than just media: media mix opens doorways to complex storyworlds, while at the same time indicating the processes that create them, the industrial structures that enable them and the fans who endlessly collect, collate and build upon those worlds. For these reasons, media mix needs to be considered not just as a key term within Japanese media discourse, but also as a constantly evolving aspect of Japan's media landscapes. However, it is also important to note that media mix is part of a constantly debated and shifting construction of Japan's transmedia worlds. It is continually being renegotiated and enmeshed within wider geographies of Japanese media economies and ecologies. To understand the "media mix," therefore, this chapter offers an investigation of media mix's conceptualization and history, as well as mapping its trajectories and evaluating its efficacy for exploring Japan's transmedia horizons.

Conceptualizing the media mix

The conceptualization of media mix as a multifaceted—and not just multimedia—phenomenon in Japan is crucial to understanding how this term is used and when and how it manifests in Japanese media. Marc Steinberg's influential definition provides a useful starting point. He writes that "Japanese media convergence has its own name: the media mix. A popular, widely used term for the cross-media serialization and circulation of entertainment franchises, the word gained its current meaning in the late 1980s" (Steinberg 2012, viii). This way of conceptualizing media mix rests on three key issues. First, there is a focus on serialized storytelling; second, an acknowledgement of distribution (and also the distributive energies of fans); and third, an invocation of Henry Jenkins's (2006) theories on media convergence as a framework for understanding the industrio-cultural processes underpinning media mix in Japan.

The inclusion of Jenkins's convergence theory in this definition creates multiple pathways to understanding the media mix. Convergence chimes with media mix because:

> By convergence, I mean the flow of content across multiple media platforms, the cooperation between multiple media industries, and the migratory behavior of media audiences who will go almost anywhere in search of the kinds of entertainment experiences they want. (Jenkins 2006, 2)

Going along this path, the use of convergence theory declares that media mix is about the diminishing distance between media producers and consumers. Jenkins tells us that, "[c]onvergence, as we can see, is both a top-down corporate-driven process and a bottom-up consumer driven process" as media fans fight for greater participatory engagement and rights in relation to popular media franchises (2006, 18). Along a separate, yet sometimes intersecting pathway, Jenkins links these industrio-cultural shifts to pre-planned forms of media franchising, in which, "[a] transmedia story unfolds across multiple media platforms, with each new text making a distinctive and valuable contribution to the whole" (2006, 97–98). Storytelling across a range of media becomes a way for franchising or media mix to manifest, and in many definitions of media mix the two have become closely intertwined. Viewed through the lenses of convergence and transmedia storytelling, then, media mix comes into focus as an industrial and narrative phenomenon; but also as result of wider processes of media globalization and shifts within trans-nationalizing media ecologies. To a degree, therefore, the appearance of media mix in Japan is suggestive of a set of globalizing forces within media production cultures in which franchising and media conglomeration dominate media production.

Similar refrains recur in other definitions of media mix. Mizuko Ito, for instance, reads convergence culture as a fact of post-industrial society (2008, 397). In Japan, she argues, this results in media mix "forms of child-oriented convergence culture that bring together television animation, comic books, electronic gaming, card games and a wide variety of merchandise" (2008, 398). Although Ito's definition uses the same theoretical starting point as Steinberg's—convergence culture—her definition is focused on a single market demographic (children). Nor is she alone in this, with studies of the global success of *Pokémon* (Tajiri Satoshi and Sugimori Ken, 1996–) and *Yu-Gi-Oh!* (Takahashi Kazuki, 1996–) similarly investigating media mix processes within the children's media market (Tobin 2004; Allison 2006;

Ito 2006). However, the children's market is not the only market that media mix informs, and its reach extends into many disparate market segments in Japan, if not all of them.

As Ito's conceptualization illustrates, efforts to define media mix frequently result in the listing of its key media forms or platforms. This can be seen in Ito's definition above, but also in a variety of other attempts to demarcate the geographies of media mix. For example, a second definition of media mix from Steinberg declares that:

> The "media mix" is a term that refers to the media environment whereby a partic- ular franchise releases interconnecting products for a wide range of media "plat- forms"—animation, comics, video games, theatrical features, soundtracks—and commodity types—cell-phone straps, T-shirts, bags, figurines and so on. (2006, 191)

This can be compared, too, with Anne Allison's description of the *Yu-Gi-Oh!* franchise as: "A media-mix complex of trading cards, cartoon show, comic books, video games, movie, and tie-in merchandise that became the follow-up global youth hit on the heels of *Pokémon*" (2006, 1). In these lists, the porousness and extensiveness of the media mix are rendered visible. Each of these definitions cites unique product mixes, and some delineate divisions between narrative and non-narrative franchise objects. Attempting to account for the inter- connectivity within Japan's media landscape, definitions of media mix can also range from the specific to the general. Where the preceding definitions provide an example of specific lists, Matthew Ogonoski's work on fan cosplaying and media mix provides an example of the latter. He writes that, "The term *media mix* refers to the many iterations of a media prop- erty across a variety of commodity types, including adaptations into different formats, and ancillary products" (2014, para. 1.3). Ogonoski's is a useful example of its type for the way it brings media mix *processes* into view—processes ranging from generalized commodification to adaptation. In addition to sometimes adopting different stances dependent on markets, therefore, these geographies of media mix are separated out by attempts to pinpoint core and peripheral media formats and processes.

What these examples further illustrate is how particular focal points in research and spe- cific scholarly objectives—in Ito's case a study of participatory child audiences; in Allison's the franchising of *Yu-Gi-Oh!*; in Steinberg's the origins of media mix in *Tetsuwan atomu* (As- troboy, Tezuka Osamu, 1952–1968 in manga) and in Ogonoski's the study of cosplaying—can work upon and shape our understanding of the meanings and aims of media mix. In one of the most compelling of such reworkings, Bryan Hikari Hartzheim analyzes the media mix around *Purikyua* (Pretty Cure, Izumi Todo, 2004–) and reassesses the significance of toy production to media mix creation. He argues that the television anime:

> broadcast, in its centralizing of media creation, becomes a kind of convergence text, tying together its producers and animators, the program and its advertise- ments, and, most importantly, its viewers to sponsored goods, into what I call a "product portal"—a toy-based narrative device that generates profits for the show, studio and supporting industries. (2016, 1063)

At one and the same time, Hartzheim's definition is generalized and specific. He locates the core medium of the media mix in anime, but sees anime itself as an intermedial text that actualizes convergence, creating a "product portal" through which and into which other media from the mix can be showcased. Hartzheim demonstrates why what we study when researching media mix matters. While in *Purikyua* the product portal is anime, he notes that for other media mix, such portals could operate out of a range of media types and formats. This suggests that our understanding of media mix can vary drastically, depending on how we approach the media involved in its creation, and how they relate to one another in their turn.

This leads to a central question about media mix: how can we start to study a phenomenon that can involve mountains of merchandising, oceans of texts and a plethora of platforms? One response, seen above, has been to unite the texts of media mixes through discussion of their transmedia storytelling. Japanese scholars have their own ways of theorizing transmedia storytelling, most notably seen in work by Ōtsuka Eiji. Ōtsuka (2010) examines the example of *Bikkuriman* stickers, which created a narrative world using mini-narratives on the reverse side of *omaketsuki* (give-away goods) stickers that came with sweets. These narrative snippets were used to foster greater engagement with the overall narrative in an effort to reveal the "grand narrative" supporting the system. As with *Pokémon*'s famous "Gotta Catch 'Em All!" catchphrase, however, this grand narrative was endlessly extendable and never fully realizable. Ōtsuka likens this to the "worldview" that sits behind large-scale media franchises like *Gundam* (Yatate Hajime and Tomino Yoshiyuki, 1979–) or video games like *Super Mario Brothers* (1983–) in Japan. Using Jean Baudrillard's simulacra as a starting point, Ōtsuka states:

> What is being consumed is not an individual drama or thing but the system itself that was supposedly concealed in the background. However since it's quite impossible to sell the system (i.e., the grand narrative) itself, consumers are tricked into consuming a single cross-section of the system in the form of one episode of a drama, or a single fragment of the system in the form of a thing. I would like to call this state of affairs "narrative consumption." (Ōtsuka 2010, 109)

Here, Ōtsuka differentiates between the worldview or grand narrative that acts as a supporting framework for a franchise, and the "small narratives," like television drama episodes, that help to sell the world. In essence, Ōtsuka explains the media mix by attending to the individual media and commodities produced as a mechanism for revealing parts of the world from which they emerge. In doing so, Ōtsuka provides a variation on transmedia storytelling theory.

Ōtsuka saw the downfall of the system in its structures, because the endless expandability of grand narratives opens them up to unauthorized fan productions. The work of Azuma Hiroki, a *"zeronendai no shisō* (thoughts from the aughts)" (Zahlten 2017a, 217) generation philosopher-turned-cultural critic took this a stage further. Azuma has built a theory of media mix on observations about how *otaku* (fans) of Japanese media consume their favored storyworlds in response to the end of grand narratives (2009). As explained by Takeshi Kobayashi:

> According to Azuma, the media mix strategy and derivative amateur works have become the norm in otaku culture since the 1990s, in which the otaku's consumptive activities are oriented toward the database-like grand nonnarrative

(ōkina himonogatari) behind individual works, exemplifying the broader social phenomena of postmodernity after the collapse of modernity's grand narratives (ōkina monogatari). (2017, 80)

As Kobayashi makes clear, Azuma's conceptualization of media mix as part of a subcultural database asks us to reconsider who media mixes are created for and consumed by within Japanese culture. Like Ogonoski, Azuma's study illustrates how deeply fan practices can work upon and shape understandings of media franchises, from the ways fans consume to the ways they produce unauthorized media texts, from cosplay to Anime Music Videos and beyond. And, perhaps just as importantly, Azuma claims that these structures sit alongside and are juxtaposed with culture writ large, and not just in relation to subcultural media consumption (and creation) practices.

Azuma's work contributes to the significance of media mix theorization in three additional ways. Each is evident in the following quotation, reproduced here at length because it is core to some of the confusion and complexity that has been emerging around conceptualizations of media mix. In it, Azuma argues that Annō Hideaki's anime *Shinseiki evangerion* (Neon Genesis Evangelion, 1995–1996), and especially its blue-haired female character Ayanami Rei, have had a dispersed influence on other Japanese media through *moe* (variously translated as the burning, nurturing or yearning emotions that characters evoke in consumers). He argues:

> *I believe that it is more appropriate to use the image of the database to grasp this current situation. The emergence of Ayanami Rei did not influence many authors so much as change the rules of the moe-elements sustaining otaku culture. As a result, even those authors who were not deliberately thinking of Evangelion unconsciously began to produce characters closely resembling Rei, using newly registered moe-elements (quiet personality, blue hair, white skin, mysterious power). Such a model is close to the reality of the late 1990s. Beyond Rei, characters emerging in otaku works were not unique to individual works but were immediately broken into moe-elements and recorded by consumers, and then the elements reemerged later as material for creating new characters. Therefore, each time a popular character appeared, the moe-element database changed accordingly, and as a result, in the next season there were heated battles among the new generation of characters featuring new moe-elements.* (Azuma 2009, 51–52)

First, Azuma introduces his "database" as a new way of understanding media mix creation and consumption, though it is not entirely dissimilar to Ōtsuka's systemic understanding of worldview systems. In Azuma's version, however, popular characters are analyzed as they emerge, are deconstructed and then re-emerge as elements of other new characters in a re-mixing database fashion. Second, Azuma positions fans as the key recipients of media mix and as participatory members in media mix creation, flattening the distinctions between the texts created by media industries and those created by fans. Third, Azuma argues that such database-construction makes what "the original is or who the original author is" ambiguous and, further, he contends that "the distinction between the original and the spin-off products (as copies) does not exist; the only valid distinction between them is between the settings created anonymously (a database at a deep inner layer) and the individual works that each artist has concretized" (2009, 39). This is a significant intervention, in that it shifts the focus away from narratives and towards the industrial side of media creation and consumption, taking us towards convergence culture and away from transmedia storytelling.

Azuma's work usefully decenters questions of authorship and originality within Japanese media franchising, and it allows for genres, popular aesthetics and tropes to be recentered in their place. However, some of Azuma's assertions create questions and problems that go unanswered. Crucially, the figure of the *otaku* becomes, as much as anything else, an idealized spectator, rather than a representative of the diverse fandoms and subcultures operating around Japanese media. The focus on *otaku* also limits the possibility of understanding how non-*otaku* audiences of Japanese media might behave in relation to, or understand, texts and their databases or storyworlds. Additionally, the idea that such *otaku* do not care about authorship is problematic in light of growing *sakuga* fandom, in which fans perform extensive work to uncover the animators behind particular sequences of anime (Suan 2018); and also in light of how much effort industry puts into the assertion of authorship and copyright in media mix franchising (Denison 2016).

Where Azuma's work has been most influential, is in the metaphor of the database itself. The database, with characters at its heart, and the flattening of hierarchies between franchise media, allows the media mix to be encountered through myriad media. It enables discussions of how consumers can dip in and out of a franchise over time or can skip across and between media experiences. This is quite different from Jenkins's construction of committed fans who seek out franchise media. It is also quite different from Ōtsuka's (grand) narratives of transmedia storytelling and collation, which inspired Azuma. The database constructs media mix at a metatextual, or at least intertextual, level without any requirements for holistic consumption. Consequently, Azuma's formulation of the database helps to explain how some media mix franchises in Japan have become multi-generational properties spanning decades, while others burn for bright, brief periods and still others appear in sporadic production cycles. With no single authorized way into media mix consumption, Azuma's database enables the study of completist and non-normative consumption patterns alike.

It is from Azuma's starting point that Steinberg builds towards his definition of the anime-centered media mix:

> *The anime media mix [...] has no single goal or teleological end; the general consumption of any of the media mix's products will grow the entire enterprise. Since each media-commodity is also an advertisement for further products in the same franchise, this is a consumption that produces more consumption.* (2012, 141)

Steinberg's focus on iterativity, intertextuality and endless consumption echoes both Azuma's claims about the *otaku* database and Ōtsuka's claims about "small narrative" consumption, but it is important to note that it is also similar to other definitions of franchising outside of Japan. Not least, Jenkins's assessment of *The Matrix* franchise, which similarly asserts: "Each franchise entry needs to be self-contained so you don't need to have the film to enjoy the game, and vice versa. Any given product is a point of entry into the franchise as a whole" (2006, 97–98). The difference between these two is slight but important: whereas consumption begets consumption in both, for Jenkins it is the experience of consumption that motivates further consumption; whereas, for Steinberg media texts are part of a promotional intertextual relay wherein mutual advertising emerges out of a database logic of media mix.

Anime is the other significant difference in these definitions. Steinberg's recognition of anime as a core medium within media mixing has been noted by several scholars and has emerged as a common thread within conceptualizations of media mix (Ito 2006; Suan 2018). For example, Thomas Lamarre has also attempted to make sense of the centrality of television anime within media mix. He writes:

> In sum, at sites of technological confluence (say, television with VCR or DVD or game box or all of these), the corporate entities struggle to unfold and refold the divergent series of animation, for profit. Ideally each jump of a character would produce a return—mandated by government fiat if necessary. Between economic convergence and media divergence, then, arises a stunning array of patterns of serialization, which are designed to build controls on divergence, to encourage the divergent paths of animetic force into those patterns that allow for greater returns. (2009, 311)

Here, Lamarre provides an alternative to the small and grand narrative metaphors, seeing industrial attempts to control media mix meanings as working in tension with those of proliferating and quasi-competing media mix texts, whose creators are determined to diverge away from the standard meanings of a franchise. In this instance, Lamarre frames anime at the center of these forces.

In more recent work, Lamarre has expanded his interpretation of media mix to include more, different and divergent media mix pathways, arguing:

> Media mix does not rely on a hierarchy of media. On the other hand, however, it generally does matter that the source for a series, or the overall emphasis of a series is a game, manga, or anime series. That source imparts a distinctive tone to it as well as a trajectory. (2018, 315)

As with his observations about the confluence of media technologies around television, Lamarre has come to view television as the heart of Japan's media ecology. He argues that "The media ecology is a holding pattern between television infrastructures, multimedia franchising, and the transmedia storytelling called media mix" (2018, 345). It is notable, however, that in order to discuss Japan's media ecology, Lamarre has siphoned off some of the meanings usually held in tension within earlier conceptualizations of the media mix. In doing so he reduces media mix to transmedia storytelling and separates it out from franchising and wider questions of media ecology.

The move away from media mix itself to discussions of the wider frames within which media mix operates in Japan can also be seen in Marc Steinberg's (2019) book, *The Platform Economy*. Steinberg organizes this transnational study of the rise of platforms in the digital era around a nested set of investigations concerning Japan's *kontentsu* (contents) industries, and how these industries became enmeshed within industrial platforming logics. Lamarre had already linked these concepts when he wrote that, "the business of media mix production came to be called the 'contents industry,' to distinguish it from production of electronics or hardware" (2018, 170). Steinberg relates contents to media mix in the following way:

> *While emerging from the realm of computer hardware firms—not unlike in the United States—in Japan the term contents is in a short order associated with particular kinds of content: anime, manga, light novels (a form of young adult fiction that has anime-style characters on the cover of the novels), and games (with film and music on the periphery), which are simultaneously the locus of "media mix" practice, whereby media are conceived and deployed in franchises.*
> (2019, 37)

There is, in both cases, an obvious cognizance between Japan's contents industries and the conceptualizations of media mix discussed above. As theoretical debates about media ecologies and economies come to the fore, therefore, it seems that media mix may be shifting into the background, replaced by alternative concepts.

This does not, however, mean that we have, as yet, adequately explained, explored or conceptualized Japan's media mix. My own work has tried to account for some of the vagaries in these appreciations, to question the centrality of industries like the anime industry and television (Denison 2019), and the "peripheral" nature of film within media mix (Denison 2016). Others, like Hartzheim (2016), have demonstrated that intermedial relations within the media mix need more attention, that we must think more about what drives consumption beyond grand (non)narratives. Still others, like Ogonoski (2014), are challenging us to look at the how fans extend and expand the media mix, whether embodying it with cosplay or rearranging its meanings through *dōjinshi* (amateur manga). Taken together with larger studies like those of Lamarre (2018) and Steinberg (2012), these recent studies suggest that Japan's media mix worlds are so varied and extensive that conceptualizing them may require not a single definition, or theoretical approach, but a multiplicity that echoes the variety and elasticity of the media mix itself.

Historicizing the media mix: From adaptation to metamedia worlds

One way of extending our thinking about media mix would be to further consider its history within Japan. As Steinberg notes (2012, viii), there is a tendency to assume that the popularization of media mix in the 1980s coincided with its creation, and that its history extends no further back than this period. To counter this impression, he traces the history of the media mix back to postwar marketing in Japan. In this early media mix of the 1960s, which Steinberg calls the "marketing media mix," marketing companies made use of a variety of licensing and tie-up deals to sell consumers on particular brands or marketing messages (2012, 138–39). So, while the marketing media mix helped to popularize the phrase in the mid-1960s, at that time it was used only as a means to point to the serialization or cross-media amplification of marketing messages.

Kadokawa Publishing (Kadokawa Shoten) has been largely responsible for the over-determination of 1980s media mix history. This is largely thanks to the oddly titled autobiography of Kadokawa Haruki, a central—if controversial—figure in the history of media mix. Kadokawa's biography—*Waga tōsō* (My Struggle, 1977)—echoes the translated Japanese title of Adolf Hitler's *Mein Kampf*, and in it he argues that Hitler's book is his "ultimate textbook" (1977, 88). Purposefully seeking controversy, and at times wilfully seeking to shock, Kadokawa's autobiography has little common ground with Hitler's Nazi manifesto and far more to do with Kadokawa's attempts to commercialize Japanese film production in the 1970s (see Steinberg 2017 for a full discussion). It suffices here to note that Kadokawa Haruki took over his family's publishing business on his father's death in 1975, founding Kadokawa Films (now known as Kadokawa Pictures), and then Kadokawa Head Office in 1976, which he used to implement his ideas around media mix.

The first phase of media mix at Kadokawa Films was experimental, and Alexander Zahlten explains that it was an attempt to bring transmedia franchising in-house; that the aim was to own not only the publishing rights for a book, but to then also produce a blockbuster-style film adaptation of it and to create and release the film's soundtrack (2017b, 104). The difference between what Kadokawa Films was doing in the mid-1970s and early forms of transmedia production in Japan was the way "Kadokawa Film marketed its business practices as part of the product" (Zahlten 2017b, 107). Zahlten summarizes the situation as follows:

> *If Kadokawa Film did not invent the strategies it presented as part of its unique identity, what it did indeed achieve was the self-reflexive packaging of a disparate group of business practices. [...] It fused these practices—rationalized and casualized production and distribution structures, use of yōga [foreign film] theaters, media-mix strategies, an economy of scale, and so on—to sociopolitical and generational discourses that charged them with meaning and created a brand that was centered around a commodifiable character, in this case Kadokawa Haruki himself. What was new was the centrality of the brand. (2017b, 117–118)*

These claims will be probed further below, especially about the coordination of "disparate" business practices and newness of branding. But, it is worth noting for now that this version of media mix, based on the triptych of book-film-soundtrack franchising, was not that different from what was happening in Hollywood cinema at the same time; akin to something that Justin Wyatt (1994) calls "the look, the hook and the book" of Hollywood high-concept film marketing.

Kadokawa Haruki's fall from grace—presaged by his arrest for cocaine smuggling in 1993—led to the reinvigoration of media mix at Kadokawa, under the leadership of Haruki's brother, Kadokawa Tsuguhiko. This new version of media mix was notably influenced by Ōtsuka Eiji, who was working at Kadokawa at the time (Steinberg 2019, 58–60). Zahlten argues that, with the new Kadokawa media mix of the late 1990s "the focus was now on building platforms on which media mixes could unfold and on which users (or audiences, readers, listeners, etc.) could participate" (2017b, 148).

Most of these commentators are clear that Kadokawa was not, in fact, the first nor only company to be invested in media mix. Zahlten notes that Kadokawa tends to suggest that its engagements with media mix have been of an evolutionary type (2017b, 150), but the most common types of media mix in Japan are not the book-film-soundtrack or platforming types developed by Kadokawa's high profile siblings. Rather, Jonathan Clements argues that Kadokawa's reputation for media mix hides wider, quieter historical changes in Japan's media industries:

> *Kadokawa's book, with its superb Annie Leibovitz cover depicting the author on a Tokyo overpass in knight's armour, is an argument for his role in the period, but is liable to overshadow the achievements of many less publicity-hungry*

entrepreneurs in the fields of, say, games, video, models or plush toys. There are sure to be other testimonials, as yet unwritten, that will present counterarguments to such an extraordinary bias. (2013, 164)

Clements' point is crucial to considering the deeper historical and industrial developments in Japan that enabled media mix from the postwar period onwards. These relate not only to the structures of industrial competition and cooperation in Japan, but extend also to developments in ever-new media technologies and fads across the second-half of the 20th and into the early 21st centuries.

Unlike the horizontal integration of US-media conglomerates seen during the 20th and early 21st centuries, in Japan Álvaro David Hernández Hernández relates that the system of media production has become "horizontally dispersed" (2018, 8). This follows from its creation of *keiretsu* (interlinked businesses; or, business groups), in which, "Japanese companies are *keiretsu* (interlocking) structures, with firms tightly conglomerated through cognate businesses, and through shared board members across different, affiliated companies" (Davis and Yeh 2008, 64–65). These *keiretsu* practices enable loosely defined networks of competition and cooperation between Japan's media industries, enabling the kinds of transmedia production that would generate media mix.

Beyond these connective tissues, too, Japan's media industries have also undertaken a variety of horizontal and vertical integration. Between the 1960s and 1990s, for example, companies began to formally conglomerate, buying up smaller business interests, investing in emerging technologies and merging businesses together. Kadokawa provides just one instance of these trends and it is by no means alone. For example, in the 1980s Tokuma Publishing (Tokuma Shoten) purchased one of Japan's major golden age film studios, Daiei, helping it to expand into transmedia production, subsequently founding blockbuster animation company Studio Ghibli, which has since become an independent mini-conglomerate in its own right (Zahlten 2017b, 116; Denison 2015). However, these kinds of conglomeration have become most obvious around television broadcasting companies, and television is now routinely argued to be "the great multiplier: fertile seed for moving images and narratives to sprout, grow and migrate to allied markets like internet, games, mobile phones and the cinema" (Davis and Yeh 2008, 70). It is the emergence of television and other constellated home media formats including video games, VHS and DVD that have led Lamarre (2018) to cite television as an ecological hub for media production and consumption in Japan.

Television broadcast companies are among some of Japan's biggest media conglomerates. For example, broadcaster Fuji Terebi (Fuji TV), part of the larger conglomerated Fuji Sankei Group, has dozens of subsidiary companies, providing an exemplar of these kinds of conglomeration and media mix production tactics. For one, Fuji TV was a member of some of the earliest forms of anime media mix, acting as the broadcaster for Osamu Tezuka's proto-media mix and proto-anime *Astroboy* (Steinberg 2012, 45). It continues today as a broadcaster for a wide variety of media mix franchises, and Fuji TV is the broadcast home to major television anime from *One Piece* (Oda Eiichirō, 1997–) through to *Chibi Maruko-chan* (Sakura Momoko, 1986–). For another, it began producing films as well as television as early as the 1950s and has since emerged as one of Japan's most popular film producers. Take, for example, its dominance in live action media mix blockbuster cinema within contemporary Japan. In 2012 alone, three of Fuji TV's media mix franchises topped the Japanese box office, including the latest films in the *Umizaru* (Satō Shūhō, 1998–) and *Odoru daisōsasen* (*Bayside*

Shakedown, 1997–) franchises, and the newer manga-anime-live action film mix produced around *Thermae Romae* (Yamazaki Mari, 2008–2013; films 2012 and 2014, Takeuchi Hideki), whose first film made approximately $60 million at the box office (Davis and Yeh 2008; Denison forthcoming). The company has also been important for providing spaces to alternative kinds of media mixing, including its *Noitamina* anime timeslot, which promotes anime media mixes (usually adapted from manga) aimed at non-standard Japanese audiences, particularly women. As this should suggest, when it comes to media mix in Japan, Kadokawa was neither the first, nor the most invested company, and many other conglomerates have more storied and consistent engagement with media mix practices.

Alongside the conglomeration of existing postwar media companies, new conglomerates have formed out of developments in Japan's media ecology. Probably the most significant industry to emerge in Japan in relation to media mix in the 20th century has been the video game industry. This industry now includes huge conglomerates that have formed through patterns of mergers, partnerships and takeovers, and unlike many of Japan's other media industries, the games industry is both a transnational and transcultural entity (Consalvo 2016). Nintendo was an early entrant into transmedia production, making deals to create transnational films and cartoons of some of their most popular arcade and console games before instantiating more top-down, controlling forms of licensing in the 1990s (Johnson 2013, 77–78). Now, Nintendo is exploring new forms of licensing, partnership and media mix production that works to extend its popular characters, like Mario, from myriad video games into ancillary productions that work to blur the lines between Mario's world and our own. As Andrew Campana (2015) argues, for example, there is a long history of capitalizing on the "flat" aesthetic of the Mario Bros. platform video game worlds to create everything from merchandizing to museum exhibitions.

Drawn into franchising, transmedia storytelling and worldbuilding just like its fellow Japanese media industries, then, the games industry makes some unique uses of media mix. For example, Mia Consalvo argues that companies like Square Enix are using media mix to "widen the scope of their product lineups […] going beyond the confines of a singular genre but also demonstrating what something like Final Fantasy might be like outside a specific form of gameplay" (2016, 111–12). As with Nintendo's complex transnational franchising practices, which routinely operate as media mix within Japan and different transnational kinds of franchising all at once (Johnson 2013, 184–85), Square Enix has similarly worked to create a media mix world that forms around the core of its gaming "worldview."

Bryan Hikari Hartzheim has also examined how mobile gaming now works within media mix. He maps some of the complex ways that games can shift in status between primary and ancillary production in media mix:

> *Within franchises from which games are adapted, spin-offs can explore segments of a manga or anime franchise in greater detail, such as the various games based around the adventure series One Piece (Toei Animation, 1997–present), while still others can be derivative games that depict alternative realities or dimensions of the original property and its characters such as the novel series Kanon (Key, 1999–2007). The financial importance of gaming content has led to increased involvement of video-game developers and publishers among the committees that handle media-mix projects; by 1998, Tokyo TV ratings reported that 60 percent*

of their sixty anime broadcasts were sponsored in part by games companies and audiovisual manufacturers. (2019, 237–38)

In observing reflexive uses of video games within wider media mix practices, Hartzheim illustrates the relational and variable processes involved within media mix. As his examples reveal, flexibility and translatability are vital aspects of media mix, and have also become hallmarks of Japanese media production.

Since the turn towards digital media that video games exemplify, the media mix has changed again, shifting focus from discrete media to the platforms that are able to deliver multiple media at once. Steinberg defines three types of platform: "(1) a layered structure often based on hardware, (2) a support for contents, and (3) a structure of mediation or enabler of financial transactions" (2019, 7). While media mix has taken place at all three of these layers, the former two types are currently losing ground to the third. Mobile games offer a particularly potent example of how media mix can now be embedded within media, shaping them in their turn through examples like in-game app purchases, pop-up advertisements and in-game collectables, all of which significantly reshaping the *moe*-style relations between player-consumers and creative industries within Japan's media mix landscapes.

Conclusion: Media mix trends and trajectories

Understanding media mix therefore requires a broader sense of how, when and where Japan's media industries have used its practices and processes to create storyworlds. The history of media mix as something wholly owned by a single conglomerated company, or formulated out of mergers, partnerships and licensing arrangements only covers part of the story of media mix's integration into the heart of Japanese media culture. A specialist industrial structure also informs the spread of media mix practices in Japan: *seisaku iinkai* (the production committee).

> *In this form of film financing, several companies, usually each representing a different ancillary market, invest in the production of a film and in return receive a portion of the rights. Often a film-production company, a television channel, a video/DVD distributor and a publishing company will be involved, dividing up the rights for their respective markets.* (Steinberg 2012, 145)

As Joo, Denison and Furukawa relate (2013), the production committee system became popular with the decline of Japan's studio system and the rise of home media and platforming across the 1980s and 1990s. Reflecting the kinds of interlocking industrial structures inherent within Japan's media industries, then, the production committee system spreads the risks of media production between a group of invested companies and organizes the pre-planning of media mix franchises. The system is flexible enough that when a media mix becomes successful, the initially short-term relationships can be extended indefinitely, creating functional oligopolies at the heart of power media mix franchises. This media mix-informed approach to film production and distribution has been the driving force behind the recovery of local films at the Japanese box office. Recently, for example, an anime feature film based on the *Demon Slayer: Kimetsu no Yaiba* manga and television anime (Demon Slayer: Kimetsu no Yaiba—*The Movie: Mugen Train, Gekijōban kimetsu no yaiba mugen ressha-hen* Sotozaki Haruo, 2020) broke all box office records in Japan, and was, in the main, produced by the same complex of interlocking companies that had created the successful television show. This trend in trans-industrial production processes has been growing increasingly visible over the past three decades, and now extends to most kinds of media mix production in Japan.

As the example of the games industry indicates, however, there are multiple different kinds of media mix operating within Japan's media markets. Steinberg (2015) has identified four major moments in the history of media mix in an Appendix to the Japanese version of his book *Anime's Media Mix*. He locates the four variants by identifying their creators: Tezuka Osamu, Kadokawa Haruki, Kadokawa Tsuguhiko and video streaming platform Nico Nico Dōga. These differing kinds of media mix move from limited transmedia serialization and expansion by industry, to tightly controlled in-house franchising, to more open forms of media production in which audiences can become active participants in media mix creation. Out of these, Steinberg considers different trends and treatments of media mix including nine key starting points: narrative, source material, chronological development, character, industrial structure, model of consumer, auteur-producer model and production model (industry and/or fans) (2015). These align with much of the existing theory conceptualizing media mix and suggest trajectories for future work in this area.

Using Steinberg's observations as a starting point, it is possible to chart several other distinct types of media mix. The most obvious, and simplest form of media mix can be found in direct adaptations. This kind of limited media mix can frequently be found in art films like *Kūki ningyō* (Air Doll, 2009) adapted from Gōda Yoshie's manga (1998–1999) by Koreeda Hirokazu, or in Ninagawa Mika's 2006 live action version of Annō Moyoco's *Sakuran* manga (2001–2003). While it might seem unusual to include direct adaptations as a form of media mix, it is worth noting that even the most straightforward adaptation also comprises ancillary merchandising and soundtracks, as well as "long tail" media production including streaming, DVD and Blurays for home consumption. *Sakuran*, for instance, was produced by a production committee that included the film's production studio, Asmik Ace, but also a host of "downstream" fashion and make-up licensees (Denison 2016). Even Japanese art cinema is thus implicated in the media mix.

Two other distinct forms of media mix would be the synchronous or simultaneous (i.e., short term) media mix and its polar opposite, the diachronic or seemingly endless media mix. Synchronous mixes can appear and disappear within a year or less. They are sometimes limited to just a few media, but they can also be trend- or fad-driven hits that appear and then quickly fade from the production landscape. For example, the adaptation of *Usagi Drop* from manga into anime happened at the same time as a live action film was made, meaning that all of the franchise texts were in production and circulation at the same time (Denison 2019). Other high-profile examples would include things like *Thermae Romae*, whose manga was adapted into anime and two live-action feature length films starring Abe Hiroshi, all of which appeared within just a few years of one another. Notably, these kinds of synchronic media mix franchises frequently seem to be centered around originating media with limited story-lengths, be it an already-completed manga series or a limited series of light novels.

At the other extreme are the huge numbers of diachronic behemoth media mixes that have made the phenomenon famous. Some like *Crayon Shin-chan* (Lamarre 2018) or *Pokémon* (Tobin 2004) stretch across decades and every medium imaginable, generating "a constant oscillating 'media ecology' of TV viewing, cinemagoing, comic-reading, and active fandom" (Clements 2013, 159). Some of these, like *Pokémon, Super Mario Brothers* or *Chibi Maruko-chan* have been around so long that the dominant media have changed through time, especially where changes in the technologies of home viewing, gaming consoles or music consumption are concerned. This demonstrates the flexibility of the production committee system in Japan, with new media companies joining committees as older forms of media production need to be replaced. However, the sheer volume of these productions, and the ephemerality of many of the media instances (broadcasts and advertising in particular) present real challenges to fully mapping or constellating the intermedial relations in diachronic media mixes.

Add to this the increasing presence of fan production in the construction of media mix and these already-massive media worlds become increasingly unknowable. Take, for example, the challenges in capturing home-made amateur manga sold by fans to other fans in Japan; or those made outside of Japan in other languages and cultures. These kinds of production create additional ancillary grey-markets of consumption relating to Japan's media mix storyworlds that significantly differ but relate to industrial forms of production (Chin and Hitchcock Morimoto 2013). This important work by fans can be considered either as a form of production in its own right, or as "synergetic production strategies that bolster brand recognizability while diversifying and consolidating distribution channels" (Ogonoski 2014, para. 3.9). Fans have already achieved what the games industry has sought in creating more porous boundaries between media production and the real world whether by bringing characters to life in cosplay, creating subtitles for otherwise lost and forgotten texts, making cakes, creating craftworks based on Japanese media or pushing whole genres of production like *yaoi* manga into the global market (Rendell 2018; McLelland and Welker 2015). In doing so, fans frequently create a volume of media mixing that industry can only aspire to equal. But, this should not suggest a flat relationship between fans, consumers and industry. Rather, creative work within Japan's media industries is the inspiration for iterative rearticulations that amplify the meanings of the industrial media mix. It is notable that some of the most intense work by fans is done, as Ogonoski and others suggest, to make up for the lack of media mix distribution in the global arena.

Within the extensive diachronic media mix there is one more issue to account for—multiple worlds. Alexander Zahlten has described the history of science fiction anime-centered media mix as following a particular trajectory. He writes that "this trajectory began as a concern with extra-terrestrial worlds that was—not incidentally—accompanied by an intensifying media mix through representative works such as *Uchū senkan Yamato* (Space Battleship Yamato, 1974)" but, that "from the beginning of the 2000s there has been a marked increase in what we can term 'multiple worlds' separated by very minor variations" (2014, 441). This trajectory helps make sense of a final type of media mix production; one in which cycles of production can pop up and fade away, before new media or an anniversary or a new creative voice inspires a new cycle. There is a nostalgic version of this story, as seen in the sporadic production around *Uchū senkan Yamato* itself, which has benefited from multiple (sometimes nostalgically oriented) treatments over time. Although dominated by its anime television origins, for example, it has periodically jumped media borders to become everything from an arcade game (in 1985) to a live action blockbuster film starring Kimura Takuya (Yamazaki Takashi, 2010).

In other cases, media mix properties are now featuring serialized arcs that shift between not only different platforms, but internally too, with shifting storylines, series and even characters. The *Sword Art Online* media mix offers a good example. It began as a series of light novels by Kawahara Reiki (2002–2008) about its protagonists becoming trapped within a virtual reality video game, but the franchise now follows arcs that continually reimagine character relationships and trans-medially created "video game" settings. Perhaps unsurprisingly, this franchise now extends to video games as well as anime, and a live action television drama series. This media mix, consequently, provides multiple storyworlds, or worldviews, and each of its media texts has either expanded its multiple storyworlds or repositioned elements of content to re-adapt central themes and settings. Here, then, the media mix may be moving beyond even the grand non-narrative, into a transmedia multiverse. Moreover, this example illustrates a tension at the heart of media mix production that the notion of transmedia storytelling overlooks; namely, the importance of repetition and iteration. While these can certainly function within Azuma's theorization of the character and *moe*-centered database, they may also suggest that character and *moe* are not the only things that keep audiences returning to media mix worlds.

Worlds built on characters that can be adapted into ever-new forms of media, who can be continually repositioned within new settings and worlds, and who can themselves be altered and adapted over time in line with the trends and trajectories of the wider media landscapes are the ever-expanding heart of media mix process. However, while the media mix has now become almost ubiquitous, it has begun to lose its discursive purchase. Swallowed by wider frames of contents, platforms, economies and ecologies, the media mix is being subsumed within debates that are themselves becoming ever more trans-medial and extensive in nature. It is worth remembering, therefore, that media mix is both a set of products and the processes that create them; that without media mix we would have neither the storyworlds nor interlocking connectivity that make Japan's media industries distinctive. Media mix therefore remains a crucial world containing multitudes of worlds, stories, characters and fans and until its impact has been fully explored we need to remain within its geographies.

Bibliography

Allison, A., 2006. *Millennial Monsters: Japanese Toys and the Global Imagination*. Berkeley: University of California Press.

Azuma, H., 2009 [2001]. *Otaku: Japan's Database Animals*. J.E. Abel and Kono S., trans. Minneapolis: University of Minnesota Press.

Campana, A., 2015 Geemu and Media Mix: Theoretical Approaches to Japanese Video Games. *Kinephanos*, 5, 77–111.

Chin, B. and Hitchcock Morimoto, L., 2013. Towards a Theory of Transcultural Fandom. *Participations: Journal of Audience and Reception Studies*, 10(1), 92–108.

Clements, J., 2013. *Anime: A History*. London: BFI and Palgrave Macmillan.

Consalvo, M., 2016. *Atari to Zelda: Japan's Videogames in Global Contexts*. Cambridge: The MIT Press.

Davis, D.W. and Yeh, E.Y., 2008. *East Asian Screen Industries*. London: BFI Publishing.

Denison, R., 2015. *Anime: A Critical Introduction*. London: Bloomsbury.

———., 2016. Franchising and Film in Japan: Transmedia Production and the Changing Roles of Film in Contemporary Japanese Media Culture. *Cinema Journal*, 55(2), 67–88.

———., 2019. Adaptation in Japanese Media Mix Franchising: *Usagi Drop* from Page to Screens. *Journal of Adaptation in Film and Performance*, 12(3), 143–61.

———., 2022. Blockbusters in Japan: Hit Film Culture and the Rise of Fuji Television as Commercial Film Studio. In D. Desser, ed., *A Companion to Japanese Cinema*. Hoboken, NJ: Wiley-Blackwell, 591–611.

Hartzheim, B.H., 2016. *Pretty Cure* and the Magical Girl Media Mix. *The Journal of Popular Culture* 49(5), 1059–85.

———., 2019. Transmedia-to-Go: Licensed Mobile Gaming in Japan. In J. Fleury, B.H. Hartzheim and S. Mamber, eds., *The Franchise Era: Managing Media in the Digital Economy*. Edinburgh: Edinburgh University Press, 233–55.

Hernández Hernández, Á.D., 2018. The Anime Industry, Networks of Participation, and Environments for the Management of Content in Japan. *Arts*, 7(42), 1–20. https://doi.org/10.3390/arts7030042.

Ito, M., 2006. Japanese Media Mixes and Amateur Cultural Exchange. In D. Buckingham and R. Willett, eds., *Digital Generations: Children, Young People, and the New Media*. Abingdon: Lawrence Erlbaum Associates, Inc, 49–66.

———., 2008. Mobilizing the Imagination in Everyday Play: The Case of Japanese Media Mixes. In K. Drotner and S. Livingstone, eds., *The International Handbook of Children, Media and Culture*. Los Angeles: Sage, 397–412.

Jenkins, H., 2006. *Convergence Culture: Where Old and New Media Collide*. New York: New York University Press.

Johnson, D., 2013. *Media Franchising: Creative License and Collaboration in the Culture Industries*. New York: New York University Press.

Joo, W., Denison, R. and Furukawa, H. 2013 *Manga Movies Project Report 1: Transmedia Franchising*. Norwich: University of East Anglia. Available at: https://www.academia.edu/3693690/Manga_Movies_Project_Report_1_-_Transmedia_Japanese_Franchising [Accessed 17 April 2020].

Kadokawa, H., 2005 [1977]. *Waga tōsō* [My Struggle]. Tokyo: East Press.

Kobayashi, T., 2017. The Media Theory and Media Strategy of Azuma Hiroki, 1997–2003. In M. Steinberg and A. Zahlten, eds., *Media Theory in Japan*. Durham: Duke University Press, 80–100.

Lamarre, T., 2009. *The Anime Machine: A Media Theory of Animation*. Minneapolis: University of Minnesota Press.

———., 2018. *The Anime Ecology: A Genealogy of Television, Animation, and Game Media*. Minneapolis: University of Minnesota Press.

McLelland, M. and Welker, J., 2015. An Introduction to "Boys Love" in Japan. In M. McLelland, K. Nagaike, K. Suganuma and J. Welker, eds., *Boys Love Manga and Beyond: History, Culture and Community in Japan*. Jackson: University of Mississippi Press, 1–20.

Ogonoski, M., 2014. Cosplaying the Media Mix: Examining Japan's Media Environment, its Static Forms, and its Influence on Cosplay. *Praxis* 16 [online]. Available at: https://journal.transformativeworks.org/index.php/twc/article/view/526/439 [Accessed 17 April 2020].

Ōtsuka, E., 2010. World and Variation: The Reproduction and Consumption of Narrative Author(s). M. Steinberg, trans. In F. Lunning, ed., *Mechademia: Second Arc: Fanthropologies*. Vol. 5. Minneapolis: University of Minnesota Press, 99–116.

Rendell, J., 2018. Bridge Builders, World Makers: Transcultural Studio Ghibli Fan Crafting. *East Asian Journal of Popular Culture*, 4(1), 93–109.

Steinberg, M., 2006. Immobile Sections and Trans-Series Movement: *Astroboy* and the Emergence of Anime. *Animation: An Interdisciplinary Journal*, 1(2), 190–206.

———., 2012. *Anime's Media Mix: Franchising Toys and Characters in Japan*. Minneapolis: University of Minnesota Press.

———., 2015. *Naze Nihon wa "media mikkusu suru kuni" nanoka* [Why is Japan a "media mixing nation"?]. Nakagawa Y. and Ōtsuka E., trans. Tokyo: Kadokawa E-Pub/Kadokawa Gakugei Shuppan.

———., 2017. Media Mix Mobilization: Social Mobilization and *Yo-kai Watch*. *Animation: An Interdisciplinary Journal*, 12(3), 244–58.

———., 2019. *The Platform Economy: How Japan Transformed the Consumer Internet*. Minneapolis: University of Minnesota Press.

Suan, S., 2018. Consuming Production: Anime's Layers of Transnationality and Dispersal of Agency as Seen in *Shirobako* and *Sakuga*-Fan Practices. *Arts*, 7(27), 19. https://doi.org/10.3390/arts7030027.

Tobin, J., 2004. Conclusion: The Rise and Fall of the Pokémon Empire. In J. Tobin, ed., *Pikachu's Global Adventure: The Rise and Fall of Pokémon*. Durham: Duke University Press, 257–92.

Wyatt, J., 1994. *High Concept: Movies and Marketing in Hollywood*. Austin: University of Texas Press.

Zahlten, A., 2014. Media Mix and the Metaphoric Economy of the World. In D. Miyao, ed., *The Oxford Handbook of Japanese Cinema*. Oxford: Oxford University Press, 440–56.

———., 2017a. 1980s *Nyū Aka*: (Non)Media Theory as Romantic Performance. In M. Steinberg and A. Zahlten, eds., *Media Theory in Japan*. Durham: Duke University Press, 200–20.

———., 2017b. *The End of Japanese Cinema: Industrial Genres, National Times and Media Ecologies*. Durham: Duke University Press.

Chapter 9
Nihilistamina: Gloomy Heroisms in Contemporary Anime

Artur Lozano-Méndez and Antonio Loriguillo-López

In contrast with optimistic shōnen protagonists, some Japanese popular franchises focus on characters that deal with psychological traumas and despondency. These young protagonists are saddled with responsibilities such as the survival of humankind. They carry out their assumed duties regardless of their mental instability. Even as reversals of fortune keep piling up, they press forward as if they had no other option. They will go as far as to sacrifice themselves for a world they reject. This chapter analyzes these works and explores the reasons why these nihilists with stamina have gained so much traction in the last decades.

Introduction: From zero to (loath) hero

In his study of the ecosystem of *Weekly Shōnen Jump*, one of the most influential weekly manga magazines since its advent in 1968 and especially since the 1980s, Bryan Hikari Hartzheim argues that although it has become a highly sophisticated publication in terms of production routines adapted to new forms of content consumption, its foundational motto "Friendship, Effort, Victory" continues to be the driving force behind the drafts that circulate at Shueisha offices (2019, 5). This seems logical considering the stable demand for the demographic genre *shōnen* (manga for boys) since the consolidation of the manga and anime markets in the 1970s. So much so that *shōnen* is the main culprit for the widespread identification of both Japanese comics and animation with the stories of self-improvement, positive values and happy endings that have dominated the market up to now.

Shōnen stories starring young action heroes have been distributed all over the world, and their sway has been acknowledged by successive Japanese administrations, which have co-opted the genre for cultural diplomacy actions. One of the most memorable moments of such diplomacy on a global scale came at the Rio 2016 Olympics closing ceremony with the brief presentation of the Tokyo 2020 Olympics (postponed to 2021 because of the COVID-19 pandemic). The inclusion of well-known figures such as Doraemon and *supokon* stars (a paradigmatic *shōnen* sub-genre) such as Tsubasa Oozora in the presentation sequence of the Japanese capital alongside athletes and Prime Minister Abe Shinzō is evidence of the extreme popularity of these heroes and their affinity with the Olympic creed: "[T]he most important thing in life is not the triumph but the struggle. The essential thing is not to have conquered but to have fought well" (The Olympic Museum 2007, 5). The self-affirmative resilience in the face of conflict displayed by canonical characters of the genre such as Goku (*Dragon Ball*), Monkey D. Luffy (*One Piece*) or Uzumaki Naruto occurs within coordinates of bright and constant optimism, even in realistic representations of a loser (e.g., Sakuragi Hanamichi in *Slam Dunk*). In all these cases, the design of the psychological dimension of the protagonists has much to do with both the classical journey of the hero (Campbell 2004) and, more specifically, with the exalted kabuki *aragoto*.[1] The *shōnen* protagonist is eager to prove his worth, has a natural aptitude for his occupation/sport and keeps a hard-working and collaborative attitude that is put forth with a smile that is difficult to break. Some of their battles can be bloody, and these heroes and heroines can express rage and even desperation. Still, the reader/viewer feels that such trials are narrative devices meant to instill a *tachiagare* (get on your feet) ethos.

The eminence of *shōnen*, a topic highlighted in manga and anime studies in recent years (Denison 2015), should not distract us from the emergence of other types of protagonists, less conventional, but which have attracted the attention of both critics and audiences in the last twenty-five years. In this chapter, we trace the emergence of a new archetype in Japanese commercial animation: the nihilistamina hero/heroine (hereinafter "NH," and "NHs" for the plural). To name this kind of character, we have resorted to a portmanteau of words that summarize their frame of mind. Relentless *nihilism* and beyond-belief *stamina* are the most striking features of these protagonists. Paradoxically, their dispirited disposition and their commitment to engage with demands support each other rather than cancelling each other out.

NHs are young people (some of them are *shōnen* and *shōjo*, but some are *seinen*/*josei*, young adults or just adults) saddled either with mental health issues or severe psychological scarring. Often, they are characters that deal with major traumas and grapple with despondency. It is frequent in *shōnen* to have the protagonist lose a dear family member or suffer some other trauma, and that becomes the catalyst for the character's growth. Unlike the Olympian bouncing back performed by *shōnen* protagonists, NHs never quite recover from the loss or grief, which becomes a ghostly, palpable presence in their journey. Because of its treatment, death is more consequential in nihilistamina fiction than in other genres. The NH harbors lingering guilt that translates to ceaseless self-doubt.

In many of these works,[2] young protagonists are burdened with such responsibilities as the survival of all humanity. They carry out their assumed duties regardless of their lack of self-worth. Even as the tragedies and reversals of fortune pile up, they press forward, reasoning that they have no other course of action (all the other options are out of the question). In a disturbingly nihilistic and unrelenting setting, these unlikely heroes, who lack confidence and conviction, who are not stoic hard-boiled types, exhibit a stamina that tests the viewer's suspension of disbelief. They will go as far as to sacrifice themselves for the slim chance of having a positive impact in a world that disgusts them. Despite their reluctant heroism, these characters are featured in some of the most influential titles in recent years in the anime scene. Ikari Shinji, the alienated teenaged pilot from the *EVA*[3] franchise has become the model of subsequent taciturn NHs, such as Homura Akemi (*Madoka*), and Levi and Mikasa Ackerman[4] (*AoT*), voted the best characters of the year by *Newtype* magazine (one of the most renowned *otaku* tribunes), in 2011 and 2013, respectively. In addition to the popularity acquired from their related manga translated into several languages, these series have also had successful distributions in adult-oriented night-time programming blocks such as Fuji TV's Noitamina or Cartoon Network's Adult Swim, and have been recognized with major awards from both the industry itself and critics.[5]

We will describe features of nihilistamina stories (hereafter NS) that distinguish them from *shōnen*, *shōjo*, and *seinen* genres. Although we are tackling a classification of the "functions of the dramatis personae" à la Vladimir Propp (2009, 25–66), we are not aiming to be fully comprehensive. We will discuss the ones that we think are more recursive and representative. Also, what delineates the NS subgenre are not particular functions (or actions), not even a set preference regarding the distribution of functions among characters ("spheres of action," Propp 2009, 79). Although a few functions seem more fundamental to the morphology of NS than to the premises of other genres, most of the elements that we will examine can be found in other genres. The NH is set apart from other heroic archetypes not because of the essence of the experiences that they endure (other heroes/heroines also bear trauma and loss), but because of the quality (the dimension of the inflicted damage and its sequels) and accumulation of such actions, and because of their lack of heroic resolve while performing the same actions as the more numerous plucky paragons of virtue.

We use the term "nihilism" as a descriptor of the outlook and the gloomy state of mind of the NHs that populate the animations that we consider to form the NS genre. NS feature protagonists that cannot bring themselves to find meaning in the social structure and the reality around them. If the optimistic attitude of main *shōnen* characters often seems unwarranted, the nihilistic outlook of the protagonists in NS stories is actually supported by the nihilistic universe being built by the creators. As the fiction mostly focalizes on the protagonists, we too witness their world sliding towards a grieving absurdity (regardless of whether the rest of humanity faces the same hell or if it concerns only the main characters).

We consider that NS stands as a genre, as its own narrative modality, because it presents a recursive set of functions and spheres of action (archetypes, although the actions of a sphere can be distributed among different characters). It also exhibits consistent narrative treatment and psychological complexity, characterized by an unflinching exploration of the darker recesses of society and the human mind. NS revolves around protagonists whose origin and vicissitudes, secondary characters and interpersonal dynamics, align with those usually found in *shōnen*, although the treatment of the situations, relationships, and story beats[6] put NS also in *seinen* territory. Due to the extreme trials that they endure and the threats that they are subjected to, NS fictions are for the most part not set in a realistic environment. On the other hand, there is no default world-building setting that we associate with NS. Thus, both *Ergo Proxy* and *Beruseruku* qualify as NS even though one belongs in SF, and the other in fantasy.

Building on the work by researchers in the history of genres, Rayna Denison claims "that genres are never definable, because they are always *in process*" (2015, 20, italics in original). One could use "NS" also as a subgenre denomination (in the way that *supokon* and *mahō shōjo* are considered subgenres of *shōnen* and *shōjo*, respectively), or we could regard NS as a term defining a trend that is replicated among works from different subgenres (mecha, historical fiction, etc). While we stand in the "genre" camp, our goal is to draw attention to the characters, conflicts and storytelling strategies favored by the works identified as NS—we do not want to bog down this study by pursuing academic disquisitions about taxonomies. These creative endeavors started at the margins of hegemonic modalities of fiction and are slowly moving to more mainstream spaces and channels of distribution (Loriguillo-López 2016).

To substantiate the existence of this archetype, we develop the figure of NHs through two main axes: the trauma that determines their existence, and their particular sense of responsibility. While our goal is a description of the genre, we also draft a provisional hypothesis that relates the popularity of NS to an increasing perception of exhaustion of capitalism (that in turn wears down its subjects), the seeping precariousness of labor, and the persisting generation gap in the social distribution of wealth and opportunities in Japan (Lozano-Mendez 2019).

After the Triple Disaster of the Tōhoku earthquake, tsunami and nuclear meltdown hit Japan, the anxieties among the Japanese reached new heights, and it became increasingly difficult to hold a positive outlook for the future. In 2007, Japan ranked second in the poverty rank of the OECD[7] with a rate of 15.3 (the first position was occupied by the US) (Allison 2013, 5). Therefore, almost 20 million live under that threshold (of a total population of 126.8 million), or more than one in every six Japanese. The unemployment rate, which reached a peak 5.5 percent in 2009, decreased consistently during the following years and, as of December 2019, it was 2.2 percent (Statistics Bureau of Japan). As flexibilization has encroached on regular as well as non-regular employment, the issue for most Japanese is not finding some job (not even when the unemployment rate was higher), but rather finding a good job (usually defined in terms of permanent employment, pay, hours, working conditions, benefits and protections, etc.) and being able to keep it and build a career (Watanabe 2018).

As these social ailments afflict many other countries, the global appeal of NS works has increased. That factor, paired with the creative investment of the creators and the remarkable quality and achievements of most of these works, has contributed to the international success and notoriety of many of these NS anime and manga.

Trauma

Traumatized characters are increasingly frequent in audio-visual post-classicism. The *mise-en-scène* of hopelessness, weakness and the futility of existence allows these stories to rise up into meaningful allegories for contemporary viewers, who witness the perpetual (re) representation of national trauma. The post-classical narratives also capture the transition from the paradigm of the unblemished action hero/heroine to the typically complex contemporary protagonist, "[s]carred and wounded, heroic nonetheless" (Shimpach 2010, 189).

The treatment of trauma in NS plots carries more weight than it does in most *shōnen* fictions.[8] Many of the NS fictions spend a little more time on average in setting up the loss or traumatic episode (thus, while *Vinland Saga* may look as prototypically *shōnen* as *Kimetsu no yaiba*, it is decidedly NS in this aspect). The weight of the setup is not released and discarded the morning after, following a resolution by the protagonist that will be reified as fate (this is often the case in other treatments of these plot premises). The effects of the trauma linger and they are embodied (sometimes somatized) and apparent in the NHs. There is, quite often, a piling up of hurt, either as a victim or as witness, and sometimes even as self-loathing perpetrator. On top of that, as the talent that particularizes the hero becomes apparent (see below "NHs sacrifice for the sake of mankind"), they are tasked with redressing the suffering of fellow team members, aiding revolutionary/messianic figures, or saving all of humankind. If

NS is mostly *shōnen* with a distinct treatment, the orders of magnitude are one of the salient features of such treatment –the magnitudes of both the trauma and the anxiety about their befallen responsibility set the NH apart from other heroic types.

Finally, magnitude does not allude to their disturbing experiences being necessarily more gruesome and more frequent than those suffered by more optimistic *shōnen* heroes (morbid accounting would not contribute to our understanding of these character types) nor are we implying that traditional *shōnen* heroes are not tasked sometimes with saving the planet. Magnitude alludes to the scarring on the character's psychology and their outlook on the world. The first trauma opens the door to nihilism, and the following ones prevent the wounds from healing up completely, thus the scar is never closed for good, and nihilism keeps seeping in.

Trauma and nihilism in anime

While nihilism is a noticeable strand in the plot threading of other popular series, we are not talking about more familiar configurations of youth disaffection or alienation—e.g., *Sora yori mo tōi basho*, *Sangatsu no raion* and *Kareshi kanojo no jijō* (Kare Kano). Some of their characters may either be fundamentally nihilistic or go through nihilistic phases, but the slice-of-life interactions prevent the world from being totally bleak. That is, NS works effectively reify the world as nihilistic by nature. In these other works, no one demands the ultimate sacrifice from the young protagonists, although they undoubtedly endure severe mental strain, for instance, competing to be the most brilliant and acclaimed student, or to win successive and increasingly difficult *shōgi* tournaments.

It is in this context of Heisei-era awakenings to the precariousness of the postwar dream that we understand the emergence of cynical and (literally) selfless heroes. Probably the most emblematic case of traumatized existence within NS settings is Ikari Shinji. The protagonist of *EVA* is perhaps the paradigmatic archetype of a character who struggles with the experience of various traumas (the death of his mother, parental neglect, the near-death experiences of citizens under his care and of his fellow pilots, for whom he takes responsibility). Although he manages to overcome some of the obstacles and save the day on more than one occasion, Shinji's nihilism—absolute denial of his own value and certainty of the meaninglessness of existence—leads him to think of himself more as a victim of circumstances than as a hero. As Michael Berman vehemently states, "Shinji is the hero who longs not to be the hero" (in Tsang 2016, 39–40).

In *Madoka*, Kaname Madoka is a carefree fourteen-year-old adolescent until her encounter with Kyubey. With its high-pitched voice, stuffed animal form, and harmless demeanor, Kyubey presents itself to Madoka as an alien capable of granting her any wish. In return, she has to become Puella Magi (a *mahō shōjo*). Madoka accompanies Kyubey and veteran Puella Magi Tomoe Mami in their battles against their natural enemies: the witches. It is not until the traumatic murder of Mami by a witch that Kyubey's increasingly insistent attempts to convert Madoka are thwarted. As she remains shocked by the images of Mami's mutilation, Madoka begins to realize that Kyubey has not been honest about its origin and its motivation to grant powers. Later Kyubey itself reveals that the mission of his species is to maintain the entropic equilibrium of the universe at all costs. In order to do so, they approach *shōjo* in their most vulnerable moments in order to make use of what they value as one of the purest and most powerful energies, the emotional bursts of *mahō shōjo*. Thus, the feelings of hope generated by the Puella Magi when they see their desires fulfilled are counterbalanced by their polar opposite, the despair that feeds witches.

Trauma and memory: Amnesiac NHs

A subtype of these traumatized protagonists is that of the amnesiac hero/heroine, the center of the story of foundational puzzle films such as the character Leonard Shelby is to *Memento* (see Buckland 2009). The instability of these characters as focalizers results in a twisting of the plot that prevents the generation of a strong enough causal relationship for viewers to build a coherent story during much of the footage. A recurrent motif in puzzle films, which are very likely to be ascribed to the psycho-thriller genre, justifies the inaccuracies of the characters on whom the narrative focuses: their psychological instability resulting from various pathologies and the compounding anxiety (Hesselberth and Schuster 2008). All these ingredients come together in representative cases of NS works.

In the celebrated light novel by Sakurazaka Hiroshi, *All You Need Is Kill*,[9] the NH, private Kiriya Keiji, becomes taciturn and obsessive about his training to perfection. Nausea creeps up on him and fellow time-looper Rita Vrataski as they progress in their learning curve to defeat the alien Mimics. As he goes through a loop over 150 times, the protagonist turns into a Laplace's demon[10] of those 30 hours in that environment. Kiriya knows everything that goes on in that frame and all the causal relations that may be established. The narration then proceeds to test the idea of determinism and how it would affect a conventional conscience instead of a superhuman, or demonic, one.

Oshii Mamoru's adaptation in 2008 of Mori Hiroshi's alternative history novel *Sukai kurora*, depicts young men and women deprived of their memories, and who are trapped inside a cycle of certain death. These "kildren," quintessential amnesiac NHs, are destined to be the cannon fodder at the service of a televised war game set by private corporations. To properly cater to this postmodern society of the spectacle (Debord 2005, 27, 28), corporations clone young pilots as "supplies" for the aircraft battles. Kannami Yūichi and the rest of kildren from his base not only need to face the threat of dying in a dogfight, but also the certainty of being replaceable (Lozano-Méndez 2015).

Despondency

The NHs are mostly teenagers, or sometimes young adults—Vincent in *Ergo Proxy*, Tsunemori in *Psycho-Pass*. Adults push upon them responsibilities that would be overwhelming even for the most skilled and cool-headed grown-up.[11] The characters internalize a sense of despondency since they do not feel that they are in control of their lives, and the people who should prioritize their welfare are the ones thrusting them into deadly situations. This predicament feeds back into their sense of being cut off and it often breeds resentment towards their "superiors." Sometimes the narration draws attention to this by having an adult supporting character comment on how the protagonist has been robbed of their childhood/youth (Leif in *Vinland Saga*, Misato in *EVA*).

Unlike mythological demigods, folk heroes and sacred religious figures, only a few NHs test the limits of what the audience can accept as feasible in human terms (*Beruseruku*, *Kurozuka*, *Vinland Saga*, *Wolf's Rain*). These NH are endowed with extraordinary strength and reflexes, but they become heroic by rote training or battling. Some *shōnen* characters are superhuman *before* they start training, although the training is required to fully materialize their superhuman capabilities.[12] On the other hand, NHs are technical heroes: they become skilled by sheer repetition and after a number of reversals (often the enemy becomes a metaphorical teacher as the character nicknamed "Teacher" in *Sukai kurora*, or a real teacher, as Askeladd does in *Vinland Saga*). In NS there is a real sense that the stakes are high and that, regardless of the nihilistic loop, NH could die at the next challenge.

Contrary to most *shōnen* fictions, the anxiety derived from having to live like this takes a toll, which compounds the lingering effects of the original trauma. Different elements index the strain—body language, facial expression, moodiness and a nihilistic worldview, listless social interactions. NHs have no real coping mechanism to deal with the situations in which they find themselves. Their strategy for "enduring the unendurable" is to withdraw themselves into the mantra-cum-topos "I have to go on":

> *I can't go on, you must go on, I'll go on,* you must say words, as long as there are any, *until they find me,* until they say me, *strange pain, strange sin, you must go on, perhaps it's done already, perhaps they have said me already, perhaps they have carried me to the threshold of my story, before the door that opens on my story, that would surprise me, if it opens, it will be I, it will be the silence, where I am, I don't know, I'll never know, in the silence you don't know, you must go on,* I can't go on, I'll go on. (Beckett 2009, 407; our emphasis)

Nevertheless, there are moments when words cannot prop them up, spaces where they are lost for words. Thus, they snap and fall into silence. This sometimes happens when the NHs are knocked down in a battle, some of them go limp or refuse to get up while the supporting characters pick up the "slack."

When they have these breakdowns, their mind finds refuge in dreams stemming out of the Imaginary. In these dreams, the person they lost is by their side. S/he acts as a mirror and allows for the reconstruction of the protagonist's dismembered ego (e.g., Thorfinn and Canute in *Vinland Saga*). Another possibility is for them to wilfully remain unconscious, senseless, thus aligning with another Lacanian concept, the Real. Falling into all-encompassing silence, the protagonists escape both the Imaginary and the Symbolic. They join a fundamental unity undifferentiated by words, where they can both discard their ego and avert any more confrontations (both Eren and Shinji are depicted in ways reminiscent of a baby in a womb).

These psychological complexities and the fact that many creators do not shun from showing unsavory recesses of the human mind lead to another widely shared trait of NS narratives from the point of view of the audiences—quite often the leads are unnerving, unlikable. This feature sets them apart from the antihero archetype of modern times, who regardless of their moral ambiguity are always charismatic and appealing (either as the silent tough figure or as the lovable, witty rogue).

The motivations of nihilists: Responsibilities and commitment in NS

The attitude of the NH regarding their responsibilities is ambivalent. Some characters welcome the "task" initially because their trauma claims for retribution, because they believe that solving a larger social issue will also solve their personal ones, etc. Regardless, at some point of the arc, it starts to look as if the protagonists would just as soon get rid of a mission that they perceive as foisted on them. One thing NHs would have going for them is that, regardless of the very real nihilism that they feel and manifest, in the end, they just press forward.

These NHs seem willing/resigned to sacrifice themselves for the cause that gives purpose to their vicissitudes. They acknowledge the premise of the story that makes it impossible for them to avoid their fate. For instance, Kiriya Keiji is trapped in a time loop, and he is killed when he tries to run away from his military base; Eren is a weapon himself, one that can change the course of the conflict; Shinji is the pilot that can achieve higher scores of compatibility and integration with the interface of the *EVA* robots, etc. The fact that they either do not have options—or that they do not feel they have any real alternatives—paradoxically hollows out, or at least diminishes, their heroism as they face likely lethal (when not outright suicidal) situations. Moreover, the narration drags the supposed higher purpose of the characters across the mud. For instance, the protagonists often realize that they serve a corrupt or morally dubious authority, or they have to acknowledge the humanity of an enemy that was supposed to remain teratological. Thus, the actions and sacrifices that the NH has performed so far are rendered pointless.

Regardless of social pressure and their level of self-indoctrination, NHs could always bow out of their predicament. The motives behind their persistence are not conventional ones or, rather, those motives reflect the conventionalisms of this day and age. The genealogy of the values endorsed in our present shows that the new values are not that removed from the old, especially as regards to practical effects and to preserving the structure of power in society. NHs do not endure out of an old-fashioned sense of honor and duty, although that may exert some influence. They know that honor is a discourse that favors the interests of the privileged and of people far from the front lines. The NHs do not profess an unconditional love of country nor have they undergone thorough institutionalization—they are acquainted with rotten apples in their organization and in the upper echelons of power. They are not fanatics with an outlook similar to 16th-century *ikkō ikki* warring monks (*sōhei*), who saw death in the service of their sect as the doorway into Pure Land paradise. While NHs often cling (for dear life indeed) to their human connections, they cannot regard their friends or colleagues as redeemers of everything that is wrong with society and the world at large. First of all, those friends are not perfect, and relationships are problematic. Second, the world, or at least the situation of the NH, is irredeemable however we slice it. Third, the ethical compass of the NH would not allow him/her to saddle another person with the task of ensuring his/her mental balance.

NS narrations make it clear that the reasons why heroines/heroes comply with the plea to sacrifice themselves have nothing to do with prospects of picture-perfect relationships. Such idealistic personal connections have no place in a nihilistic universe. They would be conjured just to showcase that the NH will never enjoy one. Worse, they could be the setting of their original trauma—it is often the case that an ideal family, relative, love interest, etc., is butchered, sometimes for no material reason (if the perpetrator gains nothing out of it, then the crime is rendered meaningless).

Sometimes, the actants that could play a role as a "holographic entry point" (Kasulis 2004, loc. 470) into the whole of humanity also play a role as mediums of ghosts of the past. Such is the case of Mikasa and Eren (*AoT*). Both experienced the same trauma of watching parents die gruesomely. Since Mikasa was adopted, she loses parents for a second time. She is more a tragic, stoic heroine than Eren, the apparent NH of the story, who often compares himself unfavorably with her. Ayanami Rei was made in the image of Shinji's mother and receives the fatherly love that Shinji never had (*EVA*). All these elements would burden the relationship between Rei and Shinji, even if she returned his attention. Tsunemori's colleagues are all criminals on parole (*Psycho-Pass*), and so developing a bond with them would hinder her ability to execute would-be murderers. Consequently, the heroism that had been hollowed out of egotistic heroism is rendered praiseworthy again, as NH would sacrifice themselves for people who are also broken, traumatized, and not always pleasant to be around.

Instilling despair: minima 'minna!' moralia

The concern for the welfare of their friends and/or crew is among the only sources of existential payoff for NHs. Thus, NS narrations will sometimes resort to the manganime trope that we call "*minna…!* moments." These are deployed when the beleaguered protagonist has been saved (or has their spirits lifted up) by supporting characters. This visual trope features a close-up of a teary-eyed protagonist who expresses their appreciation with a heartfelt "*Minna…!*" ("You guys…!").[13] Besides the attachment to people in their restricted social circle, there is a second motivator in the NH's perseverance—an awareness of essential kinship with humanity, particularly innocents that are at risk of suffering traumas similar to the ones that scarred the NH. Indeed, the protagonists could equally be moved when the population, the common folk, act virtuously in a situation where the audience would expect an "each man for himself" behavior.

Given the general nihilistic tone of these productions, *minna…!* moments are usually few and far between. The authors do not backpedal the portrayal of the world as mostly unredeemable nor suddenly fall into *supokon* team *ganba*rism. In a different narratological approach, it would have been perfectly plausible to turn a *minna…!* moment into a holographic re-entry point into humanity, a gateway into more fulfilling everyday connections and interactions. Instead, many of these works favor a conclusion that is far removed from Hollywood denouements tied with a bow. Sometimes, they are not even resolutions, and we stop being witnesses to the characters' life at a point that might even seem arbitrary. Among the NS fictions we listed, the closest one gets to a happy ending is *EVA*—having Shinji grow into accepting that nothing will make up for everything he finds lacking in his past and in present-day human interactions. Thus, he comes to grips with the limitations of human relations as well as his own shortcomings. Some other works are unrelenting, offering no compromise with nihilism and thus reaching a grim ending: *Madoka*, *Higurashi*, *Wolf's Rain*, *Ergo Proxy*, etc. Finally, there are ongoing franchises that have pummelled their protagonists for so long that any defeat of their nemesis at some point in the future will necessarily be a pyrrhic, hollow victory—*Berserk* and *AoT* are clear-cut cases.

NHs sacrifice for the sake of mankind

In the popular culture of Japan and elsewhere, sacrificial attitudes represented in popular culture tend to be rewarded—not only do the heroes/heroines not die, but they manage to save the threatened ones and to restore balance. In the case of tragic heroes, they have to experience some loss or sacrifice and, if they survive, they cannot bask in the light of the peace they have restored. NS fictions blow the misfortune out of proportion. The sacrifice of NHs is never consummated, or it takes a long time to arrive, while those near-and-dear to them either die or are transformed beyond recognition (sometimes revealing a hidden nature).

While the die-hard condition of the NH can be chalked up to demands of the classical mode of narration,[14] piling even more traumas laden with survivor's guilt stems from a choice of the authors.

In the twelfth episode of *Madoka*, the protagonist Kaname Madoka is finally transformed into a Puella Magi. This implies a supreme sacrifice, since throughout the plot it is revealed that, despite getting a wish granted in return, the inevitable fate of all Puella Magi is to become a "Witch." Madoka's wish is therefore surprising: "I want to erase all witches before they are even born. I will erase every single witch in every universe, past and future with my own hands" (Ep. 12, 01:35–01:57). At the apotheosis of her sacrifice, Madoka transcends her humanity and becomes an eternal protective entity of all the Puella Magi of all times. Far from embellishing the journey of the heroines, *Madoka's* plot flees from the idealization of the normativity of *mahō shōjo* to expose their dramatic flaws.

Higurashi's Furude Rika, an adolescent *miko*, is another case of bottomless stamina in terms of traumatic abnegation. The dramatic swap in the role of the main focalizer in the start of the second season of *Higurashi* is absolutely crucial for the filing of Rika under the NH archetype. Knowing that her death is the event that triggers the total annihilation of her village, Rika must assimilate the recurring traumas of death threats, and the ad nauseam repetition of the violent chain of events that lead to them, in order to save her community. Even though Rika tries hard to handle her pain on her own, putting on a brave face in order to not involve her dear friends, her tragic nihilism, a consequence of the emotional distress wearing her away, eventually emerges in her internal monologues.

Both Ikari Shinji and Kiriya Keiji become determined to sacrifice themselves to save everyone once their fighting becomes the lifeline of the human race in the face of alien invasion. Further from the character-centric *sekaikei* premise of these bombastic fantasies and SF, *Psycho-Pass's* Kogami Shin'ya embodies the fundamental contradiction of NHs in terms of sacrifice. As an *enforcer*, he is an individual demoted by the very society which has rejected him as a police officer. In turn, the establishment still requires him as a public safety bureau member, although under the condition of being justifiably disposable if his actions overstep the orders of Inspectors such as Tsunemori. Thus, Kogami not only faces the repudiation of society, but is also threatened with death by the very peers that he has been commanded to protect with his own life.

Conclusions: An age of reluctant champions

Humankind has always relied on myths and narrations to make sense of the world. Heroes and heroines (be they ordinary people in exceptional situations or superhumans) have worked as myths of the modern age. Thus, people will exchange memes featuring John Wick as an epitome of rightful wrath, they produce and stream shows discussing hero narratives, they will cosplay as their favorite anime characters. The heroes of Antiquity were exalted in scholarly traditions as subjects with a will that empowered them to intervene into an impermanent, unreliable world, following their own appraisal and asserting their own judgement (Thiele 1990). In modern times, after the taming of the self-affirming hero figure, the heroes have been a very active channel in the social reproduction of the Kantian approach to ethics ruled by the categorical imperative. One suspects that the myths of old, as those of the present, may have acted as galvanizers for self-actualization, but that most of the time they acted as balms against the unintelligible parcels of the world. Indeed, much has been written about how and why myths, and their heroes, do not have to be consistent and submit to reason. While NS fictions do not resemble Greek hero tales (except, perhaps, that of Medea and Jason), their account of human misery can also be both unsettling and soothing.

After *Astro Boy*'s Atom, the mecha protagonist evolves into a sombre youngster, relatable enough for the consolidation of series such as *Space Battleship Yamato* or *Gundam*. The onset of the original video animation format (OVA) was instrumental for the development of "adult anime" (Denison 2015, 92) in the eighties. Since then, darker heroes/heroines, once relegated only to niche markets of the domestic video market, proliferate. These murky champions and their mature stories have eventually found their space in the late-night slots (*shin'ya*, 11:30 p.m.–3:30 a.m.) of cable and satellite private networks. At present, the daily hours of anime broadcast at night have overtaken anime broadcast during daytime (Masuda et al. 2018, 5). This is the context of the emergence of both NS and NHs. It would be all too easy to write NS off as a strategy from weekly *shōnen* magazines and anime production committees[15] to exploit teenage angst commercially, but these productions are not pandering to the *shōnen/shōjo* youngsters (the NHs are not aspiring role models, nor are they a pleasant mirror) and NS fiction is consumed by adults around the world as well. New genres are both a continuity and a break from tradition. They speak of the present but they reflect a past that is never settled (see Guarné et al. 2019; Martinez et al. 2019). NHs are the evolution of *shōnen/shōjo* heroes/heroines in a world that has no place for the latter.

The precariatization of Japanese society (Allison 2013; Cook 2013; Toivonen et al. 2011; Toivonen and Imoto 2013) made its media market ripe for the exploration (sometimes, exploitation) of social anxieties. Widely shared fears include not being able to form a family or secure economic stability, and experiencing first-hand the crumbling of structures and supports that seemed dependable until recently (Cook 2016; Lozano-Méndez 2019). Unlike the Japanese people, NHs are not people who were victimized into surrender and then devoted themselves rebuilding the country. It is not a matter of being victim first and then heroes/heroines because of how they deal with the blow. The NHs cannot be heroes unless they are cyclically submitted to extreme tests, but they have no egomaniac desire to be heroic. Considering Achilles, James Redfield said, "(t)he hero, after all, is not a model for imitation, but rather a figure who cannot be ignored; his special excellence is not integration but potency" (1979, ix). Some NHs have distinctive physical traits and so they cannot be ignored, but most of them would rather be effaced and (re-)integrated than potent and notorious.

There is a growing scholarly literature on how the scarcity, not just of career opportunities, but of a modicum of stability is driving psychological distress and low self-respect in the successive generations that have joined the labor market in the last three decades (cf. Inui et al. 2015; Kachi et al. 2014). With further trauma potentially waiting around every bend, nihilistamina narrations prime the Japanese to be the perfect victims, ones that can be asked to sacrifice themselves again and again, without subverting the established order of things. NS fictions also allow for cathartic representations of mental scarring and for problematic personalities that are far from "hero material"—sometimes the sorrowful extremes touch the carnivalesque. This is an approach that enables audiences to find, not quite nobility, but value in failure. The pathos of the traditional Japanese heroic figures who willingly wage "their forlorn struggle against overwhelming odds" (Morris 2014, loc. 148) only to meet failure is substituted by regular people thrust into that same heroic role, which they loathe but faithfully carry out until they meet a pyrrhic victory.

Handbook of Japanese Media and Popular Culture in Transition

We are not conjuring up cultural essentialist heuristics whereby Japanese are group-oriented and conflict-averse; the previous quote could apply to other markets. We believe the rationale for the success of NS internationally is, relatively speaking (let us steer clear of both *nihonjinron* and *interpretatio romana*), the same as in Japan. It is based on the increasing tension that economic structures are placing on citizens and their shrinking social networks of kinship and trust, which simply cannot make up for the lack of stability. The increase of the international precariat has created the environment whereby these Japanese NS works can become transnational commercial successes (thanks also to new channels of distribution that make these products more readily available to the general public).

Given the way we have spoken about NS so far, one would think that they are indeed a tool of "total society" in its pursuit of conformism (Adorno and Horkheimer 2002, 29). On the one hand, NS stories seem to put all the focus on pulling through and keeping individual sanity—thereby they might be accused of relinquishing any project of social reform from the outset. On the other hand, considering the actual reality inhabited by audiences, there is a progressive framing derived from encouraging audiences to come to grips with a hostile world, develop resilience and cultivate relationships even if they are not ideal. Due to the evolution of material conditions, the stamina against all odds of NS is inseparable from a structure of feeling (Williams 1965, 64–65) that highlights precariousness and inequality. This structure is lived in by a growing parcel of the population, and it was already consolidated before the advent of the COVID-19 pandemic in 2020.

Rather than absolute abandonment in the face of a widening gap society, NS fictions stake heroism as simply making it through the day, and tending to a few human connections without losing sight of shared humanity with everyone else. Indeed, sublimation can be an instrument of conformity, but the world-building of NS and the vicissitudes of NHs do not foster any false consciousness (Engels 1893) about how wealth and success are contingent to hard work, about the power of determination or the narrative of the self-made man/woman. Instead, they are a plea not to relinquish individual agency even if it seems more and more confined and less and less transcendent.

Acknowledgements

Artur Lozano-Méndez: This work was supported by the R+D research project 'New socio-cultural, political and economic developments in East Asia in the global context' (PID2019-107861GB-I00) granted by the Spanish Ministry of Science and Innovation to InterAsia Research Group at Universitat Autònoma de Barcelona.

Antonio Loriguillo-López: This work was supported by the Universitat Jaume I for the research project Análisis de identidades en la era de la posverdad. Generación de contenidos audiovisuales para una Educomunicación crítica under Grant code 18I390.01/1; and the Valencian Community and the European Social Fund through the post-doctoral scholarship program, under grant number APOSTD/2019/067

Notes

1   "*Aragoto*—A style of Kabuki acting for male characters that emphasizes roughness and bravado. It is largely indicative of the Edo style Kabuki acting. Usually, covered with *kumadori* make-up in red, these outrageously costumed characters are among the most popular during past and present performances." (Suan 2013, 323-324). Regarding the adaptation of such archetypes to animation, see Clements and McCarthy (2006, 618).

2   The reader will find a list of works, with broadcast dates, that we consider to be part of the NS genre appended to the chapter. As a caveat, we want to point out that not every feature analyzed here as a hallmark of the genre is present in all the NS fictions that we have identified.

3   See "Abbreviations List" at the end of the chapter.

4   While the narration is internally focalized on Eren Yaeger, there are chapters that focus on Mikasa and Levi's respective original traumas, and the emotional detachment of both characters aligns them with the NH pathos in an IP that is paradigmatic of what we call *nihilistamina*. Still, both of them would also qualify as a stoic, action hero(ine).

5   *Madoka* won the Animation Kobe (2011), the Animation Award at the 15th Japan Media Arts Festival (2011), the Sugoi Japan Anime Award (2015), and the Tokyo Anime Award Festival for the franchise movie, *Rebellion* (2014). *AoT* won the Animation Kobe (2013), and the Best Title at the Anime Grand Prix by *Animage* (2013).

6   By "story beats" we refer to turns of events—especially plot points concerning character evolution—that have become commonplace to a genre or character type.

7   "The poverty rate is the ratio of the number of people (in a given age group) whose income falls below the poverty line; taken as half the median household income of the total population." (OECD, Inequality—Poverty rate).

8   We trust the readers to seek plot summaries of the shows that they have not watched yet. Also, readers should keep in mind that we will speak of major plot points.

9   See also the two-volume manga adaptation by Obata Takeshi and Takeuchi Ryosuke. This light novel has not been adapted to anime, even though there is a Hollywood live-action film featuring a not-so-*shōnen* Tom Cruise (*Edge of Tomorrow*, 2014). Nevertheless, it is quintessentially NS and, in the cross-media environment of Japan, narrative genres are also transmedia, i.e., NS is not necessarily restricted to manga and anime.

10   Laplace's demon knows the position of every atom of the universe in an instant, and the demon can identify the causes of that distribution of atoms in the cosmos as well as the consequences that those atomic dynamics will entail at every level, even regarding the behavior of complex organisms.

11   Other creatures or devices can play the same role: authority figures (such as Kyubey in *Madoka*) or an imperative of nature (such as the instinct that drives Kiba in *Wolf's Rain*).

12   *Dragon Ball* is a schizophrenic push and pull between the dimension given to hereditary genetics and epigenetic (and somewhat sadistic) training.

13   When a single support character does the assist, different forms of addressing are used according to the perceived hierarchy and degree of familiarity (*anta*, *omae*, *kimi*, *temē*, etc.).

14   According to film theorist David Bordwell, the dominant mode of representation in Hollywood films still lives on in conventional filmmaking, and remains pretty much unchanged from its splendor between 1917 and 1960. This mode of representation is characterized by presenting stories where the characters are the main means for causality, stories which hold the unified plot of the central events of the diegesis under a beginning-middle-ending structure (Bordwell 1986).

15   See Condry (2009) for a review of all the commercial and transmedia marketing considerations that go into producing anime.

Abbreviation list

AoT	*Attack on Titan*
EVA	*Neon Genesis Evangelion*
Higurashi	*Higurashi When They Cry*
Madoka	*Puella Magi Madoka Magica*
NH	Nihilistamina heroine/hero
NS	Nihilistamina stories

Nihilistamina Works

All You Need Is Kill. Sakurazaka Hiroshi. 2009 (first published in Japan in 2004 by Shueisha Inc.). San Francisco: Haikasoru, VIZ Media. See also the two-volume manga adaptation by Obata Takeshi and Takeuchi Ryosuke.

Beruseruku [Berserk], 1997–1998. [TV series]. Directed by Takahashi Naohito. Tokyo: Nippon.

Ergo Proxy, 2006. [TV series]. Directed by Murase Shūkō. Tokyo: WOWOW.

Higurashi no Naku Koro ni [Higurashi When They Cry], 2006–2007. [TV series]. Directed by Chiaki Kon. Tokyo: NHK.

Kurozuka, 2008. [TV series]. Directed by Araki Tetsuro. Tokyo: Animax.

Mahō shōjo Madoka Magika [Puella Magi Madoka Magica], 2011. [TV series]. Directed by Shinbo Akiyuki. Tokyo: MBS.

Psycho-Pass, 2012–2013. [TV series]. Directed by Shiotani Naoyoshi and Motohiro Katsuyuki. Tokyo: Fuji TV.

Shingeki no kyojin [Attack on Titan], 2013–. [TV series]. Directed by Araki Tetsuro. Tokyo: MBS.

Shinseiki evangelion [EVA], 1995–1996. [TV series]. Directed by Anno Hideaki. Tokyo: TV Tokyo.

Sukai kurora [The Sky Crawlers], 2008. [Film]. Directed by Oshii Mamoru. Tokyo: NTV, Production I.G, Warner Bros. An adaptation of the homonymous novel by Mori Hiroshi.

Vinrando Saga—Vinland Saga, 2019-present. [TV series]. Directed by Yabuta Shūhei. Tokyo: NHK.

Wolf's Rain, 2003. [TV series]. Directed by Tensai Okamura. Chiba: Chiba TV.

Additional Videography

Doragon bōru [Dragon Ball], 1986–1988. [TV series]. Directed by Okazaki Minoru and Nishio Daisuke. Tokyo: FNS.

Edge of Tomorrow, 2014. [Film]. Directed by Doug Liman. Los Angeles: Warner Bros.

Kareshi kanojo no jijō [Kare Kano], 1998. [TV series]. Directed by Anno Hideaki and Sato Hiroki. Tokyo: TV Tokyo.

Kidō senshi gundam [Mobile Suit Gundam], 1979–1980. [TV series]. Directed by Tomino Yoshiyuki. Tokyo: Nagoya TV.

Kimetsu no yaiba [Demon Slayer: Kimetsu no Yaiba], 2019. [TV series]. Directed by Sotozaki Haruo. Tokyo: Tokyo MX.

Memento, 1999. [Film]. Directed by Christopher Nolan. Los Angeles: Newmarket Films.

Naruto, 2002–2007. [TV series]. Directed by Date Hayato. Tokyo: TXN.

One Piece, 1999–. [TV series]. Directed by Uda Konosuke. Tokyo: FNS.

Sangatsu no raion [March Comes in Like a Lion], 2016–2018. [TV series]. Directed by Shinbō Akiyuki. Tokyo: NHK G.

Slam Dunk, 1993–1996. [TV series]. Directed by Nishizawa Nobutaka. Tokyo: TV Asahi.

Sora yori mo tōi basho [A Place Further than the Universe], 2018. [TV series]. Directed by Ishizuka Atsuko. Tokyo: AT-X.

Uchū senkan Yamato [Space Battleship Yamato], 1974–1975. [TV series]. Directed by Matsumoto Reiji. Tokyo: Yomiuri TV.

Bibliography

Adorno, T. W. and Horkheimer, M., 2002. *Dialectic of Enlightenment*. Stanford: Stanford University Press.

Allison, A., 2013. *Precarious Japan*. Durham: Duke University Press.

Beckett, S., 2009. The Unnamable. In *Three Novels: Molloy, Malone Dies, The Unnamable*. New York: Grove Press.

Bordwell, D., 1986. *Narration in the Fiction Film*. London: Routledge.

Buckland, W., 2009. Introduction: Puzzle Plots. In W. Buckland, ed., *Puzzle Films: Complex Storytelling in Contemporary Cinema*. Malden: Wiley-Blackwell, 1–12.

Campbell, J., 2004. *The Hero with a Thousand Faces*. Princeton: Princeton University Press.

Clements, J. and McCarthy, H., 2006. *The Anime Encyclopedia: A Guide to Japanese Animation Since 1917*. London: Titan.

Cook, E., 2013. Expectations of Failure: Maturity and Masculinity for Freeters in Contemporary Japan. *Social Science Japan Journal*, 16(1), 29–43.

———., 2016. *Reconstructing Adult Masculinities. Part-Time Work in Contemporary Japan*. London: Routledge.

Condry, I., 2009. Anime Creativity: Characters and Premises in the Quest for Cool Japan. *Theory, Culture & Society*, 26(2-3), 139–63.

Debord, G., 2005. *Society of the Spectacle*. London: Rebel Press.

Denison, R., 2015. *Anime: A Critical Introduction*. London: Bloomsbury.

Eliot, T. S., 1934. Tradition and the Individual Talent (1917). In *T. S. Eliot—Selected Essays*. London: Faber and Faber.

Engels, F., 1893. Engels to Franz Mehring. London, July 14, 1893. In *Karl Marx and Friedrich Engels: Correspondence, 1846–1895* [online]. Available at: https://www.marxists.org/archive/marx/works/1893/letters/93_07_14.htm [Accessed 14 February 2020].

Guarné, B., Lozano-Méndez, A. and Martinez, D.P., 2019. The Politics of Media and Memory Representation in Japan. In B. Guarné, A. Lozano-Méndez and D.P. Martinez, eds., *Persistently Postwar—Media and the Politics of Memory in Japan*. New York: Berghahn Books, 1–19.

Hartzheim, B. H., 2019. Making of a Mangaka: Industrial Reflexivity and Shueisha's *Weekly Shōnen Jump*. *Television & New Media* [online]. Available at: https://journals.sagepub.com/doi/abs/10.1177/1527476419872132 [Accessed 17 June 2020].

Hesselberth, P. and Schuster, L., 2008. Into the Mind and Out to the World: Memory Anxiety in the Mind-Game Film. In J. Kooijman, P. Pisters and W. Strauven, eds., *Mind the Screen: Media Concepts According to Thomas Elsaesser*. Amsterdam: Amsterdam University Press, 96–111.

Inui, A., Higuchi, A. and Hiratsuka, M., 2015. Entering the Precariat: Young People's Precarious Transitions in Japan. In J. Wyn and H. Cahill, eds., *Handbook of Children and Youth Studies*. Singapore: Springer Singapore, 583–605.

Kachi, Y., Otsuka, T. and Kawada, T., 2014. Precarious Employment and the Risk of Serious Psychological Distress: A Population-Based Cohort Study in Japan. *Scandinavian Journal of Work, Environment & Health*, 40(5), 465–72.

Kasulis, T. P., 2004. *Shinto: The Way Home*. Honolulu: University of Hawai'i Press. Kindle Edition.

Loriguillo-López, A., 2016. ¿Cómo lo haría Haruhi? La construcción del media mix de Suzumiya Haruhi [How would Haruhi do it? The construction of Suzumiya Haruhi's media mix]. In Lozano-Méndez, A., ed., *El Japón contemporáneo. Una aproximación desde los estudios culturales* [Contemporary Japan: a cultural studies approach]. Barcelona: Edicions Bellaterra, 171–92.

Lozano-Méndez, A., 2015. Mamoru Oshii's Exploration of the Potentialities of Consciousness in a Globalised Capitalist Network. *ejcjs – Electronic Journal of Contemporary Japanese Studies*, 15(3) [online]. Available at: https://www.japanesestudies.org.uk/ejcjs/vol15/iss3/lozano-mendez.html [Accessed 17 June 2020].

———., 2019. Depicting the Persistence of Being Postwar: Eden of the East. In B. Guarné, A. Lozano-Méndez and D.P. Martinez, eds. *Persistently Postwar—Media and the Politics of Memory in Japan*. New York: Berghahn Books, 143–61.

Martinez, D.P., Guarné, B. and Lozano-Méndez, A., 2019. The Persistence of Trauma. In B. Guarné, A. Lozano-Méndez and D.P. Martinez, eds. *Persistently Postwar—Media and the Politics of Memory in Japan*. New York: Berghahn Books, 182–89.

Masuda, H., Sudo, T., Rikukawa, K., Mori, Y., Ito, N., and Kameyama, Y., 2018. Anime Industry Report 2017 Summary. Tokyo: Association of Japanese Animations (AJA).

Morris, I., 2014. *The Nobility of Failure. Tragic Heroes in the History of Japan*. Fukuoka: Kurodahan Press. Kindle Edition.

OECD, "Inequality—Poverty rate" [online]. Available at: https://data.oecd.org/inequality/poverty-rate.htm [Accessed 17 June 2020].

Olympic Museum, The, 2007. *The Olympic Symbols*. Lausanne.

Propp, V., 2009. *Morphology of the Folktale*. Austin: University of Texas Press.

Redfield, J., 1979. Foreword. In G. Nagy, *The Best of the Achaeans: Concepts of the Hero in Archaic Greek Poetry*. Baltimore: John Hopkins University Press.

Shimpach, S., 2010. *Television in Transition : The Life and Afterlife of the Narrative Action Hero*. Malden: Wiley-Blackwell.

Statistics Bureau of Japan: Labour Force Survey Monthly Results -December 2019 [online]. Available at: http://www.stat.go.jp/english/data/roudou/results/month/index.html [Accessed 17 June 2020].

Suan, S., 2013. *The Anime Paradox: Patterns and Practices Through the Lens of Traditional Japanese Theater.* Leiden: Global Oriental.

Thiele, L. P., 1990. *Friedrich Nietzsche and the Politics of the Soul: A Study of Heroic Individualism.* Princeton: Princeton University Press.

Toivonen, T., Norasakkunkit, V. and Uchida, Y., 2011. Unable to Conform, Unwilling to Rebel? Youth, Culture, and Motivation in Globalizing Japan. *Frontiers in Psychology,* 2, 207.

Toivonen, T. and Imoto, Y., 2013. Transcending Labels and Panics: The Logic of Japanese Youth Problems. *Contemporary Japan,* 25(1), 61–86.

Tsang, G. F. Y., 2016. Beyond 2015: Nihilism and Existentialist Rhetoric in Neon Genesis Evangelion. *Journal of International and Advanced Japanese Studies,* 8, 35–43.

Watanabe, H. R., 2018. Labour Market Dualism and Diversification in Japan. *British Journal of Industrial Relations,* 56(3), 579–602.

Williams, R., 1965. *The Long Revolution.* Harmondsworth: Pelican Books, Penguin.

Chapter 10

A Television Flagship Sailing the Currents of a Changing Media World: NHK's Morning Drama (*asadora*) in the 21st Century

Elisabeth Scherer

The morning drama (renzoku terebi shōsetsu, *or* asadora *for short) is both an everyday ritual and an institution of collective memory: since 1961, it has entertained Japanese television audiences by telling life stories of women against the backdrop of major events in modern Japanese history. This chapter examines how the* asadora *has changed in light of transformations in the Japanese television landscape over the past decade. Digitalization and the diversification of television programming have forced the public broadcaster NHK to find new ways to address its audience. The chapter presents two areas that NHK uses to highlight the social relevance of* asadora: *first, regional identity and "place branding," especially in the context of post-3.11 revitalization efforts, and second, a "cosmetic diversity" that presents Japan as an open-minded nation through a rather superficial portrayal of minority groups.*

Introduction

Even for those who do not like it, it is hard to avoid. In Japan, the morning drama (*asadora*) greets people from the walls of subway stations and is the subject of talk shows as well as of lively discussion on social media. The series, which has been running daily on the public broadcaster NHK since 1961, is one of the most successful programs on Japanese television, with ratings of around 20 percent. The social relevance of *asadora* increases through its constant paratextual framing; NHK and other media such as daily newspapers take part in this process by making it a topic of conversation in everyday life. For NHK, the *asadora* is an important pillar of its symbolic power (Scherer 2019), alongside the news and the *taiga dorama* (an annual year-long historical series), and it also opens up marketing potential for various stakeholders, e.g., in merchandise, music, fashion and tourism.

Because of its great social and economic importance, the *asadora* is often referred to as *kokumin-teki dorama* (national drama) (e.g., Hiyama 2015, 2). In fact, the morning drama has always been closely linked to the concept of the nation; the series tells life stories, mostly of women, against the backdrop of Japan's development in modern times. The *asadora* is thus not only entertainment, but also an important institution of collective memory in Japan. On the one hand, it deals with important narratives of modern Japanese history, such as the Pacific War or postwar reconstruction, and thus contributes to the collective memory of this period. At the same time, however, media consumption (or in this case, *asadora* consumption) itself can become an object of collective memory and can serve as a connecting element for entire generations (Okamuro 2017, 6).

In many ways, the *asadora* is an old-fashioned media product, clearly influenced by the spirit of the era of linear television. Nevertheless, even this institution cannot ignore current social trends and must continually reinvent itself to retain its relevance. One important point I will discuss is the marketing of local identity, which has been a factor since the early days of the *asadora* but has significantly increased during a recent media tourism boom in Japan. There have also been efforts to include the increasing diversity of Japanese society in the plot—but so far, these have been rather superficial. Both aspects—the representation of regional identity and social diversity in the *asadora*—are characterized by a fluctuation between openness and cultural nationalism. This demonstrates that the NHK morning drama not only serves entertainment purposes but has also become part of Japanese cultural policy and nation branding.

While I was working on this chapter, the COVID-19 pandemic broke out, and more than just my writing came to a halt for a while. The broadcasting of the 102nd *asadora*, *Ēru* (Yell) in 2020, was interrupted from 26 June, because no filming was possible from 1 April to 16 June. Instead of new episodes, NHK rebroadcast the series from episode 1, and new episodes were not shown until 14 September of that year (NHK 2020c). In addition, one of the actors in the series, the well-known comedian Shimura Ken, died after becoming infected with the novel coronavirus (NHK 2020d). At the end of this chapter, I will return briefly to the effects of the COVID-19 pandemic on the *asadora*. But first, I will introduce the morning drama as a media format, and in doing so, I will also discuss the consequences of digitalization, which has added an important dimension to the series. Afterwards, aspects of regional identity and "cosmetic diversity" in the *asadora* will be the focus of this contribution.

The *asadora*: Evolutions and audiences

The *asadora*, officially titled *renzoku terebi shōsetsu* (literally "serialized television novel"), is a quarter-hour-episode series currently broadcast every morning from 8:00 to 8:15 a.m. There is also a daily rerun on NHK at 12:45 p.m. and broadcasts on NHK BS Premium at 7:30 and 11:00 p.m. It is currently the only series on Japanese television which is broadcast daily (Monday to Friday and Saturday). As with South American telenovelas, the *asadora* is not an indefinitely running series, but rather, it presents a self-contained story. From its creation in 1961 to 1974, each series ran for one year, until NHK switched to a semi-annual rhythm in 1975, which continues to this day. After approximately 130 episodes (until 2020: 150–160 episodes), the *asadora* starts anew, with a new heroine and a new story. There is no permanent staff for this format; the team changes with each story, and producers or screen-writers usually work for an *asadora* only once during their career (Takō 2012, 216).

The plot almost always focuses on a person's life story, and unlike the male-dominated *taiga dorama*, the majority of the protagonists are women. An important recipe for success, which is still used today, was developed with the sixth *asadora*, *Ohanahan* (1966–1967): a woman experiences various tragic events, always putting her family first and overcoming all difficulties for their sake. All this happens against the backdrop of important historical events that reflect the development of the Japanese nation. Often the protagonist is involved in a particular profession, art or line of business; for example, there have been a pilot, several magazine editors and doctors, a sake brewer and a translator. As Harvey points out, despite an overall conservative orientation, the *asadora* allows the portrayal of strong female figures, because they are metaphors for the development of the Japanese nation itself: "[...] the rise in women's status is part of the rhetoric of national self-improvement and development" (Harvey 1998, 134).

The *asadora* was long considered a "gynocentric genre" (Yano 2008, 104) and typical housewives' entertainment. The series is designed so that it can easily be consumed while doing housework; since there is always a narrator, you can follow the story without having to continuously watch the television screen. From the 1980s onwards, this "female orientation" also became apparent in the fact that the production and script were often in the hands of women. Meanwhile, the audience structure has changed, and the series' most loyal followers fall in the over 60 age group; according to a survey by NHK in 2018, 48 percent of people in this age group watch the *asadora* (Nihei et al. 2020, 29).

Oshin (1983–1984), the most successful morning drama ever, achieved an average market share of 52.6 percent. Since the beginning of the 1990s, however, *asadora* ratings have been declining significantly. This is in line with a general trend in Japanese television and is due to the digitalization and diversification of programming in general. Whereas previously, ratings of around 40 percent were the standard, from 1994 onwards, they were only in the 20 percent range and continued to fall until 2009, when *Uerukame* (Wel-kame) reached a historic low of 13.5 percent (Video Research Ltd. 2020, all figures for the Kantō area). NHK moved the broadcasting time from 8:15 to 8:00 a.m. with *Gegege no nyōbō* (My Husband is a Cartoonist, 2010), which was intended to attract new target groups and actually resulted in an increase in ratings. Another change in broadcasting followed in 2020: *Ēru* was only broadcast from Monday to Friday, supplemented by a summary on Saturday presented by comedian Himura Yūki. NHK announced this as "*atarashii asadora no tanoshimikata*" (a new way of enjoying *asadora*) (NHK 2020a), but the main reason for this change was probably that NHK needed to improve working conditions for the production team, which until then had always been under great pressure to deliver six episodes per week (Asahi Shinbun 2019).

The *asadora* has not only been part of the daily routine since its early days, but has also con-sistently produced very active fans. In the analog age, this was apparent, for example, in the fan mail that NHK received in large numbers. In relation to the series *Oshin*, which had particular-ly enthusiastic admirers, newspaper articles testify to what the fandom looked like back then; people met to discuss the series, published fan magazines and created *Oshin* dolls (Scherer and Thelen 2021, 137–38). Enjoying *Oshin* often also included re-enacting the story of the series. *Os-hin*'s family is portrayed in the series as very poor, which is demonstrated, among other things, by the fact that they must eat rice with radish (*daikonmeshi*) for reasons of thrift. During the broadcast of the series, it became a popular custom in Japanese families to eat *daikonmeshi* together, like the characters in the series (Shefner-Rogers et al. 1998, 9). Recreating everyday practices from the series created an intimacy with the events and characters portrayed, and the involvement of the viewers increased. To this day, food is an important factor in this process; several *asadora* cookbooks have been published[1] and fans exchange recipes online.

In the digital age, fans now have more opportunities to exchange information and are able to distribute their own fan works far more easily than before. They are not dependent on mass media, such as daily newspapers, to report on their activities. This new type of fandom achieved high visibility for the first time with the series *Gegege no nyōbo*, which tells the life story of the famous manga artist Mizuki Shigeru (1922–2015) and his wife. Around 2010, Twitter became a mass phenomenon in Japan, and the importance of social media in television consumption increased steadily. Fans began to post their own illustrations of the *asadora* on Twitter as ゲゲ絵 (*Gege-e*, "Gege-picture") and showed great creativity (Nihei and Sekiguchi 2014a, 34). This tradition continues today, and for each *asadora*, a wealth of images is published under a new hashtag. With the *asadora Ama-chan* (2013), social media activities became so widespread that one could describe it as a new way of consuming television, and NHK began to conduct extensive studies on the subject (Nihei and Sekiguchi 2014a, 2014b). Since then, alongside audience ratings, social media monitoring has become an important factor in assessing the success of an *asadora*.

Despite many options for watching the morning drama at other times or on demand, according to a survey by NHK, 46 percent of the audience still tune in at 8:00 a.m. during the main broadcast time, and for many people, the *asadora* has become a "habit" (*shūkan*) which structures their everyday life (Nihei et al 2020, 60–63). They still tune in even when the series becomes a little boring or when they dislike certain aspects. This fits in with Hansen's findings (2016, 3), which describe the NHK morning program as a "secular morning ritual" which "binds the Japanese viewing public in a shared vision of reality" and supports the construction of a common Japanese identity. Switching on while having breakfast still connects viewers in a kind of national "imagined community" (Anderson 2006), as in the golden age of television. Social media can support this effect; figures published by NHK show that the number of tweets about the *asadora* is highest at the main broadcasting time (Nihei and Sekiguchi 2014b, 8).

At the same time, social media are changing the relationship between media producers and audiences. Today, broadcasters like NHK are faced with the need to enter a dialogue with their viewers and to support their product with a communication strategy through multiple media channels. There are official Twitter and Instagram accounts for the *asadora*, the NHK website offers additional content and the *asadora*'s main actresses have become powerful social media influencers, with very large numbers of followers. Nagano Mei, the main actress of *Hanbun, aoi* (Half Blue Sky, 2018), for example, has 3.8 million subscribers on Instagram (account: @mei_nagano0924official, as of September 2021). In addition to these changes in broadcasting strategy and audience interaction, there have also been new trends in terms of the content of the *asadora*.

Asadora and regional identity

One of the *asadora*'s essential features is that it portrays regional identity and, through this, conveys a sense of national identity. This strong "local tinge" (Muramatsu 1979, 21) has been present from the beginning of the series in the 1960s. The *asadora* is produced alternately by NHK Tokyo and NHK Osaka, and both stations take great pains to offer a multifaceted view of Japanese prefectures. Since *Tsubasa* (2009), which is set in Saitama Prefecture, all 47 prefectures of Japan have been represented at least once in the morning drama. NHK is thus also following two basic principles that justify its existence (and the monthly fees paid by citizens): publicness and (national) inclusivity (Hosokawa 2010, 61). When presenting regional identity, producers pay attention to many details and integrate aspects of local history and culture in addition to landscape and sights. Important elements usually include the local cuisine and special local handicraft products, such as ceramics (Scarlet, 2019–2020) or lacquerware (Mare, 2015). Through the *asadora*, these "cultural commodities," which according to Rausch (2008) are central to the place branding of rural regions in Japan, become the center of national attention, experiencing a new popularity as a result. For example, *gohei-mochi*, rice cakes with sweet miso, from Gifu Prefecture, were literally on everyone's lips after they had been featured in *Hanbun, aoi*.

Dialect is another very important marker of local identity in the *asadora*. Since the mid-1970s, NHK has even employed dialect advisors to ensure the authenticity of the conversation in the series (Tanaka 2014, 29). However, dialect in the *asadora* is an artificial product, or as Tanaka calls it "virtual hōgen" (2014, 24), because the national audience would not be able to fully understand the actual dialect. Also, some dialects are regarded more positively by the audience than others, and a protagonist speaking in a broad dialect would not correspond to the normative Japanese ideals of femininity (Shibamoto Smith and Occhi 2009). Thus, the national audience is presented with a mixture of standard Japanese and easily comprehensible dialectal fragments. Some dialectal terms have become so popular they have entered common usage, such as the word *jejeje* from *Ama-chan*, an expression of surprise. This word was even voted Word of the Year at the national buzzwords-of-the-year contest (*Shingo ryūkōgo taishō*) in 2013, although it was hardly known in the local dialect before the series (Kinsui et al. 2014, 80–81). It has since become the "symbol of a heritage to be proud of" (Gasparri and Martini 2018, 135).

Why this attention to detail and this effort? In Japan, since the beginning of modernity, there has been a tendency to seek a true Japanese identity in rural Japan. This is where the supposed "authentic" Japanese life is to be found, in unspoiled landscapes, ancient traditions and intact social structures (family, village). Such an ideal image functions as a counterscape to "westernized" life in the cities. A term closely related to this ideal, which is marked by nostalgia, is *furusato*—which literally means "old village" but is used more in the sense of "home" or "native place." In Japan, *furusato* evokes associations of picturesque landscapes (with mountains and rice fields) and a certain aesthetic of "rustic simplicity" (Robertson 1988, 494). *Furusato* stands for the "real Japan" and as a concept contributes to the construction of a national collective identity. It has long been used by the Japanese domestic travel industry to attract tourists to rural areas (Creighton 1997; McMorran 2008; Middeleer 2016), and it also plays a major role in contemporary media tourism, also called "contents tourism" in the Japanese context (Seaton et al. 2017).

Each *asadora* is about a very specific region, whose specialities and customs often have a novelty value for the national public and are basically anything but "their own culture" for the majority of the audience. However, this regional culture is always presented as an important part of national culture, so one could say that the local is appropriated for the national. The *asadora* portrays Japan as a country of diversity, with a clear focus on an "internal diversity," characterized as harmonious and largely independent of interference "from the outside." In *Hiyokko* (Bloom, 2017), for example, which takes place in the 1960s, this becomes particularly apparent; the protagonist Mineko moves into a girls' dormitory in Tokyo, where she lives with other young transistor radio factory workers, who all come from different prefectures. All speak in their dialects, but in the logic of the series, they are united by Tokyo and by their work. As is clearly stressed by their supervisors, the girls are working for one common goal, strengthening Japan as a nation by producing an important export product. The young women also jointly explore the achievements of modernizing Japan, for example through the consumption of a new food such as instant ramen or through shopping for bikinis. Tokyo is thus presented in the series as a pan-prefectural melting pot; it is a city that takes in and unites people from all regions of Japan. Tokyo is clearly constructed as the place where the national project develops, but Japan's roots and its *furusato* are still to be found in the rural areas. The view of rural Japan is usually very beautiful in the *asadora*; while in reality, many rural communities today have to struggle with a weak infrastructure and demographic change, idyllic images of picturesque landscapes dominate the series, and the population is presented as a closely connected community.

Overall, the morning drama is more concerned with place branding than with a realistic depiction of rural Japan, since the regions in which the series is set usually benefit from positive economic effects during the time of broadcast and afterwards. Since the early days of the *asadora*, increased national visibility has ensured that tourists come to the regions to visit the filming locations. Today, local communities take various measures to promote this type of contents tourism; they advertise on social media, offer special tours, set up "tangible heritage" such as landmarks and small museums (Gasparri and Martini 2018, 132) and organize events related to the *asadora*. This works quite well at times, as for example in the case of the very popular series *Ama-chan* (2013), which gave the city of Kuji, which was affected by the triple disaster of 11 March 2011 (3.11), greater touristic relevance and increased the awareness and pride of the population for the local culture (*bunka ishiki*) (Tajima 2015, 2018). In some cases, however, the economic effects for the region are less positive than expected, as in the case of *Jun to Ai* (Jun and Ai, 2012–2013, cf. Maruta et al. 2014) or *Mare* (cf. Scherer and Thelen 2018, 2020). The following points, among others, have been observed in research as obstacles to successful tourism marketing: a lack of involvement of the local population, a restrictive copyright policy, a lack of integration into a sustainable tourism concept and sometimes (as in the case of *Mare*) unforeseeable events, such as scandals involving actors, which damage the image of the series (Thelen et al. 2020).

Due to the economic effects of the *asadora*, NHK is in a special position of power; decisions over filming locations can have far-reaching consequences for the region concerned. After 3.11, NHK deliberately used this power to strengthen the affected areas in northern Japan. For the series *Ama-chan*, the Sanriku Coast was chosen as the location. The protagonist Aki moves to her mother's home, the district of Sodegahama, which belongs to the fictional small coastal town of Kitasanriku. In the course of the story, Aki goes to Tokyo to become an idol but returns after the catastrophe to help rebuild Kitasanriku. The series was shot in the town of Kuji in Iwate Prefecture and on the Kosode Coast, which is known for its women divers (*ama*).

Nine years after the disaster, the series *Ēru* (Yell) focuses on Fukushima Prefecture—not only in a deliberate initiative to revitalize the region but also as a clear signal that the situation in Fukushima is returning to normal. The producer told the press that *Ēru* can be seen as a contribution to the run-up to the 10th anniversary of the Tohoku earthquake: "We want to create a drama that cheers up the people in Fukushima as well as the whole of Japan" (Asahi. com 2019). The inspiration for *Ēru* comes both from the composer Koseki Yūji, who was born in the city of Fukushima and wrote many well-known hits (in particular, cheering songs for sporting events) during the Shōwa period, and from his wife, the singer Koseki Kinko. *Ēru* was also expected to give a boost to the Koseki Yūji Museum, founded in 1988, which suffered a sharp drop in visitor numbers after the catastrophe (Kahoku Shinpō 2019). The theme of cheering songs also provided a link to the Olympic Games, which were supposed to take place at the time of the broadcast; in the first episode, we see Koseki Yūji composing the Olympic March for the 1964 Games. According to the minutes of a meeting of Fukushima City Council, the city has been making efforts since 2016 to encourage the production of a series about Koseki Yūji (Fukushima City 2019). This indicates that the decision to set an *asadora* in a particular location does not (as is often claimed) simply stem from an idea of the scriptwriter but is the result of marketing strategy considerations, complex negotiation processes and lobbying.

NHK's statements on *Ēru* sound very harmless—any reference to the nuclear disaster is avoided—but the background is highly political.[2] Before the series was broadcast, NHK invited the public to send in photos from Fukushima and Aichi Prefectures, which were then shown at the end of each episode. A sample photo from the competition shows a young woman happily picking a peach, with the caption "Delicious to eat, joyful to pick—Peaches from Fukushima" (NHK 2020b). Here it becomes clear that *Ēru* is countering the images of destruction and insecurity after the disaster with a panorama of positive impressions that are intended to enhance the image of the region. In the years after the disaster, there were many discussions about food safety in Japan, particularly in Fukushima (Hirata Kimura 2016; Aruga 2017; Reiher and Yamaguchi 2017), and some countries and territories continue to restrict the import of food from Japan. The *asadora* tries to present specialities (*meibutsu*) of the region independent of this context, and in doing so, it joins various efforts of the Japanese government and Fukushima Prefecture (such as the "Fukushima Pride" campaign, fukushima-pride.com) to improve the tarnished image of Fukushima food. As is customary before the broadcast of an *asadora*, the Fukushima City Tourism Association, together with local producers, developed various souvenirs which created a link to *Ēru*. *Ēru*'s theme song also creates a connection to Fukushima, as it is sung by the local group GReeeeN. Due to the COVID-19 pandemic, however, all these efforts were only partially successful, and despite various infection control measures, tourists remained largely absent. According to Asahi Shinbun, the unfortunate fate of *Ēru*, together with the cancellation of the Olympic Games, was seen as the loss of a "unique opportunity" in Fukushima (Asahi Shinbun 2020).

NHK is continuing its efforts towards revitalization; *Okaeri Mone* (Welcome Back, Mone, 2021) is set in Miyagi Prefecture, also severely affected by the triple disaster. *Ama-chan* and *Ēru* are examples of how the *asadora* is not only a media product that demonstrates national unity within Japan, but is also an important instrument of Japan's cultural policy, which is expected to have positive effects on nation branding. Iwabuchi (2015, 420–21) sees in the *asadora Oshin* the beginnings of such a "pop-culture diplomacy," whose goal is to "enhance the international understanding of Japan" and to overcome the negative image of Japan's colonial past. Efforts to introduce more diversity into the *asadora* in recent years should also be seen in this context.

"Cosmetic diversity" in the *asadora*

As mentioned above, the *asadora*, which is firmly rooted in the concept of the nation, is more concerned with similarities and unity than with differences. Nevertheless, even this serial format is not indifferent to current social developments, and the increasing diversification of Japanese society is finding its way into the stories—albeit to a limited extent. As I will show, this new diversity in the *asadora* is situated in the context of Japanese nation branding and serves more to enhance the national image than to make marginalized identities visible. I therefore describe this kind of diversity as "cosmetic diversity," in reference to Mika Ko's concept of "cosmetic multiculturalism." Ko thereby defines a "multi-culturalism which on the surface celebrates cultural diversity, but at a deeper level does not subvert the dominant structure of Japaneseness vis-à-vis 'others'" (Ko 2010, 32). Ko examines this phenomenon in connection with ethnicity in Japanese film, but her observations can also be applied to other categories of difference, such as sexual orientation and disability. Minority groups now appear more frequently in popular media in Japan, but usually only "insofar as it is considered useful for the international projection of the nation's image" (Iwabuchi 2015, 428). This "cosmetic diversity" is thus not only superficial but also impedes real efforts for mutual understanding, reinforces perceived differences and sometimes causes the actual situation of marginalized groups to recede even further into the background, as stereotypical, easily consumable images overlay the voices of those affected.

Examples of foreign characters or characters with a migrant background in the *asadora* are generally rare in the history of the series. An early *asadora* that deals with the life of immigrants in Japan is *Kazamidori* (The Weather Vane, 1977–1978), set in Kobe, where a large foreign settlement developed during the Meiji period (1868–1912). *Kazamidori* is about a German who marries a Japanese woman after World War I and opens a bakery in Kobe. As Jang (2019) points out, *Kazamidori* had a clear influence on the image of the filming location, the Kitano-chō district, which was then staged and marketed even more strongly as a "western" space. However, other aspects of local history, such as the large presence of Chinese immigrants, were pushed into the background by the image of the district conveyed by the *asadora*. Even this early example shows that diversity in the *asadora* is the result of a very specific selection of certain aspects of the "other," which, as an exotic extension, fit into the narrative of national uniqueness.

The same holds true for the series *Sakura* (2002), which focuses on descendants of Japanese migrants (*nikkei*). The protagonist Sakura, a Japanese-American from Hawaii, comes to Japan to work as an English teacher. However, *Sakura*, as Yano (2004) explains, is less about showing the complexity of *nikkei* identity (or even the prejudices against them in Japan) than about reassessing Japanese identity. The *nikkei*, who cultivate their Japanese roots in Hawaii, are presented as "nostalgic examples of who 'we Japanese' once were" (Yano 2004, 8). In a similar vein, *Massan* (2014–2015) focuses on the life of whisky entrepreneur Taketsuru Masataka and his Scottish wife Jessie Roberta "Rita" Cowan. The leading role of the Scottish wife, who is called "Ellie" in the series, was played by American actress Charlotte Kate Fox, which was seen as a revolution in the history of the *asadora*, since she was the first foreign actress to have a major role in this popular television series. As Thelen (2019) points out, however, *Massan* falls into the trap of primarily reproducing stereotypes and—in a similar vein to the Nihonjinron discourse—negotiating through the foreign character what it means to be Japanese. As Suzuki (2020) explains, Ellie's role as an outsider was also emphasized at the linguistic level. In this NHK format, multiculturalism thus becomes a concept that is marked by exoticization and difference, and *asadora* do not do justice to the real experiences of immigrants in Japan.

Furthermore, the presence of the "other" in the *asadora* is limited to very select groups; neighboring Asian countries and migrants from these countries are strongly underrepresented. It was only in the context of the Korean wave (*Hallyu*), which in the mid-2000s led to the great popularity of Korean television series and music in Japan (Chua and Iwabuchi 2008), that a Korean figure first appeared in an *asadora*. In *Dondo hare* (Happily ever after, 2007), Korean actor Ryu Si-won made a guest appearance as the Korean idol "Junso," who meets his childhood love in Japan. The producers here took advantage of the popularity of the Korean star, who actually caused the ratings to soar for a week (KBS 2007). However, as the *asadora* reduces Korean-ness to the realm of popular culture, the portrayal of the first Korean character remains one-dimensional.

Japan's Korean minority (*zainichi kankokujin*) also gained greater visibility during the Korean wave and appeared for the first time in television productions, such as the series *Tokyo wankei* (Tokyo Bayview, Fuji TV 2004). For the morning drama format, this topic is clearly still considered to be too political, but at least in the background, in *asadora* production, there are signs of progress; in *Wakaba* (2004–2005), one of the protagonist's love interests was played by actor Kyō Nobuo, who is open about his status as a third generation *zainichi* Korean. For a long time, people at the center of public interest had to hide their *zainichi* origins, partly out of fear of discrimination, but above all because their ethnicity did not fit the image of "national" stars that these actors, singers etc., embodied. In the course of the Korean Wave, an increasing number of Japanese artists began to reveal their Korean heritage to the public, which, as Dew (2016, 134) explains, was covered by the media using terms like "*kamingu auto*" (coming out) or "*kokuhaku*" (confession). Kyō began his career at a time when he was able to openly communicate his origins and even make this identity into a kind of "trademark." Thus, he used his original Korean name for his debut, and on his blog (https://ameblo.jp/kyo-nobuo/) he openly discusses issues related to his identity as a (now) Japanese citizen of Korean heritage. One could also place Kyō's attitude towards his origin within the context of what Maher terms metroethnicity—an ethnicity that is hybridized, that presents "the peripheral as a desirable object" and "difference as design and fashion" (2005, 89–90). On the one hand, the success of artists such as Kyō Nobuo increases the visibility of minority groups in Japan, but at the same time, there is always the danger that such a superficial, "cool" media portrayal of the phenomenon will cause existing social and political problems to fade into the background. Nevertheless, the fact that Kyō was able to enter the "national bastion" of the *asadora* seems to have been perceived as an important step in *zainichi* circles; Mindan, an association of Koreans living in Japan, published a statement when it became known that he had been given the role (2004).

Nevertheless, despite such small changes, the Asian neighbors still remain a blank space in the asadora. This became particularly clear in the series *Manpuku* (Full of Happiness, 2018–2019), which deals with the invention of instant ramen. While this story about Andō Momofuku and his wife Masako functions as a purely Japanese narrative about a national speciality, Andō Momofuku, the inventor of instant ramen, actually grew up as a child of wealthy Taiwanese parents in colonial Taiwan and only came to Japan as an adult. These origins are completely concealed in the *asadora*, which sometimes creates eerie gaps in the plot.

As Nojima (2018) explains, Andō himself largely severed ties with Taiwan during his lifetime, and the website of his company Nissin Foods also makes no mention of the founder's origins. Nojima assumes that in the *asadora*, it would have been difficult to tell this story about Andō's struggle for success if it centered on a member of a minority group. This might indeed not have matched the "national framing" of the *asadora* and the basic principle that it is telling *Japanese* success stories. Further, the historical background of 50 years of Japanese colonization of Taiwan (through which Andō learned Japanese as a child) was probably considered too problematic for an *asadora*. This is one of many examples that demonstrate that the collective memory of national history that *asadora* cultivates is a very selective one, concentrating mainly on aspects which can be charged with nostalgia and which do not run the risk of provoking conflict. There is no room in the *asadora* for a serious, critical confrontation with Japan's colonial past and its historically problematic relations with neighboring countries. This is, however, consistent with Japan's general diplomatic line (see Iwabuchi 2015).

The issues of disability and LGBTQ people received more attention in the runup to the Olympic and Paralympic Games in Tokyo (originally planned for 2020); in the course of this major international event, Japan wanted to present itself as a country open to all people. This can be seen in the tagline "Know Differences, Show Differences," which made diversity and inclusion important principles of the Tokyo Games. This was also the agenda of *Hanbun, aoi*, as evidenced by the fact that Kitagawa Eriko, a writer known for love stories featuring people with disabilities, was chosen for the script. Her works include the successful series *Beautiful Life* (according to Stibbe (2004), the climax of a "disability drama boom" at the turn of the millennium), in which a young woman in a wheelchair is the main character (TBS, 2000), and *Orange Days* (TBS, 2004), a series about a deaf violinist. The protagonist of *Hanbun, aoi*, Nireno Suzume, has been deaf in one ear since childhood. From the start, the first sentences spoken in the series revolve around this fact; the protagonist compares her deafness to a slightly broken umbrella and interprets this particularity as *omoshiroi* ("interesting," here in the sense of "unique" or "refreshing"). Unlike many previous Japanese television series, the *asadora* does not tell the story of disability (especially in the context of female characters) as a "form of powerlessness" (Stibbe 2004, 32); at the same time, however, a comparatively light and not very restrictive form of disability was chosen, and the series does not in fact focus on disability. It initially deals with Suzume's work as a designer of girls' manga (*shōjo manga*) and later, with her family life and her attempts to gain a foothold as a businesswoman.

The issue of disability had been raised before in the morning drama *Ten Urara* (Urara in the Sky, 1998), which addressed the issues of an ageing society and barrier-free access.[3] However, Suzume is the first *asadora* heroine with a disability, and *Hanbun, aoi* is also the first *asadora* in which an LGBTQ character appears who is explicitly marked as such; Suzume's colleague during her time as a manga artist, Tōdo Makoto (called Bokute), is openly gay. As Thelen (2021) points out, Bokute was an important step towards increasing the visibility of LGBTQ identities in mainstream Japanese media, but at the same time, the portrayal remained superficial and served popular clichés of male homosexuality. Japanese television has long portrayed gay men as "funny-peculiar" and "funny-humorous" (Valentine 1997, 64) but not as sexually active, and Bokute continues this pattern.

Hanbun, aoi appears to have been part of a trend, as there were several series with LGBTQ themes on Japanese television in 2018 (Fujita 2018, 65–67). The growing presence of LGBTQ people was linked to a political agenda; in the same year, an anti-discrimination law was passed in Tokyo (Human Rights Watch 2018), but its limitation to Tokyo Prefecture meant that it was primarily of symbolic significance in view of the Olympic Games. Even the strong media presence of LGBTQ people can be viewed as a phenomenon of "cosmetic diversity," which is intended to support the impression that Japan meets global standards in terms of minority rights. There are blind spots in the eyes of the media; As Maree (2020) states, "the resultant 'hypervisibility' of 'LGBTQ issues' has led to an increasing 'invisibility' of those who supposedly fail to fit LGBTQ narratives that pivot on specific forms of consumerism, internationalism and globalized diversity." Rückert shows in a study of queerness in Japanese television series that such media products mostly focus on private experiences of LGBTQ characters as individuals and "depoliticize the perception of queerness in the Japanese public realm" (Rückert 2019, 21). In fact, the seeming open-mindedness towards various gender and sexual identities in Japan, which has been propagated in the lead up to the Olympic Games, is contrasted with inactivity at the political level (see Khor et al. 2020); there is no national law against discrimination on the basis of sexual orientation or gender identity, and the introduction of same-sex marriage is still not an issue at the national level. Although there is the possibility for transgender individuals to legally change their gender, this is bound by very strict criteria (such as the execution of gender reassignment surgery) (Dale 2020, 62).

Similarly, the presentation of disability in the run-up to the Olympic Games was also largely devoid of socio-political context; the focus here was very much on stories of empowerment of individual athletes, who are presented like superheroes while social problems were largely ignored (van der Veere 2020). All in all, the *asadora* is taking cautious steps towards a new diversity, affording limited exposure to groups that were previously largely invisible in mainstream media. However, the focus remains on issues that can be dealt with relatively safely without causing major controversy. NHK producers only take up topics that are already present in the political discourse, and they reproduce this discourse without adding their own innovative perspectives. Innovations are generally not to be expected from a conservative media format with an "ageing" audience, like the *asadora*. Nevertheless, the introduction of new topics into the Japanese morning program is at least an indicator of the issues occupying Japanese mainstream discourse. Diversity has become an important element of Japanese nation branding, which lends the country a touch of progressiveness that is crucial in international competition. "Cosmetic diversity" in the *asadora* thus primarily serves the construct of the nation.

Conclusion: *Asadora* in times of crisis

The *asadora*, as I have shown, is a media product of great importance in Japan, and not only for everyday life. It is an important institution of national memory, it holds potential for tourism marketing, and as part of Japanese cultural policy it is used for nation branding purposes. As an object of academic research, it is immensely valuable: the *asadora* tells us a lot about Japanese memory culture, current discourses in the mainstream public realm and power relations in Japanese society. As I have demonstrated, over the last decade, one of the main trends in *asadora* has been "cosmetic diversity," a rather superficial portrayal of marginalized groups, with the intention of creating an image of an open-minded nation. At the same time, several *asadora* have been dedicated to the reconstruction of northern Japan after 3.11. Where the *asadora*'s focus will shift in the future is not yet clear—but the pandemic will certainly play a major role in this regard. Major crises which the nation has faced, most notably World War II, are a main theme of the *asadora*, which offers its own, mostly emotional-apolitical reading of these events.

The fact that even the *asadora*, which has been an uninterrupted everyday ritual in Japan for almost 60 years, came to a standstill shows the far-reaching consequences of the COVID-19 pandemic. Even after the triple disaster of 11 March 2011, the series was only stopped for one week. Nevertheless, the power of the *asadora* has not been completely lost. Although for many weeks in 2020 there was only a rebroadcast of the first 65 episodes of *Ēru*, the viewing figures still remained at 13 to 14 percent. At a time when many had to cope with disruption to their normal daily life and social contact, the *asadora* appears to have offered a sense of continuity and community, even if it had nothing new to tell. Even in times of crisis, the series provides unwaveringly optimistic images—and re-narrates Japanese history with as little controversy as possible. It will be interesting to see in which way the COVID-19 pandemic will find its way into this institution of national memory.

Notes

[1] E.g., NHK renzoku terebi shōsetsu Mare okashi reshipi bukku [NHK's Morning drama Mare: pastry recipe book], 2015; Natsusora Natsu ga tabeta oishii reshipi [Natsusora: Delicious recipes of food that Natsu is eating in the series], 2019.

[2] See Gössmann's chapter for a discussion of (the lack of) representations of the nuclear disaster in Japanese television drama.

[3] See Mithani's chapter for a discussion of the representation of disability in Japanese media.

Videography

Ama-chan, 2013. [TV series]. Tokyo: NHK.
Dondo hare [Happily Ever After], 2007. [TV series]. Tokyo: NHK.
Ēru [Yell], 2020. [TV series]. Tokyo: NHK.
Gegege no nyōbō [My Husband is a Cartoonist], 2010. [TV series]. Tokyo: NHK.
Hanbun, aoi [Half Blue Sky], 2018. [TV series]. Tokyo: NHK.
Hiyokko [Blossom], 2017. [TV series]. Tokyo: NHK.
Jun to Ai [Jun and Ai], 2012–2013. [TV series]. Tokyo: NHK.
Kazamidori [The Weather Vane], 1977–1978. [TV series]. Tokyo: NHK.
Manpuku [Full of Happiness], 2018–2019. [TV series]. Tokyo: NHK
Mare, 2015. [TV series]. Tokyo: NHK
Massan, 2014–2015. [TV series]. Tokyo: NHK
Ohanahan, 1966–1967. [TV series]. Tokyo: NHK
Okaeri Mone [Welcome Back, Mone], 2021. [TV series]. Tokyo: NHK.
Oshin, 1983–1984. [TV series]. Tokyo: NHK.
Sakura, 2002. [TV series]. Tokyo: NHK.
Scarlet, 2019–2020. [TV series]. Tokyo: NHK.
Ten Urara [Urara in the Sky], 1998. [TV series]. Tokyo: NHK.
Tsubasa, 2009. [TV series]. Tokyo: NHK.
Uerukame [Wel-kame], 2009. [TV series]. Tokyo: NHK.

Bibliography

Anderson, B., 2006. *Imagined Communities. Reflections on the Origin and Spread of Nationalism* (Revised Edition). London: Verso.

Aruga, K., 2017. Consumer Responses to Food Produced Near the Fukushima Nuclear Plant. *Environmental Economics and Policy Studies*, 19, 677–90.

Asahi Shinbun, 2019. NHK asadora, doyō wa shinsaku oyasumi. [The new NHK asadora pauses on Saturdays]. *Asahi Shinbun* [online]. Available at: https://www.asahi.com/articles/ASM5P5FS8M5PUCVL01T.html [Accessed 17 Aug 2020].

———., 2020. Koseki kōka, togirenu kitai [Hopes that the Koseki effect will not come to an end]. *Asahi Shinbun* Morning Edition 18 July. p.23.

Asahi.com, 2019. 2020 nen haru no asadora wa "Ēru" [Spring 2020's asadora is "Yell"]. *Asahi-com* [online]. Available at: https://www.asahi.com/articles/ASM2W76JNM2WUCVL02M.html [Accessed 14 August 2020].

Chua, B.-H. and Iwabuchi, K., eds., 2008. *East Asian Pop Culture: Analysing the Korean Wave*. Hong Kong: Hong Kong University Press.

Creighton, M., 1997. Consuming Rural Japan: The Marketing of Tradition and Nostalgia in the Japanese Travel Industry. *Ethnology*, 36(3), 239–54.

Dale, S.P.F., 2020. Transgender, Non-Binary Genders, and Intersex in Japan. In J. Coates, L. Fraser and M. Pendleton, eds., *The Routledge Companion to Gender and Japanese Culture*. London: Routledge, 60–68.

Dew, O., 2016. *Zainichi Cinema: Korean-in-Japan Film Culture*. London: Palgrave Macmillan.

Fujita, A., 2018. Changing Perception of LGBTQ People Through Performances—Theater and Television in America and in Japan. *Journal of Urban Culture Research*, 17, 54–71.

Fukushima City, 2019. Heisei 31 nen, 3 gatsu teirei kaigi [March 2019, regular council meeting]. Available at: http://www.city.fukushima.fukushima.jp/voices/CGI/voiweb.exe?ACT=200&KENSAKU=0&SORT=0&KTYP=2,3,0&KGTP=1,2&TITL_SUBT=%95%BD%90%AC%82R%82P%94N%81@%82R%8C%8E%92%E8%97%E1%89%EF%8Bc%81%7C03%8C%8E14%93%FA-07%8D%86&HUID=226576&KGNO=226&FINO=987 [Accessed 17 August 2020].

Gasparri, D. and Martini, A., 2018. Amachan. Japanese TV Drama and Heritage Creation in a Post-Disaster Town. In C. Palmer and J. Tivers, eds., *Creating Heritage for Tourism*. London: Routledge, 127–39.

Hansen, W., 2016. Creating Modern Japanese Subjects: Morning Rituals from Norito to News and Weather. *Religions* [online] 7(28), 1–17. Available at: http://www.mdpi.com/2077-1444/7/3/28 [Accessed 14 August 2020].

Harvey, P. A. S., 1998. Nonchan's Dream. NHK Morning Serialized Television Novels. In D. Martinez, ed., *The Worlds of Japanese Popular Culture. Gender, Shifting Boundaries and Global Cultures*. Cambridge: Cambridge University Press, 133–51.

Hirata Kimura, A., 2016. *Radiation Brain Moms and Citizen Scientists: The Gender Politics of Food Contamination after Fukushima*. Durham: Duke University Press.

Hiyama, T., 2015. NHK asadora "Mare" ni iratto suru hito no mesen [Why people are annoyed by NHK's asadora "Mare"]. *Toyo Keizai Online*, 21 Sept. Available at: http://toyokeizai.net/articles/-/85266 [Accessed 29 September 2021].

Hosokawa, S., 2010. The Uses of Routine: NHK's Amateur Singing Contest in Historical Perspective. In M. Yoshimoto, E. Tsai and J. Choi, eds., *Television, Japan, and Globalization*. Ann Arbor: University of Michigan Press, 51–72.

Human Rights Watch, 2018. Tokyo's "Olympic" LGBTQ Non-Discrimination Law. Available at: https://www.hrw.org/news/2018/10/11/tokyos-olympic-LGBTQ-non-discrimination-law [Accessed 17 August 2020].

Iwabuchi, K., 2015. Pop-culture Diplomacy in Japan: Soft Power, Nation Branding and the Question of "International Cultural Exchange." *International Journal of Cultural Policy*, 21(4), 419–32.

Jang, K., 2019. Tourism and Local Identity Generated by NHK's Morning Drama: The Intersection of Memory and Imagination in Kobe. *East Asian Journal of Popular Culture*, 5(2), 159–76.

Kahoku Shinpō, 2019. Asadora, Fukushima e "Ēru" [The asadora comes to Fukushima with "Yell"]. *Kahoku Shinpō* [online]. Available at: https://www.kahoku.co.jp/tohokunews/201904/20190424_63020.html [Accessed 28 March 2020].

KBS, 2007. Japanese Drama with Korean Actor Tops Ratings. KBS [online]. Available at: http://english.kbs.co.kr/hallyu/entertainment_news_view.html?id=&No=988&page=103 [Accessed 17 August 2020].

Khor, D., Tang, D. T.-S. and Kamano, S., 2020. Global Norms, State Regulations, and Local Activism: Marriage Equality and Same-Sex Partnership, Sexual Orientation, and Gender Identity Rights in Japan and Hong Kong. In M.J. Bosia, S.M. McEvoy and M. Rahman, eds., *The Oxford Handbook of Global LGBTQ and Sexual Diversity Politics*. Oxford: Oxford University Press, 283–300.

Kinsui, S., Tanaka, Y. and Okamuro, M., 2014. Kōkai intabyū. Hōgen to kakutō suru dorama seisaku genba (Public interview. How TV drama production is struggling with dialect). In S. Kinsui, Y. Tanaka and M.

Okamuro, eds., *Dorama to hōgen no atarashii kankei* [The new relationship of TV dramas and dialect]. Tokyo: Kasama Shoin, 52–94.

Ko, M., 2010. *Japanese Cinema and Otherness. Nationalism, Multiculturalism and the Problem of Japaneseness.* London: Routledge.

Maher, J., 2005. Metroethnicity, Language, and the Principle of Cool. *International Journal of Sociology of Language,* 175/176, 83–102.

Maree, C., 2020. "LGBTQ Issues" and the 2020 Games. *The Asia-Pacific Journal: Japan Focus,* 18(Issue 4, 7). Available at: https://apjjf.org/2020/4/Maree.html [Accessed 14 August 2020].

Maruta, K., Kanehama, S. and Tamayose, A., 2014. NHK asa no renzoku terebi shōsetsu "Jun to Ai" no hōei to Miyako-jima ni okeru juyō [The broadcast of the NHK morning TV serial story "Jun and Ai" and the reaction in Miyako island]. *Okinawa Daigaku jinbungakubu kiyō,* 16, 61–69. Available at: http://okinawa -repo.lib.u-ryukyu.ac.jp/handle/20.500.12001/11904 [Accessed 14 August 2020].

McMorran, C., 2008. Understanding the "Heritage" in Heritage Tourism: Ideological Tool or Economic Tool for a Japanese Hot Springs Resort? *Tourism Geographies,* 10(3), 334–54.

Middeleer, S., 2016. I Want to go Far Away: Discover Japan and Japanese Identity Tourism in the 1970s. *Studies on Asia Series V,* 1(1), 96–121.

Mindan, 2004. NHK asadora zainichi sansei shutsuen [A third-generation zainichi Korean is appearing in the NHK asadora]. *Mindan* [online]. Available at: https://www.mindan.org/old/front/newsDetail8e36. html [Accessed 17 August 2020].

Muramatsu, Y., 1979. Terebi dorama no joseigaku [Women's studies and television drama]. Tokyo: Sōtakusha.

NHK 2020a. Dōyōbi no, atarashii asadora no tanoshimikata ga hajimarimasu [The new way to enjoy asadora on Saturdays begins]. *Yell News* [online]. Available at: https://www.nhk.or.jp/yell/information/news/0326 .html [Accessed 14 August 2020].

———.2020b. NHK Creative Library. Available at: https://www.nhk.or.jp/archives/creative/yell/ [Accessed 17 August 2020].

———.2020c. Renzoku terebi shōsetsu Ēru hōsō saikai e. Raigetsu 14 nichi kara [NHK to resume broadcast-ing of morning drama Yell from 14th of next month]. NHK News Web [online]. Available at: https:// www3.nhk.or.jp/news/html/20200817/k10012570501000.html [Accessed 29 September 2021].

———. 2020d. Komedian Shimura Ken san shikyo. Shingata korona kansen de haien hasshō [Comedian Ken Shimura dies of pneumonia caused by novel corona virus infection]. NHK News Web [online]. Available at: https://www3.nhk.or.jp/news/html/20200330/k10012357011000.html [Accessed 29 September 2021].

Nihei, W. and Sekiguchi, S. (2014a). Asadora Ama-chan wa dō mirareta ka [How people watched and perceived the asadora Ama-chan]. *Hōsō kenkyū to chōsa* [The NHK Monthly Report on Broadcast Re-search], March, 12–41.

———. (2014b). "Sōsharu" ga umu terebi shichōnetsu!? Amachan genshō ga nagekaketa mono [Enthusi-asm for television that grows out of social networks!? What questions does the Ama-chan phenomenon raise?]. *Hōsō kenkyū to chōsa* [The NHK Monthly Report on Broadcast Research], June, 2–17.

Nihei, W., Saitō, K., Yoshikawa, K. and Kamemura, T., 2020. NHK renzoku terebi shōsetsu to shichōsha. "Asadora" wa dō mirarete iru ka [NHK morning drama serials and viewers: how "asadora" has been perceived in recent years]. *NHK Hōsō bunka kenkyūjo nenpō,* 64, 7–165. Available at: https://www.nhk.or .jp/bunken/research/domestic/20200130_3.html [Accessed 14 August 2020].

Nojima, T., 2018. Naze NHK "Manpuku" wa, Andō Momofuku no "Taiwan rūtsu" o kakushita no ka [Why did NHK's "Manpuku" hide Andō Momofuku's Taiwanese roots?]. *Gendai Bijinesu* [online]. Available at: https://gendai.ismedia.jp/articles/-/58365?imp=0 [Accessed 17 August 2020].

Okamuro, M., 2017. Goku shiteki terebi dorama shi [A very personal history of TV drama]. In Waseda Daigaku engeki hakubutsukan, ed., *Dai terebi dorama hakurankai* [Great TV drama exhibition]. Tokyo: Waseda Daigaku, 6–37.

Rausch, A. S., 2008. Place Branding in Rural Japan: Cultural Commodities as Local Brands. *Place Branding and Public Diplomacy,* 4, 136–46.

Reiher, C. and Yamaguchi, T., 2017. Food, Agriculture and Risk in Contemporary Japan. *Contemporary Japan,* 29(1), 2–13.

Robertson, J., 1988. Furusato Japan. The Culture and Politics of Nostalgia. *Politics, Culture, and Society,* 1, 494–518.

Rückert, J., 2019. Queer Desire in Japanese TV series. *Vienna Journal of East Asian Studies*, 11, 1–30. Available at: https://doi.org/10.2478/vjeas-2019-0001 [Accessed 8 June 2020].

Scherer, E., 2019. An everyday glimpse of the nation: NHK's morning drama (asadora) and rituality. *East Asian Journal of Popular Culture* 5(2), 111–26.

Scherer, E. and Thelen, T., 2021. Following Oshin and Amachan. Film Tourism and Nation Branding in the Analogue and Digital Ages. In N. van Es, S. Reijnders, L. Bolderman and A. Waysdorf, eds., *Film Tourism in Asia: Perspectives on Asian Tourism*. Singapore: Springer, 69–86.

———., 2020. On Countryside Roads to National Identity: Japanese Morning Drama Series (asadora) and Contents Tourism. *Japan Forum*, 32(1), 6–29.

———., 2018. Drama Offscreen: A Multi-Stakeholder Perspective on Film Tourism in Relation to the Japanese Morning Drama (asadora). In S. Kim and S. Reijnders, eds., *Locating Imagination in Popular Culture. Place, Tourism and Belonging*. London: Routledge, 134–50.

Seaton, P., Yamamura, T., Sugawa, A. and Jang, K., 2017. *Contents Tourism in Japan: Pilgrimages to "Sacred Sites" of Popular Culture*. Amherst: Cambria Press.

Shefner-Rogers, C. L., Rogers, E. M. und Singhal, A., 1998. Parasocial Interaction with the Television Soap Operas "Simplemente Maria" and "Oshin." *Keio Communication Review*, 20, 3–18.

Shibamoto Smith, J. and Occhi, D., 2009. The Green Leaves of Love: Japanese Romantic Heroines, Authentic Femininity, and Dialect. *Journal of Sociolinguistics*, 13(4), 524–46.

Stibbe, A., 2004. Disability, Gender and Power in Japanese Television Drama. *Japan Forum*, 16(1), 21–36.

Suzuki, S., 2020. Multiculturalism or Cultural Nationalism? Representation of Ellie Kameyama as a Conduit and the Other in the NHK Morning Drama Massan. *Japanese Studies*, 40(2), 121–40.

Tajima, Y., 2015. NHK Asa no renzoku terebi shōsetsu "Amachan" no Kuji-shi ni okeru juyō [The reception of television drama Amachan in Kuji]. *Doshisha University Social Science Review*, 116, 15–40.

———., 2018. Japanese Idol Culture for "Contents Tourism" and Regional Revitalization: a Case Study of Regional Idols. In A. Beniwal, R. Jain and K. Spracklen, eds., *Global Leisure and the Struggle for a Better World*. Basingstoke: Palgrave Macmillan, 117–39.

Takō, W., 2012. *Taisetsu na koto wa minna asadora ga oshiete kureta* [I learned the most important things from asadora]. Tokyo: Ōta Shuppan.

Tanaka, Y., 2014. "Amachan" ga hiraita atarashii tobira [How Ama-chan has opened new avenues]. In S. Kinsui, Y. Tanaka and M. Okamuro, eds., *Dorama to hōgen no atarashii kankei* [The new relationship of television dramas and dialect]. Tokyo: Kasama Shoin, 22–43.

Thelen, T., 2019. The Japanization of Wife and Whisky in NHK's Morning Drama Massan. *East Asian Journal of Popular Culture*, 5(2), 177–93.

———., 2021. Between 1990s' Nostalgia and "LGBT-Friendly" Tokyo Olympics: Representations of LGBTQ People in NHK's Morning Drama Series. *Japanese Studies*, 41(2), 241–55.

Thelen, T., Kim, S. and Scherer, E., 2020. Film Tourism Impacts: a Multi-Stakeholder Longitudinal Approach. *Tourism Recreation Research* 1–16. https://doi.org/10.1080/02508281.2020.1718338 [Accessed 14 August 2020].

Valentine, J., 1997. Skirting and Suiting Stereotypes: Representations of Marginalized Sexualities in Japan. *Theory, Culture & Society*, 14(3), 57–85.

Van der Veere, A., 2020. The Tokyo Paralympic Superhero: Manga and Narratives of Disability in Japan. *The Asia-Pacific Journal: Japan Focus*, 18(5,8). Available at: https://apjjf.org/2020/5/Veere.html [Accessed 14 August 2020].

Video Research Ltd. 2020. NHK asa no renzoku terebi shōsetsu [NHK's morning serial television novel]. Available at: https://www.videor.co.jp/tvrating/past_tvrating/drama/02/nhk.html [Accessed 14 August 2020].

Yano, C. R., 2004. Eyeing Nikkei: Portrayals of Japanese Americans on an NHK TV Drama. Available at: https://www.jamco.or.jp/2004_symposium/en/yano/ [Accessed 14 August 2020].

———., 2008. Gaze Upon Sakura. Imaging Japanese Americans on Japanese TV. In K.E. Ferguson and M. Mironesco, eds., *Gender and Globalization in Asia and the Pacific: Method, Practice, Theory*. Honolulu: University of Hawai'i Press, 101–20.

Part 4
Gender and Media

Chapter 11
Japanese Popular Fiction: Constraint, Violence and Freedom in Kirino Natsuo's *Out*

Lyle De Souza

This chapter examines Japanese popular fiction, providing an understanding of its importance during upheavals in Japanese media and popular culture, as well as within the context of major social changes. It uses as its main illustration Kirino Natsuo's (2004) novel Auto (Out), *which incorporates various social issues, including gender discrimination, an aging society, precarious employment, the (non-)belonging of minorities and violence. By examining the materiality of Kirino's fiction itself, the chapter demonstrates how Japanese popular fiction works as a lens to observing these crucial social issues facing Japanese society.*

Introduction

Japanese popular fiction is of immense economic as well as cultural importance. Yet, there have been few academic studies, particularly in the English language, assessing its significance and implications. This chapter surveys one of the most important popular fiction works in Japan in recent times, Kirino Natsuo's (2004) prominent novel *Auto* (Out), first published in 1997,[1] since it encompasses several of the most salient issues invoked in contemporary Japanese popular fiction reflecting changes in Japanese society, including gender discrimination, an aging society, a changing employment system, ethnic minorities, and violence. As well as examining the materiality of the fiction itself, this chapter demonstrates how Japanese popular fiction works as a lens to observing these paramount issues in Japanese society. By analyzing popular fiction in Japan from this multifaceted perspective it becomes possible to better understand the social issues it reflects, addresses and influences.

This chapter aims to provide readers with a broad understanding of Japanese popular fiction (*taishū bungaku*) and its relevance both within and beyond Japan. Academic scholarship on this area is neglected for a reason similar to why video games are not researched nearly as much as film, music, or other popular forms of culture.[2] They are seen as less important cultural products, even within the already lower tier of popular culture, let alone when pitted against so-called "high culture" such as literary fiction (*jun bungaku*). Notwithstanding this, the argument that popular fiction and video games should be considered purely due to their current pre-eminent economic impact is insufficient, at least when approaching them from a cultural studies perspective as this chapter does. Instead, attention should be given to thinking about how popular fiction in Japan both shapes and is shaped in time and space. It is impossible for a single essay to cover this satisfactorily, so it is necessary to establish some parameters so that the analysis comprises what can be considered the most arresting areas of cultural change in modern Japan.

First, how can popular fiction be defined? Separately, the words "popular" and "fiction" are not particularly problematic. Put together as a term, however, the meaning can vary, depending on timing, location and personalities. In Japan, the closest equivalent term, *taishū bungaku*, dates back to the 1920s with the emergence of mass media in Japan. In recent years, it has almost become a synonym of "genre fiction," a phrase coined by the publishing industry as a means of categorizing works to market to audiences who are fans of certain genres. Popular fiction has also been defined as all that is not literary fiction.[3] These delineations can be ambiguous—where is the line drawn between what is "literary fiction" and what is "popular fiction"? For example, Murakami Haruki's works are surely both? Indeed, this problem of categorization goes back as far as the beginning of the twentieth century in relation to the writings of Akutagawa Ryūnosuke and Tanizaki Jun'ichirō. To avoid the trap of overthinking categories of literature, and to fit the remit of the current work, popular fiction in Japan is defined as written works of fiction that may span different genres and formats yet have in common a mass readership based largely in Japan (although these days increasingly overseas too). Works of fiction refer to any written text where the author has created an imaginary world that is acknowledged as such by readers. The genres mentioned the most in this chapter are those that have proved the most popular and resilient in Japan over the last thirty years: children's literature, crime and detective novels, science fiction and fantasy, romance and horror. It is possible to make a case for the inclusion of other genres, too, such as comedies, historical novels, political novels, LGBTQ literature, mysteries and so on, although this brief overview cannot cover all of these. Japan is recognized throughout the world not only for its huge consumption of popular fiction but also for the innovative formats in which it is delivered to the mass market, such as cell phone novels (*keitai shōsetsu*, novels read on mobile phones). Although manga is arguably Japan's ultimate form of popular fiction, it is considered here more as a category containing all the various genres outlined above, so no special attention is paid to it except as a way of illustrating the interconnection and mixing of media formats as publishing vehicles in Japan alongside traditional printed matter, cell phone novels, electronic books and others.

There are a couple of points to note regarding the peculiarity of Japan's publishing industry in relation to its popular fiction. The sheer variety of genres and mass media formats in which they are published is a standout feature. Sumiko Asai's (2016) *Format Choice for Popular Fiction in Japan* discusses this at the macro level of understanding how the Japanese publishing industry works, showing that popular fiction in Japan has a particularly idiosyncratic link between content produced by media outlets and the format in which consumers like to read it. Much of this can be associated with technological change. For example, the postwar urbanization of Japan brought with it regular commuting for which A6-sized ("pocket-sized") paperbacks were convenient. Over the course of the beginning of the 21st century, cell phone novels have somewhat supplanted these printed books. In a manner, the message here is the medium since these media formats lend themselves to specific literary styles, such as punchy short sentences and fewer illustrations.[4]

Japanese popular fiction has recently started to be read widely beyond Japan (usually in translation), accompanying the growth of the Japanese diaspora and people interested in Japanese popular culture, especially during the "Cool Japan" period of the last couple of decades.[5] If this represents its present and near future, the importance of its past roots—folk tales, fairy tales, classical Japanese literature, as well as so-called "elite literature" (*jun bungaku*)—should also be noted.[6] The breaking down and mixing of traditional categories is a salient feature of contemporary Japanese popular fiction: "elite literature" and "mass-market literature" (*taishū bungaku*) increasingly overlap, as evidenced by the works of Murakami Ryū, Murakami Haruki, Yoshimoto Banana, and Yamada Amy (Eimi).[7]

According to the Research Institute for Publications, there was an overall decline in the sales of printed books from the peak turnover in 1996 of around 1,093 billion Japanese yen to around 754 billion yen by 2014. From around 2010 onwards, particularly with the advance and mass market appeal of digital devices such as Kobo and Kindle, the e-book sales market has grown to approximately 15 percent of the total market (Asai 2016).[8]

Sales of Japanese popular fiction peaked during the height of Japan's boom years in the 1980s until the bursting of the bubble economy in 1989 at the end of the Shōwa era. The Heisei era which followed would usher in a more sober and reflective period with greater social and economic inequality across Japan. Thus, the 1990s provide a fascinating period of change in Japan that is reflected in later popular fiction. It is now possible to consider in depth a single text from the 1990s, as well as a few other key works where applicable, to illuminate and bring together its genres, formats and sociohistorical background.

Representing gender inequalities in feminist Japanese popular fiction: Constraint, violence and freedom

> *I feel that this society takes advantage of powerless women. You could say that if you are not paying attention, something will take advantage of you. The situation is as such that it's dangerous for women unless they get smart and stand up for themselves.* (Kirino 2003)

The following analysis details the path of constraint, violence and freedom in Kirino Natsuo's (2004) novel *Out*, particularly in relation to exploring the social construction of its main female characters and related questions of representation. Kirino uses this pattern of development for her characters on each of their personal journeys—although the patterns are never quite as linear or as unambiguous as they may initially seem since Kirino is often destabilizing normative gender constructions. The analysis starts by showing how Kirino narrates the restrictions faced by women and ethnic minorities marginalized socially and economically in Japan by limiting them spatially (both physically and psychologically). It then demonstrates how, through violence and different representations of the (female) body, Kirino challenges two dualisms of modern Japanese society: (1) the male/female gender hierarchy; and (2) passivity/violence. Finally, it looks at the "freedom" attained by Kirino's female characters by the end of the novel and questions whether this is the freedom that the characters had anticipated. The analysis ends by looking at the function of violence (together with the function of sexuality) in Kirino's challenging of another dualism, that of freedom/ constraint.

Kirino is a major figure in the "third wave'" of women mystery writers in Japan (Seaman 2004, 19). *Out* tells the story of four working-class women working the night shift at a *bentō* (Japanese-style boxed lunch) factory who become embroiled in a complex plot of murder, female solidarity, revenge and struggle after one of the women murders her husband. As well as being a bestseller in Japan, the book was also controversial in the Japanese media[9] for its portrayal of an ordinary housewife as a murderer and the other housewives as being complicit in covering it up. There are few academic works published in English on Kirino, even fewer directly concerning *Out*,[10] so the following aims to fill in some of the gaps for what is one of Japan's most significant and representative (of 1990s popular fiction) works.

Each of the four main female protagonists, Yayoi, Masako, Yoshie and Kuniko, as well as the two non-Japanese characters Anna and Kazuo, suffers from being constrained in their lives within Japanese society. In the case of the four Japanese women, they are also constrained within their family home environments. Yayoi must contend with a spouse who physically abuses her, causing "hatred [...] to spread like a dark cloud and take[n] possession of her" (Kirino 2004, 56). Masako was once a successful employee at a financial company; however, after complaining that she was being paid less than a male worker who had joined the company at the same time, she was ostracized, causing her to resign. Widow Yoshie has the burden of looking after an elderly relative as well as her young grandson, who is dumped on her by her wayward daughter. Kuniko's problems are self-inflicted—a mountain of personal consumer debt, a result both of her partner leaving her and being unable to live within her means as she hopelessly strives to meet Japan's fashion media ideals of womanhood. She wishes "she were a different woman, living a different life, in a different place, with a different man" (Kirino 2004, 17). Although the sources of their problems are varied, the women are all put in the same boat by their economic necessity. As marginalized temporary and part-time workers in Japan's workforce, during a period when the lifetime employment model was being consistently eroded, the slight premium earned per hour by working the night shift at the factory helps the women. It is notable that Kirino sets up the novel in this way since these are all problems that are very relevant to the condition of women in modern Japan yet tend to be overlooked.

The two main non-Japanese characters in the book, Anna and Kazuo, also feel constrained by society, although in a different way from that of the Japanese women. Whereas no family problems are alluded to for either Anna or Kazuo, mainly because they have no family in Japan, they face even greater constraint by Japanese society than the Japanese women. Anna is portrayed as being sweet and innocent when first introduced in the novel. However, her realization that her love for Satake is unrequited unfortunately does not also open her eyes (as Satake observes) to the fact that she is being used and will be discarded once she has served her purpose in Japan. Kazuo, despite having the ostensible benefit of Japanese citizenship, also eventually realizes that he may never achieve his dreams of economic success in Japan and that he will never be truly accepted by Japanese society, as Masako's rejection of him emphasizes: "There's no point in staying any longer" (Kirino 2004, 495). There is even a case to be put forward for pimp Satake as being constrained since he is forever tainted by society, despite having paid his dues in prison and trying to rebuild his life. He must exist on the margins of society, for which his sexual impotence seems to act as a metaphor, as will be demonstrated later.

In her book *Japanese Women: Constraint and Fulfillment*, Lebra (1985) demonstrates the importance of perspective in looking at Japanese women and that constraint may sometimes hide fulfilment (and vice-versa). Kirino, although occasionally showing hints of ambiguity, tends to focus mostly on suffocating constraint in the early part of *Out* when detailing her characters and this may be to emphasize some of the major changes occurring in Japanese society since Lebra's book was published. As post-bubble Japanese society in the 1990s and 2000s became increasingly complex and its identity confused,[11] women had to try to readjust to these changes. Kirino demonstrates the effect of some of these changes on women in *Out*, touching on the themes of consumerism, domestic violence, family breakdown, sexism and ageism.

Seaman (2006) explains how Kirino uses gendered constructions of space to show how the four main characters are spatially marginalized by their gender and denied access to their desired space in the center of the urban landscape. Masako, for example, feels that she belongs to the financial industry and Kuniko desires a job in the entertainment district, each believing that this would lead to being in the center. However, the women are denied access to the center based on their gender, age, lack of perceived beauty, lack of education or other factors decided by the males who hold all the power. Instead, the women toil in a factory on the outskirts of the city which emphasizes their marginalization and, for Yayoi, also her despair:

> But in contrast to the rose-tinted world that followed along with her at the lei-surely pace of her bicycle, the rest of the world was a grimmer shade—the wet asphalt of the street, the trees on either side in their newish foliage, the tightly shuttered houses. Though the umbrella created a pink cocoon, her surroundings became more sinister and depressing. Somehow, this seemed like a symbol of her own life now that she had killed Kenji. (Kirino 2004, 112)

The women are not even allowed refuge in the traditionally matriarchal space of the family home because of the problems they face there. Thus, with no refuge either in private space or in public space they are forced to form strong friendships with each other. With such uncompromising pressures the first undercurrent of their "violence" emerges.

Constraint extends from the physical spatial reality to the inner psychological reality as the characters continue to struggle to survive. Masako has the most complex psychology. There is a tightness and a reticence to her character early on which only gradually unwinds to reveal itself as the novel progresses. At the beginning of the novel, she is uptight, reserved and trapped. However, as the reader discovers her reasons for this, and her new job seems to have a cathartic effect, she eventually appears to be able to attain some sort of freedom in her mind emotionally and possibly sexually. Yoshie is the most trapped psychologically of the four women since she is expected by everybody including her best friends to shoulder her own burden even though she worries it "would soon reach the breaking point" (Kirino 2004, 33). Her identity as a woman has been constrained in a psychoanalytical sense since the way she performs her gender roles as widow, mother and grandmother are atypical according to the norms of Japanese society, which values a "good wife, wise mother" (*ryōsai kenbo*), a phrase which encapsulated the ideal many women aspired to in postwar Japan. Women were expected to be housewifely, for example, by mastering cooking, sewing, and performing other household duties diligently, while also supporting their husband's and children's needs as required. Yoshie clearly does not fit into this mold, harried as she is between her job, caring for her mother-in-law, and providing for her greedy daughter, yet she is arguably still invested in her family as much as any other conventional "good wife, wise mother." Thus, Yoshie goes largely unappreciated both by her family and society.

The main significance of Kirino's constraining of her female characters is therefore to show the marginalized positions that women are forced to occupy in society. However, Kirino complicates this with her "ethnic" characters, Anna and Kazuo. Typically, "Orientalist discourse locates the Other as criminal, and a threat" (Munt 1994, 85). However, since Anna and Kazuo too are economically impoverished and marginalized physically and psychologically, possibly even more so than the Japanese characters, the reader cannot simply take the text as being a straightforward liberal feminist discourse speaking out on behalf of women. Indeed, gender inequality in contemporary Japan is sometimes more effectively described when it intersects with other variables, particularly social class (economic deprivation). The subordination of Japanese women to men is not only deep-seated but congenital to the economic organization of Japan Inc. as a source of a cheap, flexible and ultimately disposable form of labor. Arguably the even greater role of Japanese women is that they are required to nurture (both children and the elderly as Yoshie does) and keep their place in the pecking order of society by learning culturally appropriate behavior, rules and respect for (invariably male) authority.

Constraint is needed initially for the later pathways of violence and freedom to be duly observed. Kirino is challenging the dualism of passivity/violence whereby Japanese women are supposed to adhere to the meek "*Madame Butterfly*" stereotype. In her book, *The Newly Born Woman*, Cixous (1986) writes of the masculine framework imposed on all writing and encourages women authors to challenge and destabilize it. Kirino takes up this challenge. Putting a strong emphasis on the constraint faced by her characters at the beginning of the novel allows her to convincingly destabilize normative hierarchal binaries later through the function of violence.

The definition of "violence" used here is not simply that of physical force (although it includes it) but one that encompasses all sorts of attacks such as passive-aggressive behavior, emotional abuse and transgression of societal norms, customs and laws. Using this broad scope, Kirino uses violence not only in its most extreme and shocking forms such as murder, rape and domestic violence, but also in several other more subtle ways, too, to make her readers question these normative gender constructions in Japanese society. One example is the use of passive-aggression by some of her characters. Passive-aggression in Japanese society is often associated with women, particularly with "office ladies" who use it to rebalance some of the power in the workplace that is usually the preserve of men (Ogasawara 1998). Women in Japan have traditionally been subordinated within Japanese companies, performing gendered roles mostly based on serving their male colleagues. Ogasawara demonstrates how women can resist men's power, thwarting their managers and subverting the power structure to their advantage by shirking their duties, gossiping and other techniques. However, Kirino inverts this in *Out* by instead making some of the male characters passive-aggressive and the victims female. When Masako questions her position in the workplace she is put back in place by the men; first by the seemingly benign passive-aggression of being ignored socially, then more aggressively and painfully through being discriminated against by being denied pay rises and promotions in favor of (younger) men at the company. Masako is also on the receiving end of passive-aggression from her husband at home. By reversing gender norms, Kirino encourages her readers to re-evaluate the way they think regarding men and women.

Critics and readers tend to read *Out* in one of two ways: as a window into the trapped lives of Japanese housewives, or as a feminist work connecting the text to the growing social and political movements during Kirino's time, including a more critical look at and suspicion of the knowledge produced and disseminated by the Japanese establishment that marginalizes Japan's oppressed groups. In Japan, the former viewpoint tends to prevail whereas in the West, the latter viewpoint does (Seaman 2006, 199) while focusing particularly on the representation of women (and, to a lesser extent, ethnic minorities) and how this (alongside their social identities and subjectivity) is embedded within the complex machinations of male-controlled power structures in Japan. Kirino herself states in an interview that *Out* demonstrates how women can be "cornered" and seek "escape":

> [...] being a woman in this society is mainly an anonymous existence. I don't think the fact that the environment is such that women are nameless and overlooked is a good thing. For example, a young man once told me that until he read Out, he "never realized that regular middle-aged women actually had a life." What makes these women special is not that they committed a crime, but the circumstances around these normal women that cornered them into that situation. It's often merely convenient to depict them as seeking an escape from their life through an act of crime. (Kirino 2003)

Violence expressed in its various forms in *Out* thus offers women their only chance to escape from what is constraining them. In Yayoi's case, it is her violence against her husband which finally sets her free from him. For Masako, her violence is not a directly physical one in the same way as Yayoi's; nevertheless, the act of cutting up Yayoi's salaryman husband serves metaphorically as revenge on men for the discrimination she suffered when working in the financial sector. For Yoshie and Kuniko, becoming embroiled in the murder means a transgression of societal norms which they seem to readily embrace. But what is the purpose for shocking the reader by showing that ordinary Japanese women can become involved in such gruesome crimes?

Considering this point in more detail, it can be said that Japanese society holds certain expectations regarding gender and violence. Women, although not always acknowledged as such, are generally held by Japanese society to be the subordinate in the male-female hierarchy. Therefore, women are seen as being incapable of violence such as murder since most perpetrators are men. Women are supposed to be weak, timid, and fragile. Although women are depicted as criminals in crime fiction, it is usually as an accomplice or a *femme fatale*. Kirino depicting murder by an ordinary woman turns these conventional notions on their head.

Kirino's text complicates our understanding of these widely held hierarchal binaries since it can be read on several levels. Kirino's works have been described as "brainy writing-style mashup [...] known as 'Kirino Jynru,' or a book that borrows freely from several genres but feels beholden to none of their rules" (Rochlin 2007). Although this chapter has so far made a case for showing that women are constrained in the novel and that violence is the method they use to escape it, alternative readings are possible too. For example, some of the men in the novel (note the examples given earlier of Kazuo and Satake) are also constrained. as both men and women in Japan are expected to conform to heteronormative gender stereotypes. Alternatively, variables other than gender—economics, for example—may be more important as a determinant.

The women in *Out* have been drawn into the plot by chance and circumstance rather than by being active agents of violence. Yayoi only managed murder after "her patience snapped" (Kirino 2004, 61) so it was hardly a premeditated crime. Masako, a person who "did her best to live her life according to reason and common sense" (Kirino 2004, 6), although the leader and the most pro-active woman in the group, still needed the situation to be thrust into her lap in order to act in the way that she does. It is easy to overlook that only a single murder is committed by a single woman (should Masako's killing of Satake at the end of the novel, which is arguably self-defense, be discounted). There are other murders, rapes and horrors elsewhere in the novel, but these are all perpetrated by men. *Out* depends on this representation of men because should women be the only criminals it would provide the novel and its construction of gender with a different meaning. Why then is the focus so much upon the women's crimes and their (lack of) morality?

The answer to this may lie partly in the representation of the female body, its perceived morality, and its relation to violence. Generally, in works of fiction, women represent victims (the violated), the moral high ground and consumption.[12] In a typical crime novel, a female character is overwhelmingly more likely to be a victim of violence than a perpetrator. By switching this convention around, Kirino forces readers to re-examine their attitude towards male and female gender roles. Kirino is constantly changing meanings and allowing multiple interpretations of her text using violence, which has the effect of questioning stereotypes. Previously held hierarchies become untenable since they have apparently deconstructed themselves. However, this idea cannot be pushed too much in terms of a simple "deconstruction" of the dualisms in the novel. Although it is very important to show how and why Kirino expresses the tensions in the dualisms, Derrida's deconstruction only fits well in very specific instances where the hierarchy within the dualism is strong and where the text can easily be read in several ways. Thus, in this instance, deconstruction would appear to apply well to the dualisms of passivity/violence, and freedom/constraint though rather less well for the male/female hierarchy.

Women's bodies are usually contextualized in terms of consumption or being consumed, though in *Out* the main female Japanese characters use their bodies to help "produce" in the factory and their homes (Seaman 2006, 209). Although their bodies are constantly criticized by men for being too old (Masako and Yoshie) or too ugly (Kuniko) the body still represents both opportunities and barriers for the women. They are reclaiming their bodies from the "social" and the "political" and returning them to the "individual."[13] Through their work dismembering bodies, it is the women who gain control, and male bodies that become objectified. As ever though, Kirino complicates matters by allowing Kuniko—the consumer-victim—to herself be cut up later in the novel.

Perhaps Kuniko's violent death and later dismemberment by her "friends" has significance not just for the plot—for its dark humor and for its morality lesson—but also, because it demonstrates the abjection of the remaining three Japanese friends. As a marginalized group they are accustomed to operating outside the symbolic order of society. Thus, mutilating bodies (objects) does not present to them the same horror or violence as it may to someone belonging to the symbolic order. The murdered bodies were presumably once subjects in the cultural world, but they are just mere objects to the women, so, upon receiving Kuniko's body, the women experience the "uncanny" and yet, after a brief discussion, decide that the economic benefits from doing the task outweigh their group notions of female solidarity and morality. Another interpretation of Kirino's text, however, could be that this is the last chance for the women to redeem themselves morally by passing over this dismemberment (and stopping altogether). The body of a woman—and, moreover, a friend—"serve[s] both as a guide and locale for perfection in the symbolic order" (Slaymaker 2004, 161). By making this choice the women crystallize their position as not belonging to the symbolic order.

Iida argues that "as sexuality became increasingly commercialized, the conventional belief in the family and women's bodies as the last remaining bastions of morality, supposedly 'sacred' private realms free from commercial enterprise have undergone substantial changes" (2002, 229). The women in *Out* are willing to forego any morality to earn money by using their bodies. In the end, their morality is shredded as they become willing to cut up bodies for money, to frame Satake for a crime he did not commit, to lie and to cheat.

Have the four women achieved the freedom that they had hoped for by the end of *Out*? In Kuniko's case, depending on which perspective is taken, she has either achieved the ultimate freedom—death—or she has ultimately been deprived of her freedom by Satake. This ambiguity in how things may be construed continues Kirino's attempt to prevent her readers from taking anything for granted. In some ways, through their "violence" the three surviving women have achieved freedom. Their bodies have continued to be "productive" yet they have gained freedom from having to use their bodies for the benefit of their employer, using them instead for their own financial benefit. They control their work now, not the other way around. Indeed, the women have gained their economic freedom—certainly, at least, Masako and Yoshie—and this is significant since lack of financial freedom was the one thing that they all had in common at the start of the novel.

Whether the women are freer socially both within the private (family) and public (society) realms is debatable. Yayoi gains freedom from her abusive husband through her violence. Yoshie, too, is released from the burden of looking after her mother-in-law (although through Satake's violence, not her own). It seems that the women needed violence and their own version of justice since they were not able to rely on the law to redress having been wronged. The women find freedom socially within their own group—even though they vary significantly in age and personality—because they can identify with each other and are brought even closer in the aftermath of the murder. They realize that they are far stronger together than separately, so their solidarity gives them a collective resistance to the symbolic world they are not a part of. Interestingly, the Japanese movie version of *Out* (2003) ends instead with the women planning to move away to Hokkaido and rebuild their lives together.

Nevertheless, violence also tips the freedom/constraint dualism back towards constraint in other ways at the end of the novel. Although—tellingly or not—Kirino does not dwell upon how their crimes have affected their morality, there is certainly a squeezing effect on their conscience. Even should the women not feel remorse for what they have done—"Serves the bastard right!" as Yayoi says when recalling the murder she commits later in the novel (Kirino 2004, 113)—the moral judgement of society will forever weigh down upon them and, like Satake, they will likely be forever tainted and unable to ever rejoin society, if ever they had been a part of it previously anyway. Their friendship was what kept them going when they had little else, yet the violence has killed one of the quartet and has led to the scattering of the others by the end. Masako notes at the very end of the novel the indistinctness of freedom. She is no longer involved in other people's search for freedom and her own freedom remains elusive: "She would go and buy an airplane ticket. The freedom she was seeking was her own, not Satake's, or Yayoi's, or Yoshie's, and she was sure it must be out there somewhere" (Kirino 2004, 520).

Masako's quest for freedom is the most complex among all the characters in *Out*. She does not seem as economically underprivileged as her friends so one wonders why she works the night shift at the factory—whether it is a means to completely disassociate herself from the conventional 9-to-5 business world and to escape from her family "[b]ecause I want to be alone. Because I want to be free" (Kirino 2004, 493). It takes the catalyst of violence to wake Masako from her stupor and start in earnest her search for self-determination. First, she secures freedom for Yayoi. She then assists her friends in their search. Finally, with Satake, she both liberates him (unwittingly or not) and simultaneously achieves sexual liberation for herself.

Kirino uses sexuality in a similar way to her use of violence to cut through the dualism of freedom/constraint. At the start of the novel the women discuss a rapist lurking near their factory and are fearful of being raped. However, later in the novel Masako fantasizes about being raped:

> *The fingers tightened, and Masako went rigid with fear. But then, slowly, the warmth of his hands, the rough breathing on her neck, began to arouse a buried impulse in her: the urge to surrender, to relax and allow herself to die. Abruptly, her fear began to dissipate, as if floating weightlessly away, and in its place came a sense of blissful pleasure. She cried out in delight.* (Kirino 2004, 378)

In the closing stages of the novel Masako is raped by Satake. Curiously, the rape is not what is expected: with the combined force of violence and sexuality working together, Kirino hammers at the freedom/constraint dualism by making us question whether rape can in some cases provide self-determination to a woman rather than oppress her. Yayoi, after her act of violence and the freedom she finds as a result, is also shown by Kirino to exude even greater sexuality than before. Masako emerges from her own rape and her killing of Satake materially richer, freer and more satisfied than at any other time.

The mixing of violence, sexuality and fear is an irresistible combination to Masako during her rape. This contradicts the portrait Kirino steadily built of Masako early in the novel of a constrained, self-effacing woman with no sexual appetite who cares little for her appearance and is generally fearful. Yet again, violence—and this time sexuality, as well—is used to destabilize a dualism (freedom/constraint). The "buried impulse" of fear within Masako is open to interpretation though could be linked to the primeval fear humans used to experience of being attacked while engaging in sex.[14] Ironically, it is through "regressing" in such a way rather than by participating in Japan's postmodern culture that a woman such as Masako is able to find her own freedom and peculiar *jouissance*. Kirino is questioning Japan's gender norms and ageism through Masako, who no longer equates with the submissive Japanese woman stereotype, and in doing so sheds light on the deeply entrenched misogynistic workings of (corporate) Japan. Masako's freedom comes at the cost of having to live on the margins of society. Admittedly, as a woman she already occupied a marginalized position, but her new freedom at least affords her the ability to break from some of society's constraints.

Satake is a complex character who on the face of things ought immediately to be marked as deranged. He is violent through and through—a murderer, a rapist and a general sociopath.

However, he elicits sympathy for the way that he is shunned by society by continuing to be tainted despite having paid his dues in prison and for being unfairly held for the murder committed by Yayoi. Satake demonstrates his human side in the way he cares for Anna and, in a different way, his "relationship" with Masako. His sexual impotence acts as a metaphor for his restriction from society. When he violently rapes Masako—perhaps the only way, given his lowly social position, that he can exert any power—his penetration of her is also literally a "re-entering" of the symbolic order in the center of society and how he regains his freedom:

> He hadn't been with a real, flesh-and-blood woman since that day in Shinjuku, since that dark dream. The thing deep in his soul began to writhe, rise up and become real, promising to take him with it wherever it was going. To hell, and heaven. It was only in the final moments of sex with her that the gap between them could be bridged. This was what he'd been born for, and this was what he would die for. (Kirino 2004, 502)

That Kirino allows Satake—represented as male, misogynist[15] and a criminal—his freedom too, again complicates reading the text as a transgressive, feminist work of crime fiction. Indeed, it could even be argued that *Out* portrays women in an unfavorable light as passive, weak, cold, calculating and greedy and demonstrates that they are willing to violate the norms of society should it bring them material gain. This pattern of shifting boundaries and testing dualisms can also be found in her other works. Copeland (2004) demonstrates how Kirino tests the binaries of marriage and pornography; passivity and violence; and homosexuality and heterosexuality. In *Angels*, Kirino "questions the constructedness of gender and the unnatural enforcement of identities dictated by these constructions" (Copeland 2004, 266). In *Out*, Kirino's questioning of the bond between logocentrism and phallocentrism in literature follows Cixous.[16] Although her technique of constantly challenging dualisms makes readers giddy—being spun in one direction then the opposite—in the final evaluation it produces a work that forces readers to consider the changes in gender relations, gender hierarchies and gender lifestyles currently evolving in modern Japan.

As a result of this, *Out* is a critical novel as an in-road into the popular fiction of Japan, not just as a work in itself but also for the very salient social issues it traverses as well as its multiple forms of dissemination beyond the novel itself (in addition to the film, it was also adapted for television) which is a feature of Japanese popular fiction. The novel encapsulates the period of time just after the "peak" of popular fiction (considered in terms of sales and cultural prevalence) at the start of the 1990s, so is useful in being able to be both critical of the excesses of bubble-era Japan while also alerting readers to the rapidly deteriorating and ongoing social problems in Japanese society, particularly those relating to women, the aged, minorities and the poor. In particular, its contribution towards influencing the representation of women and associated norms regarding their positions and roles in contemporary Japanese society is nuanced yet considerable. It skillfully avoids didacticism by refusing to align itself with any particular school of feminism while portraying women characters using a full array of humanity normally afforded only to male protagonists ranging from the monstrous feminine to the good wife, wise mother. Women should not be viewed in universal or essentialist terms, but with full appreciation of their variety, differences, oppressions, victories and femininities, allowing their subaltern voices to speak and be heard among the louder voices of western feminism and the Japanese patriarchy. By bringing the otherness of the Japanese woman's voice into frame, Kirino guides readers towards an understanding of the antithetical specificity yet vastness of the feminine mind and condition, something that might ultimately be unknowable, as Irigaray (1993) suggests. Along with Yoshimoto Banana, Kawakami Hiromi and Tawada Yōko, Kirino has led the way for a plethora of other Japanese women writers of popular fiction including Murata Sayaka and MotoyaYukiko to blossom and also resist dominant gender paradigms and the patriarchal construction of the nation Japan.

Conclusion

The social changes that *Out* references have become even more important in recent times and have also been addressed by later Japanese popular fiction, especially that written by women. A case in point is Murata Sayaka's (2016) novel *Konbini ningen* (*Convenience Store Woman*) which won the prestigious Akutagawa Prize in its year of publication. Based on the author's own experiences working at a convenience store, the novel uses this space as a representation of the same issues covered by Kirino in *Out*. The heroine, Furukura Keiko, works in a convenience store for eighteen years after leaving school at the age of eighteen. During her school years, Keiko was shunned by her peers and adults around her for her non-conformist character and behavior. The convenience store offers Keiko a modicum of status in society albeit tempered by its precarious contract, long and unpredictable working hours and male-dominated hierarchies. By entering into a contract with the convenience store (which acts as a proxy for Japanese society), the protagonist experiences the same progression of constraint, violence and freedom as demonstrated in Kirino's *Out*. The convenience store acts as a microcosm of Japanese society, which remains male-dominated and beset by rigid rules that seem only to serve to perpetuate such domination. Women such as Keiko are structurally subordinated by this patriarchy—simply by being born as women—to positions in which they need to learn how to adapt and find their freedom amidst a culture of conformism, much in the same way as Kirino's female characters in *Out* must too.

Japan is clearly at a crossroads regarding its treatment of women, its elderly and its attitude towards immigration and minorities. Postwar norms of gender expectations and family structure[17] propagated by an alliance of government, industry and social organizations were stretched by the bursting of the economic bubble in the 1990s. Still, this historically contingent heterosexual matrix remains resilient. In fact, as Ayako Kano (2015) has noted in her writing on gender relations and politics in the aftermath of the East Japan Earthquake Disaster in 2011, various conservative divisions in Japan blamed working women and women's liberation feminism dating from the 1970s for the consequent economic decline. Japanese popular fiction has an important role to play not just in reflecting social changes but also in giving voice to these groups, thus its future direction is likely to become increasingly political, eclectic and fragmented.[18] The role of popular fiction in Japan, despite its relative decline both in turnover and share of the overall popular culture market,[19] is expanding in terms of the demographics of its authors and readers in both Japan (more women and elderly) and abroad (more Japanese diaspora and other general readers as a result of more translations from Japanese into other languages),[20] thus it will still be important and influential for a long time to come.

Acknowledgements

This work was supported by JSPS KAKENHI Grant Number 21K12957.

Notes

[1] *Out* is one of Kirino's most successful novels to date. It won Japan's top mystery award (Grand Prix for Crime Fiction) and its English translation was nominated in the "Best Novel Award" category in 2004 by the Mystery Writers of America's Edgar Allen Poe Awards (Seaman 2006, 197).

[2] Ozaki Hotsuki's (1964) *Taishū bungaku* (Popular literature) and Nakatani Hiroshi's (1973) book of the same name, although both now out of date, at least attempted to address popular fiction in Japan as a subject worthy of academic attention. Other researchers on the topic include Cécile Sakai and Tsurumi Shunsuke although their work also dates to the 1980s, hence, the need for new research based on more recent developments in the genre.

[3] Several categories for literature exist in Japan. Washburn (2013) lists the following: *Nihon bungaku* (Japanese literature); *kindai bungaku* (modern literature); *gendai bungaku* (contemporary literature); *taishū bungaku* (popular literature); *jun bungaku* (pure or elite literature); *puroretaria bungaku* (proletarian literature); *seisan bungaku* (productivity literature); *nōmin bungaku* (rural or peasant literature); *dōwa bungaku* (children's literature); *joryū bungaku* (women's literature); *posutomodan bungaku* (postmodern literature).

[4] For more on media mix and how it leads to certain textual strategies see Zahlten (2014).

[5] "Cool Japan" was a campaign to boost Japan's cultural industries orchestrated by the Japanese government. See Otmazgin and Ben-Ari (2013).

[6] For an overview of Japan's reading culture see Kamei-Dyche (2017).

[7] The works of these authors are mostly eclectic. Since this chapter aims to show the patterns and trends in Japanese popular fiction over recent decades, it focuses mainly on works by women authors concerning changing Japanese society and the place of women within it.

[8] Since 2020, however, the impact of COVID-19 has led to more purchases of printed books for reading at home in place of reading on electronic devices while commuting or at offices. See The Shuppan Kagaku Kenkyūjo website: https://shuppankagaku.com/statistics/paperback/.

[9] See Kirino's reaction to this in her interview with Andrew Duncan in IndieBound (Kirino n.d.).

[10] Pre-eminent is Amanda Seaman's (2006) journal article "Inside OUT: Space, Gender and Power in Kirino Natsuo."

[11] For an overview of these changes see Yoda (2000), Iida (2000) and Kingston (2004).

[12] See chapter 2, "The (gendered) discourse and a (woman's) body" in Slaymaker (2004, 31–42).

[13] See Segal et al. (2003) especially chapter 14 "Bodies in Transition, or the Unbearable Lightness of the "Traditionless' Self" by Márta Csabai and Ferenc Erős.

[14] See "The Predator Narrative," chapter 6 in Fry (2019).

[15] "You hate me, don't you? Just like I hate you." "But why?" "Because you're a woman." (Kirino 2004, 504)

[16] See Cixous and Derrida (1994, 35–46).

[17] See Senda (2011, 16) and Ochiai (1997).

[18] Women have recently dominated Japan's most prestigious literary awards. All six nominees for the 2019 Naoki Award were women, as were all four recipients of the Akutagawa Award in 2020 and 2021. See https://www.bunshun.co.jp/shinkoukai/.

[19] Latest figures show that this downturn was reversed during the coronavirus pandemic (nippon.com 2021).

[20] Yoko Tawada's *The Emissary* won the 2018 National Book Award in the United States for best translated work.

Bibliography

Asai, S., 2016. Format Choice for Popular Fiction Books in Japan. *Publishing Research Quarterly*, 32(2), 75–83.

Cixous, H., and Derrida, J. (1994). *The Hélène Cixous Reader*. London: Psychology Press.

Copeland, R., 2004. Woman Uncovered: Pornography and Power in the Detective Fiction of Kirino Natsuo. *Japan Forum*, 16, 249–69.

Fry, C. L., 2019. *Primal Roots of Horror Cinema: Evolutionary Psychology and Narratives of Fear*. Jefferson, NC: McFarland.

Iida, Y., 2000. Between the Technique of Living an Endless Routine and the Madness of Absolute Degree Zero: Japanese Identity and the Crisis of Modernity in the 1990s. *positions: East Asia cultures critique*, 8 (2), 423–64.

———., 2002. *Rethinking Identity in Modern Japan: Nationalism as Aesthetics*. London: Routledge.

Irigaray, L., 1993. *An Ethics of Sexual Difference*. Ithaca: Cornell University Press.

Kamei-Dyche, A.T., 2017. *Reading Culture in Japan*. [online] Oxford Research Encyclopedia of Literature. https://doi.org/10.1093/acrefore/9780190201098.013.287.

Kano, A., 2015. The Future of Gender in Japan: Work/Life Balance and Relations between the Sexes. In F. Baldwin and A. Allison, eds., *Japan: The Precarious Future*. New York: New York University Press, 87–109.

Kingston, J., 2004. *Japan's Quiet Transformation: Social Change and Civil Society in the Twenty-First Century*. London: RoutledgeCurzon.

Kirino, N., (2003). *Natsuo Kirino*. Available from: http://www.japanreview.net/interview_Natsuo_Kirino.htm [Accessed 8 January 2021].

———., *Natsuo Kirino Interview*. Interviewed by Andrew Duncan [online]. Available at: http://www.indiebound.org/author-interviews/kirinonatsuo [Accessed 8 January 2021].

———., 2004. *Out*. London: Vintage.

Lebra, T.S., 1985. *Japanese Women: Constraint and Fulfillment*. Honolulu: University of Hawai'i Press.

Munt, S., 1994. *Murder by the Book? Crime Fiction and Feminism*. London: Routledge.

Murata, S., 2018. *Convenience Store Woman: A Novel*. New York: Grove Press.

Nakatani, H., 1973. *Taishū bungaku* [Popular literature]. Tokyo: Togensha.

nippon.com, 2021. *Koronaka de hon no juyō zōka: 2020 nen no hanbaigaku wa suitei 1 chō 6000 oku en ni* [Increased demand for books due to corona stagnation: Sales in 2020 estimated at 1.6 trillion yen]. [online] nippon.com. Available at: https://www.nippon.com/ja/japan-data/h00937/ [Accessed 6 September 2021].

Ochiai, E., 1997. *The Japanese Family System in Transition*. Tokyo: LTCB International Library Foundation.

Ogasawara, Y., 1998. *Office Ladies and Salaried Men: Power, Gender, and Work in Japanese Companies*. Berkeley: University of California Press.

Otmazgin, N. and Ben-Ari, E., 2013. *Popular Culture and the State in East and Southeast Asia*. London: Routledge.

OUT. 2003. [DVD] Directed by Hideyuki Hirayama. Japan: 20th Century Fox Home Entertainment Japan.

Ozaki, H., 1964. *Taishū bungaku* [Popular literature]. Tokyo: Kinokuniya Shoten.

Rochlin, M., 2007. *Grotesque: Natsuo Kirino's Dark World*. LA Weekly. Available at: http://www.laweekly.com/2007-07-05/art-books/grotesque-natsuo-kirino-s-dark-world/ [Accessed 8 January 2021].

Seaman, A.C., 2004. *Bodies of Evidence: Women, Society, and Detective Fiction in 1990s Japan*. Honolulu: University of Hawai'i Press.

Seaman, A.C., 2006. Inside OUT: Space, Gender, and Power in Kirino Natsuo. *Japanese Language and Literature*, 40 (2), 197–217.

Segal, N., Taylor, L. and Cook, R., 2003. *Indeterminate Bodies*. Basingstoke: Palgrave Macmillan.

Senda, Y., 2011. *Nihon gata kindai kazoku doko kara kite doko e iku no ka* [The model Japanese family: where did it come from, where is it going?]. Tokyo: Keisō Shobō.

Slaymaker, D., 2004. *The Body in Postwar Japanese Fiction*. London: RoutledgeCurzon.

Strecher, M. C., 1996. Purely Mass or Massively Pure? The Division Between "Pure" and "Mass" Literature. *Monumenta Nipponica*, 51(3), 357–74.

Tawada, Y., 2018. *The Emissary*. New York: New Directions Publishing.

Washburn, D., 2013. Bungaku/Literature. *Review of Japanese Culture and Society*, 25, 116–26.

Yoda, T., 2000. A Roadmap to Millennial Japan. *The South Atlantic Quarterly*, 99 (4), 629–68.

Zahlten, A., 2014. Media Mix and the Metaphoric Economy of World. In D. Miyao, ed., *The Oxford Handbook of Japanese Cinema*. New York: Oxford University Press, 438–56.

Chapter 12
Intersections of Difference: Sex, Gender and Disability in Japanese Visual Media

Forum Mithani

The sexual lives of disabled people in Japan are becoming more visible as activists and media makers seek to interrogate long-standing taboos around the subject. This chapter uses an intersectional feminist lens to examine representations of disability, gender and sexuality in Japanese visual media, demonstrating the ways in which such images both push and simultaneously reinforce the boundaries of acceptable discourse. Using an approach that combines theories from feminist film studies and disability studies, the chapter highlights the synergies between the two fields, suggesting the potential for future avenues of inquiry.

Introduction

The Tokyo 2020 Paralympics (delayed due to the COVID-19 pandemic until late summer 2021) brought renewed focus to the potentialities of people with disabilities on an international scale. The host nation was keen to present itself as a beacon of diversity and inclusion under the banner "know differences, show differences" (*chigai o shiri, chigai o shimesu*). Indeed, people with disabilities were not only shown, they were celebrated during the two-week global event. However, this progressive-sounding slogan obscures the complex reality of attitudes towards disability, which, as Stevens (2013, 27) suggests, is embraced when it brings fortuitous circumstances and shunned when it is considered burdensome to society. Despite efforts to move from a medicalized view of disability to a model that sees it as a consequence of social restrictions to participation, disability continues to be stigmatized in Japan as something undesirable and to be avoided (Okuyama 2020; Stevens 2013). This is exemplified in the Japanese term most commonly used to refer to disability, *shōgai*, which combines the Chinese characters *shō* (interfere or hinder) and *gai* (harm) (Okuyama 2020, Kindle loc. 404).

Such attitudes come into sharp focus in discussions of the sexual and reproductive rights of people with disabilities. The historical practice of forced sterilizations, legally enshrined in the Eugenic Protection Law (*Yūsei hogo hō*, 1948–1996) (Hovhannisyan 2021), as well as a lack of adequate sex education provision in special needs schools (Satō and Miyazaki 2014) are indicative of a reluctance to address issues of sexuality and desire among people with disabilities. Gender brings an additional dimension to this difficult terrain: although there now exist a range of sexual services aimed at the disabled community, most are designed to fulfil male needs, ignoring the sexual desires of disabled women.

This reluctance to view women with disabilities as sexual beings has manifested itself in cinematic representations, which have tended to romanticize disabled women as persevering, heroic and essentially asexual. However, the recent film *37 sekanzu* (37 Seconds, Hikari 2019), the story of a young woman with cerebral palsy who embarks on an exploration of her sexuality, confronts the stigmatization of non-normative female bodies from the fore with its frank depictions of nudity and sexual desire. Furthermore, the decision by director Hikari to cast a disabled actor in the lead role makes the film truly ground-breaking. As such, it both complements and contrasts with other recent Japanese films that explore similar themes from a male perspective. This chapter uses a feminist lens to examine representations of disability, gender and sexuality in Japanese visual media, demonstrating the ways in which such images both push and simultaneously reinforce boundaries of acceptable discourse in relation to gender, sexuality and non-normative bodies.

Disability through a feminist lens

The primary aim of this chapter is to demonstrate how feminism can provide a useful lens for better understanding representations of marginalized people in Japanese visual media. In the context of disability studies, the feminist approach has been adopted by a number of anglophone scholars, including Susan Wendell (1996) and Rosemary Garland-Thomson (1997), who note the parallels between the way womanhood and disability are perceived. In a discussion of female and disabled bodies, Garland-Thomson observes that "Both are cast as deviant and inferior; both are excluded from full participation in public as well as economic life; both are defined in opposition to a norm that is assumed to possess natural physical superiority" (1997, 19). Meanwhile, Wendell has argued that it is no coincidence that architectural designs that make it difficult for those with disabilities to access also present challenges to pregnant women and mothers of young children (in Markotić 2016, 10).

As Garland-Thomson argues, viewing disability through a feminist lens can

> *challenge existing social relations; resist interpretations of certain bodily con-figurations and functioning as deviant; question the ways that differences are invested with meaning; examine the enforcement of universalizing norms; interrogate the politics of appearance; explore the politics of naming and forge positive identities.* (Garland-Thomson 1997, 22)

In turn, approaches and insights from disability studies enable feminist inquiry to acknowledge and accommodate the diverse experiences of women more thoroughly (Garland-Thomson 1997, 24). Garland-Thomson argues the physically disabled body "constructed as the embodiment of corporeal insufficiency and deviance, becomes a repository for social anxieties about such troubling concerns as vulnerability, control, and identity" (1997, 24). Thus, disability discourse need not limit its politics to a specific minority but has the potential to recognize how disability informs national ideologies of identity beyond that which might not explicitly relate to those that identify as disabled.

The concept of intersectionality, first introduced by Kimberlé Crenshaw (1989) to explain the particular oppression faced by black women in the US (which differs from that experienced by black men or white women), provides an additional framework within which to view the experiences and representations of disabled women. Crenshaw argued that because the intersectional experience of black women was "greater than the sum of racism and sexism," existing structures of analysis and discourse focused on these issues were not sufficient to address their subordination (Crenshaw 1989, 140). Since then, intersectionality has been widely taken up and expanded to include additional categories of difference, including gender identity, sexual orientation, class, ability, nationality and so on, recognizing that the female experience is by no means universal. In the Japanese context, where historical notions of citizenship have perpetuated a tendency to view women as a homogenous mass, intersectionality is rarely discussed. Nevertheless, feminist scholars of disability have begun to embrace it as a structure for examining the particular experiences of disabled women in Japan (Kawaguchi 2019).

This chapter uses feminist theories of gender and sexuality to analyze representations of disability in recent Japanese television and film. Through a feminist interrogation of these cultural products, it aims to shed light on intersecting discourses of disability, sex and gender which have hitherto received little attention within Japanese (media) studies. In particular, it focuses on one television drama, *Pāfekuto wārudo* (Perfect World, Fuji TV 2019), and two films, *Pāfekuto reboryūshon* (Perfect Revolution, Matsumoto Junpei 2017) and *37 Seconds*, to demonstrate how visual culture can perpetuate and/or challenge (dis)ableist discourses and, in the case of *37 Seconds*, how diversity in representation can reveal the freedoms and constraints faced by multifarious categories of women in Japan. Before I move on to my analysis of media, I would first like to provide some context by talking about disability, gender and sexuality in Japan.

Disability, gender and sexuality in Japan

The complex interplay between disability, gender and sexuality has deep roots, and can be traced back to early myths and legends. Take, for example, the story of Hiruko, the child of the Japanese gods Izanagi and Izanami, who are credited with the creation of the islands of Japan. According to Shinto legend, Hiruko was cast into the ocean by his parents for being born with a physical disability (Okuyama 2017). As Yoshiko Okuyama (2017, 2020) observes, this story posits disability as a justifiable reason for infanticide. Of particular relevance to the present discussion is the cause given for Hiruko's disability—the supposed transgression of his mother, Izanami, who had initiated relations with her husband, behavior considered unbefitting of the female gender. Thus, one finds in this legend a number of interweaving discourses that demonstrate the close relationship connecting disability, gender and sexuality: the abjection of the imperfect child, the subordination of women and the blame and punishment meted out to the mother for her sexual assertiveness.

The ways in which discourses of disability, gender and sexuality have intersected to marginalize and discriminate against certain members of society are also apparent in Japan's recent history. Between 1948 and 1996, the Eugenic Protection Law enabled the practice of forced sterilizations of those considered to be suffering from hereditary disabilities, echoing the age-old notion that a disabled life was not a desirable one. The law had a disproportionate effect on women, who made up 70 percent of those subjected to sterilization (Hovhannisyan 2021).[1] The state has only recently accepted responsibility for depriving thousands of their reproductive rights with an apology and compensation (Hurst 2019). Furthermore, reports that women from Fukushima are being labelled "damaged goods" (Haworth 2013), unsuitable for marriage due to unfounded beliefs that the effects of radiation poisoning can be genetically inherited, suggest that such discrimination has not disappeared.

Sex itself is seen as a "private issue" in Japan and social workers who work with disabled people receive almost no training on the sexual needs of service users. According to Yonemura Mina, social workers operate under the mantra "let sleeping dogs lie," which suggests that, if they just ignore the issue, it will not rear its head (AERA 2018). Such attitudes came to the fore during an incident in 2003 involving the Nanao Special School in Tokyo, which became the target of a campaign after it introduced sex education classes for students with learning disabilities. The school had devised a special curriculum, including the use of visual aids and a song that featured terms for genitalia, which was designed specifically with the needs of their students in mind. However, it was branded obscene and excessive by conservative politicians and the right-wing press, who believed the students were being unnecessarily exposed to such information far too soon and moved to have the classes stopped, teaching materials confiscated and teachers punished. The school was eventually successful in bringing a lawsuit against the authorities and the media (Ogawa 2018).

Although these events occurred during a wider backlash against "gender-free" policies and sex education in schools, the social discourse surrounding them is indicative of the extent to which people with disabilities are infantilized as innocent and passive, incapable of autonomous thought or expression. Normative social discourses linking adulthood to productivity reinforce the perception that disabled people can never become mature, fully-formed members of society (Veere 2020, 3). However, somewhat contradicting the assumption that sex education would put improper thoughts in the minds of innocents, it was revealed that Nanao Special School devised the curriculum in the first place because teachers had already observed sexual behavior among the students (Ogawa 2018). The more recent case of a Japanese woman with a mild intellectual disability who was charged with abandoning her new-born baby in a toilet has once again highlighted concerns over the inadequacy of sex education for disabled people (Takebayashi 2020).

In recent years, disability rights activists have increasingly pushed back against the stereotype of disabled people as sexually innocent and passive. Kumashino Yoshihiko (2021), who describes his work as "helping horny disabled people," founded the non-profit organization NPO Noir to campaign for better awareness of the sexual needs of people with disabilities. Kumashino, a wheelchair user born with cerebral palsy, speaks and writes extensively on disability and sexuality, including accessible love hotels and sex worker services. He published a memoir about his experiences that became the basis for the Japanese romantic comedy *Perfect Revolution* released in 2017, starring Lily Franky in the lead role (which I discuss in more detail below).

Due to the activism of Kumashino and others, there now exist a range of sexual services aimed at the disabled community. However, most are designed to fulfill male needs, ignoring the sexual desires of disabled women. For example, Yasuda and Hamilton (2013, 47) noted that while there was a support service to help physically disabled men masturbate, there did not appear to be equivalent assistance for women. Indeed, disabled women with strong sexual desires can feel stigmatized or shamed (Kawaguchi 2019, 56). When disabled women do engage with their sexuality, their experiences may range from positive encounters of self-validation to highly negative interactions that can even involve force (Yasuda and Hamilton 2013). Disabled women often remark that their femininity or sexuality are denied by those around them. They may be discouraged from wearing feminine clothing and taking an interest in fashion (Kawaguchi 2019, 51–52; Yasuda and Hamilton 2013, 49). They may also be told that their desires for love, marriage and children are hopeless, and even be encouraged to have a hysterectomy to eliminate menstruation or the possibility of getting pregnant, because raising a child as a disabled woman is considered impossible (Kawaguchi 2019; Yasuda and Hamilton 2013). It is no wonder then, that some disabled women feel devalued and suffer from a negative self-image (Kawaguchi 2019, 51).

An interview with disabled activists Nakajima Ryōko and Umetsu Eri reveals the extent to which disabled women talking about sex continues to be a taboo in the mainstream media. The interviewer opens with the question: "Why did you decide to co-operate with this article on sex, revealing your real name and face?" (Itō 2019). Undeterred by the allusion to the stigma surrounding the subject, wheelchair users Nakajima and Umetsu spoke openly about their experiences of love and romance as disabled women in their 30s and 40s. Umetsu, who was keen to become a mother, described the rehabilitation she underwent to prepare her body for sex with her husband. However, she admitted she was only able to ask for help because her occupational therapist was a young woman; she believed that most disabled women would struggle to request the assistance they might need, both out of a sense of embarrassment and a wish not to burden others (Itō 2019). Disabled women in Japan face extreme social pressure not to be a burden to others, which often discourages them from asserting their needs and desires. When they do so, they may face rejection or abuse (Yasuda and Hamilton 2013). Meanwhile, Nakajima spoke frankly of her experience of online dating and sex as a woman with paraplegia, including details such as the risk of bladder leakage during intimacy (Itō 2019). Nakajima and Umetsu founded BEYOND GIRLS (n.d.), an all-female collective that actively engages with the media to dispel stereotypes of disabled women and celebrate their femininity.

The ableist gaze

The reluctance to view disabled women as sexual beings has manifested itself in representations of disability on screen, which have tended to romanticize disabled women as persevering, heroic and essentially asexual. Martin Norden uses the term "sweet innocent" to describe such cultural representations. A sweet innocent is typically a child or young unmarried woman who is "respectful, humble, gentle, cheerful, godly, pure, and exceptionally pitiable [...] far more reactive than proactive and [seems] to bring out the protectiveness of every good-hearted able-bodied person who [comes] his or her way" (1994, 33). Through this archetype, we see the way in which heteronormative discourses of disability and femininity intersect to produce cultural stereotypes of disabled women as passive, naïve and in need of a savior. While there is a dearth of research when it comes to representations of disability in recent Japanese film and media, Arran Stibbe (2004) has previously observed that Japanese television dramas featuring disabled characters of the 1990s and 2000s conformed to the traditional gender dynamic. Disabled female characters were idealized for displaying perseverance (*gaman*)—enduring their suffering without complaint—and were often protected by men, while male disabled characters often acted as the protectors of able-bodied women. More recently, in her study of manga, Okuyama (2020) has observed how disability, which is tied to negative stereotypes of victimhood and weakness, can be framed as a sign of diminished masculinity. Such stereotypes continue to be perpetuated in contemporary Japanese media, as evidenced by the 2019 television drama *Perfect World* (Fuji TV).

Perfect World encapsulates many of the ableist discourses that have invited criticism from disability activists and scholars. In particular, the series, an adaptation of the popular, award-winning manga of the same name,[2] offers a textbook example of the ableist gaze in practice. Derived from the concept of the male gaze, which originated in feminist film studies, the concept of the ableist gaze not only signifies the perspective from which a disabled person is looked at—that of the non-disabled majority—but also signifies a system of power relations, whereby the gazer, the abled, is superior to the object of its gaze, the disabled. Admittedly, *Perfect World* is clearly written from the perspective of able-bodied Tsugumi, who falls in love with wheelchair user Itsuki. Even so, the opening scene, where Tsugumi learns for the first time that Itsuki is disabled, presents us with the ableist gaze at its most extreme.

Tsugumi joins a group of work associates for a social gathering at an *izakaya*, where she sits next to Itsuki, the handsome former schoolmate she once had a crush on. Reuniting after several years, the pair are excited to see each other again and have an enjoyable time. However, it is only as Itsuki leaves the venue that Tsugumi realizes that Itsuki, once a star player on the school basketball team, is no longer able to walk. By repeatedly cutting back to Tsugumi's crestfallen face as she watches Itsuki use his arms to manoeuvre himself across the room and into his wheelchair, the focus remains very much on her reaction to the discovery. The sentimental music underscoring the scene further emphasizes the ableist perspective, underlining the shock, disappointment and pity that Tsugumi and the (presumably able-bodied) viewer is meant to feel for her one-time crush (Pāfekuto wārudo 2019). At the same time, the extended shots of Itsuki settling himself into his wheelchair, as he puts on his shoes, enables us to indulge in what disability studies scholars refer to as "staring" (Okuyama 2020). From the safety of their home, the viewer is able to indulge in their curiosity and desire without any risk of social opprobrium. While Okuyama (2020, loc. 1610) has criticized this practice, it should be noted that others recognize that some forms of "staring" offer a "generative potential" that can transform the ways in which disability is viewed, thus distinguishing the concept from the oppressive "gaze" of feminist film studies (Garland-Thomson 2009; Fraser 2015). Later in this chapter, I discuss another opportunity for "staring" that embodies this transformative potential.

Perfect World doubles down on the pity factor: later in the episode, Itsuki has an emotional breakdown after accidently wetting himself in public and is hospitalized with terrible sores from extended wheelchair use. In both cases Tsugumi comes to his rescue, shielding him from embarrassment and helping him to meet work deadlines from his hospital bed. Demasculinized by his inability to control his body or his emotions, Itsuki is seen by the audience as unfortunate. His protestations that he does not want to be pitied by others—said through frustrated tears as he lies prone on the floor of his hospital room—ironically only serve to induce more pity. Seeing him in such a wretched state in this first episode, the viewer is induced to admire not only Itsuki's subsequent bravery in overcoming his difficulties but also Tsugumi's sacrifice in choosing the difficult path of becoming the partner of a disabled person. Modeling a patriarchal view of gender relations, Itsuki and Tsugumi's relationship faces resistance from her father, who believes that, as a disabled man, Itsuki will not be able to take on the "protector" role that is traditionally expected of a husband. It is only after Itsuki saves his future father-in-law's life and offers emotional support to Tsugumi during her father's hospitalization that he is able to regain his masculinity and acceptance as a suitable son-in-law.

Perfect World is a clear example of what disability activists and scholars have named inspiration porn—cultural and media representations that are designed to evoke an emotional response from consumers through stories of disabled people overcoming adversity. Activist and wheelchair user Stella Young (I'm not your inspiration, thank you very much 2014) spoke eloquently of how the media objectifies disabled people for the benefit of non-disabled people, who consume these images to make them feel better about themselves. She rejected the notion that disabled people should be considered brave or noble simply for living their lives. As Markotíc (2016, 4) notes, the flipside of such admiration is pity, as it implies that a life with disability would be too overwhelming for a so-called normal person to bear.

Inspiration porn, known as *kandō poruno* (lit. emotion porn) in Japanese, has also faced criticism from within the Japanese media itself. In 2016, the NHK show *Baribara* (Barrier-Free Variety Show), which features disabled presenters and guests and regularly tackles issues related to disability and diversity, introduced and discussed the topic of inspiration porn. The episode featured a parody of the typical inspiration porn documentaries that use sentimental stories of disabled people overcoming adversity to elicit emotions from viewers. It was widely considered to be a barely veiled attack on commercial broadcaster Nippon TV's annual *24-Hour Television*, a charity fundraiser airing at the same time as the *Baribara* episode that featured inspirational videos of disabled people taking on difficult physical challenges (Huffington Post 2016). During the *Baribara* episode, a survey of viewers revealed that, while 45 percent of non-disabled people admitted to enjoying inspiration porn programs, only 10 percent of disabled people felt the same (Baribara~Shōgaisha jōhō baraetii~ 2016).[3]

Furthermore, inspirational stories of disabled people defying apparently insurmountable barriers to achieve feats that prove challenging for abled people—the so-called "supercrip" narrative—risk fostering unrealistic expectations of what disabled people can accomplish, thus reinforcing the notion that it is the individual, and not society, that needs to change (Berger 2004, 798). Veere (2020, 2) points out the chasm between media coverage of the Paralympics celebrating elite athletes, who have access to the latest mobility technology, and the experience of an ordinary disabled person, who does not have such access. As Okuyama (2020) argues, manga centered on disabled superheroes can be entertaining but offer little in terms of advocacy.

Resisting the ableist gaze: *Perfect Revolution*

There is clearly some work to do in order to diversify the kinds of images and messages of disability that appear in the mainstream media, and which have an enormous influence on the way society perceives people who identify as disabled. One film that has gone some way towards resisting ableist and inspirational representations of disability is the 2017 film *Perfect Revolution*, which, as mentioned above, is based on the memoir of Kumashino Yoshihiko. The film follows the tumultuous relationship between best-selling author Kuma (also known as Kuma-chan), played by Lily Franky, and sex worker Mitsu, played by Seino Nana. While the film is essentially an uplifting romantic comedy, its unapologetic celebration of the sexuality of disabled people and its refusal to conform to the "sweet innocent" stereotype is noteworthy. From the very first scene, as we watch him lecherously peering up the skirt of a young woman standing on a ladder, we are made explicitly aware that Kuma-chan, a middle-aged wheelchair user with cerebral palsy, does not fit the mould of the pure-hearted, asexual and passive victim that mainstream society has come to expect. He is a cynical single man who has given up on finding love but has a strong sex drive, a situation that would be relatable for many disabled and able-bodied men alike in contemporary Japan. While the scene is far from politically correct in terms of its objectification of a woman's body, it does serve to humanize Kuma-chan who, to use his own words, is neither monster nor saint. As such, it avoids the trap of simplistic binaries of "good" and "bad" that representations of disability often fall into (Okuyama 2020).

The film is highly critical of the way the mainstream media portrays disability. For example, at a press event to publicize Kuma-chan's book, a photographer asks if he can take a picture of only his hands, which are a visible marker of his difference. Kuma-chan, who up until that moment was in good spirits, suddenly tenses up. While the attention of the able-bodied photographer and his camera fix upon Kuma-chan's hands, the video camera and the viewer is focused on his face, capturing his discomfort at being reduced to his non-normative body parts. The marked shift in tone, from light-hearted to sombre, further enables the audience to identify with the "staree" rather than the "starer," while the frame-within-a-frame provokes us to question our own motives when we "look." This scene marks a stark contrast from the one described earlier in *Perfect World,* which privileged the able-bodied perspective, thus demonstrating the objectifying, dehumanizing impact of the ableist gaze.

Further criticism appears later in the film, when a television crew comes to shoot an interview with Kuma and Mitsu for what is clearly planned as an inspiration porn segment. Unhappy with their cheerful appearance and demeanor, crew members ask them to tone down their clothing and make up and focus on the hardships they have encountered, to create a mood more in keeping with disability. Mitsu is also asked not to speak so positively about her sex work. The scene demonstrates how stereotypes of disability, gender and sexuality are perpetuated by the media through what scholars refer to as framing or packaging (Okuyama 2020, loc. 850), By emphasizing certain messages and eliminating others, the media is able to frame the way in which disability is portrayed and, thus, influence the perceptions of the audience.

Perfect Revolution also reveals the contrasting ways in which visible and invisible disabilities are perceived by society. Scholars have noted that the latter can struggle more than the former to navigate public spaces and are more likely to be misunderstood, due to society's perception of what disability should look like (Markotić 2016; Okuyama 2020). This is made apparent in the different ways in which Kuma-chan, a physically-disabled man, and Mitsu, an able-bodied woman with a personality disorder, are treated by society. Kuma-chan, whose disability is made visible through his non-normative body and use of an electric wheelchair, is more successful in navigating public spaces, even forging a career as a bestselling author. He is accommodated through a range of strategies, such as the provision of ramps, the assistance of a carer or being physically carried on his brother's back. Mitsu, on the other hand, fails time and again to conform to the expectations of others. Because her disability, mental illness, is not immediately visible, society expects her to act as a non-disabled person would and is less accommodating of her difference. Thus, when she fails to meet these expectations by, for example, physically attacking others or throwing food, she loses her right to access social spaces, and is eventually institutionalized.

This underscores the disparities in the extent to which society is able or willing to accommodate different types of disability, in Japan and elsewhere. Having said this, the representation of Mitsu's illness is not unproblematic. Some would justifiably object to the depiction of her attempt to commit murder-suicide by dragging Kuma-chan's wheelchair into the sea, which may serve to reinforce negative stereotypes of people suffering from mental illness as dangerous, not only to themselves but also to others. This aside, *Perfect Revolution* offers a representation of disability that feels refreshing, honest and authentic. The involvement of disabled people in the production, including Kumashino, who not only wrote the source material but also acted as an onset consultant during filming, was no doubt a significant factor in creating a sense of authenticity. A close friend of lead actor Lily Franky, the two spent many hours together so Franky could observe his mannerisms (Pāfekuto reboryūshon 2017). As such, it shares similarities with the film *37 Seconds*, which features a similarly frank story of a wheelchair user exploring their sexuality, but focuses on a woman's point of view.

Authenticity, gender difference and sexuality in *37 Seconds*

37 Seconds (2019) tells the story of Takada Yuma (portrayed by Kayama Mei), a paraplegic manga artist who breaks free from the restricting confines of her sheltered life to embark on a journey of sexual and personal discovery. US-based Japanese writer-director Hikari has a history of creating progressive narratives of sexuality: her previous work includes *Tsuyako* (2011), a short film centered on a lesbian love affair in postwar Japan. She was inspired to create *37 Seconds* after meeting wheelchair users, therapists working with disabled clients and disabled activists, including Kumashino Yoshihiko, who also has a small role in the film (37 Seconds filmpartners 2021).

What sets *37 Seconds* apart from *Perfect Revolution* and the vast majority of other Japanese feature films centered on disabled characters is the casting of Kayama, a wheelchair user born with cerebral palsy, in her first acting role. Hikari has revealed that for her, this was non-negotiable (37 Seconds Filmmaker Hikari in the Corner Booth 2020). This groundbreaking decision had a significant impact on the production process: the crew put in place a number of provisions to accommodate the needs of Kayama during filming, including engaging a carer to support her and scheduling more than double the time normally required for a typical shoot. During the scriptwriting process, Hikari also rented a wheelchair herself to get a better understanding of her protagonist (37 Seconds filmpartners 2021). This perspective is translated to the screen in the scenes where the camera is positioned at Yuma's height, giving the viewers an opportunity to see the world through her eyes.

Focusing on a female heroine was another progressive choice, as stories of women with disabilities exploring their sexuality are rarely told.[4] One of the most striking scenes in *37 Seconds* comes early in the film—a mere three-and-a-half minutes in—when protagonist Yuma, a 23-year-old Japanese woman born with cerebral palsy, is carefully undressed and washed by her mother, Kyoko. While the camera is unflinching as Yuma crouches nude on the bathroom floor, it does not linger in an excessive or intrusive manner. The scene is almost mundane in its depiction of a daily ritual, yet the image of a non-normative body in naked form within the soothingly familiar setting of a shared family bath—a juxtaposition that is both "visually quiescent and eye-catching" (Garland-Thomson 2009, 9)—is undoubtedly significant and powerful. In allowing us a rare look at a disabled female body, and thus making an "extraordinary sight ordinary" (Garland-Thomson 2009, 9), the scene demonstrates the potential for "staring" to "disrupt habits" and enable the viewer to "revisit assumptions" around difference (Fraser 2015, 64).

The first part of the film charts Yuma's sexual awakening, as she watches pornographic videos, masturbates and tries online dating. These early moments—Yuma's knowing smirk after she lies to her mother about where she is going, the comically awkward first dates, the disappointment of being stood up—are all the more resonant for their relatability as universal experiences of youth. Nevertheless, the film does not shy away from the specific challenges that come with being a sexually mature woman with a disability in Japan. Hikari and producer Yamaguchi Shin aimed to highlight the gender disparity in the recognition of the sexual rights of people with disabilities. This discrepancy is made apparent in the contrasting sexual experiences of the two disabled characters who appear in the film, protagonist Yuma and Mr. Kuma (portrayed by Kumashino).[5] The sensual connection between Mr. Kuma and his paid companion Mai (Watanabe Makiko) is undeniable. As she lovingly caresses his earlobe and talks to him affectionately, it is clear they have developed a sexually fulfilling relationship based on her sensitive understanding of his needs and desire. The encounter between Yuma and sex worker Hide, whom she hires for her first experience of sexual intimacy, is awkward and ultimately disappointing. In contrast to Mr. Kuma's erotic excitement at Mai's sensual touch, Yuma appears uncomfortable as Hide undresses her. Meanwhile, Hide is taken aback by her wheelchair, refuses to kiss her and expresses repulsion when she accidently urinates during foreplay. This unvarnished depiction not only exposes a very real issue for paraplegic women navigating sex and intimacy—bladder leakage—it also highlights the need for greater empathy in the treatment of people with disabilities.

These disparate experiences expose the way in which disability and gender intersect to marginalize the sexual needs of women with disabilities. As Yasuda and Hamilton (2013, 45) have observed, disabled women must contend with the double burden of the limitations posed by their disability and the cultural and social constructions of womanhood that exist in Japanese society. From an early age, Japanese women are socialized to conform to a definition of femininity that embodies innocence, passivity and nurturance, while men become accustomed to having their needs met, first by their mothers and later by their wives. Such stereotypes can prove challenging for a woman whose disability prevents her from taking on a caregiving role. The situation is compounded by the extreme social pressure they face not to be a burden to others, which often discourages them from asserting their needs and desires. This is represented in the film in the contrasting reactions of Mr. Kuma and Yuma. While he eagerly encourages Mai to continue her erotic stimulation, Yuma meekly acquiesces to the conditions imposed by Hide on their interaction.

The constraints and performativity of gender

Nevertheless, this negative experience does not dampen Yuma's enthusiasm, and instead becomes a conduit to a more satisfying relationship—friendship with fellow social outsider, Mai. It is with the support of open-minded Mai, who acts both as female confidante and nurturing maternal figure, that Yuma is able take the next step in her journey of self-discovery and independence. For Yuma, who has struggled to find her place in conventional society, Mai is one of the few people to see beyond her wheelchair and accept her as an equal. Her other relationships with women appear to evoke the unequal power dynamic that, according to Yasuda and Hamilton (2013, 53), can exist between disabled women and the able-bodied women around them. Former schoolfriend Sayaka, for whom she works as a manga ghost-artist, happily takes the credit for Yuma's talent without giving any acknowledgement, even refusing to be seen in public with her. Meanwhile, Yuma is also trapped in a suffocating relationship with overprotective Kyoko, who not only bathes her, but also monitors where she goes and even what she wears. Denied the flowery pink dresses she loves to wear, Yuma is restricted to simple shirts and trousers in neutral colors—a necessary measure, Kyoko insists, against the legion of "creepy men" who would attempt to sexually violate the daughter she sees as innocent and helpless.

However, in its depiction of the complex relationships between female characters, *37 Seconds* not only reveals the ways in which women with disabilities are denied mainstream social acceptance, it also exposes the strictures that bind able-bodied women who do appear to adhere to their socially prescribed roles. We see this in the hyper-feminized persona of the *kawaii kogyaru* (cute and fashionable teenage girl) manga artist Sayaka presents to her fans, her pastel-colored wigs and bright bows contrasting with the sombre, casual attire she wears when not in the public eye. Her anxiety over her image—"Doesn't my fringe look strange?" she worries at one point (37 sekanzu 2019)—underlines the level of performativity, to use a Butlerism (2006), involved in creating and maintaining her highly gendered persona, as well as the extent to which she has become entrapped by its necessitated repetition.

Furthermore, we learn that smothering Kyoko is just as much a victim of the co-dependent relationship that exists between mother and (adult) daughter, which has imprisoned both in a permanent stasis that denies either the opportunity to become fully realized, independent women. If Yuma is infantilized because of her disability, Kyoko is also trapped in what Asai Michiko (1990) refers to as the "maternal fantasy," an idealized image of purity and selflessness that came to dominate Japanese discourses of motherhood during the second half of the twentieth century. Kyoko's refusal to allow Yuma to wear feminine clothing signifies a fear of her daughter's transition to adulthood and eventual independence, which could make the mother's role redundant. It also indicates Kyoko's fear of her own sexuality, which, following Asai's theory, was stunted the moment she became the mother of a child with a disability, and came under social pressure to relinquish her identity as a woman in order to devote her life to caring for her daughter. This fear is neatly captured in the horrified shriek Kyoko emits when she discovers Yuma's dildo. Thus, when Kyoko polices Yuma's sexuality, she is arguably also attempting to restrain her own. Nevertheless, Kyoko is no beacon of purity; her repeated warnings of "creepy men" indicate the extent to which she herself has become preoccupied by sex. As Foucault (1998) might say, this attempt to repress her daughter's sexuality, as well as her own, only pushes it into the realm of secrecy, subconsciously creating a space for it to flourish.

Kyoko's fear is exposed in an argument mother and daughter have in a scene that, sharing an ironic symmetry with the one discussed earlier, also takes place in the bathroom. Yuma acknowledges her mother's fears and confronts her with them when she yells: "You act like you are sacrificing yourself for me, but you're just afraid of being alone!" (37 Sekanzu 2019). She has pulled herself into the bath to prove to her mother that she is not the helpless child she has been perceived to be. However, it is when she disappears from Kyoko and Sayaka's lives that we can truly appreciate how much more they rely on her than she on them. This turning of the tables on Yuma's part underscores the fragility of the able-bodied women's identities, dependent as they are on performing a narrowly defined stereotype of femininity.

But perhaps Yuma's greatest ability lies in her rich imagination and creativity. Unlike Sayaka, who is forced to appropriate the talent of others because she has none of her own, or Kyoko, who finds solace in the creativity of others—namely, Shakespeare, whose plays she reads in her spare time—Yuma can both visualize and recreate in manga form a world of her own design. A world that extends beyond the boundaries of existing gender norms or even humanity as we know it. One that allows her to escape her wheelchair and reinvent herself as the great queen of an alien race on a quest to mate with the finest human male specimen she can find.

This freedom allows Yuma to eventually break free from the toxic relationships that have stymied her and strike out on her own. However, her journey does not necessarily lead her where one might expect, and it is here that the narrative risks reverting to stereotype. Two-thirds of the way through, the film shifts gear, as Yuma uses her new-found independence not to embark on further sexual adventures, but to search for her long-lost father and, ultimately, the sister she was unaware of. This change of direction in the narrative reflects a similar deviation during the production process that occurred after Hikari cast Kayama for the role of Yuma. Although the film had originally meant to be a love story, on meeting Kayama at her audition, the filmmaker decided a romance would seem unnatural for the "pure and youthful" woman and rewrote the script. Kayama's high-pitched tone appeared to bring out Hikari's maternal side: "She has such a cute voice—it hums like a mosquito. I just wanted to wrap my arms around her" (Ishitobi 2020). In another interview, she added: "The other auditionees had serious expressions on their faces, but Mei-chan giggled and blushed shyly. I was attracted to her innocence" (Kurata 2020). With these comments, the director was perhaps, if inadvertently, revealing her own preconceived notions of women with disabilities as childlike and asexual and how these may have influenced her characterization of Yuma. Hikari's description of Kayama is reminiscent of the "sweet innocent" archetype of disability discussed earlier. It may explain why, much like other "sweet innocent" types, Yuma is, for the most part, respectful, gentle and humble to everyone she meets and brings out the protectiveness of good-hearted able-bodied people such as Mai and carer Toshiya.

Alternatively, one could argue that by abandoning the love story, Hikari has avoided the pitfall that other Japanese films featuring disabled protagonists have fallen into by not excessively romanticizing relationships. Indeed, *37 Seconds'* greatest strength is its refusal to patronize its subject by depicting her as especially valiant or spirited. This attitude is most effectively conveyed in the scene in which Yuma submits a sample of her work to an editor of erotic manga. Rather than suggest she use her disability to market her manga—according to Sayaka's editor, pity sells—the editor judges Yuma on merit, and is frank in pointing out what the artist needs to do to improve, suggesting that she try sex for herself before drawing it. There is no question in the editor's mind that Yuma is capable of having sex, if she puts her mind to it. This simple instruction opens up a world of possibilities for the heroine. As Hikari has noted, "regardless if she's in a wheelchair or not, it's a story about this girl who's trying to make it work for her" (37 Seconds Filmmaker Hikari in the Corner Booth 2020). The fact that Yuma is ultimately unsuccessful in her quest to have sex is perhaps beside the point. More important is that she has proved she can.

Handbook of Japanese Media and Popular Culture in Transition

Conclusion

Scholars have noted the importance of realistic representations of disability as "agents of so-cial change" (Okuyama 2020). The "supercrip" narrative has come under particular criticism for obscuring broader social issues concerning disabled people in Japan by focusing on the superhuman feats of a small (often fictional) minority (Okuyama 2020; Veere 2020). Images and messages of disability in the mainstream media, such as those found in the television drama adaptation of *Perfect World* (which was also made into a feature film) suggest that inspiration porn continues to be embraced by creators and viewers alike. Such stories may seem sympathetic and uplifting, but only serve to reproduce stereotypes of "sweet innocents" and reinforce an ableist gaze that objectifies and patronizes people with disabilities, while ignoring their real-life hopes, desires and worries. Within this context, diversifying represen-tations of disability to encompass everyday concerns is long overdue.

Films such as *Perfect Revolution* and *37 Seconds* contribute to this process of diversifi-cation by challenging entrenched perceptions of disabled people as passive, innocent and asexual. Examining such representations through a feminist lens has provided insight into the ways in which the media exploits and objectifies disabled people with its ableist gaze. It also reveals how factors such as (in)visibility or gender intersect with disability to ensure that equal levels of social acceptance, accessibility and agency are not afforded to all. In turn, my analysis of the female relationships in *37 Seconds* also demonstrates how the study of disability narratives can benefit feminist inquiry by better elucidating the constraints that all women, regardless of ability, face in a society that expects them to conform to narrow heteronormative roles and predetermined life-courses. When Yuma finally breaks free of her metaphorical shackles, this represents not only her own liberation, but that of her mother and Sayaka too.

While neither *37 Seconds* nor *Perfect Revolution* are without flaws in their representation of disability, each reverting to stereotype at times, the involvement of disabled people in these productions, both on and off camera, played a pivotal role in creating narratives that challenge normative discourses and should be seen as a positive step forward. Whether the example set by *37 Seconds* will be taken up by others is more doubtful; the costs involved in accommodating disabled actors are likely to be too great a price for many producers of film or television. Japan has yet to have its Sia moment;[6] nevertheless, the positive reception the film has received, both within and beyond Japan, offers hope that disabled people will be allowed a more active role in telling their own stories.

Notes

[1] Although outside the scope of this chapter, any mention of eugenics legislation in Japan, in particular when framed within a discussion of women's rights, must acknowledge the role of some Japanese feminists in promoting eugenicist arguments that supported selective abortion on grounds of fetal deformity. The conflict between women's rights and disability rights eventually led to a reframing of feminist discourse in the 1970s. For more details see Kano (2016: 84–103).

[2] For an analysis of the manga, see Okuyama (2020).

[3] The program can be viewed at: https://www.youtube.com/watch?v=mLOC9d_8OJc [Accessed 18 June 2021].

[4] Shonali Bose's *Margarita with a Straw* (2014) explores similar themes, but its wheelchair-using protagonist was portrayed by an able-bodied actress.

5   Not to be confused with Kuma-chan, the protagonist of *Perfect Revolution*. Both characters are derived from the same, real-life person and have the same name. To minimize confusion, I refer to the character in *Perfect Revolution* as Kuma-chan and the character in *37 Seconds* as Mr. Kuma.

6   Singer-songwriter Sia attracted widespread criticism for her film *Music*, which featured an abled actor playing a disabled character. For an analysis of the film's (dis)ableist narrative, see Alison Wilde's (2021) opinion piece.

Videography

37 Seconds Filmmaker Hikari in the Corner Booth. 2020. Netflix Film Club. Available at: https://www.youtube .com/watch?v=pLoVyrOOul4 [Accessed 21 June 2021].

37 sekanzu [37 Seconds], 2019. [Film]. Directed by Hikari. Available through: Netflix [Accessed 15 February 2020].

Baribara~Shōgaisha jōhō baraetii~ [Barrier Free variety show], 2016. NHK. 28 August.

I'm not your inspiration, thank you very much, 2014. [Online video]. Directed by S. Young. Available at: https://www.ted.com/talks/stella_young_i_m_not_your_inspiration_thank_you_very_much [Accessed 18 June 2021].

Pāfekuto reboryūshon [Perfect Revolution]. 2017. [Film DVD] Directed by Matsumoto J. Tōei.

Pāfekuto wārudo [Perfect World], 2019. [TV series]. Fuji TV.

Bibliography

37 Seconds filmpartners, 2021. *Eiga "37seconds" kōshiki saito* [Film "37 Seconds" official website]. [online] Available at: http://37seconds.jp/ [Accessed 21 June 2021].

AERA, 2018. "Shōgai ga attemo suki na hito to shitai" sei no kunō kakaeru shōgaishatachi no sakebi [A cry from disabled people agonizing over their sex lives: "I might be disabled, but I still want to do it with the one I love"]. *AERA*. [online] 28 May. Available at: https://dot.asahi.com/aera/2018052400034 .html?page=1 [Accessed 16 June 2021].

Asai, M., 1990. "Kindai kazoku gensō" kara no kaihō o mezashite [Towards a liberation from the "fantasy of the modern family"]. In Y. Ehara, ed., *Feminizumu sensō—70 nendai kara 90 nendai e* [Feminism debates: From the 1970s to the 1990s]. Tokyo: Keisō Shobō, 87–117.

Berger, R.J., 2004. Pushing Forward: Disability, Basketball, and Me. *Qualitative Inquiry*, 10(5), 794–810. https://doi.org/10.1177/1077800403261857.

BEYOND GIRLS, n.d. [online] BEYOND GIRLS. Available at: https://beyond-girls.tokyo/ [Accessed 17 June 2021].

Butler, J., 2006. *Gender Trouble: Feminism and the Subversion of Identity*. London: Routledge.

Crenshaw, K., 1989. Demarginalizing the Intersection of Race and Sex: A Black Feminist Critique of Anti-discrimination Doctrine, Feminist Theory and Antiracist Politics. *University of Chicago Legal Forum*, (1), 139–67.

Foucault, M., 1998. *The Will to Knowledge: The History of Sexuality, Vol. 1*. Translated by R. Hurley. London: Penguin Books.

Fraser, B., 2015. *Cognitive Disability Aesthetics: Visual Culture, Disability Representations, and the (In)Visibility of Cognitive Difference*. Toronto: University of Toronto Press.

Garland-Thomson, R., 1997. *Extraordinary Bodies: Figuring Physical Disability in American Culture and Literature*. New York: Columbia University Press.

———., 2009. *Staring: How We Look*. Oxford: Oxford University Press.

Haworth, A., 2013. After Fukushima: Families on the Edge of Meltdown. *The Observer*. [online] 24 Feb. Available at: https://www.theguardian.com/environment/2013/feb/24/divorce-after-fukushima-nuclear -disaster [Accessed 30 September 2021].

Hovhannisyan, A., 2021. Preventing the Birth of "Inferior Offspring": Eugenic Sterilizations in Postwar Japan. *Japan Forum*, 33(3), 383–401. https://doi.org/10.1080/09555803.2020.1731570.

Huffington Post, 2016. *24-jikan terebi o shōgasha no "kandō poruno" to shiteki, NHK ga parodi ura bangumi nama hōsō de makkō shōbu* [NHK live broadcast of parody program competes directly with 24-Hour TV, labelling it "inspiration porn"]. [online] Hafuposuto. Available at: https://www.huffingtonpost.jp/2016 /08/28/24hours_n_11756598.html [Accessed 6 May 2021].

Hurst, D., 2019. Victims of Forced Sterilisation in Japan to Receive Compensation and Apology. *The Guardian*. [online] 18 Mar. Available at: https://www.theguardian.com/world/2019/mar/18/victims-of-forced -sterilisation-in-japan-to-receive-compensation-and-apology [Accessed 15 September 2021].

Ishitobi, N., 2020. Kurumaisu no wakamono, jiritsu e tobidasu eiga "37 sekanzu," HIKARI kantoku [Director Hikari on a young wheelchair user taking a leap towards independence in "37 Seconds"]. Asahi Shinbun, 7 February, 4.

Itō, A., 2019. *Josei no shōgaisha ga kataru "sei no nayami" yoru no seikatsu "imajinēshon no sekai"* [Disabled women describe their "worries over sex," their romantic lives and a "world of imagination"]. [online] withnews. Available at: https://withnews.jp/article/f0190216002qq000000000000000W02110101qq00001 8753A [Accessed 17 June 2021].

Kano, A., 2016. *Japanese Feminist Debates: a Century of Contention on Sex, Love, and Labor*. Honolulu: University of Hawai'i Press.

Kawaguchi, N., 2019. Difficulties Disabled Women in Japan Face with Regard to Love, Marriage, and Reproduction. *Ars Vivendi Journal*, 11, 48–60.

Kumashino, Y., 2021. *Kumashino yōgisha (51) (@kumashino)* [Kumashino Yoshihiko's official Twitter feed]. [online] Twitter. Available at: https://twitter.com/kumashino [Accessed 16 June 2021].

Kurata, T., 2020. Shōgaisha no jiritsu egaku, eiga "37 sekanzu" nōsei mahi no watashi, tōei Ōsaka-fu shusshin Kayama Mei san shuen [It's my authentic self on screen—Osaka-born actress with cerebral palsy, Kayama Mei, on film depicting disabled person's independence, 37 Seconds]. *Mainichi Shinbun*, 8 February, 7.

Markotić, N., 2016. *Disability in Film and Literature*. Jefferson, North Carolina: McFarland.

Norden, M.F., 1994. *The Cinema of Isolation: A History of Physical Disability in the Movies*. Montclair, NJ: Rutgers University Press.

Ogawa, T., 2018. *Gimu kyōiku de seikō o oshienai no wa "seiteki dōi nenrei 13-sai" to mujun shimasenka (Nanao yōgo gakkō jiken o furi-kaeri tsutsu)* [Doesn't failing to teach sex education during compulsory schooling contradict the "age of consent of 13?" (reflecting on the Nanao Special School incident)]. [online] Yahoo! Nyūsu. Available at: https://news.yahoo.co.jp/byline/ogawatamaka/20180328-00083247/ [Accessed 3 December 2018].

Okuyama, Y., 2017. Semiotics of Otherness in Japanese Mythology. *Disability Studies Quarterly*, [online] 37(1). https://doi.org/10.18061/dsq.v37i1.5380.

———., 2020. *Reframing Disability in Manga* (Kindle version). Honolulu: University of Hawai'i Press.

Satō, T. and Miyazaki S., 2014. Chiteki shōgaji no seikyōiku shidō ni okeru genjō to kadai [The sex education of intellectually disabled children: its current status and issues raised]. *Chūō daigaku hoken taiiku kenkyū-jo kiyō* [Chuo University Journal of the Institute of Health and Sports Science], 32, 161–70.

Stevens, C.S., 2013. *Disability in Japan*. [online] London: Routledge. Available at: http://ebookcentral .proquest.com/lib/cardiff/detail.action?docID=1143866 [Accessed 14 September 2021].

Stibbe, A., 2004. Disability, Gender and Power in Japanese Television Drama. *Japan Forum*, 16(1), 21–36. https://doi.org/10.1080/0955580032000189311.

Takebayashi, S., 2020. Sex Ed. for Those with Disabilities in Japan: the Focus in Woman's Trial over Baby's Death. *Mainichi Daily News*. [online] 26 Aug. Available at: https://mainichi.jp/english/articles/20200826 /p2a/00m/0na/037000c [Accessed 16 June 2021].

Veere, A.P. van der, 2020. The Tokyo Paralympic Superhero: Manga and Narratives of Disability in Japan. *The Asia-Pacific Journal: Japan Focus*, 18(5), 1–12.

Wendell, S., 1996. *The Rejected Body: Feminist Philosophical Reflections on Disability*. London: Psychology Press.

Wilde, A., 2021. *Music—a Cacophony of Disableist Representation*. [online] Disability Arts Online. Available at: https://disabilityarts.online/magazine/opinion/music-a-cacophony-of-disableist-representation/ [Accessed 23 June 2021].

Yasuda, H. and Hamilton, C., 2013. Investigating the Sexuality of Disabled Japanese Women: Six Autobiographical Accounts. *Women's Studies Journal*, 27, 44–53.

Chapter 13
Marketing Men (,) Silencing Men: The Sapporo Beer-Mifune Campaign and Perspectives on Gender in Japanese Advertising

James X. White

This chapter examines the discourse around gender in the media by analyzing a Japanese beer advertising campaign from the 1970s. Its major objective is to explore how discussions of advertising campaigns, across decades, reveal an underutilized, but rich and diverse trove of understandings about gender. To this end, the first section discusses the advertising discourse, the choice of product, its connection to gendered depictions and the background of this particular campaign. The various interpretations and discussions of the model of masculinity featured in this campaign are then analyzed and placed in historical context before a conclusion which summarizes these findings and highlights the importance of this approach.

Introduction

In 1970, Mifune Toshirō, star of countless *jidaigeki* and noted collaborator of Kurosawa Akira, sauntered to the bow of a ship, opened a bottle of beer and quaffed it. This performative act of consumption was in service of an advertising campaign for Sapporo Beer under the rubric "*Otoko wa damatte...Sapporo Biiru*" (Men are silent... Sapporo Beer). Utilizing Mifune's image garnered from many years of playing loners, rough outcasts, and authoritative men, this campaign presented beer consumption as a masculine, Japanese and solitary activity. Lauded by authors and commentators as a success despite, or because of, its unique singular image of manhood, it gained a reputation both as one of the advertisements of 1970 and of this period. Its overt depiction of hyper-masculinity has continued to resonate, serving as a touchstone for the idea of what Japanese masculinity is, and what it should be. This vision has continued to inform depictions of men in contemporary advertisements and continues to be used as a reference for how men should act in order to be men.

This campaign was not without criticism, however, with contemporaneous commentators negotiating and challenging the meaning and significance of the depiction they saw in their newspapers, homes and in other media. To date, there has been little interrogation or examination of such interpretations and their evolution and importance within Japan's mediascape in the postwar period. This chapter maps these changes in perspectives on gender and masculinity in Japan by critically analyzing the writings of the critics, creatives and corporate entities that constitute the advertising discourse. The variety and diversity of these interpretations expand our understanding of gendered depictions within advertisements and demonstrate the importance of incorporating these perspectives into any analysis of advertising in Japan.

The Japanese advertising industry is massive, ubiquitous and influential in its reach. In terms of expenditure, it was the second largest in the world until recently surpassed by China (Cramer-Flood 2020). Advertising permeated Japanese society in the postwar, not only promoting products, but also actively shaping the programming watched between advertisements (Yamaki 1992; Prieler and Kohlbacher 2016, 38; Galbraith and Karlin 2012, 5–12). Its images, increasingly prevalent and inescapable (Amano 2002, 5), dominated the visual landscape.

Across Japan, campaigns depicting "correct" practices and sites of consumption featured equally "normative" models of gender: certain products marked as masculine were for certain men; others, feminine and for particular women. These images are one aspect of a wider discursive realm, however, subject to scrutiny and analysis, to contestation, to challenge and to praise, which serve to both support and undermine the images that they featured. The way gender was understood through these critics' voices is an important element of advertisement analysis without which these images can only partially be understood. Existing approaches, while valuable for revealing systematic and stereotypical depictions of gender, are inadequate historically as they prioritize contemporary lenses while ignoring the specific historical context of advertising campaigns' production and reception.

Both quantitative methods (cf. Furnham, Abramsky and Gunter 1997; Arima 2003) and qualitative ones (Roberson 2005) can be criticized for being too grounded in the text itself, neglecting both advertising traditions and the perspectives of coeval writers who found the representations ground-breaking or mundane. That is, the context of advertisements, and the practices and knowledge of the industry that shape their production, as Morris Holbrook (1987) and Brian Moeran (1996, 27–32) have argued. Indeed, critical industry writings are often marginalized in scholarly advertising studies despite the extensive debates and high degree of scrutiny. Roberson's rigorous examination of the representation of masculinity in Japanese energy-drink advertisements (2005), for instance, does not take into account prior analyses that came to some of the same conclusions, such as Niki Etsuko's 1971 critique in *Fujin kōron* (Women's review) (Niki 1980). Other scholars (Johansson 1994; Prieler et al. 2010; Ford et al. 1998; Martin 2012; Okazaki and Mueller 2008; Creighton 1997) have equally failed to incorporate the broader industry and popular discourse when looking at Japanese advertising.

Considering advertisements and their critical contexts together as advertising discourse addresses the demands of various scholars to adopt a multiplicity of perspectives when examining cultural texts (Kellner 2003; Holbrook 1987; Moeran 1996). This provides a historical dimension to the analysis of advertisements while foregrounding the existing critical voices writing in Japanese. Interrogating corporate, creative and critical examinations of the campaigns in this way is thus a key contribution to debates on the representation of gender. This more integrated approach deepens our understanding of the social and cultural construction of gender in the postwar period and illuminates a relatively unexamined archive.

Discourse as used here is based on Lynda Nead's definition, adapted from Foucault, to describe the critiques and surrounding commentary on female sexuality in 19th-century art. For Nead, discourse is "a particular form of language with its own rules and conventions and the institutions within which the discourse is produced and circulated" (1988, 4). Just as it becomes possible to talk of medical or art discourses in the context of Foucault and Nead's work respectively, I suggest an "advertising discourse" that discusses masculinity and femininity, gender, sexuality and correct and ideal ways to live using its own conventions and rules is equally possible. Criticism plays an equal role alongside the visual forms within the discourse in categorizing and defining (Nead 1988, 2) depictions, contributing, through praise and critique, to the establishment of parameters of idealized and laudatory forms of masculinity and femininity.

Why beer?

The gendering role of beer combined with its universality and its accessibility as a topic makes the depiction, and descriptions, of its consumption in advertisements ideal for examining understandings of gender. Firstly, beer itself, more so than other non-durable consumable products, is an influential and effective means of demonstrating and regulating gender practices. The social and public sites where it is consumed, and the choice of drinking companions, provide a means to perform and to police gender (Heath 1995, 2; Plant 1995, 294; Joffe 1998). Masculinity and heavy drinking are so closely entwined that the (visible) ability to withstand alcohol's effects often publicly affirms one's manhood (Mandelbaum 1979, 16–17; Sargent 1979, 278–80) as seen in various Japanese social practices, from dinner parties (Befu 1986) to pottery gatherings (Moeran 1998, 250-56).

Secondly, beer's pricing and availability helped it become *the* postwar drink in Japan, essential to quotidian social practices (Smith 1992; Francks 2009, 95, 127, 157–59; Alexander 2013, 177) and ostensibly the drink of men, occupying as it did the "dominant role in masculine social life" (Francks 2009, 127). An "affordable accompaniment" (Francks 2009, 166–67) to men's social practices, beer complemented both the father's meal at home and men's corporate post-work practices. Conversely, the postwar period can also be characterized by both increasing numbers of women consuming beer publicly and by commentaries upon this subject (see Tanaka 1995, 79–80; Takayama 1999, 253). The "*Otoko-wa-damatte*" campaign encapsulates many of these debates.

Masculinizing beer

In 1970, Sapporo Beer concluded that *Sapporo Lite*'s "feminine" image was directly responsible for its commercial failure. To masculinize their brand image they subsequently utilized the actor Mifune Toshirō (Matsuura 1970, 53; Kamo 1975, 263; Sapporo Biiru KK 1996, 791), shifting the representation from a refreshing and sharp image—qualities perceived as feminine—to a full-bodied, bitter, and thus more masculine, profile (Sapporo Biiru KK 1996,

791). Both Sapporo Beer (1996, 791) and historian Jeffrey Alexander (2013, 225) called it a "huge hit" (*daihitto nari*) while its impact was "immense" (Aoyanagi 2001, 8) with the Tokyo Copywriters' Club (TCC) ranking it as one of the top 11 advertisements for 1970 in their 1972 review of the previous decade (Tokyo Copywriters' Club 1972, 239). Later commentators saw it as particularly representative of the year, and period (Yamakawa 1987, 8; Focus 1998, 51). For two and a half years, Mifune consumed beer aboard a ship in the Sea of Enshū (off Shizuoka Prefecture); towering over the arid landscape of Monument Valley (U.S.); sitting among yellow flowers in indistinct meadows; and riding horses in the fields of Erimo on the island of Hokkaidō (Kamo 1975).

This campaign became emblematic of Japanese manhood by explicitly linking Mifune's masculinity with these spaces, which were understood as free and independent, both in terms of what he could do there and what he was free from—the feminine and, by extension, the domestic (White 2007). Understandings of gender such as these informed the conception of this campaign, its production, and the evaluations of these processes. The explicitly gendered image of Mifune, for instance, was partly to create a talking point (Matsuura 1970, 53), but also to clearly delineate their masculine product from the more "feminized" competition. The campaign thus became representative of Japanese beer advertising and of a transhistorical Japanese masculinity.

Its slogan, "Men are silent… Sapporo Beer," was both prescriptive—pronouncing that to be a man, to be considered masculine, one should be silent—and descriptive, describing how men act, that is, that men *are* silent. It was extremely popular and appeared to resonate culturally, subsequently being recycled and re-used (Lebra 1976, 78; JAC 1991, 151). It appeared on a Judo club recruitment poster as *Otoko wa damatte… Judo* (Men are silent . . . Judo) (Dentsu hō 1970, 3); it connected silence and masculinity to the Japanese Self-Defence Forces (Morigaki 1998); and it was also used to link carnivorous and voracious consumption to masculinity. A Kyoto ramen restaurant, for example, used this phrase to promote their huge meat servings (Yamadera 2018). The centrality of silence and meat consumption within masculinity is seen as natural and can also be seen in recent non-normative models of masculinity such as those categorized as "herbivore men" (*sōshokukeidanshi*) because of an apparent disinterest in "carnivorous" activities such as sex or the typical salaryman life-course (Yuen 2014, 222). This recycling provides an interesting insight into how certain activities and interests are seen as masculine and also connect to previous models of masculinity.

The way this slogan resonated in the popular imagination enabled Sapporo to integrate it within their corporate identity. It was so successful in this regard that print media were still using it as shorthand for the company two decades later. The headline for the 1990 *Sunday Mainichi* interview with Sapporo Beer's president, "The Fierce Great Beer War—Men are Silent and Hokkaido!?" (Sunday Mainichi 1990, 5) demonstrated that editors clearly expected their readers to still understand this reference. The campaign's enduring appeal lies precisely in its continual reiteration within a range of commentary, including scholarship that referenced it to explain the appropriateness of silence for men (Lebra 1976, 78) or the essential role of beer within masculinity (Sugiyama 2000; Christensen 2010). These repetitive references in the media, in corporate recollections and in academic commentary have contributed to its continued use and helped to valorize and emphasize this campaign over its competitors.

Competing masculinities

While the *Otoko wa damatte* campaign became the most iconic representation of idealized masculinity, extant industry and social criticisms were neglected and competing campaigns, and their depictions of gender, were marginalized and eventually ignored despite these being understood at the time to be at least as successful as the Mifune campaign. It is essential to explore the very different masculinities presented by Sapporo's competitors because they alter our understanding of the Mifune campaign's status from a representative depiction to an outlier.

The Mifune campaign, one of the most evocative promotional campaigns of the postwar, did not operate in a vacuum. Its masculinizing re-branding was to directly challenge, and undermine, Kirin Beer's dominance. The later exclusion of Kirin's advertisements from debates was not commensurate with contemporaneous events—Kirin's campaign won awards and helped Kirin maintain their market share.

Kirin used the married actors Nakaya Noboru and Kishida Kyōko to promote their beer with the tagline "*dō iu wake ka, Kirin*" (for some reason, somehow, it's Kirin). Their activities—train trips, bicycling on the beach—contrast starkly with Mifune's solitary presence. The *Dō iu wake ka* campaign was recognized as a departure from the norm. Kirin's previous advertising had favored men (Dentsu hō 1970, 3), while for Shimamori Michico, Kishida contrasted with the usual representation of women: the "my home mama [...] who was a good wife and good mother" (Shimamori 1984, 122–25). Kishida instead reflected a new era where women were free to travel or seize the initiative (Takishima 2000, 28–29). The campaign was seen as appealing to women (Sunday Mainichi 1973, 135), specifically young women because of their proclivity for travel (Shimamori 1984, 122–25), and to married couples (Brain 1971, 123) with Kishida and Nakaya considered an ideal example (Josei Seven 1977, 174).

This campaign, however, has been neglected in narratives of the *Otoko wa damatte* campaign and ignored in discussions of masculinity in Japanese beer advertisements partly because Nakaya's particular model of masculinity does not match Mifune's. Only certain models of masculinity are viewed as masculine by commentators, with Kishida's practices—trouser-wearing, beer-drinking, and travelling—notably not seen as masculine. Critics clearly defined masculinity and femininity through these exclusions. In applying certain terms to their descriptions of Mifune, and not Nakaya, these critics provide insight into how the idealized form of masculinity was constructed.

Commentators tend to define Mifune Toshirō in this campaign as hyper-masculine. This quality was essential to this campaign and he was considered indispensable by Sapporo Beer (Sapporo Biiru KK 1996, 791) with no other man in Japan capable of properly embodying this idealized image of masculinity (Aoyanagi 2001, 8). This understanding of Mifune's masculinity as dominant is reflected in articles separated by some 18 years. The magazine *Josei Seven* described the *Otoko wa damatte* catchphrase as perfect for its period, specifically, that this was the "era when men were still manly" (*mada otoko ga otokorashikatta jidai*) (Josei Seven 1988, 46). This direct (and negative) comparison to the then-contemporary masculinity of the 1980s positions the men of that time as inauthentic and lacking in comparison to Mifune.

The advertising critic, Okada Yoshirō, similarly categorizes Mifune's masculinity. Writing in the trade journal *Sendenkaigi (Marketing and Creativity)* Okada's evaluation (2006, 92) is noteworthy because he directly relates the Mifune campaign to its competitors and because he defines masculinity as performed only by certain men. This included men such as Takakura Ken, whose tagline for Asahi advertisements—"*Nonde moraimasu*" (now you will drink) (Asahi Beer 1970)—referenced his Yakuza films with a line that often preceded an antagonist's death: "*Shinde moraimasu*" (now you will die). Okada describes the competition between the Takakura and Mifune advertisements as a "contest of manliness" (*otokorashi-sa*) (2006, 93). For Okada, Takakura and Mifune personified masculinity; Nakaya did not though he does not specify why. The suffix *rashii/sa* often roughly corresponds to those behaviors and practices which are culturally, socially and emotionally appropriate (Itō, Kimura and Kuninobu 2002, 7; Lebra 1976, 78); *otokorashii* itself is often used to emphasize practices or an individuals' proximity to a gender stereotype (Robertson 1992, 421). A lack of loquacity in particular is one of the socially accepted prohibitions for men (including not crying or showing weakness) that Itō Kimio has defined as the constrictions of *otokorashisa* (2003, 9).

Mifune's silence is masculine because it fits preconceived notions of practices appropriate for men. Takakura and Mifune are thus manly according to Okada (2006, 92) because of their proximity to a gendered stereotype of how a man should be. Nakaya does not meet this gendered stereotype despite engaging in activities in conjunction with his wife. This exclusion is particularly jarring given the role that marriage has played in mainstream narratives of being considered a (male) adult (Taga 2003, 138). The practices promoted within what Taga calls the *sarariiman-sengyōshufu* regime (the professional salaryman-housewife model) (2003, 137), such as marriage, children, work and home-buying, clearly contrast with the practices (engaged in by Mifune and Takakura) lauded within the advertising discourse as manly. On the contrary, these responsibilities actually appear to preclude men from this definition within the advertising discourse as defined by these critics.

We can see how gendered terms are used to describe, and thus regulate, various practices and behaviors and how gender is used in quotidian language. Designations such as *otokorashii* were reserved for "hyper-masculine" men, such as Mifune, whose performance fit preconceived notions of what masculinity is. Yet it should be noted that there was contemporaneous criticism of this campaign's linking of taciturnity and masculinity and praise of Nakaya's masculinity. Such critiques are important for revealing dialogues between critics and industry practitioners. Writing in *Fujin kōron*, Niki Etsuko (1980, 32–33) considered Mifune's depiction "*otokorashii*" but found it problematic rather than praiseworthy. In doing so, Niki discusses masculinity in terms of multiple and varying masculinities which, while now widely recognized within Japanese scholarship (Dasgupta 2009, 84–89), is rare within discussions of these campaigns.

Niki described this campaign, and others, as an "*otokorashisa* movement," a reaction to societal trends. These *otokorashii* men's identity—centered on "their ability to silently, and earnestly, walk their own path"—contrasted with the constraints on women or children who could not act similarly (1980, 32–33). For Niki, these depictions were part of an ongoing reactionary trend that operated within a system of oppression with Mifune's masculinity, situated as it is within a system of independence composed of themes of loneliness, isolation, and hardship, neither laudable nor aspirational. Sapporo's evaluation of this independence and isolation was more positive, identifying it as the "sorrow or pathos" (*kanashisa*) of being a man (Sapporo Biiru KK 1996, 791). The company emphasizes and highlights these moments throughout the campaign by situating Mifune away from social networks or urban locations.

Sapporo also addressed the criticism of the campaign as reactionary. Responding to an Asahi Shimbun columnist who also suggested that the campaign was a reaction against "the tide of society," thwarting and neglecting the age of women by limiting beer to men, Matsuura Iwao, Sapporo's head of marketing, introduced and summarily dismissed this criticism on two grounds: that it was not valid because it came from a man; and that many women seemed to like this advert, as the company had received no complaints (1970, 51–53). Women, he argued in part, enjoyed transgressing what they saw as gendered boundaries because they were able to gain a feeling of masculinity when they drank beer and it thus made sense to use men such as Mifune in these advertisements.

Mifune's hypermasculinity was thus a point of resistance that women could protest by drinking the beer that promoted this image. Matsuura's argument contradicts Sugiyama Gaku's evaluation of the campaign as signifying beer as a drink explicitly for men with beer-drinking women described as being like old men (*oyajikusai*) (Sugiyama 2000, 117). However, in the postwar, beer consumption by women was an opportunity to challenge gendered norms. The actresses Kuji Asami, Izumi Kyōko, and Koro Tomoko discussed how their drinking practices played a democratic and equalizing role in challenging men's monopoly on the public consumption of beer (Asahi Graph 1957). In these cases, women used their alcohol choices to challenge men's right and role to publicly consume, but the question of whether the further promotion of beer as a manly man's drink led to enjoyment when transgressing these boundaries remains. Niki's article, meanwhile, contradicts Matsuura's contention that all women necessarily liked the campaign.

Niki's criticism of Mifune also provides access to perspectives on competing models of masculinity. She compares Mifune's dominant masculinity with Nakaya Noboru, specifically drawing attention to Nakaya's contrasting physique and actions. Nakaya is not "one of those burly men, swelling with muscles," she writes, "but instead gives off a refined air and, most importantly, his male image is one type of masculinity" (1980, 32–33). Nakaya's refined air was also mentioned in a *Brain* article looking at celebrities in advertisements (Fukunaka 1971) and another which categorized performers and products into a typology of gender, with Nakaya seen as knowledgeable (*chiseiteki*), wise (*kenjitsu*) and refined (*jōhin*) (Brain 1972), but not masculine. Kishida, however, was deemed feminine (*joseiteki*) in contrast.

Niki's description of Nakaya as one model available from multiple masculinities within a women's magazine is notable because this was apparently the target demographic for the *Dō iu wake ka* campaign. The various demographics of each company's campaigns were widely discussed in both the media and specialist advertising literature (cf. Brain 1971, 123) with Kishida and Nakaya competing "on the 'women front' (*josei rosen*); Sapporo and Asahi […] using Mifune and Takakura on the 'men front' (*dansei rosen*)" (Sunday Mainichi 1973, 135). Nakaya's masculinity was understood in the popular media as appealing to women in conjunction with his wife. Men, on the other hand, were attracted to hypermasculine men who were free from their family or wives in the form of Mifune and Takakura.

Masculinities: Hyper-, hegemonic- and vicarious-

The magazine articles mentioned above are useful in clarifying the issue of later commentators' situating Mifune as hypermasculine despite Mifune's actual model of masculinity not matching what many consider the hegemonic Japanese masculinity of the time. The concept of hegemonic masculinity explains how gender relations work by culturally exalting and socially privileging one form of (ideal) masculinity over others (Light 2003, 103) with other men subordinated, complicit or marginalized. It was the salaryman (Hidaka 2010, 2–3; Dasgupta 2013, 118) who was "the principal normative embodiment of Japan's postwar economic success [...] a cultural icon and ideological model" (Matanle 2003, 8–9).

The designation of Mifune as hypermasculine complicates both the positioning of salaryman masculinity as the hegemonic ideal and this categorization of his own model. Indeed, the *Otoko wa damatte* campaign appears to challenge the salaryman model by representing themes of escape as essential to the performance of masculinity. This contrasts with the salaryman who would need to divest himself of his accoutrements to engage in these activities, which was not uncommon in this period. Weekly magazines discussed *datsusara*, the trend of salarymen rejecting the constrictions of this lifestyle while also subtly highlighting the risks of a "free" life running petrol stations and ramen shops (Aono 1972; Shūkan Sankei 1972). The company's explanation of the desired target clarifies this issue.

Broadcast on Sunday nights during baseball games, this campaign was primarily designed to appeal to salarymen, namely heavy-drinking men in their 30s to 40s, according to Matsuura (1970) and not to dislodge or destabilize their lives. The advertisers did not necessarily want these salarymen to engage in similar activities to Mifune—to abandon their work, lives, families etc., to live a liberated life—as this would remove their ability to buy this beer. Instead, the masculinity embodied by Mifune was a fantasy, appealing to these men precisely because it was unobtainable. Mifune's peripheral sites of beer consumption, far from the urbanized centers, differentiated him from the inflexible salaryman, but this performance is actually one embodiment of the many masculine fantasies, such as mendicant monks and wanderer poets, which frequently stress the mobile in Japan. Ambulatory fantasies contrast with the static in models of masculinity in Japan, according to Tom Gill (2003), with the stable, central pillar in the home (the *daikokubashira*) often likened to the salaryman's role. As part of this fantasy element, Mifune's appearance in remote locations played an important function.

The rural sites of Mifune's masculinity were similar to those of Tora-san—the itinerant peddler whose travels around Japan in a long-running series of films (*Otoko wa tsurai yo* 1969–1995) inevitably resulted in heartbreak. Ian Buruma has attributed Tora-san's popularity to the way he allows those confined by regularity and routine to vicariously experience the pleasures and failures of travelling and to thus reassure themselves of their own life choices (1995, 218). Actors such as Takakura Ken and Ishihara Yūjirō similarly offered "an alternative imagining to the increasingly bureaucratized, regulated reality of lives of [...] salarymen" (Dasgupta 2013, 35). The Mifune model also fulfils this function yet differs markedly by offering practices to redefine one's masculinity.

While the Tora-san films offered a partial respite from, and a cultural reference for, the stresses of ordinary life, the Mifune model was a means for salarymen, through their consumption (of Sapporo Beer), to enact a stoic and laconic masculinity which would be recognized by other men. This campaign, recognizing the inconsistencies of the salaryman ideal, used themes of freedom and movement to convince men who did not enjoy such liberties that they could present an image of being so through consuming this beer. This small change, selecting a different beer, would apparently enable them to define their identity in similar terms to Mifune. This masculinity could thus be performed without risking any of the elements that defined their core identity—job, home or family. Essentially, it allowed men to live this identity through consumption, without acknowledging the demands of the domestic sphere or of the office. While beer brands were "powerful symbols of professional identity and affiliation" for individual salarymen (Alexander 2013, 191), Sapporo clearly hoped their beer would become part of the performed identity of these men despite the reality of the restrictions on their lives.

The use of a hypermasculine, but non-hegemonic, man to appeal to men situated within the hegemonic ideal explains why Mifune's masculinity appears both challenging (in that it undermines the salaryman lifestyle) and complicit (in that it upholds it). Expanding the definition of vicarious masculinity from male spectators sharing athletes' masculinity through possession of a similarly sexed body (Crawley, Foley and Shehan 2008, 132) to Mifune's model has some validity here. It contributes to a more nuanced understanding of gender relations within the media and affirms the complexity of a depiction which allowed men to enact practices that defined their masculinity differently from that same ideal.

Forging masculinity

The multiple interpretations of Mifune as hypermasculine in this campaign are also helpful for understanding how referent systems, or influences, work to define gender in advertising. Judith Williamson (2005, 19) has described the transferal of a priori meanings of objects or people within advertisements to the product as a referent system. It was Mifune's acting history rather than his in-scene activities which helped to cement his meaning and establish the longevity of this campaign. Most uses of Mifune's referent system were partial, however, with only certain elements used and others ignored or neglected.

With roles ranging across Japanese history, Mifune embodied a transhistorical Japanese masculinity unchanging across periods or regions: he was Imperial Japan (as Admiral Yamamoto Isoroku) in 1968's *Rengō kantai shirei chōkan: Yamamoto Isoroku* (Admiral Yamamoto); he was Edo-period Japan (as *Yōjimbō*, 1961); and he was modern Japan, playing salarymen (*Warui yatsu hodo yoku nemuru* (The Bad Sleep Well), 1960), gangsters (*Yoidore tenshi* (Drunken Angel), 1948), and policemen (*Nora inu* (Stray Dog), 1949). These roles positioned his masculinity clearly within national frames and presented him as a timeless embodiment of a (masculine) Japanese spirit, entwining his masculinity so deeply with the idea of Japaneseness that he was labeled Mr. Japan (*Misutaa Nippon*) (Shūkan Yomiuri 1969, 104).

Despite Mifune's range of roles, and the number of meanings available within his referent system, commentators focused on the "feudal" samurai as the key marker of Mifune's masculinity rather than the more controversial imperial or militarist masculinities he had represented. He was described as an embodiment of "the samurai of Japan" (Okada 2006, 92), while his stoic silence was linked to his samurai characters silently cutting through his enemies (Yamazaki 1973, 148). This connection was not undesired. Sapporo actively incorporated elements of Mifune's film roles into the campaign. This included creating a visual connection between the cinematic and advertising realms by commissioning the *Shichinin no samurai* (Seven Samurai 1954) poster calligrapher to recreate the "intense" (*kyōretsu*) calligraphic style for the catchphrase, "*Otoko wa damatte ... Sapporo Biiru*" (Sapporo Biiru KK 1996, 791) and making this connection to Mifune's *jidaigeki* screen roles clear to consumers and viewers.

The trope of the samurai helped to construct a national image both masculine and ostensibly universal (Mason 2011, 68–70); it was also instrumental in creating Mifune's image, which was parlayed into this campaign. The highlighting of this element by creators, critics, and commentators explicitly reveals the relationship between masculinity and national myths and narratives. References only to Mifune's samurai roles demonstrate how restricted a referent system can be. While Williamson's (2005) use of binary oppositions to explain how referent systems work has been criticized (Cook 1992, 63–65), we can see here that some of Mifune's multiple meanings were constrained and not necessarily available. Most commentators specifically avoided any connection between masculinity and silence to militarism. This was not unusual. The postwar rehabilitation of bushidō from the wartime imperial version relied on the popular understanding that it was "an ancient tradition corrupted by militarists" during the early Shōwa period (Benesch 2014, 222, 241). Reverting back to an "uncorrupted" pre-Meiji-era version meant that critics could reference samurai (and Mifune) as exemplars of bushidō and avoid any associations with an uncomfortable wartime past.

The lack of reference to militarism is particularly discordant, however, when the genesis for the slogan is examined. Despite the calligraphy, and Mifune's role as a silent samurai, the idea of emphasizing silence within this campaign apparently originated from a film set during the Second World War, *Taiheiyō kiseki no sakusen: Kisuka* (Miraculous Military Operation in the Pacific Ocean, 1965). According to Kamo Kazumasa the creative catalyst came from a scene where Mifune's character, Admiral Omura, contemplates in silence before taking decisive action (Kamo 1975, 240)—action that was in the wartime service of the Japanese Empire. The model of masculinity that Mifune portrays in the advertisement is therefore directly drawn from a representation of militaristic and imperialistic masculinity, a point largely overlooked in later commentary.

Attesting to the variety and diversity of thought at the time of broadcast, however, contemporaneous commentators did critique this advertisement for its emphasis on silence as integral to masculinity and its connection to militarism. The social critic Yamazaki Masakazu adopted a Barthesian notion of myths as constructed narratives to critique this campaign. Yamazaki highlighted the danger of positioning silence as integral to masculinity, noting that perpetrators of massacres are described after the event as quiet office workers (1973, 148–49). These unassuming workers contrast with such exemplars of masculine virtue, namely the Meiji Restoration leaders, who spoke out and "made modern Japan." He then discusses how remaining silent allowed those with louder voices to rise to positions of dangerous power during the war. In this way, he shows the ahistorical nature of this simple equation of silence and masculinity. Yamazaki's analysis suggests a more critical take on the *Otoko wa damatte…* campaign's meaning. Not only was it popular enough to be a topic for consideration, but the linkage of silence with masculinity was not necessarily a desirable trait. Drawing on national historical events, Yamazaki also undercut the idea that silence was a transhistorical ideal practice for Japanese men.

Niki was equally critical of this marriage of silence with masculinity, viewing the promotion of this silent endurance as fraught with danger, carrying with it the risk of increased nationalism. Niki specifically warned that this campaign's depiction of silent masculinity was one step towards Yasukuni Shrine (Niki 1980, 34), the site of the enshrinement and veneration of Japan's war dead, including some war criminals, and consequently the subject of numerous controversies. Niki felt that this campaign was helping to shift the parameters of what was acceptable in popular discourse by helping to rehabilitate pro-militaristic perspectives. Yamazaki and Niki's criticism, combined with Kamo's recollection of this campaign, indicates that at the time of the campaign's production there was an understanding of the link between militarism, masculinity and this model of behavior and that there was a willingness to utilize these elements in a bricolage that both created and promoted a model of masculinity that concealed these influences.

These two contemporaneous critics' interpretation that the silence-masculinity nexus is directly linked to militarism contrasts with the elision of this connection by later commentators who instead, distanced from the war and discussions of defeat, laud this depiction. When viewed against these cautionary critiques, the claim that this was an age when men were manly requires an equal acknowledgement that pre-1945 practices of masculinity continued to be implicated within this postwar manliness. The men deemed most manly at this time had been involved and participated in wartime activities while representations utilized a number of tropes and values leftover from this period to inform their then current advertising campaigns. Mifune himself was linked to militarism not only by his film roles but also through his wartime service. This was not necessarily by choice (Wise and Baron 2002, 132) as military service was part of a normative life course for men at this time (Sewell 2003, 99; Cook 2008, 260) but this apparent lack of wartime agency did not affect Mifune's significant, active, and voluble role in creating a militarized model of masculinity that became a key part of his referent system. When making *Hell in the Pacific* with Lee Marvin, Mifune advocated to ensure that "no damage was done to the prestige of the Japanese military [which was] one way to repay the spirits of the war dead who remain in this place." He also rejected an instruction to cry, saying that "Japanese soldiers don't cry; they cry only in their souls" (*Nippon gunjin wa nakan. Kokoro no naka de shika nakan motsu da*) (Shūkan Yomiuri 1969, 104–5).

The links between militarism and masculinity in this campaign can thus be traced to Mifune's film roles and Mifune himself. The absence of these links in canonical interpretations of the campaign shows how uncomfortable associations were avoided and controversial issues unaddressed. While commentators such as Yamazaki and Niki, who wrote closer in time to the campaign and the war, did address these connections, most analyses of gender in this advertisement rested on the samurai as the mythical epitome of Japanese masculinity. Part of the reason for this continued use of Mifune as samurai and as masculine was because of his referent system but also because other references were uncomfortable for later commentators.

Conclusion

Throughout the postwar period and into the 21st century, advertising and beer industry professionals presented an idealized world of beer drinking to the Japanese public. One such endeavor, the Mifune campaign, positioned silence as an integral practice in masculinity alongside a rejection of the feminine. The discussion of this campaign's iteration of masculinity in trade journals, magazines and in contemporary articles revealed boundaries and conceptualizations of gender which differed by time and between industry professionals and critics.

Significant differences in understandings of what constituted masculinity manifested themselves according to the temporal proximity of the commentators. While contemporaneous thought gave credence to the concept of multiple masculinities and hierarchies and contested the linking of silence to masculinity, retrospective works positioned this model of masculinity as hypermasculine with a highly selective reading of Mifune's referent system while neglecting other associations, such as militarism. This was especially problematic given it was Mifune's role in war films that had provided the genesis of the campaign.

Critiques by contemporaneous critics such as Niki and Yamazaki, who did highlight militarism's link with silence, offer resistance to the more visible corporate understandings and narratives and attest to the importance of examining the advertising discourse. Challenges such as these also drew attention to wider trends within society and within advertisements themselves. This campaign's model of masculinity was understood to be a reaction against the advances that women were making at this time, and thus a further subordination of women and non-normative models of masculinity. In doing so, these critiques revealed a diversity of thought and perspective on hegemonic and subordinate forms of masculinity. By referencing competing campaigns and including performers such as Nakaya Noboru in their analyses, these critics acknowledged the variety of models available, their apparent subordination to that represented by Mifune, and their validity as men despite this subordination. In doing so they showed an understanding of hierarchies of gender which was both sophisticated and highly prescient, hinting at future theorizations of gender such as hegemonic masculinity.

Advertising campaigns were a looking glass to the events and changing narratives of the postwar period, offering idealized images of what life could and should be like against the backdrop of actual social change. As seen here, the advertising discourse analysis of these images reveals a wider picture featuring a dialogue of images and respondent voices, discussing, critiquing, and praising these distorted, idealizing images. The existence of diverse perspectives on the gender performances of individuals depicted within the media highlights the diversity and variety of available practices and behaviors. It is essential that these voices be considered when looking at ads because they are an integral and important resource revealing ephemera about campaigns, perspectives that have since vanished, and points of contestation that fade into the condescension of posterity.

Bibliography

Alexander, J.W., 2013. *Brewed in Japan: The Evolution of The Japanese Beer Industry*. Vancouver: UBC Press.

Amano, Y., 2002. *Kōkoku ronkōgi* [Lectures on the theory of advertising]. Tokyo: Iwanami Shoten.

Aono, I., 1972. Esso Shōhō ni miru gaishi no teguchi [The M.O. of foreign investment which resembles Esso's operation]. *Shin'hyō*, March.

Aoyanagi, S., ed., 2001. *Ketteiban! Terebi CM daihyakka: 50 nenkan no terebi CM ga subete wakaru!!* [Special edition! A hundred television advertisements: understand all advertisements from 50 years]. Tokyo: Enterbrain.

Arima, A.N., 2003. Gender Stereotypes in Japanese Television Advertisements. *Sex Roles*, 49(1), 81–90. https://doi.org/10.1023/A:1023965704387.

Asahi Beer, 1970. *Nonde itadakimasu* [Now you'll drink]. Advertisement in the Yomiuri Shinbun, 30 May, 12.

Asahi Graph, 1957. Bīrutō joyūretsuden [Biographical series: movie actresses who love beer]. *Asahi Graph*, 21 July, 12–13.

Befu, H., 1986. An Ethnography of Dinner Entertainment in Japan. In T.S. Lebra and W.P. Lebra, eds., *Japanese Culture and Behavior: Selected Readings*, Rev. ed. Honolulu: University of Hawai'i Press, 108–20.

Benesch, O., 2014. *Inventing the Way of the Samurai: Nationalism, Internationalism, and Bushidō in Modern Japan*. [online] Oxford: OUP. Available at: http://site.ebrary.com/id/10909669 [Accessed 10 October. 2016].

Brain, 1971. Asahi Biiru—"Kyōkan" to "jōzetsu naru taiwa" o motomete [Asahi Beer—demanding "empathy" and "a loquacious dialogue"]. *Brain*, 11(11), 122–25.

———., 1972. Gendai CM talento no imēji bunseki [Analysis of contemporary advertising celebrity images]. *Brain*, 12(2), 8–27.

Buruma, Ian., 1995. *A Japanese Mirror: Heroes and Villains in Japanese Culture*. London: Vintage.

Christensen, P., 2010. *Struggles with Sobriety: Alcoholics Anonymous Membership in Japan*. PhD, University of Hawai'i. Available at: https://www.academia.edu/574665/Struggles_with_Sobriety_Alcoholics _Anonymous_Membership_in_Japan [Accessed 7 April 2014].

Cook, G., 1992. *The Discourse of Advertising*. London: Routledge.

Cook, T.F., 2008. Making "Soldiers": The Imperial Army and the Japanese Man in Meiji Society and State. In B. Molony and K.S. Uno, eds., *Gendering Modern Japanese History*. Cambridge: Harvard University Press, 259–94.

Cramer-Flood, E., 2020. *Comparing Total Ad Spend in the US, China and the Rest of the World*. [online] Insider Intelligence. Available at: https://www.emarketer.com/content/how-our-ad-spending-outlook-has-changed-us-china-rest-of-world [Accessed 30 December 2020].

Crawley, S.L., Foley, L.J. and Shehan, C.L., 2008. *Gendering Bodies*. Lanham: Rowman & Littlefield Publishers.

Creighton, M., 1997. Consuming Rural Japan: The Marketing of Tradition and Nostalgia in the Japanese Travel Industry. *Ethnology*, 36(3), 239–54. https://doi.org/10.2307/3773988.

Dasgupta, R., 2009. The "Lost Decade" of the 1990s and Shifting Masculinities in Japan. *Culture, Society and Masculinities*, 1(1), 79–95. https://doi.org/10.3149/csm.0101.79.

———., 2013. *Re-reading the Salaryman in Japan: Crafting Masculinities*. London: Routledge.

Dentsu hō, 1970. "Mūdo" jūshi no keikō—kateiteki ya danseiteki nado [The important trend of "mood": domestic and masculine etc.]. *Dentsu hō*, 9 May.

Focus, 1998. Focus Best Channel—Sapporo Biiru CM. *Focus*, 7 October.

Ford, J.B., Kramer Voli, P., Honeycutt Jr., E.D. and Casey, S.L., 1998. Gender Role Portrayals in Japanese Advertising: A Magazine Content Analysis. *Journal of Advertising*, 27(1), 113–24.

Francks, P., 2009. *The Japanese Consumer: an Alternative Economic History of Modern Japan*. Cambridge: Cambridge University Press.

Fukunaka, H., 1971. Biiru CM no narēshon [The narration of beer commercials]. *Brain*, 11(12), 76–79.

Furnham, A., Abramsky, S. and Gunter, B., 1997. A Cross-Cultural Content Analysis of Children's Television Advertisements. *Sex Roles*, 37(1–2), 91–99. https://doi.org/10.1023/A:1025692804434.

Galbraith, P.W. and Karlin, J.G., 2012. Introduction. In P.W. Galbraith and J.G. Karlin, eds., *Idols and Celebrity in Japanese Media Culture*. Basingstoke: Palgrave Macmillan, 1–34.

Gill, T., 2003. When Pillars Evaporate: Structuring Masculinity on the Japanese Margins. In J.E. Roberson, and N. Suzuki, eds., *Men and Masculinities in Contemporary Japan: Dislocating the Salaryman Doxa*. London: Routledge, 144–161.

Heath, D.B., 1995. An Introduction to Alcohol and Culture in International Perspective. In D.B Heath, ed., *International Handbook on Alcohol and Culture*. [online] Westport, CT: Greenwood Press. 1–6. Available at: http://www.questia.com [Accessed 1 May 2013].

Hidaka, T., 2010. *Salaryman Masculinity: Continuity and Change in the Hegemonic Masculinity in Japan*. Leiden: Brill.

Holbrook, M.B., 1987. Mirror, Mirror, on the Wall, What's Unfair in the Reflections on Advertising? *Journal of Marketing*, 51(3), 95–103. https://doi.org/10.2307/1251650.

Itō, K., 2003. "*Otokorashisa" to iu shinwa—gendai dansei no kiki o yomitoku* [The myth of "masculinity"— closely reading the current men's crisis]. Tokyo: Nihon Hōso Shuppansha.

Itō, K., Kimura, M. and Kuninobu, J., 2002. *Joseigaku—danseigaku: jendā ron nyūmon* [Women's studies— men's studies: an introduction to gender theory]. Tokyo: Yuhikaku Arma.

JAC, 1991. *Shōwa no CF100Sen: Best 100 Japanese Commercial Films 1961-1988*. Tokyo: Seibundo-Shinkosha.

Joffe, A.H., 1998. Alcohol and Social Complexity in Ancient Western Asia. *Current Anthropology*, 39(3), 297–322. https://doi.org/10.1086/204736.

Johansson, J.K., 1994. The Sense of "Nonsense": Japanese TV Advertising. *Journal of Advertising*, 23(1), 17–26.

Josei Seven, 1977. Kishida Kyōko-Nakaya Noboru no rikon ga ōhamon [The ripples from the divorce of Kishida Kyōko-Nakaya Noboru]. *Josei Seven*, 22 September.

———., 1988. Biiru no umasa to ano sutā [The taste of beer and the stars]. *Josei Seven*, 7 July, 45–52.

Kamo, K., 1975. Case Study 5: Mifune Toshirō—Otoko wa damatte Sapporo Biiru. In R. Kondō and Y. Kaji, eds., *Tarento kōkoku: saidai kōka wa kō shite tsukurareru* [Celebrity advertisements: The most effective are made like this]. Tokyo: Diamond.

Kellner, D., 2003. Cultural Studies, Multiculturalism, and Media Culture. In G. Dines and J.M. Humez, eds., *Gender, Race, and Class in Media: a Text-reader*, 2nd ed. Thousand Oaks: Sage Publications, 9–20.

Lebra, T.S., 1976. *Japanese Patterns of Behavior*. Honolulu: University Press of Hawai'i.

Light, R., 2003. Sport and the Construction of Masculinity in the Japanese Education System. In K. Louie and M. Low, eds., *Asian Masculinities: the Meaning and Practice of Manhood in China and Japan*. London: Routledge, 100–17.

Mandelbaum, D.G., 1979. Alcohol and Culture. In M. Marshall, ed., *Beliefs, Behaviors, & Alcoholic Beverages: a Cross-cultural Survey*. Ann Arbor: University of Michigan Press, 14–29.

Martin, D., 2012. Foreign Women in Japanese Television Advertising: Content Analyses of a Cultural Convergence Paradigm. *European Journal of Marketing*, 46(1/2), 157–176. https://doi.org/10.1108/03090561211189275.

Mason, M.M., 2011. Empowering the Would-be Warrior: Bushido and the Gendered Bodies of the Japanese Nation. In S. Frühstück and A. Walthall, eds., *Recreating Japanese Men*. Berkeley: University of California Press, 68–90.

Matanle, P.C.D., 2003. *Japanese Capitalism and Modernity in a Global Era: Re-fabricating Lifetime Employment Relations*. London: RoutledgeCurzon.

Matsuura, I., 1970. "Otoko wa damatte Sapporo Biiru" Kyanpēn kēsu [Campaign case: Sapporo Beer—men are silent]. *Māketingu to kōkoku* [Marketing and advertising], 9 (September).

Moeran, B., 1996. *A Japanese Advertising Agency: an Anthropology of Media and Markets*. [online] Available at: http://search.ebscohost.com/login.aspx?direct=true&scope=site&db=nlebk&db=nlabk&AN=641008 [Accessed 20 January 2014].

———., 1997. *Folk Art Potters of Japan: Beyond an Anthropology of Aesthetics*. Honolulu: University of Hawai'i Press.

———., 1998. One Over the Seven: Sake Drinking in a Japanese Pottery Community. In J. Hendry, ed., *Interpreting Japanese Society: Anthropological Approaches*. 2nd ed. London: Routledge.

Morigaki, H., 1998. Otoko wa damatte sentōki [Men are silent and fighter planes]. *Securitarian*, 62–64.

Nead, L., 1988. *Myths of Sexuality: Representations of Women in Victorian Britain*. Oxford: B. Blackwell.

Niki, E., 1980. Otoko no naka no otoko kenkyū—CM senba no yukimonotachi [Research on men of men—the brave men of the advertising battlefield]. *Fujin kōron*,1971/9. In H. Yamakawa, ed., *Terebi 25 nen no kiroku—CM gurafiti* [Ad graffitti—a record of 25 years of television] Tokyo: Seibundō Shinkōsha.

Okada, Y., 2006. "Sapporo Biiru—otoko wa damatte Sapporo Biiru" jidai no kibun o utsusu gōkai na CM ["Sapporo Beer's otoko wa damatte Sapporo Biiru"—a lively CM which reflects the spirit of an age]. *Sendenkaigi* [*Marketing and Creativity*] (700), 92–93.

Okazaki, S. and Mueller, B., 2008. Evolution in the Usage of Localized Appeals in Japanese and American Print Advertising. *International Journal of Advertising*, 27(5), 771–98. https://doi.org/10.2501/S0265048708080323.

Plant, M.A., 1995. The United Kingdom. In D.B. Heath, ed., *International Handbook on Alcohol and Culture*. [online] Westport, Conn: Greenwood Press. 289–99. Available at: http://www.questia.com [Accessed 1 May 2013].

Prieler, M. and Kohlbacher, F., 2016. *Advertising in the Aging Society: Understanding Representations, Practitioners, and Consumers in Japan*. Basingstoke: Palgrave Macmillan.

Prieler, M., Kohlbacher, F., Hagiwara, S. and Arima, A., 2010. Older Celebrity versus Non-Celebrity Television Advertising: A Japanese Perspective. *Keio Communication Review*, 32, 5–23.

Roberson, J., 2005. Fight!! Ippatsu!! "Genki" Energy Drinks and the Marketing of Masculine Ideology in Japan. *Men and Masculinities*, 7(4), 365–84. https://doi.org/10.1177/1097184X03261260.

Robertson, J., 1992. The Politics of Androgyny in Japan: Sexuality and Subversion in the Theater and Beyond. *American Ethnologist*, 19(3), 419–42.

Sapporo Biiru, KK, 1996. *Sapporo 120 nenshi* [120-year history of Sapporo Breweries]. Tokyo: Sapporo Biiru, KK.

Sargent, M.J., 1979. Changes in Japanese Drinking Patterns. In M. Marshall, ed., *Beliefs, Behaviors, & Alcoholic Beverages: a Cross-cultural Survey*. Ann Arbor: University of Michigan Press, 278.

Sewell, B., 2003. Postwar Japan and Manchuria. In D.W. Edgington, ed., *Japan at the Millennium: Joining Past and Future*. Vancouver: UBC Press.

Shimamori, M., 1984. *Kōkoku no naka no jōsei-tachi* [Women in advertisements]. Tokyo: Daiwashobō.

Shūkan Sankei, 1972. Kinmōke Seminā ramen "Nihon ichi" ni manabu datsusara shikō [The trend of stopping being a salaryman—No 1 Study: Ramen] (Interview with President Komazawa Kiyomi). *Shūkan Sankei*, 6 October

Shūkan Yomiuri, 1969. Mifune Toshirō ni okeru nihonjin no kenkyū [Research into the Japanese in Mifune Toshirō]. Shūkan Yomiuri, 104.

Smith, S.R., 1992. Drinking Etiquette in a Changing Beverage Market. In J.J. Tobin, ed., *Re-made in Japan: Everyday Life and Consumer Taste in a Changing Society*. New Haven: Yale Univ. Press, 143–58.

Sugiyama, G., 2000. Daisanshō: Otoko to onna no shinboru kōkoku ni okerudanjo no kigōgaku [Chapter 3: men and women as symbols—the semiotics of men and women in advertisements]. In H. Ishikawa and H. Takishima, eds., *Kōkoku kara yomu onna to otoko: jendā to sekushuariti* [Reading men and women from advertisements: gender and sexuality]. Tokyo: Yuzankaku Shuppansha, 99–126.

Sunday Mainichi, 1973. Shin biiru sensō: neage ato mo—damatte nonde moraimasu [New beer war—even after the price rise we'll have you be quiet]. *Sunday Mainichi*, 28 October.

———, 1990. Gekiretsu biiru daisensō ni otoko wa damatte "Hokkaido"!? [The severe great beer war—men are silent and "Hokkaido"!?]. *Sunday Mainichi*, 28 July.

Taga, F., 2003. Rethinking Male Socialization: Life Histories of Japanese Male Youth. In K. Louie and M. Low, eds., *Asian Masculinities: the Meaning and Practice of Manhood in China and Japan*. London: Routledge, 137–54.

Takayama, F., ed., 1999. *Asahibīru sendengaishi—yōranki no eikō to zasetsu* [An unofficial history of Asahi Beer's publicity section]. Tokyo: Chūō Ado Shinsha.

Takishima, H., 2000. Kōkoku kara yomu onna to otoko no 50 nen: Sengōkōkoku 50 nen no sukecchi [Fifty years of reading women and men in advertisements—a sketch of the fifty-year postwar advertisements]. In H. Ishikawa and H. Takishima, eds., *Kōkoku kara yomu onna to otoko: jendā to sekushuariti* [Reading men and women from advertisements: gender and sexuality]. Tokyo: Yuzankaku.

Tanaka, Y., 1995. *Contemporary Portraits of Japanese Women*. Westport, CT: Praeger.

Tokyo Copywriters' Club, ed., 1972. *Advertising Copy Annual '72*. Tokyo: Kawasaki.

White, J., 2007. *The Promise of Sex and Fun: An Inquiry into the Construction of Gender in Japanese Beer Advertisements*. MA Thesis. University of Sheffield, School of East Asian Studies.

Williamson, J., 2005. *Decoding Advertisements: Ideology and Meaning in Advertising*. London: Marion Boyars Publishing Ltd.

Wise, J.E. and Baron, S., 2002. *International Stars at War*. Annapolis, MD: Naval Institute Press.

Yamadera, 2018. Kyoto—ramen Banrai-ya de otoko wa damatte nikuzō 300gram ni chōsen [Kyoto rāmen shop—Banraiya's men are silent and 300g meat challenge]. Available at https://www.youtube.com/watch?v=YhNtOJtOYf0 [Accessed 22 September 2021].

Yamakawa, H., ed., 1987. *Shōwa kōkoku 60-nenshi* [A 60-year history of Showa advertisements]. Tōkyō: Kōdansha.

Yamaki, T., 1992. *Nihon kōkokushi: keizai, hyōgen, sesō de miru kōkoku hensen* [Japanese advertising history: economy, expression]. Tokyo: Nihon Keizai Shinbunsha.

Yamazaki, M., 1973. Otoko wa damatte [Men are silent]. In S. Komatsu and M. Yamazaki, eds., *Gendai no shinwa* [Modern myths]. Tokyo: Nihon Keizai Shinbunsha.

Yuen, S.M., 2014. From men to "boys"—The cooking danshi in Japanese mass media. *Women's Studies International Forum*, 44, 220–227. https://doi.org/10.1016/j.wsif.2013.08.002.

Chapter 14
Japanese Men's Magazines: (Re)producing Hybrid Masculinities

Ronald Saladin

This chapter traces the development of the magazine medium in Japan, with a specific focus on men's magazines. Elaborating on the content of the early magazines for men appearing in the late 19th and 20th centuries, the focus shifts to a "new kind" of men's magazines that boomed in the 1990s. Using the magazine BiDaN as an example, this chapter elaborates on how these magazines were structured, how they differed in content from their predecessors, and how the idea of masculinity they construct can be read as an exemplification of changing gender perceptions of society.

Introduction

Magazines are among Japan's most visible print products and as such one of its most prominent artefacts of popular culture. Kiosks and bookshops brim over with an uncountable number of journals geared towards an equally vast array of different target audiences. One section of the magazine market that is relatively new and propelled in size during the 1990s are magazines for men. This chapter discusses the development and current state of Japanese men's magazines with the aim of understanding the meaning of this medium for its audiences and Japanese society in general. It will elaborate on the history and characteristics of the magazine medium in Japan, focusing on the emergence of magazines that cater towards gendered target audiences and, in so doing, will discuss the meaning of a product of popular culture with regard to the gender perceptions of society. Focusing on the appearance of men's magazines in the late 20th and early 21st centuries, the chapter discusses one example of a typical Japanese lifestyle magazine for young men—the magazine *BiDaN*. The aim is to show what topics are being addressed in this "new" kind of magazine, how this is done and what the analysis of these magazines reveals about the development of Japanese society.

Products of popular culture allow us to understand the issues being discussed in society. They play a part in the discursive construction of topics that are deemed important or interesting and thus participate in shaping the everyday reality we live in. Hence, analyzing products of popular culture allows us to understand how society is evolving. Magazines enable the discussion and negotiation of topics that a great number of people are interested in. Reading a magazine, like the consumption of all products of popular culture, is voluntary. Hügel (2003, 6) explains:

> Popular Culture—there is no doubt about it— is no culture of compulsion. Without the freedom of reception, which has to be understood as both the freedom to choose what to receive and to participate in shaping the processes of creating meaning as well as uses—in other words, without civic liberties—there is no popular culture.

This means that it is possible to understand which topics are of interest for the readership of a particular magazine by analyzing magazines and their content. The way magazines are purchased in Japan in particular highlights the voluntary nature of their consumption. Japanese magazines tend to be purchased actively by readers (Morohashi 1998a, 193). They usually buy them at a kiosk, convenience store or a bookshop, most likely on their way to the train station or while they are taking a break from work etc. While many magazines now also offer subscriptions and/or online issues[1] as well, buying a print copy of a magazine in a shop has been (Cooper-Chen 1997, 83–84), and continues to be (Kurata et al. 2017, 888), the most typical method of purchase.

It must not be forgotten, however, that the reader creates the meaning of the magazine content within a creative process of perception and interpretation. Therefore, we cannot assume that the readers take in any magazine content as it appears in the magazine. Readers interpret the information conveyed by a magazine and possibly decode it in contradictory ways.[2] Nevertheless, a look into a magazine can allow us to draw conclusions as to which fields of information are of interest to readers without having to ascertain how a specific reader interprets the information conveyed by the magazine.

The development of the magazine medium in Japan

The first print publication ever to be called a magazine (*zasshi*) in Japan appeared in 1867 (Nojiri 1991, 27). At the time, Japan was undergoing a period of radical renewal, politically, socially, academically and scientifically, with the aim of catching up with the western world. One way to bring western knowledge into the country was to translate and publish news and information on scientific developments achieved in the West. Yanagawa Shunsan, a well-educated scholar who later reached high-ranking positions at the Kaiseijo, an institute that was a predecessor of the University of Tokyo, was dedicated to spreading this kind of knowledge by means of a new medium—the magazine. Yanagawa's *Seiyō zasshi* (lit. Western magazine) which published translations of foreign academic and scientific articles, therefore, became the predecessor of the magazine genre in Japan (Woldering 2005, 93–105). Even though the *Seiyō zasshi* hardly resembles today's magazines, it included some features that have become characteristic of modern magazines. First and foremost, its contents suggest that it was produced for a relatively small and highly educated layer of Japan's society. Having a narrowly defined target audience remains the standard for the vast majority of Japan's magazines and the Japanese magazine market today. As Japanese media scholar Morohashi Taiki puts it:

> It is, therefore, sufficient to align the topics of a magazine with its respective
> target audience. There is no need to "offer something for everyone" as is the
> case with television or newspapers. This phenomenon is called "segmentation of
> magazines" or "distribution of subject-specific information." This means nothing
> else but the congruence of the magazine content with the needs of the readers.
> (Morohashi 1998b, 266)

On the one hand, the Japanese magazine market is highly diverse in terms of the vast number of target audiences it caters to. On the other hand, these magazines are very narrow with regard to their contents and aim at one of those clearly defined target audiences. Brian Moeran, who has analyzed advertising in Japanese magazines, explains that:

> Magazines offer advertisers something no other media can supply: a selected
> target audience, which is likely to be interested in a particular product. Not only
> do those who read a particular magazine have certain specialized interests ca-
> tered to by the magazine's content, they are also usually members of a particular
> narrowly-defined age group, and of one gender rather than the other. (Moeran
> 1996, 200)

Therefore, Japanese magazines of the 20th and 21st century are a medium with an unparalleled degree of specialization (Nojiri 1991, 290).[3] This kind of specialization was already evident in the many magazines that were published in the 19th century after *Seiyō zasshi*. Between 1867 and 1869, more than 180 different magazine titles appeared. Some were very closely connected to political parties, which is why they often disappeared soon after their publication due to governmental censorship. From 1883 onwards, most magazines catered to specific interests such as the natural sciences, society, literature, religion, etc. (Nojiri 1991, 27).

Audience segmentation based on gender and age came soon after. The publisher Jitsugyo no Nihon Sha, for example, started to produce magazines for a wider variety of audiences: men, women, children, boys and girls. Thus, women's magazines were published for the first time in Japan and became an economic success. In 1906, Jitsugyo no Nihon Sha published the women's magazine *Fujin sekai* (Women's World). Within three years it would achieve a circulation of 400,000 issues a month, the highest number of copies printed for a magazine in Japan at the time (Nojiri 1991, 28). These magazines were clearly perceived and branded as women's magazines which were usually focused on educating and supporting the idea of the *ryōsai kenbo*, meaning "good wife, wise mother," a state-supported conception of the role of women in Japan (Wöhr 1997, 75). This demonstrates that, very early on, magazines in Japan were starting to participate in discourses on how a member of society should live his or her life. Thus, magazines were part of everyday-life negotiations of issues and topics that were both very private and social matters at the same time.[4]

The fact that women were specifically targeted by magazines through branding—such as using the word *fujin* or something similar in the title— is significant. At the same time, there were magazines for a male readership as well. The so-called *sōgō zasshi*, the general interest magazine, was a typical magazine that was targeted at a male audience. As Christopher Keaveney (2013, 34) puts it: "These *sōgō zasshi* (comprehensive magazines) were intended for a wide audience of non-specialists and generally included articles and editorial commentaries about a far-ranging variety of issues including politics, economics, the arts and society." The first magazine of this kind, *Kokumin no tomo* (The Nation's Friend), appeared in 1887. Many more magazines like it followed in the late 19th century and have since found great success. Among the titles of this genre was, for example, *Chūō kōron* (The central review), which is still published today. The fact, however, that these magazines neither catered to a specific field of interest nor targeted a specific gender—as women's magazines did—is noteworthy. It is not the case that women were not interested readers of these magazines as well. However, two other aspects need to be taken into consideration here, as I have already stated elsewhere (Saladin 2019, 112) referring to Morohashi (2005, 231):

1. The content of magazines targeted at women was deemed gender-specific and, therefore, these magazines needed to be marked explicitly as magazines intended for a female readership.
2. Men, apparently, were not assumed to be interested in reading magazines that targeted women. Otherwise, the label "women's magazine" which excludes a male audience would have been misleading.

The way magazines in Japan were produced and marketed, then, demonstrates that the late 19th and early 20th century were highly gendered times. It also shows that a look at magazines and the magazine market can be very insightful in terms of revealing the fundamental and underlying fabric of the gender order. Men were perceived as the norm, therefore there was no need to brand magazines targeting men as "men's magazines." It would take several decades until the category of "men's magazines" would appear in Japan. According to Morohashi (2005, 231), the first time the category of "men's magazines" was incorporated into an analysis of the Japanese magazine market was the year 2003.

The line between men's and women's magazines, however, cannot be drawn that easily. This becomes apparent when looking at weekly general-interest magazines. These magazines often do not market themselves as magazines that are geared towards one gender or the other and, according to Morohashi (1998b, 276), therefore fall into the category of "genderless weekly magazines." However, Morohashi also points out that those magazines that feature articles on sex and erotica are targeted more towards a male readership than a female one. Typical examples of these magazines include *Shūkan posuto* (Weekly Post), *Shūkan hōseki* (The Weekly Magazine Hoseki, lit. "weekly jewel"), or *Shūkan gendai* (Weekly Gendai, lit. "modern weekly") (Morohashi 1998b, 276). Hence, the analysis of magazines can be an insightful approach to understanding the ongoing discourse about gender in society. It is with this in mind that I now take a closer look at Japanese men's magazines and their development.

Men's magazines

The fact that some Japanese magazines cater specifically to men was by no means a new development of the 2000s. There were magazines that did so before this time. The 1960s saw the birth of several titles, for example, *Heibon panchi* (lit. Ordinary Punch, 1964), *Shūkan pureibōi* (Weekly Playboy, 1966) or *Young Man* (1964) that were clearly aimed at a male readership. These so-called *gurabia* (from the English gravure) magazines featured erotic images of women and were perceived distinctly as men's magazines (Nanba 2009, 54–55; Nojiri 1991, 31; Shūeisha n.d.). This new genre of magazines was distinct from *sōgō zasshi* in that it did not aim at a diverse audience. Rather, it specifically targeted men with articles on sex together with erotic imagery, reports on cars, sports and even culture and comics (Morohashi 1998b, 278). These magazines could therefore be understood as a new genre of entertainment magazines that covered a great variety of topics in which men were assumed to have an interest.

A new category of men's magazines appeared in the latter half of the 20th century. These magazines were much more intriguing as they did not cater to the erotic desires of men to the extent that *gurabia* magazines did. In 1954, the fashion magazine *Men's Club* started publication and in 1986 the magazine *MEN'S NON-NO* was the first magazine in the Japanese market to target a young male audience, offering very different content from the men's magazines that existed until then. *Japan's Periodicals in Print* describes it as follows:

> *A fashion magazine that offers carefully selected information to men who want to live a more comfortable and refined everyday life. About 80 percent of the readers are males between 15 and 24 years of age. Most readers are fashionable and aware of trends.* (Media Risāchi Sentā 1978–, 266)

MEN's NON-NO is the sister magazine of the women's magazine *NON-NO*, which was established in 1971. This demonstrates the close link between the development of a new generation of men's magazines and women's magazines. In fact, in most cases, women's magazines would be the predecessors of men's magazines; the latter would often be established as "men's versions" of the former. As such, men's lifestyle magazines modeled themselves on women's magazines in terms of structure and content (Morohashi 2002, 86–88).

Tsuji Izumi (2013, 2017) has produced the most recent comprehensive assessment of Japanese men's magazines, employing a scheme of quantitative content analysis first introduced by Inoue Teruko and her research group (2001). Examining the overall structure of men's magazines in terms of the types of features that they incorporated, Tsuji came to the conclusion that men's lifestyle magazines share similar tendencies. In his analysis, Tsuji (2013) looked first at the proportion of articles, advertisements and a format that combines an article with an advertisement called *kōkoku kiji* (advertisement article). These *kōkoku kiji* feature product information, such as pricing and brand names, but are still editorial parts of the magazine. They, therefore, differ from the advertorials that appear in western magazines, which are strongly influenced by the companies and brands that pay for them, and usually have to be marked as promotional content, which is not the case with *kōkoku kiji*. In his quantitative analysis, Tsuji combined advertisements and *kōkoku kiji* (since the latter are arguably a form of advertisement as well) into one category, showing that at least 40 percent (in about half of cases more than 50 percent) of nearly every men's magazine he analyzed was made up of advertising, with the rest comprising articles (Tsuji 2013, 37). This ratio of advertisements to articles mirrors the way women's magazines are structured.

There is also a high degree of similarity in the content of men's and women's magazines. Men's lifestyle magazines focus to a great extent on fashion, leisure and lifestyle, with the former being exceptionally prominent. *Oshare* (being fashionable) content accounted for at least half of all content in the magazines in Tsuji's (2013, 38) analysis. Many magazines, including *MEN'S NON-NO*, the forerunner of modern men's lifestyle magazines, dedicate about 70 percent or more of their content to style and fashion. Between 11 percent and 38 percent of magazine content relates to leisure, while 5 to 15 percent addresses lifestyle issues (Tsuji 2017, 53–59). According to Tsuji, comparing these results with a content analysis of women's magazines shows that men's magazines not only focus on similar topics as women's magazines but also exceed women's magazines in doing so. "Men's lifestyle magazines place a greater emphasis on outward appearance and pay less attention to lifestyle issues than the women's publications" (Tsuji 2013, 40).

Tsuji explains that magazines that belong to this new category of lifestyle or fashion magazines for men can be considered a distinct genre since they differ markedly from earlier men's magazines in terms of content. It is intriguing that in most of these new men's magazines discourse on sex is completely absent. As I have shown elsewhere, discourses on sex can be understood as a line of demarcation in terms of the kind of masculinity these new lifestyle magazines for young men are constructing (Saladin 2011/2012). Magazines that incorporate features on sex tend to reproduce notions of Japan's hegemonic masculinity to a greater extent than those that completely lack such discourses, such as *MEN'S NON-NO*. This brings us to another important factor that needs to be considered when examining Japan's men's magazines: the construction of notions of gender.

Magazines and gender

The shift in content in Japan's men's magazines that began during the 1980s opened up a new segment of the Japanese magazine market. New magazines started to feature information that was usually found in women's magazines: fashion, cosmetics, hairstyle and other information related to one's outward appearance. This process of "men's magazines becoming like women's magazines" (Morohashi 1998a, 215) gave rise to a boom in men's magazines during the 1990s (Saladin 2011/2012, 190), that mirrored that of women's magazines in the 1970s. According to Inoue Teruko, the boom in women's magazines in the 1970s expressed a change in perceptions of the female gender (Inoue and Josei zasshi kenkyūkai 1989, 3). These "modern" women were not the old fashioned "good wife, wise mother" type of women anymore; they were much more adventurous and fashion-conscious. They were more interested in enjoying their life than getting married (Holthus 2009, 109). New women's magazines like *NON-NO* or *An An* catered to this new kind of readership. These magazines were so influential that their names became synonymous for those magazines that followed their model, commonly known as "annon"-type magazines (Inoue and Josei zasshi kenkyūkai 1989, 37).

The boom in men's magazines such as *MEN'S NON-NO* in the 1990s is comparable to the boom of women's magazines in the 1970s in terms of what it reveals regarding societal gender constructions and perceptions. Magazines that addressed fashion, style and outward appearance gained a large readership. From 1990 to 2011 the number of monthly printed issues roughly tripled (Saladin 2011/2012, 190). The predominantly male readership of these magazines was clearly interested in topics that used to be understood as topics of women's interest (Nishiyama and Tanimoto 2009, 52–65). These men were seen as being men who tended to be less masculine and more effeminate. The immensely popular expression *femi-o* (Watanabe 2005, 39), which was used to refer to these "new" men and derives from the English word "female" and the Chinese character for "man" (*o*), expressed this perception. Men who paid attention to their fashion and hairstyle, who would use make-up and perfumes etc., in order to create their outward appearance, were seen as a new kind of man who differed distinctly from men of former generations. They would buy magazines as manuals or guidebooks on creating style (Saitō 2003, 333). These magazines taught their readers everything they needed to know about outward appearances in order to express themselves.

The popularity of these magazines was a sign of changing gender perceptions in Japanese society. The 1990s were a period of significant social change: the collapse of the economic bubble triggered drastic changes in the way Japanese companies had operated for decades. Since Japan's economic rise in the 1960s, the salaryman had become the manifestation of Japan's hegemonic masculinity.[5] However, with the recession and economic restructuring (including the liberalization of the labor market) that followed the burst of the bubble economy in the 1990s, companies had to change their business models. Many Japanese employees no longer earned the income they used to in exchange for their long working hours, and de facto lifetime employment was no longer guaranteed. Hence, becoming a salaryman became more difficult as other kinds of employment, such as contract or dispatch work, became more popular with struggling companies. As a result, becoming a salaryman not only became less realistic, it also lost appeal as an ideal to strive for (Dasgupta 2013, 38–42).

The 1990s, thus, were a period that was seen in a very negative light, especially as far as economic development was concerned. The young people of this decade who were meant to enter the job market but found it difficult to secure permanent employment were called the *ushinawareta sedai* (lost generation). However, the 1990s can also be seen in a different light. The economic crisis that prevented many young men from becoming salarymen opened up new opportunities as well. With the salaryman ideal losing ground, gaps appeared that could be filled with different conceptions of masculinity and men's magazines were one of the main media to negotiate these new notions.

In order to better understand what a typical Japanese magazine for young men looks like, the following section presents a detailed examination of the magazine *BiDaN*. It reveals how this magazine addressed issues of outward appearance or lifestyle and how these topics were connected to gender constructions.

BiDaN: a typical lifestyle and fashion magazine for young men

I have chosen the magazine *BiDaN* as an example of a typical magazine during the peak period (roughly the 1990s and 2000s) for lifestyle magazines for young men in print. As such, it serves as a good indicator of the style and content of Japanese men's lifestyle magazines. The following aspects apply to the magazine:

1. A male readership with a typical age-range for lifestyle and fashion magazines (15–25 years of age)
2. Content focused on fashion, hairstyle and beauty (more than 70 percent)
3. Monthly issue

BiDaN was first launched in 1996 and it ceased publication in 2011. During that time, *BiDaN* underwent a number of changes. Initially it was published by Bauhaus, later moving to Index Communications. Its last publisher was Jack Media Capital. Likewise, the magazine's title and subtitle changed. The first subtitle read: "HAIR & BEAUTY FOR MEN." Later, this was modified to "REAL BOOM HAIR, FASHION & CULTURE MAGAZINE." From 2010, the magazine was titled *B-st*. However, these transitions appear to be purely cosmetic, as the content of *BiDaN* remained the same for the most part. The most significant development in content occurred when the title changed to *B-st*. The magazine began to include pages on sexual issues and erotic imagery of women, which had previously been absent.[6] The recurrent revisions of title and the eventual ceasing of publication are typical of a men's magazine.

The magazine market in Japan is highly dynamic: magazines appear, cease publication or are modified in content quite frequently.

The title of the magazine offers the first clue to the content the reader can expect. Although it is written in Latin script, *BiDaN* could possibly be written with the Chinese characters for "beautiful" (bi) and "man" (dan) giving the magazine title the connotation of "handsome man." Accordingly, the content of *BiDaN* largely corresponds to topics that deal with beauty in the broadest sense: cosmetics, body care, body shaping (workout), perfumes, hairstyles and even the correct shaping of the eyebrows etc. Approximately 50 percent of *BiDaN*'s magazine content covers these issues. Another approximately 25 percent addresses fashion—i.e., clothing, shoes, accessories, etc. Taken together about 75 percent of *BiDaN* focuses on how men can shape their external appearance positively—that is, beautifully. The rest of the magazine is divided into a variety of subject areas, but separately are insignificant in terms of overall space occupied: about three percent deal with feature-related topics, such as films or music, while another three percent feature women or pin-up girls.[7]

The large proportion of advertising in *BiDaN* is also very typical of men's magazines of the 1990s. Only a little over 25 percent of the content is dedicated to articles. In contrast, pure advertising accounts for over 30 percent. Adverts feature heavily and in a condensed form, especially in the last quarter of the magazine. Again, this is very typical for men's lifestyle magazines with many magazines featuring similar or even the same advertisement, demonstrating that men's magazines tend to address the same topics of fashion, beauty and outward appearance.[8]

Like many other magazines in Japan, *BiDaN* features *kōkoku kiji*—roughly 40 percent of the magazine's content is this mixed article-advertisement format—with heavy emphasis on cosmetic products, hairstyle and haircare products and cosmetic and beauty clinics and institutes. Combined with "street snaps"[9] these article-advertisements assure readers that the featured styles are not unusual and that they can be adopted without the reader having to feel that he may be viewed negatively if he follows them.

The following headlines can all be found in the same issue of *BiDaN*—March 2006: "*Snapshots: The front-line of attractive hair*"; "*Training: Men's 'attractive skin'*"; "*The attractive man's art to wearing a suit*"; "*'Attractive hair' and 'attractive clothes' in spring*"; "*Must-have 'hair' and 'clothes' for attractiveness in spring*" (BiDaN 2006/03, 1). Attractiveness in *BiDaN* is connected with discourses on physical outward appearance: the magazine's main goal is to support the male reader in becoming a *mote-o* (attractive man) to enhance his ability to attract women. In this sense, *BiDaN* reconstructs Japan's hegemonic masculinity, which is based on heterosexuality.[10] No other forms of sexuality are mentioned. In the following sections, I take a closer look at how and in which contexts being attractive is addressed by *BiDaN*.

Being attractive: hairstyle

As the above-mentioned headlines, which appear on the front cover of *BiDaN* 2006/03, show, the magazine suggests that attractiveness can be achieved with, among other things, the right hairstyle. In "Basics for style-beginners" (BiDaN 2006/03, 40), an article of several pages in the same issue, various hairstyles and the methods of creating them are set out in detail. Underlined in red on the same page is the note that this guide is a "book" that will undoubtedly lead to a change in style that brings with it an enormous increase in attractiveness:

"Attractive guy no.1 in spring makeover complete version" (BiDaN 2006/03, 41). The subtitle of the article furthermore suggests that this article will assist the reader in choosing the right style among the examples presented here in order to increase his own attractiveness. It reads: "We teach you how to prevent any possible mistake when choosing a 'hairstyle' and 'clothes' that make you attractive" (BiDaN 2006/03, 41).

Hairstyles make up a considerable part of the content of *BiDaN*, with every issue featuring articles that link hairstyles with attractiveness. Of particular importance is the great variety of styles for a range of people and occasions presented by the magazine. There are styles for any hair length and color, as well as styles that are especially fitting, for example, for a date or for a particular season of the year. These are not inimitable works of art that would only suit very special people but rather styles which any reader can adopt to become more attractive. Literary critic Saitō Minako points out that teaching readers how to become attractive is typical for men's lifestyle magazines. She writes referring to the magazine *MEN'S NON-NO*: "'Learning from the stylist' is the typical article-type of 'MEN-NON'" (Saitō 2003, 333).[11]

Being attractive: fashion

According to *BiDaN*, attractiveness can be increased not only through hairstyles, but also through an appropriate outfit—i.e., clothing and fashion style. Articles or *kōkoku kiji* that promise attractiveness, be it through hairstyles or clothing, are quite similar. Again, there is no clearly defined fashion style with specific features that is particularly favored over other styles. A great variety of possible design options is presented and there is no characteristic feature that belongs to every single style. In turn, only one message is implied: all the different styles introduced by the magazine are, in themselves, attractive.

The magazine uses an important rhetoric strategy: by sanctioning various and different styles as appropriate, good looking and fitting to their readers, the magazine discursively creates what can be called "habitual security." Readers gather information about outward appearance via the magazine, which is also read by their peers. Hence, the whole readership of the magazine evaluates fashion, hairstyle and any other means of creating outward appearance based on the same standards—the standards conveyed by *BiDaN*. As a result, the readers can rest assured that while creating their own outward appearance within the (very broad) boundaries of style as they are conveyed by the magazine, they will not risk having a style that others might interpret as unfitting, strange or unattractive.[12] The magazine, therefore, can secure a relatively broad readership by not having too narrowly defined style boundaries. At the same time, however, it still constitutes itself as the institution that creates the standards to which readers with an interest in outward appearance want to adhere.[13]

Being attractive: beauty care

A third area that addresses attractiveness is cosmetics or beauty care in general. Articles or *kōkoku kiji* on this topic cover a variety of products and services. Typical magazine content features treatments for acne and the use of cosmetics such as creams, lotions and face washes. The magazine explains to its readers, for example, that "the keyword for attractive men is the treatment of pimples" (BiDaN 2005/10, 64). Hence, in order to be an attractive man, it is essential to have well-groomed and well-cared-for facial skin. Accordingly, this *kōkoku kiji* explains how a cosmetic institute addresses this problem and treats its customers. However, the magazine does not just explain to the readers where to go for skin-care treatment—it also educates the readers about how to do it themselves. Often, these articles not only introduce different products but also the correct techniques that should be employed when using them. In so doing, the magazine actually encourages its readers not to rely only on experts and their knowledge, but to acquire such knowledge and, thus, become experts themselves.[14]

Apart from cosmetics in the narrower sense, *BiDaN* also introduces other ways to create a beautiful outward appearance. Dieting products (BiDaN 2005/11, 202), for example, aim at helping the readers to have a slender and muscular body, which, according to the magazine, is what draws the attention of women. The magazine also introduces practices that used to be understood as distinctly female, such as shaping the eyebrows with scissors, comb and pencil. Additionally, these magazines frequently address the topic of body hair removal, which is a popular service offered in beauty parlors for men (Miller 2003, 40). Through its features on beauty care, *BiDaN* conveys information on practices of creating outward appearances for men that did not belong to the male habitus for most of the 20th century, as already mentioned in the "Magazines and gender" section. It is, therefore, typical of men's magazines that started to appear in the 1990s and contributed to negotiating and exploring different masculinities. The question remains, however, what to make out of these "new" masculinities?

Conclusion: Men's magazines as vessels of hybrid masculinity

As mentioned above, being attractive is a means the magazine introduces to its readers in order to make contact with the opposite sex. Furthermore, the strategies for improving one's outward appearance introduced by the magazine had been exclusively feminine ones for much of the 20th century. Hence, the question arises whether men presented by *BiDaN* are becoming effeminate. Interestingly, regardless of the topic discussed, while employing strategies that once were predominantly perceived as female, the magazine links its content on outward appearance time and again with masculinity. All the styles that are presented aim not only at creating an attractive outward appearance, but are also defined as something that men (can) do without sacrificing their masculinity. The ways of enhancing one's appearance as presented by the magazine never give rise to doubts that they might be unusual for men. On the contrary, it introduces them as if they were the most "natural" thing for a man to do. Hence, the magazine creates a concept of masculinity that clearly differs from what can be perceived as Japan's hegemonic masculinity for the greatest part of the 20th and early 21st century. To the editors and readers of *BiDaN* these formerly feminine techniques are as masculine as anything else a "man" does. This suggests that the norms of masculinity have changed significantly.[15]

From this perspective, the development of (not only) Japanese masculinities might best be viewed through the lens of what has been coined hybrid masculinities. This term was introduced to the analysis of masculinities around the year 2000 (Bridges and Pascoe 2014, 246). It conveys the notion that masculinities are not solid and stable but prone to change. They are not as closed and clearly defined as they may appear. Bridges and Pascoe argue (like many others, too) that "the emergence of hybrid masculinities indicates that normative constraints are shifting but that these shifts have largely taken place in ways that have sustained existing ideologies and systems of power and inequality" (2014, 247). That is to say, masculinities as they appear in *BiDaN* are changing by incorporating practices that used to be associated with the female gender and therefore might be interpreted as a feminization of masculinity.[16] However, the concept of hybrid masculinity allows us to understand that masculinity is changing by incorporating aspects that did not belong to it before (e.g., taking care of outward appearance) without infringing its own legitimacy. The concept of masculinity is broadened without losing touch with its core ideas. In other words, the aspects at the core of the hegemonic construction of masculinity[17] are not pushed aside but remain valid, while the overall idea of masculinity is being extended by adding aspects that did not belong to it before. For example, the idea that the man has to be the breadwinner led to many men believing that it was not "manly" to care about outward appearance in terms of being fashion-conscious or interested in cosmetics, which explained the lack of interest in these areas. Men becoming more fashion conscious nowadays does not mean that they do not have the aspiration to still be the breadwinner. Therefore, it is misleading to speak of a feminization in the sense of a power shift between masculinity and femininity. As core values of masculinity remain unharmed, so does its position within the gender order.

This examination of men's magazines has demonstrated how societal changes are reflected within and likewise reproduced and propagated by a medium of popular culture. Lifestyle magazines produced for young men during the 1990s and 2000s are particularly useful in revealing changing gender perceptions in Japan. Notions of how a man should behave or dress are also broadening. One of the most visible examples of a discourse on how change in masculinity is connected to outward appearance in Japan concerns the "herbivore man" (*sōshoku (kei) danshi*).[18] Lifestyle magazines for young men promote ideas of how men should interact with women or fashion styles that were associated with this kind of masculinity.[19] Although journalist Fukasawa Maki coined the term "herbivore man" originally to denote a positive change in men (Saladin 2019, 85) and did not connect it to a certain clothing style,[20] it quickly became associated with a "softie masculinity" that was judged in public discourse as a negative and problematic development. This negative perception of "herbivore masculinity," which is in many respects contradictory to the "old-fashioned" idea of a man in Japan, proves that, even though the shape of masculinity is changing, a fundamental shift in society-wide power relations cannot yet be observed.

Notes

[1] As is the case, for example, with the magazine *Men's NON-NO* (see "Men's Non-No") or *FINEBOYS*, which can be purchased not only in a store but also by mail order or by subscription (See FINEBOYS 2021).

[2] Stuart Hall elaborated on this dynamic in his encoding-decoding model (1993, 515–17).

[3] That is not to say, however, that there were no magazines that addressed a broader audience, as will be discussed later.

[4] Likewise, the women's movement in Japan also started with the magazine *Seitō* (1911).

[5] For more information on the concept of hegemonic masculinity see Connell (2005).

[6] Since these changes occurred very shortly before the magazine ceased publication they will not be addressed here.

[7] Author's assessment based on the scheme developed by Inoue and Josei zasshi kenkyūkai (1989).

[8] Of course, as magazines are targeting a very narrowly defined audience, each magazine differs from the next. Due to the fact that many magazines feature the same advertisements, however, the analysis of featured advertisements can only produce limited results when trying to investigate differences between magazines.

[9] Street snaps are reports "from the streets," which normally involves a team of reporters and photographers going out on the streets (usually of big cities) to interview and take photos of passers-by, which are then

selectively incorporated into the magazine. These street snaps are usually centered around topics of outward appearance such as fashion or hair style. Some magazines, however, also cover other topics with street snaps, e.g., the life of couples.

[10] See, for example, Dasgupta (2013, 23) and Meuser (2006, 104).

[11] *MEN-NON* is the abbreviation for the magazine *MEN'S NON-NO*.

[12] See also Saladin (2019, 3–4, 2011).

[13] Regarding young people wanting to belong to a particular peer-group, see White (1995, 269).

[14] For a more thorough discussion of this see Saladin (2019, 163–64).

[15] Of course, gender constructions are never "natural." However, character traits which are deemed typically "masculine" or "feminine" are often assumed to be associated with some kind of "essential gender ideal," which in turn, is connected to and perceived as "natural."

[16] There was a comparable development in the West in the emergence of discourse around metrosexual men in the 1990s.

[17] For more information on Japan's hegemonic masculinity, see e.g., Dasgupta (2013).

[18] The term "herbivore man" is a metaphor coined by journalist Fukasawa Maki to describe an alleged change in especially younger generations of Japanese men. According to Fukasawa, men of the older generations used to be very "aggressive" in terms of being proactive when approaching women with a clear mind set of looking for the opportunity to enter into a sexual relationship—they would "hunt" women like carnivores would hunt their prey. The "herbivore men" of younger generations do not strive for sexual encounters and show therefore a more "courteous" attitude towards women, connecting with them emotionally and not being guided by the mere goal of having sex. For more information on "herbivore men" see Fukasawa (2009).

[19] For more information on herbivore men within men's magazines see Saladin (2019).

[20] This happened later with the publication of Morioka Masahiro's book on herbivore men (see Morioka 2013).

Bibliography

BiDaN, 2006 3. Tokyo: Index Communications.

———, 2005 10. Tokyo: Index Communications.

———, 2005 11. Tokyo: Index Communications.

Bridges, T., and Pascoe C. J., 2014. Hybrid Masculinities: New Directions in the Sociology of Men and Masculinities. *Sociology Compass*, 8 (3), 246–58.

Connell, R., 2005. *Masculinities*. 2nd ed. Cambridge: Polity Press.

Cooper-Chen, A., 1997. *Mass Communication in Japan*. Ames, Iowa: Iowa State University Press.

Dasgupta, R., 2013. *Re-Reading the Salaryman in Japan: Crafting Masculinities*. London: Routledge.

FINEBOYS. 2021. Fineboys. Hinode Publishing Co., ltd. Available at: https://hinode-publishing.jp/?page_id =77 [Accessed 10 August 10 2021].

Fukasawa, M., 2009. *Sōshoku danshi sedai: Heisei danshi zukan* [Generation of herbivorous men: illustrated encyclopedia of Heisei men]. Tokyo: Kōbunsha.

Hall, S., 1993. Encoding, Decoding. In S. During, ed., *The Cultural Studies Reader*. London: Routledge, 507–17.

Holthus, B., 2009. *Paarbeziehungen in japanischen Frauenzeitschriften seit 1970: Medien und Geschlecht in Japan* [Partner relationships in Japanese women's magazines since 1970: Media and gender in Japan]. Lewiston, NY: Edwin Mellen Press.

Hügel, H.-O., 2003. Einführung [Introduction]. In H.-O. Hügel, ed., *Handbuch Populäre Kultur: Begriffe, Theorien und Diskussionen* [Handbook of popular culture: Terms, theories and discussions]. Stuttgart: J.B. Metzler'sche Verlagsbuchhandlung und Carl Ernst Poeschel Verlag GmbH, 1–22.

Kurata, K., Ishita, E., Miyata, Y. and Minami, Y., 2017. Print or Digital? Reading Behavior and Preferences in Japan. *Journal of the Association for Information Science and Technology*, 68, 884–94.

Inoue, T., 2001. Jendā to media: zasshi no shimen o kaidoku suru [Gender and media: decoding magazine pages]. In M. Suzuki, ed., *Media riterashī no genzai to mirai* [Current state and future of media literacy]. Kyoto: Sekai Shisōsha, 118–39.

Inoue, T. and Josei zasshi kenkyūkai, 1989. *Josei zasshi o kaidoku suru: Nichi Bei Mekishiko hikaku kenkyū = comparepolitan* [Decoding women's magazines: A comparative study of Japan, the USA and Mexico = Comparepolitan]. Tokyo: Kakiuchi Shuppan.

Keaveney, C., 2013. *The Cultural Evolution of Postwar Japan: The Intellectual Contributions of Kaizo's Yamamoto Sanehiko*. New York: Palgrave Macmillan.

Media Risāchi Sentā. 1978–. *Zasshi shinbun sō katarogu* [Japan's Periodicals in Print]. Tokyo: Media Risāchi Sentā.

Men's Non-No. Available at: https://flagshop.jp/fs/shop/g/g200MNN/?utm_source=hpplus&utm_medium =referral&utm_campaign=subsc [Accessed 10 August 2021].

Meuser, M., 2006. *Geschlecht Und Männlichkeit: Soziologische Theorie Und Kulturelle Deutungsmuster* [Gender and masculinity: Social theory and cultural patterns of interpretation]. Wiesbaden: VS Verl. für Sozialwissenschaften.

Miller, L., 2003. Male Beauty Work in Japan. In J.E. Roberson and N. Suzuki, eds., *Men and Masculinities in Contemporary Japan: Dislocating the Salaryman Doxa*. London: Routledge, 37–58.

Moeran, B., 1996. *A Japanese Advertising Agency: An Anthropology of Media and Markets*. Richmond, Surrey: Curzon Press.

Morioka, M., 2013. A Phenomenological Study of "Herbivore Men." *The Review of Life Studies* (4): 1–20. Available at: http://www.lifestudies.org/press/rls0401.pdf. [Accessed 27 October 2016].

Morohashi, T., 1998a. Nihon no taishū zasshi ga egaku jendā to "kazoku" [Depictions of gender and the "family" in Japan's general interest magazines]. In Y. Muramatsu and H. Gössmann, eds., *Media ga tsukuru jendā: Nichi-Doku no danjo, kazokuzō o yomitoku = Das Geschlecht als Konstrukt der Medien* [Gender as a construct of the media: Deciphering the images of Japanese-German women, men and families]. Tokyo: Shin'yōsha, 190–218.

———., 1998b. Stereotype Geschlechterrollen in Frauen- Und Männerzeitschriften [Stereotypical gender roles in women's and men's magazines]. In H. Gössmann, ed., *Das Bild der Familie in den Japanischen Medien* [The depiction of the family in Japanese media]. München: Iudicium, 265–81.

———., 2002. *Jendā no katarare kata, media no tsukurare kata* [How to tell gender, how to create media]. Tokyo: Gendai Shokan.

———., 2005. Zasshi ni okeru jendā: Kategorī no kōchiku [Gender in magazines: Creating a categorization]. In Kitakyūshu shiritsu danjo kyōdō sankaku sentā 'mūbu', ed., *Jendā hakusho: Josei to media* [Gender-whitebook: women and the media]. Mūbu sōsho. Tokyo: Akashi Shoten, 214–36.

Nanba, K., 2009. *Sōkan no shakaishi* [Sociology of first issues]. Chikuma shinsho 763. Tokyo: Chikuma Shobō.

Nishiyama, N., and Tanimoto T., 2009. Buzokuka suru oshare na otoko tachi: Joseiteki na goi to "otokorashisa" no tanpo [Tribes of fashionable men: female vocabulary and security of "masculinity"]. In S. Miyadai, I. Tsuji and T. Okai, eds., *"Otokorashisa" no kairaku: popyurā bunka kara mita sono jittai* [The pleasure of masculinity: Reality depicted in popular culture]. Dai 1-han. Tokyo: Keisō Shobō, 49–78.

Nojiri, H., 1991. *Medien in Japan: Der Einfluss Neuer Medien auf die Entwicklung Traditioneller Medien in Japan* [Media in Japan: The impact of new media on the development of traditional media in Japan]. Hochschul-Skripten. Medien 32. Berlin: V. Spiess.

Saitō, M., 2003. *Danseishi tanbō: minna ga yondeiru ano zasshi o uocchingu* [Exploring men's magazines: a look into the magazines everybody reads]. Tokyo: Asahi Shinbunsha.

Saladin, R., 2011. *Gyaru-o zasshi ni egakareru jendā* [Gender in gyaru-o magazines]. *Sociologist*, 13 (1), 197–230.

———., 2011/2012. Japanische Modezeitschriften Für Junge Männer. Eine Genderorientierte Kategorisierung. [Japanese fashion magazines for young men. A gender oriented categorization]. *Nachrichten der Gesellschaft für Natur- und Völkerkune Ostasiens* (NOAG), 2011/2012 (187–188), 183–209.

———., 2019. *Young Men and Masculinities in Japanese Media: (Un-) Conscious Hegemony*. Singapore: Palgrave Macmillan.

Shūeisha, n.d. *Shūeisha*. Available at: https://www.shueisha.co.jp/magazines/man.html [Accessed 23 December 2019].

Tsuji, I., 2013. Zasshi ni egakareta "otokorashisa" no henyō: Dansei fasshon shi o naiyō bunseki kara [A content analysis of men's fashion magazines in contemporary Japan: From the viewpoint of changes in masculinity]. *Jinbun gakuhō*, (467), 27–66.

———., 2017. Changing Masculinities: From a Content Analysis of Men's Fashion Magazines in Contemporary Japan and Germany. *Sociologist*, 19 (1), 43–67.

Watanabe, A., 2005. *Sutorīto fasshon no jidai: Ima fasshon wa sutorīto kara umareru* [Street fashion]. Tokyo: Meigensha.

White, M., 1995. The Marketing of Adolescence in Japan: Buying and Dreaming. In L. Skov and B. Moeran, eds., *Women, Media and Consumption in Japan*. Richmond: Curzon Press, 255–73.

Wöhr, U., 1997. *Frauen zwischen Rollenerwartung und Selbstdeutung: Ehe, Mutterschaft und Liebe im Spiegel der japanischen Frauenzeitschrift Shin-shin-fujin von 1913 bis 1916* [Women between role expectation and self-interpretation: Marriage, motherhood and love reflected by the Japanese women's magazine Shin-Shin-Fujin from 1913–1916]. Wiesbaden: Harrassowitz.

Woldering, G., 2005. Seiyō zasshi (1867–69): Die erste japanische Zeitschrift [Seiyō zasshi (1867–69): The first Japanese magazine]. In S. Köhn, ed., *Facetten der japanischen Populär- und Medienkultur* [Facets of Japanese popular and media culture]. Wiesbaden: Harrassowitz, 93–126.

Part 5
Audiences and Users

Chapter 15
Japanese Audiences, and Japanese Audience Studies

Jennifer Coates

Audience studies is experiencing renewed interest in Japanese media studies. This chapter explores the potential of working with audience members to understand the daily uses of various popular media in Japan, as well as the impacts of that media on social imaginaries, life worlds and senses of self. Providing an overview of the earlier history of studying media audiences in Japan, this chapter offers an account of the development of audience studies in early Japanese cinema history and shares some findings from a recent study of memories of cinema-going in the Kansai region of western Japan.

Introduction

At the time of writing, audience studies is experiencing renewed interest from scholars in a number of the fields of research which comprise Japanese media studies. Why might the study of media audiences be of interest (again) to contemporary researchers, and what can we learn about media from studying audiences? The opening section of this chapter explores these questions, outlining the potential of working with audience members to understand the daily uses of various popular media in Japan, as well as the impacts of these media on social imaginaries, life worlds and senses of self.

While audiences, users and gamers have been a central feature of scholarship on gaming and digital media since the beginning of research on the topic (Hjorth 2007; Galbraith 2017; Whaley 2018), the histories of audience studies in earlier eras of Japanese film have looked slightly different. Providing an overview of the earlier history of studying media audiences in Japan, the next section of this chapter offers an account of the development of audience studies in early Japanese cinema history. Moving through the introduction of audience and reception studies to the 1950s, this overview ends with an assessment of new developments in the field unfolding today.

I conclude by sharing some findings from a recent study of memories of cinema-going in the Kansai region of western Japan, generated from an ethnographic research project that I conducted from 2014–2018. This section introduces a variation on audience studies in the form of the ethno-history (Kuhn 2002), a mode of researching memories of viewership in past times, which blends audience studies approaches with methods of research and analysis drawn from memory studies. This contemporary case study is offered to illustrate the potential of new and divergent modes of studying audiences, and so suggest some complementary fields to which audience studies can have relevance, for example, Japanese history, anthropology and gender studies.

Ask the audience: Why study media audiences and reception?

Since the introduction of cinema apparatus, if not from the earlier eras of mass saturation of radio and print media, a significant portion of our time has been devoted to the consumption of media texts. Our exposure to media today is almost constant, from the advertisements that illustrate public spaces, including our streets and public transport, to the media content that addresses us from our phones and the many screens that populate our lives. A survey of audience studies across this diverse range of media is outside the scope of this chapter, which will focus more closely on the study of film reception in Japan. Regardless of the genre or type of media that we study however, the significant time investment of everyday people in media consumption should identify the topic as an appropriate focus of study in itself.

Yet time spent consuming media does not in itself always constitute audience support for, approval or enjoyment of a certain text. Studying audiences offers the opportunity to access narratives of media consumption outside the top-down expectations of producers, sellers and advertisers of media texts. The ethnographic methods discussed in the second part of this chapter can be particularly useful in uncovering unexpected or divergent audience behaviors and opinions about media texts. Media that may have been assumed to have a specific effect by creators is often received, analyzed and used very differently by audiences, and so audience studies can give a fuller picture of the life of a media text outside the design decisions and aspirations of its creators.

This view becomes particularly useful when we look at media texts produced under conditions of censorship, technological restriction or other kinds of restraint or coercion. Across Japanese history, as in many parts of the world, popular media production has been co-opted by governments, military forces and organizational institutions, which have imagined film technologies as a means to influence citizens at different times and for a variety of ideological purposes (Coates 2017). The consistent use of popular entertainment to persuade or attempt to manipulate viewers keeps the question of what (and how) media means to viewers at the forefront of any inquiry that seeks to determine what media does. The case study that concludes this chapter demonstrates the use of audience studies for determining where censorship and media-based coercion or persuasion can fail.

Finally, which media texts we consume, in what formats and for how long, as well as how we assess those texts and their roles in our lives can tell us a lot about a particular moment in time, or the life-worlds of a particular group of people. Where audience studies borders the fields of history and anthropology, we can use an understanding of an audience's relation to a particular text, creator or star to understand more about how everyday people make sense of the socio-political and historical particularities of their times. In the concluding case study, I demonstrate how audience studies can offer new ways of looking at certain periods of history, as well as a more nuanced understanding of how everyday people navigate their environments and understand their place in the world. Before introducing this specific example however, the next section offers a brief overview of trends in Japanese audience studies that focus on film.

Japanese audience studies: A brief history

We begin our brief history of audience studies in Japan with the introduction of cinema apparatus, near-simultaneously arriving in Japan from the USA and France in 1896 and 1897 respectively. Japan's first film critics and scholars were immediately concerned with the impact of commercial cinema on public attitudes and behaviors. Early film scholar Gonda Yasunosuke's *Minshu goraku no kicho* (The foundations of popular entertainment, 1922) presented an account of audiences as members of a new class generated by the growth of capitalism (Fujiki 2014, 78). Gonda criticized other theorists for not engaging with the everyday realities of "the people," arguing for movie-going as a learning process through which viewers "unintentionally trained themselves as social subjects conforming to the current regime" (Fujiki 2014, 80). As Fujiki Hideaki notes, Ministry of Education bureaucrats and cultural critics tended to conflate "audiences" with "the people," however, Fujiki reminds us that then, as today, "'the people' is an unavoidably idealized or abstracted concept" (Fujiki 2014, 80). Fujiki cautions that both "the masses" imagined by the bureaucrats of the 1920s, and "the nation" as imagined in the 1930s, "were all nothing more than ideals, and very far removed from reality" (Fujiki 2014, 92). In this early example of audience studies developing in Japan in the 1920s then, we already encounter the problem of essentializing the audience, an issue that will raise questions about how to use audience studies as part of a multi-method film studies, given the subjectivity of the audience as individual and localized group.

Nonetheless, the possibility of imagining the audience as a homogenous block recommended this area of scholarly inquiry to government and other agencies intent on surveying and shaping popular opinion. Gonda's imagined audience was not only in dialogue with the bureaucracy however, but with the film itself, both as text and interface. Aaron Gerow notes that Gonda emphasized "how lower-class spectatorship becomes the 'subject' of film entertainment, effectively finishing the film as it is viewed in the theater" in a conceptualization that Gerow argues could be understood as "an early form of British cultural or reception studies" (2010, 37). Gonda's were among the first audience surveys in Japan, positing the viewer as "the subject of culture" and the film as a text in which spectators could "insert their everyday emotions and ideas" (Gerow 2010, 40). He suggested that "viewers' selves are projected out (*tobidasu*) because of their work with the photoplay to turn the flat into the three-dimensional, an unconscious but difficult task" (Gerow 2010, 41). Gonda imagined viewers as engaged in active interaction with the film and its subject matter, rather than passive consumers of media content.

In *Katsudō shashin no genri oyobi ōyō* (The principles and applications of the moving pictures), Gonda described a "viewer-self" (*jiko*) who is "active" and relatively independent. To illustrate this point, he uses as an example an incidence of observing film audiences crying at different moments during a screening, whereas he imagines that a theater audience would cry at the same moment (Gonda 1914, 415). In this earliest of Japanese audience studies, we see the film audience imagined as a room full of independent individuals, moved by the film content but in a variety of ways, as different elements of the film speak to different elements of each viewer's life and consciousness. By contrast, film studios of the same era surveyed audiences for commercial purposes, focusing on mass preferences that could be translated into production and marketing. In the end, this conceptualization of viewer as mass, rather than Gonda's argument for the film viewer as individual, proved more appealing to the institutions that sought to understand the audience as a group which could be educated in the national ideals of militarizing Japan through cinema propaganda.

After Japan's defeat in the Second World War (1945) and Fifteen Years War (1931–1945), studios, newspapers and university groups continued audience surveys, focusing largely on demographic and content issues (Fujiki 2019, 295). These surveys tended to continue the wartime understanding of the audience as a mass. During the Occupation of Japan (1945–1952), the Motion Picture and Theatrical Division of the Civil Information and Education Section (hereafter CIE) of the General Headquarters of the Occupation, led by the Supreme Commander for the Allied Powers (SCAP), conducted wide-ranging censorship of all popular media (Coates 2018b). This process is discussed in more detail in the case study to follow, but it should be mentioned here that while occupation censorship documentation records an aim to promote the values of a modern capitalist democracy, including a positive valuation of individuality (SCAP 1945, 1948; Allen 1945; Conde 1945), propaganda initiatives largely imagined the Japanese cinema audience as an ill-defined mass whose homogenous ideas could be changed all together in the same direction (Coates 2017, 2018b). Viewers were counted and surveyed rather than interviewed, with some conflicting results. Studios also continued their surveys of audience demographics and behaviors for commercial purposes, such as the Sunday Audience Survey conducted by the *Hōga rokusha seisaku shiryo chōsa kai* (Six domestic film company production materials survey group).

Japanese sociologists and anthropologists also engaged in audience studies in the 1950s and 1960s, often for popular publications as well as academic surveys. For example, a 1950 article on "The state of couples in the movie theater" sought to explore the use of cinema-going in relation to new postwar dating conventions, for a popular readership. Sociologist Fukuoka Takeo reported that couples in the cinema often responded physically when a scene with "sex appeal" (*sei teki appiiru*) appeared on screen. Such scenes are described as including "dialogue containing the words 'I love (*ai*) you,' 'I like (*suki*) you,' 'marriage,' 'body,' and 'pregnancy,'" or scenes including "a kiss or some other physical resolution" (Fukuoka 1950, 165). Fukuoka reports observing couples kissing or interacting physically with one another during these scenes, while other audience members called out commentary. In this way, audience studies of the 1950s were used not only for commercial and coercive purposes, but also to understand the impacts of the social reforms introduced by the Occupation of Japan.

Audience and reception studies of the 1960s, 1970s and 1980s tended towards an emphasis on television and home viewership patterns, emerging in the wake of the mass saturation of television ownership in the late 1950s and 1960s. In classical film studies, a turn towards investigating the conditions of early film theaters in the 1990s led to a renewed focus on film audiences. Katō Mikiro's studies of the cinema theaters around Kyoto contain valuable information about audience behaviors during the 1940s and 1950s, from attendance across the range of first, second and third-tier cinemas to evidence of cinema theaters engaging with their audiences in the public press (1995; 1996). Hiroshi Kitamura's study of the Marunouchi Subaruza theater similarly connects innovations in theater design, furnishings and programming with the development of new audience behaviors in the Occupation era (2004). Kitamura and Sasagawa's research on the marketing and screening of Hollywood cinema in postwar Japan provides fascinating details about the innovative marketing and advertising used to draw key audience demographics to certain film screenings, as well as an account of the workings and communications of fan clubs, particularly the groups and gatherings that grew around the journal *Eiga no Tomo* (Film Friends) (Kitamura, H. 2010; Kitamura and Sasagawa 2017).

Japanese language scholarship has recently begun to use audience memories to reconstruct attitudes from key periods of Japanese viewership. For example, Kitamura Kyōhei's study of audience responses to Kurosawa Akira's *Waga seishun ni kuinashi* (No Regrets for Our Youth, 1946) demonstrates a significant gap between the attitudes of older and younger audiences to this early example of censored Occupation-era cinema content (2017). Kitamura's study draws from the recorded memories of men who became famous film directors or cultural critics, including director Ōshima Nagisa.

As I mentioned in the introduction, audience studies is currently experiencing a resurgence in Japan. Fujiki Hideaki's (2019) recent book *Eiga kankyaku to wa nani mono ka: media to shakai shutai no kin-gendaishi* (Who is the cinema audience?: A history of media and social subjects, 1910s–2010s) offers the ultimate survey of the Japanese cinema audience over more than 100 years of film viewership in Japan. Fujiki's (2011) earlier edited volume *Kankyaku e no apurōchi* (Approaching the audience) compiled essays on the topic of audience studies from a variety of perspectives and periods of Japanese cinema history, focusing largely on archival material and the personal recollections of senior contributors. *Eiga kankyaku to wa nani mono ka* radically reconsiders recent historical writings on Japanese cinema, introducing issues of historical contingency and transmediality, framed through a study of changing audience demographics and shifting conceptualizations of subjectivity. The case study that follows introduces a complementary project that employs ethnographic methods drawn from anthropology to further investigate the question of subjectivity as it relates to engagement with films and cinema culture, offering the first ethno-history of Japanese film viewership.

Case study: Growing up in the cinemas of postwar Kansai, 1945–1975

The ethno-historical approach pioneered by British Cultural Studies researchers and feminist film historians (Radway 1984; Ang 1985; Stacey 1994; Kuhn 2002) combines ethnographic research methods within a memory studies framework to examine the impact of popular culture texts on the everyday lives of their consumers. This case study draws from four years of interviews, participant observation, questionnaire surveys and written communications with over 100 study participants in the Kansai region of western Japan to explore the role of cinema in the formation of self in the aftermath of war and defeat.

The project takes the Allied Occupation of Japan as both historical starting point and framing device. As noted above, from the very beginning of the Occupation, SCAP GHQ identified the cinema as a means to reshape popular attitudes in an American-inspired democratic capitalist mode, re-educating Japanese citizens away from the nationalist ideologies that had characterized wartime. Beginning with the simple question, "Can cinema content change social attitudes?" this ethnographic audience studies project evolved into a consideration of the role of cinema-going and film viewership, broadly conceived, on the formation of a sense of self in the generation that grew up under the Occupation.

In a "Memorandum Concerning Elimination of Japanese Government Control of the Motion Picture Industry" circulated on October 16, 1945, SCAP GHQ directed an end to wartime censorship, "to permit the industry to reflect the democratic aspirations of the Japanese people" (Allen 1945, 3). A new occupation censorship process was designed to channel viewers' conscious and unconscious responses, aiming to shape film viewers into modern subjects, imagined in the democratic capitalist mode modeled by the occupiers themselves (Kitamura, H. 2010, 36). Information Section personnel instructed Japanese filmmakers in the kind of content understood by the occupiers to be desirable, assessing synopses and screenplays before final film prints were censored or suppressed. The Motion Picture division of the CIE, while not officially recognized as a censoring body, checked synopses, screenplays and filming plans, while the Civil Censorship Detachment (hereinafter CCD) examined prints (Mayo 1984). Finished products were often sent back to the studios for cuts or reworking; yet SCAP influence over film content was quite uneven and changed over time (Coates 2016, 35).

Initially scenarios were examined by head of the Motion Picture division David Conde, despite having no knowledge of the Japanese language (Iwasaki 1978, 308). He was assisted by a number of Japanese-American officers, whom Iwasaki alleges had "less than perfect command of Japanese" (1978, 308). Conde was replaced in July 1946 by George Gerke, a member of the Information Division with prewar experience in the American film industry. In June 1949, contents control was ceded to Eirin (Film Ethics Regulation Control Committee). Although independent from the Occupation and the Japanese government, Eirin followed guidelines similar to those of the CIE, continuing to ban depictions of militarism and nationalism, and limiting the number of period films (Hirano 1992, 98). Overall, impressing new social values on young Japanese minds was a central goal of film contents control between 1945 and 1952.

On September 22, 1945, David Conde met with film and theater producers and forty Japanese Bureau of Information officials (Brandon 2006, 18). Reading from a draft document entitled "Memorandum to the Japanese Empire," written two days earlier, he urged those present to cooperate with the Occupation's goals, particularly in promoting "fundamental liberties" and "respect for human rights" (SCAP 1945). Conde advised producers to develop entertainments to educate citizens about democracy, individualism and self-government (Brandon 2006, 18). On November 19, 1945, a list of thirteen themes and topics identified as problematic followed. Number nine targeted media narratives that "dealt with, or approved of, the subordination or degradation of women" as undesirable, while number twelve warned against stories and images that "approved the exploitation of children" (Kitamura, H. 2010, 36; Brandon 2006, 94). Filmmaker Iwasaki Akira, who was forced to work closely with the censors, recalled that the Occupation personnel "were convinced that cinema was a most important instrument for effecting the necessary changes to make Japan a peaceful and democratic nation" (1978, 304).

But could cinema really have such an impact? Do we form our attitudes through engagement with popular media to this extent, and can that same media change our attitudes? Taking the Allied intervention in film production and exhibition as a starting point, this ethnohistory project explores how we interface with and through cinema, and what that means for our understandings of our place in the world. Focusing on the discourse around cinema, rather than a close reading of cinema texts, the project is an ethnographic study of the role of cinema in the lives of everyday citizens in postwar Japan. Extending the ethno-historical research methods developed by Annette Kuhn (2002) and Jackie Stacey (1994), this study draws not only on discourse analysis of participant-generated written and spoken materials, but also from visual analysis of filmed interviews with study participants (Coates 2018a). Weaving analyses of gestural expression, self-presentation, word-choice and emphases together to create an evocative ethnography reveals the deep significance of the cinema, and talking about cinema, in the life experiences and memories of this generation.

This grounded ethnography of the Japanese cinema audience covers the most intensive period of production and cinema attendance (peaking in 1958), and diverges from much extant scholarship in its focus on the Kansai region and neighboring areas of western Japan, while many studies are Tokyo-based, or survey the whole nation, subsuming regional difference. In western Japan, the cities of Kyoto, Osaka and Kobe all claim to be the very first sites of cinema in Japan. An ethnography of cinema culture in this area offers an account of regional difference in cinema-going and film-viewing, as well as an urgent reminder that we cannot take Tokyo as emblematic of the whole of Japan. In this section, I aim to offer nuanced approaches and perspectives on key areas of assumed knowledge in the field, including background information on the gender demographics of the audience and testimony that problematizes the use of box office statistics to determine a film's popularity, by bringing the voices of everyday audience members into the scholarly discourse on Japanese cinema.

Methodology

The design of this study was inspired by studies published in the 1980s and 1990s in English that re-shaped scholarly understanding of the methods available for the study of popular media and literature. Developing contemporaneously with the ascendance of British cultural studies, the Anglophone areas of film studies and English literature turned to the question of reception, and began to employ ethnographic methods drawn from the field of anthropology to collect and analyze the responses of popular culture consumers. Janice Radway's *Reading the Romance: Women, Patriarchy, and Popular Literature* (1984), Ien Ang's *Watching Dallas: Soap Opera and the Melodramatic Imagination* (1985), Jackie Stacey's *Star Gazing: Hollywood Cinema and Female Spectatorship* (1994) and Annette Kuhn's *Dreaming of Fred and Ginger: Cinema and Cultural Memory* (2002) opened up new methods and questions for the study of literature, television and film.

Designed as an ethno-history, this study most closely resembles Kuhn's ethno-history of 1930s cinema-going in Britain (2002). Yet several key differences became apparent from the first stages of fieldwork. Like Kuhn's interviewees, participants in this study first attended the cinema at a time with relatively few other entertainment options (Koyama 2016). The ways participants watch films have also changed greatly, as run-on program viewing, the "stuffing system" (*tsumekomi shiki*) of packing theaters, and standing and temporary seating no longer feature in today's mainstream cinemas. Both ethno-histories present a cinema culture now past. While Kuhn's interviewees have largely retired from cinema culture, watching favorite films at home on television rather than attending public screenings, a number of participants in my study are still actively involved in public cinema cultures. In fact, I first encountered many participants at public retrospective screenings and film clubs. Furthermore, while only two of Kuhn's interviewees were members of film clubs or fan appreciation societies, a large number of the participants in this study meet regularly with other viewers to watch and discuss films in the "circle" (*sākuru*) group structures particular to modern Japan. In this sense, the ethno-history presented here stretches up to the present day, revealing how elderly film fans in western Japan continue to engage with cinema in their daily lives.

Yet no matter how many viewers we interview, no matter how many letters or questionnaires we collect, we will never be able to surmise with any degree of certainty what exactly a viewer is experiencing in the cinema. Kuhn and Stacey raise the question of memory in relation to this issue; after all, a viewer's account of their experience is necessarily a question of recall, whether the memory in question is from five minutes or fifty years before the interview. My participant observation at retrospective film programs and in film circles suggests that personal memory plays a key role not only in the encounter between interviewer and interviewee, but also in discussions between viewers before or after a screening. Following Kuhn and Stacey's examples, I treat my ethnographic materials as individual memory testimonies, or personal narratives about cinema, rather than historical facts (discussed in more detail below). To avoid "leading" questions, I generated interview questions from the words, phrases and topics introduced by participants in my large-scale written survey, rather than from my own research design.

I attempted throughout this study to lead from the words of my participants, mirroring the emic imperative common to anthropological study. In practice, this means using the terms and phrases of my research participants and their cultural sphere, rather than imposing categories from outside. I began my research project with two years of participant observation at the retrospective screening programs held at the Kyoto Bunka Hakubutsukan (Kyoto Culture Museum), known locally as the Bunpaku. This large museum is situated on the central Sanjō street, just off Karasuma Street in downtown Kyoto. On the third floor, a film theater with a capacity of 180 seats hosted two daily screenings at 1:30 p.m. and 6:30 p.m. Programs ran for around one month, focusing on one particular aspect of Japanese cinema. Program themes ranged from a focus on the work of a particular director, scriptwriter, camera operator, composer or cinematographer, to more abstract concepts such as "Eating on Film" (*Taberu eiga: eiga de no shoku no yakuwari*, November 10 to 29, 2015). With the exception of specially organized events such as an annual student film festival, and the rare program devoted to European art-house cinema, all programs featured Japanese studio films made between 1910 and 1980. Each film was repeated four times in a program, twice per day on two days of a single week. Tickets were comparatively cheap at 500 yen ($4.50 USD) for non-members and 400 yen ($3.60 USD) for members, or 4000 yen ($36.50 USD) for a yearly pass (whereas a single commercial cinema ticket would be closer to 2000 yen). Viewers were relatively free to come and go as they please, though two yellow-jacketed attendants attempted to discourage visitors from entering the theater during the last thirty minutes of a screening.

The museum houses an archival collection of materials related to Kyoto's film history. A scholarly approach was also apparent in the changing displays in the small lobby area in front of the theater entrance, which showcased archival materials related to the screening program, including contemporary posters, magazine articles, critical coverage, published interviews with directors and stars and on-set photographs. The changing lobby displays also provided an opportunity to observe how viewers interacted with film materials other than the film texts themselves, and the roles film ephemera played in interpersonal conversations between viewers.

The location, surroundings and access arrangements of the Bunpaku film theater ensured a diverse audience in terms of personal interest and expertise as well as class, educational and financial background. The central area of Kyoto city is quite easily accessible and the film theater includes access for the disabled, not guaranteed in the smaller commercial cinemas, and indeed many viewers with mobility impairments attended screenings regularly. In its position on the third floor of a large museum which featured a permanent exhibit on Japanese culture and history as well as several temporary exhibits on topics as diverse as The English Country Garden (May 2016) and classical Japanese painting, the Bunpaku film theater also attracted patrons who had not come to the building with the specific intention of watching a film, but found the theater an interesting or convenient place to visit after an exhibition. Patrons purchasing tickets for any exhibition could enter the cinema theater for free. The low price of tickets and availability of an affordable yearly pass further suggested that viewers at the Bunpaku theater ranged from dedicated film fans to first-time visitors, and people attended the screenings for reasons of personal convenience and curiosity as much as long-term interest in Japanese cinema. As a participant observer at the Bunpaku film theater, I was able to observe the viewing practices of both regular and occasional viewers. The range of casual and committed viewers who visited the Bunpaku presented a rare opportunity to incorporate casual viewer participants into my study.

After two years, I obtained permission to conduct a questionnaire survey at the Bunpaku film theater. In formulating the questionnaire, I was mindful of leading my respondents, or confining their responses to specific topics. I hoped to produce a survey that would allow and encourage respondents to write at length on the topics most important to them. I planned to generate questions for in-depth recorded interviews from any patterns that emerged from the questionnaire survey.

As this is the first ethnographic study of general cinema viewership practices in Japan, I was determined to impose as little of my own assumptions on the language as possible. I attempted to keep the phrasing of the questions neutral, aiming to generate free responses from which I could identify recurring patterns in word choice and viewer preferences. Finally, I aimed to generate a set of responses on which I could conduct discourse analysis, with the aim to construct not only an ethno-history of the period, as Annette Kuhn has done for viewership in the UK in the 1930s (2002), but also some theoretical innovation in the field of ethnographic audience studies. The planning of the questionnaire took six months, after which I conducted a one-week survey at the Bunpaku film theater from 18 May to 24 May 2016. Stamped addressed envelopes left in the museum lobby, and word of mouth transmission of the project's goals, enabled me to continue collecting questionnaire responses for three months after the Bunpaku survey ended, and introduced me to the film screening clubs that would become my next sites of participant observation.

Further to the pre-prepared questionnaires, an accompanying information sheet invited participants to send letters and emails to my university office. The first letter arrived on the second day of the survey; hand delivered by a lady who had completed the questionnaire the day before. Her letter, and those which followed, confirmed a tendency also evident in the questionnaire responses to draw a strong connection between memories of cinema and events in the respondent's personal life. This connection was so strongly assumed by participants that many began both letters and questionnaires with a version of the *jikoshōkai*, or self-introduction used when meeting a new person in Japan. This standard format includes the following personal information: name, place of birth, place of residence and perhaps year of birth or job description. It seemed surprising that questionnaire respondents would volunteer this information despite my repeated promises, both verbal and in printed information materials, to anonymize personal data. Several participants and interviewees also produced personal life narratives structured like published biographical information presented in a magazine or newspaper. These were delivered by post or in person, with an accompanying personal letter or a completed questionnaire. Study participants would also contact me to correct details they had misremembered, particularly in relation to the name of a film or actor.

Twelve Bunpaku patrons volunteered to take part in a filmed interview lasting around two hours, and every one initiated lengthy communication by telephone, post, or by email in the months between first contact and interview. In addition to discussing practical matters such as the time and place of the interview, all interviewees requested a set of sample questions before filming. The filming element appeared to have inspired interviewees to prepare materials as though for a job or television interview. I conducted a number of interviews with audio recording alone, as well as a series of informal unscripted interviews with a group of 20 female friends who had married cinema industry personnel in the 1960s. These interviewees engaged in preparation activities in the same manner as the others, and I concluded that the camera was not the only factor in this common approach to participating in the study. In addition to conversational emails and letters, interviewees also sent unsolicited life narratives, most often organized in the form of a biographical chart, as well as clippings from newspapers and publications that the participant perceived to be relevant to my study. One man with a high-profile public persona sent clippings and a DVD of his own media appearances, while another interviewee sent a package of academic articles on the topic of Kansai film clubs.

As these donated materials indicate, the results of this study were varied, and offered a number of new perspectives on Japanese cinema history and audience attitudes (see Coates 2017, 2018a, 2018b, 2020). The larger theoretical findings of the study however, relate to how we understand the encounter between film text and viewer, as well as the role played by the screening space and the viewers' surroundings. Re-focusing on audience experiences outside the personal experiences of the researcher, I would like to ask what exactly we can know about another's viewing experience from ethnographic study. It seems that all we can apprehend with any certainty is that an interlocuter has brought themselves to the moment of the encounter in order to communicate something, and to produce some kind of mutual or collective meaning. This is true of the face-to-face encounter in an interview situation, whether formal or informal, and also true of encounters conducted by email or by post. It is also the case in participant observation, where participants have chosen to attend a public screening despite the availability of the same film online, and in DVD rental stores, libraries, or shops. This study focuses on these encounters, aiming to understand how accounts of cinema viewership can become tools to communicate, both to another, and to oneself.

In asking the question "What does cinema viewership do?" then, I am really asking how we use the cinema in our daily lives, and what kinds of avenues of expression, communication, meaning-making and understanding film viewership affords. In speaking with film viewers about their experiences and memories of postwar cinema, I had a strong sense that cinema discourse often becomes a tool to convey personal, perhaps unrelatable, experience and feeling, and to make that experience mean something, both socially and historically. I wondered if my interviewees and fellow viewers were even drawn to the cinema for this particular affordance. Was the cinema a window that viewers used to try to make sense of deeper questions of being, both for themselves and for others? Can we make ourselves more knowable to others by thinking and communicating through cinematic engagement?

While constructing an audience study can lead us towards these more philosophical questions about interaction with media texts, and the influence of those texts on our understanding of our experiences, audience studies also offers a means of testing assumptions about the more basic aspects of a media text or era of media consumption. The findings of the study described above include memories of cinema-going that suggest that we may want to re-think some of our most basic assumptions about the demographics and behavior patterns of the cinema audience in postwar Japan.

For example, the existence of genres understood as women's films, from the *hahamono* or "mother film" to the *josei eiga*, which we might translate as close to "chick flick," the language of postwar Japanese cinema culture can lead us to assume that the cinema audience was significantly, or even disproportionately female. Anecdotal evidence from visitors to Japan has occasionally been extrapolated to suggest a dense concentration of female audiences for particular films (Russell 2008), which in turn is extrapolated into the notion that cinema audiences in postwar Japan were largely female.

Yet collecting memories of cinema-going in the Kansai region gives a different picture. Female participants in my study largely reported memories of restriction and frustration in relation to accessing the cinema. Going to the cinema alone was often considered bad behavior for a girl or young woman (Coates 2018), while many remembered having to convince family members or friends to accompany them, and thereby deferring to their companion's choice of film. Archival evidence supports the idea that the cinema audience was in fact disproportionately male (Uryū 1967).

Prior to the Occupation, wartime surveys show the general female audience to have been on average significantly less than fifty percent of the total (Hori 2018, 88). Studies of particular theaters show some outlying data, particularly around the central Tokyo district. For example, a poll taken in the Shibuya and Ginza districts of Tokyo in late 1941 recorded a turnout of 41.1 percent female viewers, but this was considered "an absolute predominance" (*danzen yūsei*) at the time (Eiga junpō 1941, 54). In light of these figures, Hikari Hori argues that "it is safe to assume that women viewers were in the minority," and moreover, "immediate postwar statistics do show that more men saw movies than women in the late 1940s and early 1950s" (2018, 88). Survey takers found that female viewers were generally students and working women, both with disposable incomes (Hori 2002, 55). An audience survey from 1946 estimates the nationwide audience between the age of ten and twenty years old at 10 percent, viewers between twenty and thirty years old at 70 percent, viewers in their thirties at 12 percent and viewers in their forties at only 3 percent (Eiga geijutsu nenkan 1947, 118).

The Sunday Audience Survey, which sampled the audience demographics on selected Sundays at cinemas around the country, indicates that the total postwar female audience peaked in 1956 with a turnout of 37.4 percent (Uryū 1967, 89). Between 1955 and 1957, female viewers younger than nineteen averaged 10.7 percent of the total national cinema audience (Uryū 1967, 89). While I have not been able to find comprehensive figures for the gender demographics of the audience during the Occupation period, taking the later 1950s gender demographics together with wartime surveys as well as anecdotal evidence from my ethnographic study, it seems reasonable to suggest that female viewers were in the minority throughout the Occupation, and that girls below the age of twenty may have been even less than five percent of the general commercial film theater audience in the 1940s.

Female viewers, and particularly younger girls, were disproportionately underrepresented in cinema audiences compared to their numbers in the general postwar population. In 1945, the population was 47.1 percent male and 52.9 percent female, with four million more female citizens than male; by 1950, female citizens outnumbered men by one million, or 51 percent to 49 percent, a demographic trend that continues today (Ministry of Internal Affairs and Communications 2017). People under nineteen years of age made up 47.6 percent of the total population of Japan in 1945, with girls at 23.7 percent, but by 1950 the percentage of under-19s fell slightly to 45.7 percent, with girls at 22.5 percent.

Why might the gender of the postwar cinema audience matter? As described above, the cinema was one of SCAP's key vehicles for social reform, and among General MacArthur's five priority reforms at the beginning of the Occupation was gender equality, at least as it was understood at the time. Yet these carefully planned and executed interventions into popular cinema culture were surely undermined if indeed the target audience of young women was not in the cinema theater in the first place. While male audience members were also expected to learn from SCAP's censored cinema content, a cornerstone of the implementation of new gender relations in Japanese society was understood to be women and girls insisting on their new rights. If they were not among the audiences of the cinema texts designed to inform and persuade citizens about these new rights, at least in the numbers expected, the censorship process had failed before it was even tested.

The demographic make-up of the cinema audience therefore has implications for how we understand censorship, political upheaval and social reform in Japan. However, audience studies can also reveal gaps and omissions in our data on audience numbers and demographics itself. For example, in addition to the restrictions that many female study participants reported, a number of male participants recalled entering the cinema without paying, by tricking ticket desk employees or letting friends in through side doors (Coates 2017). Not only does this suggest that the male proportion of the cinema audience was larger than recorded, it also offers a caution against taking box office figures as an indication of the number of people who watched a particular film. This granular detail about the daily conditions of the cinema theater is one of the major contributions of audience studies to how we understand media consumption and interaction.

Conclusion

As this brief history has demonstrated, the study of audiences has fallen in and out of favor over the history of Japanese media studies, and media studies in Japan. Audience studies also encompasses many methods, and new approaches are borrowed from cognate fields and disciplines regularly, renewing and expanding the sub-field of scholarship which seeks to understand the experiences of audiences. As the case study detailed above indicates, understanding audience experiences can have implications for how we think of key periods in Japanese history, as well as moments of historical, political and social change. Speaking with audiences can give the researcher a healthy degree of scepticism when dealing with survey and demographic data, reminding us that human behavior often falls outside the limits of what we can track. Finally, audience studies offers a mode of investigating the role that media plays in the lives of those who engage with a media text, demonstrating the various interactions possible between human and screen, as well as the use to which those interactions are put in communications between humans about media. In thinking from the perspective of audiences, we can see media not only as an entertainment in and of itself, but as a mode of understanding, situating oneself in and communicating about our world.

Bibliography

Allen, H. W., 1945. Elimination of Japanese Government Control of the Motion Picture Industry. *SCAPIN* 146, October 16, 1945. Box 8565, Folder 31, SCAP records, National Archives (and online). http://dl.ndl. go.jp/info:ndljp/pid/9885209 [Accessed 3 January 2019].

Allison, A., 1996. *Permitted and Prohibited Desires: Mothers, Comics, and Censorship in Japan.* Boulder: Westview.

———., 2002. Playing with Power: Morphing Toys and Transforming Heroes in Kids' Mass Culture. In J.M. Mageo, ed., *Power and the Self.* Cambridge: Cambridge University Press, 71–92.

Ang, I., 1991 [1985]. *Watching Dallas: Soap Opera and the Melodramatic Imagination.* London: Routledge.

———., 1996. *Living Room Wars: Rethinking Media Audiences for a Postmodern World.* London: Routledge.

Brandon, J. R., 2006. Myth and Reality: A Story of Kabuki during American Censorship, 1945–1949. *Asian Theatre Journal,* 23(1), 1–110.

Coates, J., 2016. *Making Icons: Repetition and the Female Image in Japanese Cinema, 1945–1964.* Hong Kong: Hong Kong University Press.

———., 2017. Socializing the Audience: Going to the Cinema in Postwar Japan. *Participations,* 14(2), 590–607.

———., 2018a. Alternative Viewership Practices in Kyoto, Japan. In A. Magnan-Park, G. Marchetti and S.K. Tan, eds., *The Handbook of Asian Cinema.* London: Palgrave Macmillan, 221–44.

———., 2018b. Rethinking the Young Female Cinema Audience: Postwar Cinema-Going in Kansai, 1945–1952. *US-Japan Women's Journal,* 54(1), 6–28.

———., 2020. Bodies in the Dark: The Postwar Cinema Audience and the Body as Ground Zero. In I. Holca and C. Sapanaru Tamas, eds., *Forms of the Body in Contemporary Japanese Society, Literature, and Culture.* London: Lexington Books, 237–58.

Conde, D., 1945. Consolidated Report of Civil Information and Education Section Activities, Daily Report to Brigadier General Ken R. Dyke, Chief of CI & E, November 16, 1945, from Mr. D. Conde, Motion Picture and Visual Media Section. GHQ/ SCAP Records, National Diet Library, Tokyo.

Eiga geijutsu nenkan, 1947. *Eiga geijutsu nenkan* [Motion picture arts yearbook 1947]. Tokyo: Jiji Tsūshinsha.

Eiga junpō, 1941. Kankyaku dōtai chōsa [Audience demographic survey]. *Eiga junpō,* (December 1), 54–56.

Fujiki, H., 2011. *Kankyaku e no apurōchi* [Approaching the audience]. Nagoya: Nagoya University Press.

———., 2014. Creating the Audience: Cinema as Popular Recreation and Social Education in Modern Japan. In D. Miyao, ed., *The Oxford Handbook of Japanese Cinema.* Oxford: Oxford University, 79–100.

———., 2019. *Eiga kankyaku to wa nani mono ka: media to shakai shutai no kin-gendaishi* [Who is the cinema audience?: A history of media and social subjects, 1910s–2010s]. Nagoya: Nagoya University Press.

Fukuoka, T., 1950. Eigakan ni okeru abekku no seitai [Lifestyles of couples in the movie theater]. *Chuō kōron,* (December), 162–67.

Galbraith, P. W., 2013. Maid Cafés: The Affect of Fictional Characters in Akihabara, Japan. *Asian Anthropology,* 12 (2), 104–25.

———., 2017. RapeLay and the Return of the Sex Wars in Japan. *Porn Studies,* 4 (1) 105–26.

Gerow, A., 2010. The Process of Theory: Reading Gonda Yasunosuke and Early Film Theory. *Review of Japanese Culture and Society,* 22, 37–43.

Gonda, Y., 1914. *Katsudō shashin no genre oyobi ōyō* [The principles and applications of the moving pictures]. Tokyo: Dojinsha.

———., 1922. *Minshu goraku no kichō* [The foundations of popular entertainment]. Tokyo: Dojinsha.

Hirano, K., 1992. *Mr Smith Goes to Tokyo.* Washington: Smithsonian Institute Press.

Hjorth, L., 2007. The Game of Being Mobile: One Media History of Gaming and Mobile Technologies in Asia-Pacific. *Convergence,* 13 (4), 369–81.

Hori, H., 2002. Eiga o mirukoto to katarukoto: Mizoguchi Kenji "Yoru no onnatachi" (1948) o meguru hihyō, jendā, kankyaku ["Women of the Night" (1948) as framed by the Occupation era in Japan: negotiations between text, critics, and female spectators]. *Eizōgaku*, 68, 47–66.

——., 2018. *Promiscuous Media: Film and Visual Culture in Imperial Japan, 1926–1945*. Ithaca: Cornell University Press.

Iwasaki, A., 1978. The Occupied Screen. *Japan Quarterly*, 25 (3), 302–22.

Katō, M., 1995. Eigakan to kankyaku no rekishi: Eigatoshi Kyoto no sengo. *Eizōgaku*, 55, 44–58.

——., 1996. A History of Movie Theatres and Audiences in Postwar Kyoto, The Capital of Japanese Cinema. *Cinemagazinet! No. 1*. Available at: http://www.cmn.hs.h.kyoto-u.ac.jp/NO1/SUBJECT1/KYOTO.HTM [Accessed 31 January 2017].

Kitamura, H., 2004. "Home of the American Movies": The Marunouchi Subaruza and the Making of Hollywood's Audiences in Occupied Tokyo, 1946–9. In M. Stokes and R. Maltby, eds., *Hollywood Abroad: Audiences and Cultural Exchange*. London: BFI, 99–120.

——., 2010. *Screening Enlightenment: Hollywood and the Cultural Reconstruction of Defeated Japan*. Ithaca: Cornell University Press.

Kitamura, H. and Sasagawa, K., 2017. The Reception of American Cinema in Japan. *Oxford Research Encyclopedia of Literature*, (November), 1–15.

Kitamura, K., 2017. Sukurīn ni tōeisareru "seishun": Kurosawa Akira "Waga seishun ni kui nashi" no ōdiensu [Projected youth on the screen: the audience of Kurosawa Akira's "No Regrets for Our Youth"]. *Masu komyunikēshon kenkyū*, 90, 123–42.

Koyama, M., 2016. Interviewed by Jennifer Coates and Nozomi Matsuyama. Kyoto, domestic address, 17 October 2016.

Kuhn, A., 2002. *Dreaming of Fred and Ginger: Cinema and Cultural Memory*. New York: New York University Press.

MacArthur, D. and staff, 1994. Reports of General MacArthur: MacArthur in Japan: The Occupation: Military Phase vol. 1. Department of the Army.

Mayo, M., 1984. Civil Censorship and Media Control in Early Occupied Japan: From Minimum to Stringent Surveillance. In R. Wolfe, ed., *Americans as Proconsuls: United State Military Government 1944–1952*. Carbondale, IL: Southern Illinois University Press, 263–320.

Ministry of Internal Affairs and Communications, 2017. *Official Statistics of Japan*. http://www.e-stat.go.jp/SG1/estat/List.do?bid=000001007702&cycode=0 [Accessed 27 September 2017].

Motion Picture Producers Association of Japan (Eiren), 2017. *Statistics of Film Industry in Japan*. http://www.eiren.org/statistics_e/index.html [Accessed 27 October 2017].

Radway, J., 1984. *Reading the Romance: Women, Patriarchy, and Popular Literature*. Chapel Hill: University of North Carolina Press.

Russell, C., 2008. *The Cinema of Naruse Mikio: Women and Japanese Modernity*. Durham: Duke University Press.

SCAP (Supreme Commander for the Allied Powers) General HQ., 1946–1949. 000.076 Women's Affairs, February 1946–January 1949, Folder 28, Box 2879.

——., 1945. Indication of Production Principles of IDS. Draft Memorandum to Japanese Empire, issued by General Headquarters of Allied Forces, September 22, 1945, Box 8563.

——., 1948. Political Information-Education Program. National Archives II at College Park, Maryland, RG 331, GHQ/SCAP, CI&E, Box 5305, file 12 and 15.

Stacey, J., 1994. *Star Gazing: Hollywood Cinema and Female Spectatorship*. London: Routledge.

Toki, A. and Mizoguchi, K., 1993. A History of Early Cinema in Kyoto, Japan (1896–1912). *Cinemagazinet! No. 1*. http://www.cmn.hs.h.kyoto-u.ac.jp/NO1/SUBJECT1/INAEN.HTM [Accessed 31 January 2017].

Uryū, T., 1967. Eiga fukkō wa josei no dōin kara: josei kankyaku genshō no donsoko wa sugita [Cinema recovery begins with women's mobilization: female audience decrease hits bottom]. *Kinema Junpō*, 450, 88–91.

Waga seishun ni kui nashi [No Regrets for Our Youth], 1946. [Film.] Directed by Kurosawa Akira. New York: Criterion Collection. DVD.

Whaley, B. 2018. Who Will Play Terebi Gēmu When No Japanese Children Remain? Distanced Engagement in Atlus' Catherine. *Games and Culture*, 13 (1), 92–114.

When Cinema Was King, 2018. [Film.] Directed by Jennifer Coates. https://vimeo.com/231839981.

Chapter 16
The Serious Business of Song: Karaoke as Discipline and Industry in Japan

Laurence Green

This chapter explores, by way of a literature review, the evolution of karaoke—the act of singing along to a pre-recorded vocal-less audio track—from its origins in 1970s Japan to the medium's current manifestation among diverse international audiences. Looking to the wider literature on the medium to examine how karaoke as a systemic part of a specifically "Japanese" musical culture is often obscured; the chapter looks to evidence a distinct in-group/out-group dynamic within Japanese karaoke culture and its value-creation processes, proposing that karaoke was, and continues to be, a key force in the evolution of the Japanese music industry as well as the way Japanese interact with music.

Introduction

Karaoke, or the act of singing along to a pre-recorded vocal-less audio track (often accompanied by visuals), has drawn a considerable amount of attention as one of Japan's foremost pop-cultural exports. Book-length studies such as Hosokawa and Mitsui's *Karaoke Around The World* (1998), Drew's *Karaoke Nights: An Ethnographic Rhapsody* (2001), Zhou and Tarocco's *Karaoke: The Global Phenomenon* (2013) and Brown's *Karaoke Idols: Popular Music and the Performance of Identity* (2015) have viewed the narrative of karaoke's journey from Japanese invention to global success story as one fundamentally mediated by "local" uptake; karaoke as a medium that adapts technologically and performatively depending on where it is being consumed. However, this view of karaoke "by-satellite," as a series of interconnected but disparate local scenes, obscures a key dimension: karaoke as systematically informed by Japan's socio-cultural forms and spaces, as opposed to being merely a "product" of Japan. Can the Japanese karaoke experience instead be re-situated as part of something larger—both a vital component in a thriving domestic music sector, but also as a key node linking together the ideas of "practice" and "pastime"? Is it possible to read karaoke in Japan as not merely a playful form of musical interaction, but one in which wider, pre-existing structures and systems of social capital formation are re-enacted and given firmer meaning?

Answering these questions is important because they can help us to understand better the inherent tension that exists between descriptions of karaoke as something to be approached as simple entertainment—a means of unwinding after a long day at work—and as something serious that needs to be "practiced." The recent *Be More Japan*, a glossy hard-cover volume aimed at a populist audience, is typical of this friction; on one hand describing karaoke as a jubilant means of "team-bonding" among a "hardworking Japanese population," while simultaneously introducing the notion that despite initial protestations that proficiency level does not matter, it actually *does* (Beidas and Moul 2019, 159). This is most apparent in concepts such as the *jūhachiban* (lit. "number eighteen"), a term taken from traditional theater form kabuki and used to refer to one's favorite song, or specifically, the one you excel at singing best (Kelly 2005, 163) and the phenomenon of *hitokara* (solo karaoke), often done so the singer can practice and improve their favorite song (Matsumoto 2016, 3428). These terms underscore the presence of a systematic approach to karaoke in Japan defined by the identifiable "value" of skill and excellence on the part of the singer, whereby they are expected, or feel obliged to practice in order to meet a certain standard. It is here that the crucial nuance alluded to in the "discipline" mentioned in this study's title can be found; namely, that discipline can encompass both the means of training, through practice, to obey a certain code of conduct or behavioral norms, but also stand for an identifiable branch or body of knowledge.

Taken together, these two nuances form the backbone to what we might term the karaoke "system" in Japan, or a Japanese "model" of karaoke. More than simply a technological interface to enable amateur singing within a public sphere, the suggestion here is that karaoke in Japan is far more along the lines of a lubricant or service, enabling an interconnected web of social systems to thrive by virtue of a body of knowledge (songs, and the capacity to sing them) in common among its participants. By identifying and then synthesizing "markers" or symbols of discipline identified in a spread of prior case studies on karaoke into a composite picture, it is possible to re-approach the history of karaoke with a view to how audiences in Japan find value in these systems of practice. This will take the form of a number of distinct sub-sections of discourse analysis that in turn considers karaoke performance as something one is able not only to practice, but also to improve via the processes of routinization and incentivization. In each of these sections, these components will be shown as crucial in reinforcing and perpetuating karaoke as a *disciplined* system, to which these standards are constantly measured and sought to be met by karaoke audiences, even if in a subjective, unquantifiable manner. Today, karaoke finds itself one of countless words (file next to "karate" and "katsu") to join an "intercultural" lexicon of Japanese aestheticism (Wong 2004, 72), so much a part of popular mass culture that their original meanings begin to blur. By dissecting the various dynamics that define karaoke as both a form of entertainment and a driver of social capital, that blur can be brought back into clear focus.

Opting in to the in-group:
Practice and participation as pastime in Japan

Of the existing studies of karaoke, William H. Kelly's *Training for Leisure—Karaoke and the Seriousness of Play in Japan* arguably comes closest in its approach to codifying and linking karaoke as it is performed in Japan to a set of wider cultural concepts and practices that exist beyond the pastime itself. This approach is rooted in what he sees as a natural extension of the idea of *kata* (forms) and *dō* (paths) found in the ideology of arts (both aesthetic and martial) in Japan (Kelly 2005, 153). Kelly looks at the phenomenon of "training" for karaoke via a series of organized classes which, crucially, turn the training process into an observable system or pattern of "senso-motoric coordination" that plays on a deeper-seated aesthetic of "repetition in learning." Here, mastery comes through frequency, or what Chiesa (2005, 194) terms the "ethics of effort"; namely, that the concerted and integrated act of practice among individuals working in concert on an activity can in many ways simultaneously become both the means and outcome of a training regimen. Much like the compulsory choir classes in Japanese high schools, the implication is clear; through sheer number of hours spent on singing, a kind of national "base aptitude" is achieved (Kelly 2005, 157).

Practice provides a measurable scale by which practitioners of an activity can gauge not only their acumen at that particular point in time, but more crucially, are made cognizant of the steps they must follow to reach a level occupied by their peers. When everyone is equal, and we play by the rules (implicit or otherwise), our position within the group is justified—we know where we stand. But this position—this sense of being "among equals"—is inherently reliant on a constant, minute-level jockeying for position, an endless recalibration of individual anxieties and self-pride, and it is this that drives us to improve. A "bad" performance at karaoke would destroy this self-pride, and by extension the self that exists as part of the group (Kelly 2005, 165). Individually, our self-value is difficult to determine, but when placed in proximity to others, suddenly the distance (or closeness) between us becomes all the clearer.

The "performance" of karaoke extends beyond the actual singing itself to an entire periphery of "rules" that dictate an acceptable experience, as presented in Japanese women's magazine *Josei Seven*—in this instance aimed at fresh employees who have just joined a new company:

1. Listen respectfully to the singing of the boss
2. Practice and be able to sing at least three duet songs so that you are able to accompany your boss on request
3. Take care not to sing the boss's favorite song as he is likely not to be able to sing too many different songs
4. Take care to avoid songs which are likely to have a depressing effect, such as those which are nostalgic or about separation and lost love
5. Take care to avoid songs which are unfamiliar to others since they are more likely to chat during your performance if they do not know the song
6. Avoid sexy songs which are likely to offend senior office ladies
7. Choose a song the boss has heard at least once before
8. Wear a suit rather than a sexy dress out of respect for senior office ladies
9. When not singing, be sure to maintain an awareness of and express an interest in those around you

(Josei Seven 22 April 1993, trans. in Kelly 2005, 159)

Beyond the face-value humor of these "rules" lies a far darker tinge of peer-pressure, a world rife with the dangers of corporate hazing and the implication of playing up or shutting up. Karaoke, as seen here, is a "compulsory company activity [...] especially for female staff and new recruits to the company," so much so that they feel "duty-bound" to comply (Zhou and Tarocco 2013, 41). Implicit in that repeated "Take care" is a far stronger "Do not!" while the language of "respect," "offence" and "awareness" presents an intimidating cocktail of obstacles to avoid. Not even foreigners are excused—Shitamachi suggests that any foreigner invited to karaoke while conducting business in Japan would be well advised to steer clear of *My Way*, *Yesterday*, or anything by Elvis Presley because "the chances are you've chosen the one song they can sing in English and taken away their opportunity to impress you" (Shitamachi 2015, 103). The Beatles' *Eleanor Rigby* is cited as occupying a particular category of its own: "songs that are too fast paced *for a typical Japanese to master* yet are still well known" [my emphasis] (Shitamachi 2015, 103). The more serious takeaway from both Shitamachi's account and the rules presented in *Josei Seven* is that the practice of karaoke is not only about what one should do, but also what one should *not* do. This codification of karaoke has gone as far as driving the spread of special "karaoke courses," offered in many cities to professionals looking to avoid an embarrassing faux pas (Kelly 2005, 154).

This need to practice runs in tandem with a corresponding awareness of "taking part." Wong sees this dynamic of taking part as a performative activity, one in which value is created through the act of participation: "The point is simply to take part—to demonstrate good humor and good manners by taking one's turn, as well as by expressing appreciation of others' singing" (Wong 2004, 78). In performing karaoke, we perform by the rules of societal expectations of what constitutes an acceptable, appreciable karaoke performance. Thus, it is not so much the act of "taking part" that is important here, but rather the *ability* to take part. We might not be the *best* singer among our peers, but notions of "good humor" and "good manners" imply that our act of performing karaoke fundamentally rests on objective standards that must be practiced and met. Rather than soldier on with a horrendous dud performance that offends and disrupts the sensibilities of the in-group, better to opt out entirely. In this, a darker sensibility can be read—that the "emphasis is on participation rather than skill" (Wong 2004, 78) precisely because anyone with a truly awful voice is already in the safely negligible out-group, and only those within the appreciable base level of skill remain. Kelly's study affirms this in his observation that in karaoke, the maintenance of a "good atmosphere" is crucial, and that this is accordingly constituted by a sensitivity to the likes, dislikes and most importantly, the expectations of others (Kelly 2005, 163).

An interesting parallel can be observed among the owners of karaoke bars. West (2005) introduces the case of fifty-year-old Hasegawa Junji, who had been running a karaoke bar in a small Kyushu town for fifteen years. Tight policing of his establishment including hefty insulation and well-observed closing hours have ensured his bar has never been a concern in terms of noise pollution for nearby residents, and as such, he has become a valued, trusted member of the community. "Everybody in this community knows everybody else. I see my neighbors at the grocery store. I play golf with the kindergarten principal next door. If I'm the neighborhood nuisance, who is going to respect that? Nobody would even talk to me," he tells West (2005, 115). His feelings are backed up by other members of the community, one of whom comments, "The owner knows everybody and doesn't want to cause trouble... About three weeks after we moved in, I saw him while I was taking out the garbage. He came right up to me and introduced himself" (West 2005, 115–16).

Hasegawa's careful efforts to play by the rules and "take part" in his community have seen him greeted with the same kind of "appreciation" reserved for participants during karaoke performances. By first being aware of, and then following, an objective set of "good manners" dictated by his peer group (the local residents), the success of his livelihood is preserved. It is possible to read here the same kind of "minutiae of performance" that Kelly sees in karaoke

Handbook of Japanese Media and Popular Culture in Transition

itself, where the value remains very much in the detail (Kelly 2005, 161). Here, Hasegawa has mastered the social codes of the community, and in his statements, makes open that which is implicit—codifying the "rules of life" that largely go unwritten. By re-affirming the "familiar" to both himself and the community that he has moved into, he assures a frictionless presence among the wider group. Brown, drawing on political scientist Robert D. Putnam, identifies the clear benefits to society that can result from "the collective membership of individuals in groups" (Brown 2015, 113). As in the case of Hasegawa, these groups do not need to be overt, but are instead organically generated through a sense of "social capital" or "civil society" by those living in or utilizing localized spaces. In karaoke, as in the everyday life of the communities we inhabit, notions of practice or the accumulation of the knowledge of what to do or not do help provide a framework by which to better define membership of these communities, and the familiarity that comes from knowing those codes of conduct are observed in common.

Local music on a national stage:
Karaoke as contest, and the "potential" to improve

The opening pages of Brown's *Karaoke Idols: Popular Music and the Performance of Identity* turns the spotlight on how previous work on karaoke has frequently taken an ethnographic approach (Brown 2015, 6–7) in an attempt to better understand the construction of identity enacted by performers through their engagement with the medium. However, this continuing focus on the performer throws into stark contrast the relative lack of material linking this performative aspect with the role karaoke takes within the wider music industry, and leaves open the question as to why it has achieved such ongoing durability as a medium of popular entertainment. This question of durability, of karaoke's continuing perpetuation, is key to moving toward a clearer systemization of it. Why are people who have never before attempted karaoke drawn to it, and more importantly, why do they keep coming back? What is it that, years after the medium's advent, keeps so viable the simple concept of amateurs singing along to a backing track? When we engage with the act of performing karaoke, we do so at our most vulnerable—presenting ourselves on a public or semi-public stage, all in an attempt to inject a sense of "meaning" into our wider social sphere (Drew 2001, 70). Again, discipline provides a potential answer here, via the feedback mechanism present in a constant sense of improvement; the idea that by investing time and effort now, we open the possibility to an imagined future self that is superior to where we currently stand.

Central to this dynamic, Drew suggests, is the distinction between local and national music scenes. For him, the concept of "local music" is defined by music that touches our "daily lives and relationships," our "personal affiliations" (Drew 2001, 16). Put simply, it is the difference between seeing a famous, untouchable pop idol on the television screen, and watching your best friend sing a version of their song at the karaoke venue ten minutes down the road from your house. In the US, Drew suggests that the kind of local music scene characterized by bedroom producers plugging away on a Casio keyboard, small town bar circuit bands and karaoke "stars" are something to constantly get "beyond." Local music is nothing more than an "appendage to the national" (Drew 2001, 13) and karaoke offers merely a short-lived fantasy of being a real star. But in Japan at the turn of the millennium more than half of the population performed karaoke at least once a year, and 80 percent of Japan's 350,000 bars were equipped with karaoke systems (Drew 2001, 12–13). More recent figures, discussed later in this chapter, suggest some degree of change in these habits, but at the dawn of the 21st century, the local and national could very much be said to occupy a shared space. Drew explains that "karaokists and all local musicians must deal with the sense of redundancy that comes from making local music in a culture dominated by mass music" (Drew 2001, 17), but once again, what if—as in the case of Japan—it is precisely that kind of personally affiliated local music that becomes the "mass music" of a nation at large? I would suggest that here, the transposition of the self from the local to the national level, when audiences engage in a karaoke performance, holds more tangibility in Japan, precisely because it occupies a majority space as a social activity. By engaging in karaoke, a Japanese audience inherently moves into, and further swells, that majority.

This backdrop of creating a "national" stage for the performance of karaoke plays into what Drew sees as a potential arena for not only "validating personal and social identities" but also "performing and testing those identities before others" (Drew 2001, 120). The friction created by this "testing" can manifest itself in a number of ways. For Drew, and his study of karaoke in the US, an increasing trend toward contest-like "competitive karaoke" formats brings karaoke far closer to the "winner-take-all world of pop stardom" (Drew 2001, 122). Audiences watch the performers with quiet, rapt attention before bursting into applause at the end of each song, and there is an "edgy seriousness to proceedings"; a model that bears marked similarity to the kind of karaoke seen in Japan. Viewed negatively, this edgy seriousness can be seen as stemming from potential feelings of "vocal inadequacy," the reminder that someone else is better than us. Drew points the finger at "classically trained vocalists," at those with time, effort and money to invest in bettering their performances and at those "concerned with standards" (Drew 2001, 120). This sense of objective standards, of a distinction between the trained and untrained, falls in line with the earlier observations regarding the discipline of majority in Japan; for standards to emerge, they rely on a majority to first form a clear consensus on what they actually are. Likewise, what if, instead of these contest-like elements provoking feelings of inadequacy in us, it is precisely this competitive spirit that drives us, en masse, to get better at singing? In other words, inadequacy is only inadequacy if we believe we cannot improve, that each and every one of us cannot be idols ourselves. Do we fully acknowledge and adopt the idea of objective standards, buckle up for some serious practice and "play the game," or do we "opt out," leaving the serious business of song to the real stars?

Karaoke as the ordinary un-ordinary: Authentic simulations of reality

The "serious" approach to karaoke outlined above—the idea that karaoke is about something more than just enjoying a good time singing with your friends—can best be framed within the lens of the degree to which the act of singing exists as something "ordinary," as opposed to something professionalized—limited to the domain of pop superstars and those whom society dubs "singers." It is important to note here that the everyday-ness of singing does not imply lack of application or discipline, rather, it is precisely because singing is "ordinary" (and thus expected) as part of everyday life that application and discipline become part and parcel of it. If the practice of karaoke outlines the method of correctly performing it within a social context, and the notion of improvement outlines a route to do so more effectively, then the next vital ingredient is the solidifying of these concepts as something normal and in keeping with a person's character. In essence, karaoke, and by association, public singing in general, needs to become routine.

To throw this distinction into better contrast, it is useful to observe Drew's analysis of how singing has become "un-ordinary" in contemporary North America. He paints a picture of an American world of song, withered away and lost to time—a world where, 150 years ago, "singing was the center of social life" (Drew 2001, 119). Here, piano-side singalongs were a staple ingredient of middle-class home life, as was the piano itself. Choral societies and other such groups were prolific, and singing could be expected at school, work and—most obviously—at religious services. These days, "public singing has become a rarity to many of us, limited to clumsy iterations of 'Happy Birthday' and 'Auld Lang Syne'" (Drew 2001, 119). Drew sees the causes of this decline as manifold, but suggests that "our own feelings of vocal inadequacy, as well as our vague sense that music making is alien to the real business of life" are chief among them (Drew 2001, 119). In other words, we, collectively, have decided that we are just too bad at singing to sing, preferring instead to opt-out entirely, or if we do choose to sing, to do so ironically, occupying the conveniently prescribed larger-than-life role of "karaoke performer" (Drew 2005, 378). Ill-prepared for public performance, Drew sees us as "touristic" onlookers viewing with ironic detachment—"as if from behind glass"—the karaoke spectacle as remote and exotic (Drew 2001, 73).

The question of irony—as placed in direct opposition to authenticity, or the sense that our actions and self are not only genuine and congruent with our beliefs, but that they remain relatively consistent despite varying external forces—recurs frequently in discussions of karaoke. This opposition can be read alongside questions of coolness, highbrow versus lowbrow culture, and even a certain dismissiveness from middle-class audiences toward the lower classes (for whom karaoke is seen to primarily belong to). Drew's imagined put-down from a snooty onlooker: "These guys think they're on TV" (Drew 2001, 69), is typical of this attitude—the idea that karaoke performers are somehow "acting up," breaking out of the humdrum of their small, local everyday lives and donning the guise of a nationally famous musical star. But to read a karaoke performance in this manner is to oversimplify the dynamic at play here. Adams gets closer to the heart of the idea: "karaoke is thus not a representation but a simulacrum of fixed and singular authenticity. This does not mean the performance is not real. On the contrary, it means that the simulation is the reality" (1996, 510–11). In essence, when we perform, it is not that we are really "thinking" we are on television, but that by engaging in the medium of karaoke, we are comfortably fulfilling one part of a wider system (or simulation) that naturally engenders this kind of behavior. Television *is* our reality, so it is only right and proper that we should exist within its extended periphery.

I would suggest that a Japanese model of karaoke thrives in a nested layering of these "versions" or ways of life. If karaoke is to be seen as a performative manifestation of the self, it is one based on an idealized vision of that self; part of the everyday, but also apart from it. Karaoke is selling a dream—one created and fashioned by members of a moneyed higher class (the music industry), to members of a lower class who desire to be part of that higher echelon (by becoming a pop idol, if only for a short while) (Brown 2015, 89). This economic "rift" is perhaps better envisioned as a kind of looped conveyor belt, one where the simulation engendered through the karaoke performance perpetuates itself into a kind of never-ending "present" in which the user finds themselves inhabiting a very particular kind of middle-class life halfway between the lowbrow and highbrow. To a Japanese audience, these versions of selfhood can comfortably co-exist without giving rise to questions of an inauthentic engagement with the world around them. Sone draws on Barthes' famous discussions of *honne* (true) and *tatemae* (facade) to suggest that "a Japanese individual is conscious of these two selves coexisting in oneself and in others in social situations. The Japanese are expected to alternate these two 'faces' according to circumstances" (Sone 2014, 203). Of course, a varying of the "presented" self, depending on the social context, is certainly not unique to Japan, but it is the self-consciousness of this presentation that Sone alludes to that is particularly relevant to my argument here, contributing to a kind of hyper-awareness of constant re-calibration, depending on the self that is "needed" at that point in time. Thus, the highly coded, performative actions of karaoke are implicitly understood as by no means false, imitative or inauthentic, as they already exist within a situation where this "self" is socially expected. Once again, the simulation becomes the reality.

The rise of this kind of upward mobility-via-song evidenced in the global popularity of television talent show franchises like *The X Factor* and *American Idol*, or Japan's *Sutā tanjō!* (lit. a star is born!) and *Nodo jiman* (lit. proud of my voice) has historically had the capacity to horrify some audiences precisely because it thrusts this dynamic into the spotlight (Raftery 2008, 43). The cultural democracy of song—the allowance of "all members of society equal access to a cultural space" (Brown 2015, 89) was terrifying because it offered a voice to all, giving everyone—rich or poor—the "permission" to sing, no matter how bad they were at it. It was not so much a question that passive consumers had suddenly become active, but that we could *see them doing it*, and had to reconcile these seemingly inauthentic selves with the concrete social reality of the world around us. For some, the karaoke performance is, and always will be, thoroughly inauthentic; an "acting up" of the self that takes us too far from the material, concrete, knowable world. It is a canned, borrowed imitation of the genuine, authentic article. But at the same time, one could argue—as Wong does—that by performing karaoke, we seek to reclaim the same hegemonic force that the mass-media nature of karaoke seems to so wholly represent (2004, 72). Karaoke, at its most basic level, is something above and beyond a passive, sit-back engagement with popular music; it is utterly reliant on us as users, as performers, to place ourselves within it and fill its emptiness. The backing track might be canned, but through our voice, we inject liveness back into it and—by extension— our own lives and their place within the mass-media system.

Drew grapples with the question of the "imitative" quality of a specifically "Japanese karaoke" and how this can easily become a hastily trotted out, mechanistic stereotype of Japanese conformity, including humorous appellations of a karaoke-*dō* (way of karaoke) where imitation is a necessary phase in the path to mastery. More interesting though is his analysis of the wider Japanese music scene, which he sees as having benefited from a much-needed boost in the late 1980s and early 1990s, when the mass popularization of karaoke via the advent of karaoke boxes increased demand for singable pop music. Suddenly, million-plus selling singles were no longer the exception to the rule, but common-place, with over ten hitting the charts every year (Drew 2001, 19–20). The implication is clear: karaoke, and the need it engendered for catchy pop hits had been thrown into a symbiotic embrace, not only feeding off each other commercially, but laying down a framework by which its users could fit themselves. As Drew rather neatly puts it, "In Japan, songs are for singing, the tools through which one learns to sing, displays singing competence, adopts singing roles" (2001, 20). It is the last of these that perhaps warrants the closest examination, recalling as it does the earlier comments about the functions of *honne* and *tatemae* in the presentation of the self

Handbook of Japanese Media and Popular Culture in Transition

in Japan. In attributing "singing roles" to Japanese karaoke-goers, it is not simply the pop-idol versions of themselves that are seen, but also the *role* this slippage between selves plays in their own lives. In Drew's statement, there is clear use-value for the song, and singing, and it is this value—this incentive—that has not only made karaoke an indispensable social tool in Japan, but also made millions for the country's music industry.

Incentive: Karaoke as service, and moving beyond technological one-upmanship

West frames his history of the rapid rise of karaoke's popularity in 1980s Japan as premised by two driving factors: a wider selection of songs and lower cost (West 2005, 93). In essence, both operate on presenting the user with the freedom of choice: freedom to choose whatever song they desire (and thus to perfect their performance of favorites) and freedom to choose which locale they perform in, selecting one from among countless karaoke venues. West goes on to explain that the advent of the karaoke box format (small, dedicated private rooms in which to perform among friends or colleagues) saw the focus shift from drinking as the primary focus of the social gathering (with the singing as a sideshow) to the reverse, which in turn engendered a shift in the demographic of people drawn to karaoke. Now, all—young and old alike—felt included, when previously they would have felt hesitant about spending time in drinking establishments. The karaoke box experience offered music-as-service. Now it was not only the drinks that were on tap, but the music too, via an hourly charge (West 2005, 93–94). The concept of the karaoke box, what Ogawa (1998, 47) calls "enclosed" kara-oke space, is so prevalent within Japanese karaoke culture that it can even be read as having semantic significance in how the Japanese refer to karaoke—namely, that it is something that you go to (*karaoke ni iku*) (ALC Press Inc. n.d.), not just something that you do. All this helps frame another key component in the conceptualization of karaoke as discipline and system: the question of incentive. The kinds of feedback loop explored earlier regarding the self-validation of karaoke consumers in terms of their perceived improvement and accrued social capital is on its own not enough to explain the perpetuation of the medium. For that, it is crucial to also consider the commercial forces behind the production of karaoke, and more importantly, the symbiotic relationship of supply and demand they engender among consumers.

The effect the transformative changes, outlined by West above, had on the Japanese ka-raoke industry (for it was by the turn of the millennium, an industry) cannot be underes-timated. West's (2005, 96) headline figure, taken from a 2000 White Paper on the leisure sector, sees total annual revenue from karaoke at $10 billion USD, split between $3.8 billion USD in bars, $5.6 billion USD in karaoke boxes and $560 million USD in other assorted sites including hotels, tour busses and restaurants. The picture at the turn of the millennium seemed rosy, but there is a bitter sting in the tail. From the mid-2000s onward, karaoke was becoming, in some ways, a victim of its own success—61 percent of karaoke businesses cited competition from others as a major concern—and West (2005, 96) details the number of users falling slowly each year. By the end of the decade, things look far more nebulous, and Brown's 2015 study openly acknowledges the difficulty in finding accurate, up-to-date figures for the economic impact of the medium—figures which also often fail to include food and drink sales at karaoke booths, as well as the royalties generated for artists by the performance of their songs. Nevertheless, like West, he sees the industry maintaining its status as a multi-billion-dollar earner in Japan, albeit with a turnover in 2010 in the region of $10 billion USD, one that has flatlined to a degree, unable to move beyond its early 2000s peak (Brown 2015, 34). More recent figures from an All-Japan Karaoke Industrialist Association report (2017) indicate revenue has since declined to an annual total of around $5 billion USD, split between $1.4 billion USD in bars, $3.5 billion USD in karaoke boxes and $416 million USD in other establishments.

Commercial pictures of the karaoke industry and their emphasis on the physical, real-world space in which karaoke happens—in which performances are made possible via the assembled technology of microphones, television screens and databases of songs—is born out in much of the existing writing on the medium. As early as the mid-1990s, Kelly aired his frustrations at how "contemporary constructions of karaoke's history [...] are invariably concerned with identifying the first authentic karaoke system [...] This is generally accomplished by defining what exactly constitutes karaoke and then christening the earliest system which fits this definition as the first karaoke machine" (Kelly 1997, 72–73). Part of the trouble in rooting histories of karaoke in this technologized space is that they age fast. For example, Zhou and Tarocco's *Karaoke: The Global Phenomenon*, first published in 2007, already sounds hopelessly outdated with its talk of then-cutting-edge "polyphonic karaoke songs" and how in 2003, 80 billion JPY ($729 million USD) was made on ringtones and mobile karaoke in Japan (Zhou and Tarocco 2013, 174–75). At the time, these downloadable tunes proved particularly popular with 20-something women and middle-aged men, and were perfect for users that "like to rehearse before heading for the karaoke box" (Craft 2003). Here there is an echo of similar discussions around the earlier advent of television screens with scrolling lyrics replacing printed songbooks and how it was claimed this helped "ease the tension" of the singers, while simultaneously proving more engaging for those watching too (they had something else to look at as well as the singer themselves) (Wong 2004, 76). In this manner, each new technological advancement is met with enthused accolades that it enhances the karaoke experience, adds further steps to the ritualistic dance of performance. We are sucked further in—the singer, gazing at the lyrics on the screen, performing, their audience, watching too, each in their own way, performing.

Instead of attributing narrative primacy to technological "precedence," the importance of "defining" exactly what karaoke is, and when it "first" emerged, perhaps it is better to envision karaoke in its current state—delivered via high-speed data cable—as a new chapter in the medium's story, linked to, but also fundamentally "beyond" what has come before. Brown (2015, 90) sees the beginnings of this kind of shift in Tim O'Reilly's Web 2.0 and the success of internet behemoths like Google and Amazon in the decade following the Dot Com crash of the early 2000s. These companies thrived because, unlike others, they delivered services rather than software; harnessing the collective energy of millions of users and their aggregated consumer habits (Brown 2015, 90). Leonhard and Kusek develop this idea further in their discussion of a "Music 2.0" (2005, 55), in particular relation to the emergence of streaming services, where, just like the rise of the net service economy seen in Web 2.0, we have seen a shift from music as "software" to music as "service." We no longer purchase music on a CD, insert it into our hi-fi or computer and press "play." Instead, the music is, quite literally, never-ending—an almost infinite library of genres and songs are made available to us via streaming service catalogues, aided by clever recommendation algorithms that will continue to suggest further material that fits our tastes. All this for the simple cost of a monthly subscription fee.

Thus, in a theoretical "Karaoke 2.0," the conversation moves away from a constant "one-upmanship" of technological progress and becomes more about how karaoke seamlessly integrates itself into a person's life, how it might systematically (and continuously) deliver value and drive consumer habits. For Drew, this shift has seen us arguably lose our status as "audiences"—we are now users, "actively incorporating bits and pieces of media content into our personal and social lives" (2001, 25). Likewise, Brown sees clear evidence of this in social media, where the likes of Facebook and Twitter allow consumers to become producers (or rather, the pro-sumers first suggested by Toffler (1980) in his classic study *The Third Wave*). He looks also to the popularity of interactive karaoke-esque videogames like *Rock Band* and *Guitar Hero* (Brown 2015, 34) that allow players to both mentally and physically envision themselves as rock stars, not only singing along to their favorites but playing along too. Hindsight has, of course, shown us that consumer tastes for both social media and these kinds of videogames can also be incredibly fickle (Stuart 2011), but they highlight how the incentive for users to engage in these forms of technology is not necessarily inherent on the technology itself, but rather the absorption and routinization of those technologies into daily social practice. If this disappears, then so too does the incentive to engage with them.

Karaoke, in all its iterations, has survived for so long not because of its technological platforms, but in spite of the technology. Viewed in this way, it is clear that the value of karaoke is not in the delivery mechanism itself, but in the social capital conveyed via its performative aspect. When commentators observe the technological peculiarities of engagement with karaoke depending on the locale, it presents an image of bubbles of frenetic activity, rising to the surface at any given time before eventually bursting. Crucially, while the stream of bubbles might ebb and flow, it continues on nonetheless. Japan, through its endemic karaoke box format, has arguably already mastered the nature of karaoke-as-service, a wholescale enveloping of the medium's value and self-validation system into everyday, local, ordinary life. For Japanese audiences, there is a clear incentive to perform karaoke; through its morphing into a nationally prolific service-style medium in the form of the karaoke box, it becomes more than a technological mediator of entertainment, and begins to take on the form of a designated destination "space" that enables and lubricates social interaction. By visiting karaoke space, Japanese audiences are offered a constantly evolving opportunity to engage as active consumers in the output of the country's music industry; this "closeness," this blending of countless interstices of local engagement with national output firming up a symbiotic relationship that benefits both parties.

Conclusion

Karaoke as a "global phenomenon" continues to have impressive staying power precisely because of its ability to manifest in a multitude of manners within any given local context. In this chapter, I have attempted to highlight the centrality and importance of singing not only as a pastime, but as a specifically *public* pastime—and how this creates important changes in how we view the practice authentically or ironically. Through our engagement with karaoke, we not only shape our social interactions with the world, but also how we define ourselves in relation to both our immediate peers, members of our class, and— ultimately—the nation as a whole. When we sing karaoke, what face is it that we present to the world? Ours, or the face of the star we are emulating? What happens when karaoke becomes a competition, and was it always one to begin with?

The relentless impetus behind the karaoke system in Japan is best viewed against the backdrop of the medium's remarkable commercial success in the country. While the growth seen in the late 1980s and 1990s has since flatlined and now begun to decline, the sheer scale and proliferation of spaces in which to participate in karaoke in Japan remains impressive. The karaoke box format provides a useful way of framing wider shifts in how the experience is delivered to its users, going beyond a procession of technological upgrades toward a more holistic understanding of karaoke-as-service; fundamentally plugged into the everyday-ness of its participants' lives.

By engaging with both the idea and *ideals* of karaoke, as opposed to the delivery mechanism in isolation, it is possible to move closer to an understanding of karaoke in Japan as not only fundamentally driven by the structures and systems of social capital, but also a useful lens by which to observe these played out on a national level, both informing and informed by its symbiotic relationship with the Japanese music industry and its corresponding flow of financial capital. The karaoke box exists because it needs to exist. An empty box, much like the titular *empty orchestra* of karaoke itself, waiting to be filled.

Bibliography

Adams, V., 1996. Karaoke as Modern Lhasa, Tibet: Western Encounters with Cultural Politics. *Cultural Anthropology*, 11 (4), 510–46

ALC Press Inc., n.d. "karaoke ni iku" to "karaoke e iku" wa dō chigau? [How are "karaoke ni iku" and "karaoke e iku" different?]. Available at: https://www.alc.co.jp/jpn/article/faq/03/225.html [Accessed 8 July 2021].

All-Japan Karaoke Industrialist Association, 2017. Ippan shadanhōjin zenkoku karaoke jigyō-sha kyōkai, 2017—Nendo no yūzā ichiba kibo [All-Japan Karaoke Industrialist Association user market size report]. Available at: http://www.karaoke.or.jp/05hakusyo/2018/p4.php [Accessed 8 July 2021].

Beidas, E. and Moul, R. eds., 2019. *Be More Japan: The Art of Japanese Living*. London: DK Eyewitness Travel.

Brown, K., 2015. *Karaoke Idols: Popular Music and the Performance of Identity*. Bristol: Intellect Books.

Craft, L., 2003. Karaoke Versus Keitai. *Japan Inc*. Available at: https://www.japaninc.com/article.php?articleID=1113 [Accessed 8 July 2021].

Chiesa, S. D., 2005. When the Goal is not a Goal: Japanese School Football Players Working Hard at Their Game. In J. Hendry and M. Raveri, eds., *Japan at Play*. Abingdon: Routledge, 186–98.

Drew, R., 2001. *Karaoke Nights: An Ethnographic Rhapsody*. Lanham: Rowman Altamira.

———., 2005. "Once More, with Irony": Karaoke and Social Class. Leisure Studies, 24(4), 371–83.

Hosokawa, S. and Mitsui, T. eds., 1998. *Karaoke around the World: Global Technology, Local Singing*. Abingdon: Routledge.

Kelly, W. H., 1997. *Empty Orchestras: an Anthropological Analysis of Karaoke in Japan*. Doctoral dissertation. University of Oxford.

———., 2005. Training for Leisure: Karaoke and the Seriousness of Play in Japan. In J. Hendry and M. Raveri, eds., *Japan at Play*. Abingdon: Routledge, 152–68.

Leonhard, G. and Kusek, D., 2005. *The Future of Music: Manifesto for the Digital Music Revolution*. Boston: Berklee Press.

Matsumoto, J., 2016. Differences of Characteristics of Music Singing between in usual Karaoke and in Hitokara. *The Journal of the Acoustical Society of America*, 140(4), 3428.

Ogawa, H., 1998. The Effects of Karaoke on Music in Japan. In S. Hosokawa and T. Mitsui, eds., *Karaoke around the World: Global Technology, Local Singing*. Abingdon: Routledge, 45–54.

Raftery, B., 2008. *Don't Stop Believin': How Karaoke Conquered the World and Changed My Life*. Cambridge, MA: Da Capo Press.

Shitamachi, H. R., 2015. A Karaoke Perspective on International Relations. In T.J. Craig, ed., *Japan Pop: Inside the World of Japanese Popular Culture*. Abingdon: Routledge, 101–5.

Sone, Y., 2014. Canted Desire: Otaku Performance in Japanese Popular Culture. *Cultural Studies Review*, 20(2), 196–222.

Stuart, K., 2011. Guitar Hero Axed: Five Reasons Why Music Games are Dying. *The Guardian,* [online] 10 Feb. Available at: https://www.theguardian.com/technology/gamesblog/2011/feb/10/guitar-hero-axed [Accessed 8 July 2021].

Toffler, Alvin., 1980. *The Third Wave*. New York: Bantam Books.

West, M. D., 2005. *Law in Everyday Japan: Sex, Sumo, Suicide, and Statutes*. Chicago: University of Chicago Press.

Wong, D., 2004. *Speak it Louder: Asian Americans Making Music*. Abingdon: Routledge.

Zhou, X. and Tarocco, F., 2013. *Karaoke: The Global Phenomenon*. London: Reaktion Books.

Chapter 17
Studying Digital Media in the Diasporic Transnationalism Context: The Case of International Migrants in Japan

Xinyu Promio Wang

This chapter explores the complexity of migrant communities in Japan through the lens of digital media. It aims to illustrate how migrants' everyday diasporic experiences and their digital media usage are manifested in the Japanese context, so as to explore the intersection of digital connectivity and human mobility. The first section dissects the concept of "migrants in Japan," followed by an introduction to transnationalism as a theoretical toolkit for digital migration studies. This chapter is then concluded by a case study focusing on digital media appropriation among Chinese migrants in Japan, demonstrating migrants' indigenized application of digital media and transnational social engagement.

Introduction

With the rise of digital technologies, the time we are living in is marked by two interlocked phenomena, namely globalization and digitization. Globalization brings an easier means of transport together with evolving and transgressing technologies, leading to the increasing interaction, interpenetration and interdependence of economic, social and political activities across national boundaries. Meanwhile, digitization facilitates these transnational activities. Digital media, such as the internet and internet-based hardware (i.e., computers and smartphones) and software (i.e., social networking services, digital communication technologies and online streaming), have expedited the global process of interconnectivity and digitalized exchange, where flows of ideas and ideologies, languages and cultures contribute to the construction of a borderless world.

The increasingly interconnected and transnational media may also transform the meanings of being mobile and the logic of migration. Although transnational connections have always constituted an intrinsic element of human mobility, the instant communication and constant contact contemporary migrants enjoy differentiate them from their counterparts in other periods of history. Using digital media to mediate texts, images, sounds, discourses and ideologies, migrants today are able to engage in continuous contact with the homeland and at the same time negotiate the local reality in their host society as well as while on the move. In the context where digital media turn mobile individuals into connected dots (Diminescu 2008) that together compose a transnational social formation (Vertovec 1999), digitally connected migrants are no longer just a group of displaced people. Instead, through their development of new modes of social organizations, group actions, as well as collectively interpreted diasporic experiences (Guarnizo and Smith 1998; Wang 2020a), they are now designated as "transnational communities" (Anderson 1983; Retis and Tsagarousianou 2019; Ponzanesi 2020).

This concept of "transnational communities," as Appadurai (1996) argues, is essential to understand the role of digital media and its culture in mediating and facilitating today's complex ethnoscapes, mediascapes, technoscapes, financescapes and ideoscapes. In addition, it also helps scholars to narrate social and political mobilizations among various diasporic groups, particularly in the case of Japan. For instance, in contrast to other popular immigration countries such as the US, Canada and Australia, Japan persistently refuses to identity itself as an immigration country, instead promoting a national identity that emphasizes the myth of ethnic homogeneity and cultural uniqueness (Liu-Farrer 2020). In a society where migrants are institutionally, culturally and socially considered foreign and alien (Liu-Farrer 2020), using "transnational communities" as a framework allows us to understand how migrants negotiate and adjust their self-positioning in the Japanese social context, and produce varying narratives of belonging as a response to their perceived marginality in Japanese society. Indeed, recent research indicates that for many migrant communities in Japan, such as the Chinese and the Brazilian, digital media have become a crucial tool to grapple with the distinction between themselves and an ethnonationalist Japanese society (Retis 2020; Liu-Farrer 2020).

Against this backdrop, this chapter explores the use of digital media among international migrants, particularly Chinese migrants living in Japan. It illustrates migrants' negotiation between themselves and the Japanese social context from a digital and transnational perspective, to explore the intersection of digital connectivity, human mobilities, and social networks (Castells 2010). Before I discuss how and why digital media has emerged as a key space for migrants to interact with both local and global socio-cultural conditions, I first dissect the concept of "migrants in Japan." What are the characteristics and variations among migrant groups in Japan? How is their media usage different from those of local citizens? After providing an overview of the migrant population in Japan, the following section introduces transnationalism as a theoretical toolkit for digital media and migration studies. I then conclude this chapter by sharing some findings from a recent study of digital media appropriation and transnationalism among Chinese migrants in Japan. I offer this case study, a combination of interview records together with complementary survey data, to demonstrate the indigenized application of transnational digital media, and how the interaction between everyday diasporic experiences and digital media usage is manifested in the context of Chinese migrants in Japan.

Understanding migrant populations and their use of digital media in Japan

The first question researchers often need to address when studying migrants' media use is how to do justice to their diversity and complexity. In the case of Japan, at the end of December 2020, statistics indicate that the country was hosting approximately 2.89 million mid- to long-term[1] migrants (including permanent residents and informal migrants) (MOJ 2020). About 76 percent of this culturally and ethnically diversified population was constituted by migrants from China (778,112), Vietnam (448,053), South Korea (426,908), the Philippines (279,660), Brazil (208,538) and Taiwan (55,872). On the one hand, this highly diversified migrant population is attributed to changes in migration policy and economic conditions in both the sending and receiving countries. Le Bail (2013) indicates that Japan's significant migrant population is partially a result of its continuous effort[2] to attract (un)skilled migrant workers as a strategy to overcome labor shortages and increase global competitiveness. On the other hand, Japan's diasporic population profile is also a reflection of socio-cultural factors, subject to migrants' individual manifestations, and has its own historical roots. For example, in terms of the significant presence of Brazilian migrants in Japan, from the existing empirical evidence we understand that many of them are *nikkeijin* (ethnic Japanese), whose origins lie in more than 100 years of Japanese emigration to Brazil (Higuchi 2005). Their "return" to Japan is therefore often perceived as mutually supported by Japan's Immigration Control and Refugee Recognition Act in 1989 (Higuchi 2005),[3] as well as the desire to find their ethnic and cultural roots and the imagination of affinity to Japan manifested by blood ties (Saenz and Murga 2011; Nishida 2018).

Many other diasporic groups in Japan, such as the Korean community, share a similar level of complexity. As the third largest diasporic population in Japan[4] after the Chinese and Vietnamese (MOJ 2020), its complexity is not only represented by its population size, but also by the fact that about two thirds of this community are *zainichi* Koreans—Koreans who came (or were forcibly brought) to Japan before and during World War II as colonial subjects, or their descendants (Mizuno and Mun 2015). Despite the fact that over 80 percent of *zainichi* Koreans were born in Japan and a significantly large proportion of this demographic is constituted by second, third and fourth generations, they remain institutionally and legally categorized as *gaikokujin* (foreigners) (Lee 2012). In this sense, Japan is considered a nation with fourth-generation immigrant issues derived from its exclusivist policies and fantasies of racial homogeneity in dealing with diasporic populations, particularly colonial subjects.

The cases of *nikkei* Brazilians and *zainichi* Koreans reflect the complexity and diversity of diasporic populations in Japan in their aggregate social form. On an individual level, we can also observe migrants' heterogeneity from their personal diasporic experiences, individual predispositions, expectations as well as motivations, which often lead to their diversified migratory patterns as well as post-migration life trajectories. For instance, some ethnographic studies on Chinese migrants in Japan reveal that their imaginations of Japan as a country full of educational and economic opportunities serve as a major pull factor that encourages their China-Japan emigration (Liu-Farrer 2012, 2020). For many of them, this China-Japan movement therefore represents their ideal of success and the hope of achieving a better life (Coates 2019). In contrast to their desired lifestyles, however, the post-migration reality faced by many is employment in the 3K industries. Since the implementation of the foreign technical intern system in 1993, migrant workers have become an indispensable force in Japan's *kiken*, *kitsui* and *kitanai* (dangerous, demanding and dirty) industries, such as agriculture, cattle breeding, textile manufacturing and food processing, and are largely perceived as a source of low-wage labor for unskilled jobs. By the end of 2020, there were 73,000 Chinese technical interns, constituting 9.3 percent of the Chinese population in Japan. The majority work in the 3K industries, facing various forms of social marginalization such as discrimination, language barriers, mental and physical abuses, as well as low-income levels (Ochiai 2010). In this context, some Chinese migrants perceive their diasporic experiences in Japan as a paradoxical sense of simultaneous accomplishment and failure (Ochiai, 488). While their mobility to Japan illustrates the constant effort made to achieve their object of desire, the post-migration reality serves as a reminder that they are still far away from reaching that goal.

Moreover, it is worth mentioning that the construction of national identity in China relies on positioning Japan as the ultimate "other" (He 2013). In this context, Chinese migrants' awareness of the fact that they are living in the land of the ultimate "other" results in diversified diasporic experiences and self-identifications (Wang 2020b). Digital media influence these experiences and self-identifications in a couple of ways. Firstly, empirical evidence indicates that while Chinese migrants can enjoy instant contact with the homeland, this also means that their everyday life experiences are now mutually shaped by a compound set of spatial and social factors in both home and host societies (Coates 2019). Secondly, recent findings reveal that through the current global terrain that populates cross-border flows, Chinese migrants in Japan are capable of domesticating and internalizing the diasporic experiences of fellow overseas Chinese in other regions, which may result in different self-identifications not only between the homeland and the host society, but also in relation to the transnational Chinese community (Wang 2020b).

In this regard, many scholars have been discussing migrants' transnational networks in relation to digital media.[5] For instance, Georgiou (2011) describes contemporary migrants' lives as characterized by "multilocality" and "accessibility." On the one hand, "multilocality" indicates that migrants increasingly find themselves engaging in social lives across national boundaries with the help of digital media, which inextricably locate them in a transnational context (Castles 2017; Vertovec 1999). On the other hand, "accessibility" suggests that migrants' transnational practices are largely actualized by the availability of digital media (Tsagarousianou 2019). Although these studies reflect different digital media and migration studies paradigms depending on the scholarly positions informing them (Candidatu et al. 2019), they commonly conceptualize migration as a dynamic movement and as networked webs of information exchange and knowledge transfer through the lens of digital media (Alonso and Oiarzabal 2010).

However, while we try to understand how digital media provide migrants with a mediated and connected network to re-construct, re-ground and transfer their diasporic experiences (Beck and Cronin 2014), it is equally important to acknowledge that such transnationality is largely subject to digital accessibility. Therefore, the migratory experiences of those who do not have access to digital media, as well as the differences in terms of media practices among different generations and migrant groups should be well recognized (Dhoest et al. 2013). For instance, in the case of Japan, a comparison in terms of the possession rate of smartphones as well as the usage rate of digital media[6] between Japanese citizens and different migrant groups illustrates the importance of avoiding romanticizing and generalizing media usage behavior across generations and populations (MIC 2016). A report released by the Ministry of International Affairs and Communications (2016) indicates that the younger generation (i.e., individuals between 20 and 29) of both migrant groups and Japanese citizens generally share a higher smartphone possession rate and digital media usage frequency. However, compared with Japanese citizens, US and UK migrants, Korean migrants[7] and Mainland Chinese migrants demonstrate a significantly higher dependence on digital media. Specifically, for Korean migrants, the report points out that the highest usage rate of digital media is attributed to migrants aged 30 to 49. For Chinese migrants in Japan, although the 30-49-year-old population cohort has the highest smartphone possession rate, it is only 0.5 percent higher than their younger counterparts (MIC 2016).

Furthermore, by comparing the smartphone possession rate between Japanese citizens and migrant populations, one finds that although all migrant groups demonstrate a significantly higher rate than local citizens, the difference is most visible among older generations. Compared to the fact that only 44.5 percent of Japanese citizens who are aged 50 or above have smartphones, the rate among migrant populations is, on average, 33 percent higher. Moreover, for Korean and Chinese migrants, smartphone possession rates are more than double that of Japanese citizens' (MIC 2016).

These data are indicative of migrants' dependence on distant interaction and sociability through digital connectivity. In addition, the data also imply that, compared to non-migrant populations, migrants most clearly exemplify broader evolutions brought by globalization and digitalization (Appadurai 1996), in the sense that they are globally and transnationally connected through the use of digital media.

As digital media are increasingly embedded within our social infrastructures (Miller and Slater 2003), observing migrants' use of digital media allows us to more clearly understand and conceptualize the role of such media in the processes of human mobility, both in a geographical and social sense. Geographically, migrants' media use exemplifies the way information from the "home" country flows to the "host" country, as well as how this information flow safeguards interpersonal connections, family ties, cultural heritages, social norms and practices transnationally. Various empirical studies (e.g., Adams and Ghose 2003; Pertierra 2012; Sofos and Tsagarousianou 2013) reveal that while information travels across national boundaries through digital media, it also helps with creating transnational networks among individuals, groups and organizations. Such transnational networks in turn serve the diffusion of awareness of better lifestyles, economic gain and wealth, leading to chain migration (Alonso and Oiarzabal 2010). In this way, digital media permits the understanding of migration as a social product—an outcome that reflects the individual, economic and political parameters of both homeland and destination societies (boyd 2010).

Furthermore, some scholars describe migrants' participation in both home and host countries' social, economic and political activities through digital media as a process of "deterritorialization" and "reterritorialization" of the nation (Duara 1993; Dirlik 2004). It is deterritorializing because through digital media, migrants can actively participate in social, economic and political activities of not only their homelands, but also other remote regions (Duara 1993). Therefore, their transnational social practices and engagements challenge the traditional understanding of national boundaries, questioning the self-evidence of the national and the practice of using it as the default basis for migration studies.

Digital media-based transnational networks can also be interpreted as the reterritorialization of a nation. While migrants are able to construct codes of communication and cross boundaries between "us" and "others" that were once defined by static physical demarcations (Diminescu 2008), empirical evidence indicate that migrants' transnational communities are often defined by ethnic boundaries. For instance, in the case of Chinese migrants living in the US and Japan, it has been found that their senses of belonging to the transnational Chinese community are predominantly defined by Mainland Chinese ethnicity, membership to which is not accessible to ethnic others (Dirlik 2004; Wang 2020b). In this context, the transnational community can be perceived as the reconstruction of the ethnic nation on a transnational scale, which Ang (2004) describes as "transnational nationalism."

Although the studies mentioned above focus on different migrant communities and groups, they commonly illustrate that with digital media, migrants' identity and self-identification are not a matter of essence but positioning, constantly changing in correspondence to different contexts and in response to different events (Gillespie 2007, 285). To a certain extent, these works portray digital media as a medium that surpasses the assumed disjuncture between migrants and their homelands, allowing them to renegotiate their identities and senses of belonging. This approach, which emphasizes transnationalism and migrants' transnational networks, has become a substantial body of theoretical consideration and empirical research in the field of media and migrant studies. Transnationalism theories contribute to a shift from a more essentialist notion of homeland, nation, locality, race and ethnicity to a focus on transnationality, imagination, hybridity and heterogeneity that takes shape and is activated through diasporic mobility and connectivity (Tsagarousianou 2019).

Studying digital media and its impact on migrants in Japan

Although studies that focus on the digital media usage among migrants in Japan are not abundant, recent scholarship has begun to illustrate how certain migrant communities (i.e. (*zainichi*) Korean, *nikkei* Brazilian and Mainland Chinese) transfer and reground practices and meanings derived from specific geographical locations and cultural and historical contexts in the host society (Hyun 2011; Retis 2020; Wang 2020b). With an eye to Japan's multiple history- (and exclusivist policy-) derived issues in dealing with its diasporic populations, many of these studies indicate that to a certain extent, migrants' extensive use of digital media can be seen as a reactive outcome to the historical context as well as the liminality they experience in Japanese society. For instance, against the background of Japan's colonization of the Korean Peninsula, which led to the forced migration of more than three million Koreans in the 20th century (Hyun 2011, 33–34), Hyun (2011) explores the media consumption of the Korean diasporic community in Japan, arguing that Korean ethnic media serve a crucial role in unifying those dispersed Korean populations, including Korean migrants, *zainichi* Koreans as well as Chinese Koreans.[8] In this regard, the transnational community for Korean migrants in Japan is similar to its Chinese counterpart, with ethnicity becoming a colloquial referent (Ang 2004) for a collectively interpreted sense of belonging through the use of digital media.

For *nikkei* Brazilians in Japan, Retis (2020) argues that with the rise of digital media, the self-identification of contemporary *nisei* (second generation) and *sansei* (third generation) is largely based on their distinctive cultural identities. Upon their return to Japan, many *nikkei* Brazilians face discrimination due to lack of fluency in spoken Japanese (Watanabe 1995) as well as cultural differences (Tsuda 2004). Empirical evidence indicates that this perceived discrimination in turn leads to a series of reactive initiatives to further broaden the cultural distinction between themselves and the local citizens through the consumption of ethnic media (Retis 2020). In doing so, they can "sustain a cultural continuity and distinct identities while keeping links with what they identify as their original homeland: Brazil" (Retis 2020, 302).

Similarly, Chinese migrants' transnational connectivity is largely actualized through digital media. Digital forms of communication not only allow them to live transnationally, but also to negotiate their senses of belonging transnationally. For instance, through a 4-year ethnographic research project on this diasporic group, I found that digital media played an important role in making sense of their everyday diasporic experiences so they could engage in a constant imagining of being Chinese (Wang 2020b). This not only involves using digital media to maintain social ties with left-behind contacts in the homeland, but also using it to validate their overseas lives, making their diasporic experiences meaningful and referable to their lives and memories pre-migration. For example, some of my interviewees, including those who had become naturalized Japanese citizens, indicated that their daily consumption of ethnic media contents as well as communication with families and friends back in China serve as a self-fulfilment process that enables them to reconfirm their Chinese identity. These activities evoke memories and a sense of familiarity between their life experiences pre-immigration and their ongoing, everyday experiences post-immigration (Wang 2020b). However, it is worth noting that while this "(re)confirmed" Chinese identity represents migrants' desire to remain culturally and socially related to China, it also illustrates their wishes to be de-linked from China politically. For instance, when conflicts occurred between Japan and China, such as the heated territorial dispute over a group of uninhabited islands in the East China Sea,[9] many of my informants elaborated on how they would rely on different information sources, from Mainland China, Japan and other Chinese-speaking regions and countries such as Hong Kong, Taiwan and Singapore, in order to obtain a politically unbiased perspective. For some of my informants, the ability to freely access various information via digital media gives them the opportunity to challenge "historical facts and truth" that are subject to national regime and political ideologies of the Chinese government. Given the fact that information that is considered politically sensitive or subversive to the Chinese Communist Party's ruling regime is often restricted from dissemination within Mainland China (Schneider 2016), many informants perceive their ability to access such information as something that differentiates them from their left-behind counterparts. In this sense, I argue that digital media provide Chinese migrants with not only a transnational public space for them to maintain their cultural identity of being Chinese, but also an alternative for remaking a Chinese identity that may diverge from the Chinese state's political ideologies.

Transnational media practice among Chinese migrants in Japan

In response to the need to address transnationalism among migrants in Japan through the lens of digital media, I now use Chinese migrants as a case study to further elaborate the complex dynamics between digital media practices and their senses of belonging. Factors that contribute to this complexity include the cultural and political relations between Japan and China that are deeply characterized by the wounds of previous wars, especially the Second Sino-Japanese war (1937–1945) (Schneider 2016). They also include the conflict in

Handbook of Japanese Media and Popular Culture in Transition

national identity building strategies between Japan and China—while the Japanese government has repeatedly promoted a national identity that emphasizes historical revisionism and democracy, China constructs itself on the basis of national reinvigoration, socialist values and the resolve to defend its core interests (He 2017). In this context, focusing on Chinese migrants' digital practices in Japan provides us with an entry point to investigate migrants' identity building, their cultural and heritage beliefs, as well as political agency "from below" (Leurs and Smets 2018). This bottom-up approach allows us to observe closely how they are placed in the center of the Sino-Japanese power geometry (Castles 2017), and re-emphasizes the importance of understanding diasporic belonging and identity as something that is actively produced by migrants, instead of merely the product of Japan-China power relations.

The analysis reported in this chapter is based on empirical research, including 415 online surveys and 61 in-depth interviews[10] I conducted with Chinese migrants in Japan between June 2017 to April 2020. The online survey aimed to understand how Chinese migrants consume and appropriate digital media in their diasporic lives, including the forms of digital media they use, usage frequency and with whom they are building connections. The interviews focus on the divergent subjectivities of Chinese migrants' notions of belonging and illustrate digital media's role in shaping these notions and mediating their daily interactions with their homeland and host society. My informants comprised entrepreneurs (13), business investors (7), skilled workers (39) and spouses of Japanese citizens (2). They were recruited according to the following criteria: length of residence in Japan, educational attainment, income and Japanese language skills.[11] These control measures ensured that only the insights from migrants who were economically independent and had stable living conditions in Japan were collected, so the use of digital media was the only prominent variable in the research. Finally, in order to protect my informants' privacy and ensure their anonymity, no identifiable information, such as their real name and residential address, was collected. All names mentioned in this paper are therefore aliases proactively provided by the interviewees.

Digital media as the basis for migrants' social engagement

It is worth mentioning that while no control measures regarding digital media usage behavior (i.e., hours spent on digital media per day) were introduced during the participant recruitment stage of both the qualitative and quantitative researches, all participants indicated that they at least hold one form of digital media device (such as a smartphone, laptop or tablet PC). In fact, the majority (47.3 percent) of online survey participants stated that they have four to five digital media devices, while those who only possess one device for digital media engagement comprised the smallest proportion (9 percent) among the surveyed population. In addition, when participants were asked about hours spent on digital media consumption and its purposes, it is revealed that 36.4 percent of participants (151), the largest group within the dataset, spend on average 2-3 hours per day on digital media. In terms of the purpose of their digital media appropriation, participants reported that they rely on digital media for tasks such as banking and investment related activities (23.5 percent), household maintenance tasks such as paying bills and online shopping (70.4 percent), recreational activities such as watching videos and playing games (44.6 percent), communicating with friends and families (65.6 percent), as well as obtaining news and information (66.3 percent). These descriptive data indicate that divergent forms of digital media serving various purposes have created a comprehensive media environment within which Chinese

migrants are highly engaged. More importantly, the fact that more than 70 percent actively use digital media in their daily household maintenance tasks illustrates that to a certain
degree, digital media has become part of the social infrastructure in Japanese society, and
serves as an important, supportive role to Chinese migrants' diasporic experiences. Indeed,
as 28-year-old entrepreneur Yuxuan explained, "I can definitely feel that the world today is
totally digitalized...I honestly can't imagine how anyone could live without digital media.
That would be so scary as basically you are blind with no source to obtain any information."
It is clear that for migrants such as Yuxuan, making use of and consuming a range of digital
media has become a significant channel to connect to the social environment and carry out
social interactions. In this sense, Chinese migrants' use of digital media is not a peculiarity,
but a fairly common part of a continuous integration and engagement of online and offline
elements in their mediated lives.

Digital media and the negotiated belonging

While Chinese migrants use digital media to sustain their transnational lifestyles in ways
that are similar to other diasporic groups, they more importantly present a paradigmatic
example of how such media may pose a significant influence on migrants' sense of belonging,
which in this case, is still characterized by complex Sino-Japanese dynamics. For instance,
my informant Tangyue, who migrated to Japan in 2011 to pursue higher education, serves
as a good example to illustrate how digital media, together with the conflicts of the national
identity construction strategies between Japan and China, pose an influence on her sense
of belonging. When I interviewed her in 2018, Tangyue stated that with her language skills
in both Japanese and English, her world value and political perspectives had changed drastically during the first few years living in Japan. Because, unlike China, where information
that is considered sensitive or threatening to the Chinese Communist Party's ruling regime
is filtered from its media ecology (Schneider 2018), Japan for her is a "liberal land" (自由的
国度 ziyoude guodu) where she can freely access media content produced by non-Chinese
agents. Tangyue indicates that accessing this information allows her to compare and contrast
how a particular international affair may be narrated differently by different media agents
representing different state ideologies:

> When I read news written by foreign media, sometimes I can't help but wonder
> what the (Chinese Communist) Party is trying to hide from us...I do understand
> that for many international controversies, it is often your words against mine,
> and no states really have a solid and unbiased standpoint...but the fact that
> such information is filtered out in China has made me suspicious of our national
> regimes of truth. (Tangyue 2019)

For Tangyue, transnational media contents not only contribute to the forming of a Chinese subjectivity (Ong and Nonini 1997) that is increasingly independent of the Party-state
agenda and political ideologies, but also provide her with an alternative to Chinese ideals for
remaking her identity. She elaborates that:

> The difference in public opinion between China and Japan shocks me. I remem-
> ber back in 2011 when some Chinese news reported on the Tōhoku earthquake,

I saw so many horrible comments on Weibo [...] like "this is the karma for what they have done to us" [...] and when I finally got the chance to learn how Japanese audiences reacted to our national tragedy, like the 2008 Sichuan earthquake, I was astounded over the empathy expressed by them, and this kind of information is screened out in China [...] Ever since I came here [Japan], I feel they [Japanese] are actually quite friendly to us [Chinese]…contrarily, I feel our public opinions are always driven by hatred towards them and I'm not proud of it. While our government always talks about "remembering the history," I'd rather remember the good part [of the history], like our cultural richness, and get rid of thoughts that always see Japan as an enemy. I mean, it's the year 9102 already.[12] (Tangyue 2019)

From Tangyue's narratives, we can clearly see how media contents help her to navigate between national ideologies promoted by Japan and China respectively. As He (2017) argues, through the constant reminiscence of a particular period of modern Chinese history, the Chinese national identity has become, for the most part, defined by the collective memory of suffering, as well as struggle, in resisting foreign aggressions. In this context, the Second Sino-Japanese War provides the crucial soil for the CCP (Chinese Communist Party) to cultivate its vision of a nationalism that is parallel to the Party-state agenda (He 2017), and Japan has become the ideal object for the CCP to establish the boundary between in- and out-groups (the "us versus them" narratives observed by Callahan (2010)), linking the Chinese national identity with anti-Japanese sentiments. However, it is clear that for Tangyue, access to variant narratives and national ideologies transmitted online, combined with her diasporic experiences, have offered her new ground to (re)negotiate the way she understands her Chinese identity. Consequently, she not only holds a suspicious attitude towards "(the Chinese) national regimes of truth," but also proposes a Chinese identity that is defined by "cultural richness," instead of a politically motivated patriotism that "always see(s) Japan as an enemy."

Similarly, some of the other interviewees, such as 44-year-old Ningjing, a mechanical engineer, point out that emotions and ideologies transmitted through digital media have encouraged him to rethink his Chinese identity:

Last year, when my friends in China asked me what I would do on 13th December,[13] I said I'd go to work just like any other ordinary day…I mean, what would they expect me to say? I know I'm a Chinese living in Japan, but this doesn't mean that my life should be defined by the history…and although I do think what they did in Nanjing is vicious and immoral, when a certain piece of history is constantly used as a political tool, it loses its sentimental value to me. (Ningjing 2019)

Ningjing's statement not only indicates how Chinese migrants in Japan are constantly positioned at the center of the Sino-Japanese power negotiations, but also reveals that China's propaganda strategies may serve as a double-edged sword to the CCP. On the one hand, the question proposed by Ningjing's left-behind friends indicates that such anti-Japanese ideology helps to construct a sense of national unity (Schneider 2018). On the other hand, it is clear that digital media endows Chinese migrants such as Ningjin with opportunities to negotiate the perceived conflict between China's political ideologies and their actual daily experiences in Japan, thereby redefining the meaning of being Chinese in ways that do not necessarily legitimate the ruling regime.

Transnationalism in what sense?

The cases of Tangyue and Ningjing provide us with an insight into how digital media allow Chinese migrants in Japan to renegotiate their self-positioning and identification within the Sino-Japanese dynamics. Throughout the interview, I also found that such media help with the construction of a transnational Chinese community, where Chinese migrants in Japan can internalize and domesticate the narratives of other globally dispersed Chinese communities and make sense of other co-ethnics' experiences of grievance and injustice. For instance, Pingzong, a 29-year-old winemaker who migrated to Japan seven years ago, expressed a feeling of connection with Chinese migrants in remote locations when facing hardships:

> My friends and I started to call Trump and the Hakone restaurant owner[14] "Jian-guo" [literally translates as nation-building] after we came across their hatred of Chinese on WeChat... The harder they discriminate against China and overseas Chinese, the more we will show our solidarity... as this is something we can all relate to as overseas Chinese. This pandemic has made me realize that you can only expect help from your own people. (Pingzong 2020)

During the interviews, many informants resonated with Pingzong and talked about how some recognisable and interchangeable negative diasporic experiences have contributed to a collective interpretation of Chinese identity. For instance, when 33-year-old accountant Hening elaborated on her use of different social media platforms in obtaining first-hand information on the COVID-19 pandemic in Japan, she also expressed sympathy for Chinese migrants living in other territories, such as the United States and Italy:

> I can only imagine how scared and confounded they become when all flights get cancelled, the city is in lockdown, having no access to medical supplies, and are nowhere near their families [...] Because I'm also an overseas Chinese, I know how much our families weigh on our hearts, so I could emphasize with their feelings. (Hening 2020)

The compassion expressed by many interviewees indicates the formation of a collectively interpreted Chinese diasporic identity that is characterized by recognisable and interchangeable experiences of injustice and hardship, as well as traits that reflect Chinese ideologies and virtues, such as family-oriented values. In this way, the membership of this Chinese identity is expanded into a broader, global context that includes not only the homeland and the host society, but also other territories based on the recognition of fellow Chinese communities living further afield.

However, it is also clear that this membership is largely based on, and defined by, Chinese ethnicity. Through the digital mediation of emotions, diasporic experiences and life stories, Chinese migrants in Japan are able to construct an inclusive but equally exclusive sense of transnational connectedness, in a way that focuses less on self-identification based on physical localities and demarcations, but places more emphasis on ethnic boundaries. This finding in turn indicates that we should be aware of the difference between the transnationalism that defines the transnational community (Anderson 1983) and the transnationalism that shapes migrants' transnational consciousness (Castles 2017). With regards to the former, Chinese migrants' transnationalism can be understood as their engagement in a digitally mediated social field that exceeds nation-states and territorial boundaries. Whereas for the latter, it is evident that although the transnational community is characterized by its interconnectivity, "being Chinese" has become the crucial identifiable and connecting quality that enables this connectivity, hence representing a form of revalorization of exclusionary ethnic identity that Ang (2004) describes as "transnational nationalism."

More research needs to be undertaken to clarify to what extent this "transnational nationalism" is representative of diasporic communities. Indeed, some may argue that the way my informants sympathize with their fellow co-ethnics can be seen as exceptional cases as my observations were collected during the global pandemic of COVID-19. However, as I have suggested elsewhere (Wang 2020b), instead of trying to draw definitive conclusions from the above analysis, which may risk glossing over migrant individuals' heterogeneity and the dynamics of a constantly changing social context, it is more important to acknowledge that the self-identification and positioning among Chinese migrants in Japan can indeed be context- or situation-based, and that it is fluid, hybrid and constantly changing direction in a way that suits the unique set of socio-political contingencies they engage with. Furthermore, these findings also conceptually illustrate how power dynamics, connectivity and mobility shape diasporic identity and community formations. Understanding Chinese transnationalism as something that is both inclusive (as it involves multiple territories) and exclusive (in terms of ethnicity) gives us the opportunity to understand how positionalities are created through migrants' engagement with transnationalism and online-offline continuity, hence contributing to the reconceptualization of migration as part of imaginaries on the move (Appadurai 1996).

Conclusion: Some reflections on Chinese migrants' transnationalism and digital practices: Rethinking the role of digital media in diasporic lives in Japan

As the case study on Chinese migrants in Japan has demonstrated, if we are to speak of migrants' self-identification and sense of belonging, it is important to acknowledge this as essentially context- and situation-based, shaped by the intersections of various power negotiations, and under the influence of circulations of identifiable traits and emotions through digital media. On the one hand, for some Chinese migrants, different ideologies transmitted through digital media provide them with alternatives to renegotiate their self-identity. Such identity is in large part culturally defined, characterized by a Chinese subjectivity that is increasingly independent of the party-state agenda, and conscious of the national regimes of truth. On the other hand, it is also clear that while digital media endow Chinese migrants in Japan with a transnational consciousness, such Chinese transnationalism is largely based on an exclusionary Chinese ethnic identity, which calls for caution when we attempt to understand and conceptualize Chinese migrants' transnationalism. In addition, as the discussion detailed above indicates, in order to better understand how migrants position themselves between the homeland, the host society and the transnational community through their daily practices of digital media, it is crucial for researchers to perceive the positioning process as essentially a socio-political one, which involves migrants' constant imagination and reimagination of the nation, and thereby the ongoing negotiation of "who we are" in relation to concurrent cultural, social and political changes. In this sense, through the lens of digital media, we can better understand migrants' sense of belonging as something that is actively constructed and produced by diasporic individuals in accordance with the context they are situated in, instead of as a nostalgic effort to maintain or preserve their identity.

Focusing on diasporic populations enables us to see digital media as fundamentally transnational and capable of transmitting variant cultural, social and political traits, as well as emotions. Digital media allows migrants to become connected with and engaged in a transnational social field, a site where they become aware of fellow migrants' diasporic experiences and are capable of domesticating and internalizing these experiences for the construction of a collectively interpreted identity. In an increasingly globalized world, studying digital media together with migration inspires us to think about how dispersed individuals are turning into transnational actors, and to challenge the conventional state-centered logic that emphasizes national borders and the static geography of the locality.

Notes

[1] See http://www.moj.go.jp/content/001234018.pdf for a definition.

[2] See Hamaguchi (2019) for details.

[3] The 1989 Act opened a side-door to second- and third-generation *nikkeijin* to enter Japan to live and work. See Higuchi (2005) for more details.

[4] The Korean community had been the second largest migrant population in Japan from 2010 until June 2020 (MOJ, 2020). It was the largest migrant population in Japan between 1920 and 2009 (MIC 2010).

[5] For example, see Diminescu (2008), Madianou and Miller (2012), and Retis and Tsagarousianou (2019).

[6] In the source file, digital media consist of 13 categories: social media, net shopping, information search, news, online videos, music and audio, maps and navigation, e-books, online banking, ticket reservations, cloud storage services, social games and online games.

[7] There is no clarification in the source file as to whether *zainichi* Koreans are included in the sample.

[8] Contemporary Chinese Koreans are mainly the offspring of emigrants from the Korean Peninsula to China after the Japan-Korea Annexation Treaty in 1910. From 1910 to 1945, about two million Koreans settled in China, either to escape from Japan's rule or were forcibly brought to China as labor forces due to Japan's occupation of Northeast China and consequently the establishment of Manchukuo in 1931. About half of them repatriated to the Korean Peninsula by 1949 before the establishment of the PRC. Those who remained were later officially recognized as Chinese Koreans (中国朝鲜族 zhongguo chaoxianzu) by the PRC and are categorized as one of the 56 ethnic groups in China. See (Ri, Funahashi and Nitta 2001, 281–84) for details.

[9] This island group is located east of China, west of Okinawa (Japan), northeast of Taiwan, and known as Diaoyu Islands in China, Senkaku Islands in Japan, and Tiaoyutai Islands in Taiwan.

[10] The group comprised 35 women and 26 men, corresponding to the gender ratio of the Chinese migrant populations in Japan (MOJ 2019). 55 out of 61 participants were interviewed in person, and the remaining 6 participants were interviewed during online video calls due to the COVID-19 crisis.

[11] All participants had at least three years of residence in Japan, an educational attainment level of higher education and above, 200,000 JPY monthly income before tax and had passed the highest (N1) level of the Japanese Language Proficiency Test.

[12] 9102 is the year 2019 rendered backwards. This convention was initially introduced by the internet buzzword "7102" in year 2017, and this expression is often used to ridicule or sarcastically comment on conservative and outdated thoughts.

[13] The anniversary of the Nanjing-Massacre, a national memorial day in China.

[14] Pingzong was referring to an incident on 21st January 2020, when a dessert shop owner in Hakone city posted a statement announcing that "Chinese are corona virus and are not allowed to enter this shop. This statement does not apply to Taiwanese from the Republic of China," which caused outrage on China's social media sites such as Weibo and WeChat.

Bibliography

Adams, P. and Ghose, R., 2003. India.com: The Construction of a Space Between. *Progress in Human Geography*, 27(4), 414–37.

Alonso, A. and Oiarzabal, P., 2010. The Immigrant Worlds' Digital Harbors: An Introduction. In A. Alonso and P. Oiarzabal, eds., *Diasporas in the New Media Age: Identity, Politics, and Community*. Reno: University of Nevada Press, 1–18.

Anderson, B., 1983. *Imagined Communities: Reflections on the Origin*. London: Verso.

Ang, I., 2004. Beyond Transnational Nationalism: Questioning the Borders of the Chinese Diaspora in the Global City. In K. Willis and B. Yeoh, eds., *State/Nation/Transnation: Perspectives on Transnationalism in the Asia-Pacific*. London: Routledge, 179–98.

Appadurai, A., 1996. *Modernity at Large Cultural Dimensions of Globalization*. Minneapolis: University of Minnesota Press.

Beck, U. and Cronin, C., 2014. *Cosmopolitan Vision*. Oxford: Wiley.

boyd, d., 2010. Social Network Sites as Networked Publics: Affordances, Dynamics, and Implications. In Z. Papacharissi, ed., *Networked Self: Identity, Community, and Culture on Social Network Sites*. London: Routledge, 39–58.

Callahan, W., 2010. *China: The Pessoptimist Nation*. Oxford: Oxford University Press.

Candidatu, L., Leurs, K. and Ponzanesi, S., 2019. Digital Diasporas: Beyond the Buzzword: Toward a Relational Understanding of Mobility and Connectivity. In J. Retisand R. Tsagarousianou, eds., *The Handbook of Diasporas, Media, and Culture*. New Jersey: John Wiley & Sons, 31–47.

Castles, S., 2017. Transnational Communities: A New Form of Social Relations under Conditions of Globalization? In S. Castles, ed., *Migration, Citizenship and Identity: Selected Essays*. Cheltenham: Edward Elgar Publishing, 335–51.

Castells, M., 2010. *The Rise of the Network Society*. Chichester: Wiley-Blackwell.

Coates, J., 2019. The Cruel Optimism of Mobility: Aspiration, Belonging, and the "Good Life" among Transnational Chinese Migrants in Tokyo. *positions: asia critique*, 27(3), 469–97.

Dhoest, A., Nikunen, K. and Cola, M., 2013. Exploring Media Use among Migrant Families in Europe: Theoretical Foundations and Reflections. *Observatorio*, [online] (Special issue: Introducing Media, Technology and the Migrant Family: Media Uses, Appropriations and Articulations in a Culturally Diverse Europe). Available at: http://obs.obercom.pt/index.php/obs/article/view/663 [Accessed 29 May 2020].

Diminescu, D., 2008. The Connected Migrant: An Epistemological Manifesto. *Social Science Information*, 47(4), 565–79.

Dirlik, A., 2004. Intimate Others: [Private] Nations and Diasporas in An Age of Globalization. *Inter–Asia Cultural Studies*, 5(3), 491–502.

Duara, P., 1993. De-Constructing the Chinese Nation. *The Australian Journal of Chinese Affairs*, 30, 1–26.

Georgiou, M., 2011. Diaspora, Mediated Communication and Space. In M. Christensen, A. Jansson and C. Christensen, eds., *Online Territories: Globalization, Mediated Practice and Social Space*. New York: Peter Lang, 205–21.

Gillespie, M., 2007. Security, Media and Multicultural Citizenship. *European Journal of Cultural Studies*, 10(3), 275–93.

Guarnizo, L. and Smith, M., 1998. *Transnationalism from Below*. New Brunswick, N.J.: Transaction Publishers.

Gubrium, A. and Harper, K., 2013. *Participatory Visual and Digital Methods*. Walnut Creek, CA: Left Coast Press.

He, Y., 2013. Forty Years in Paradox: Post-Normalisation Sino-Japanese Relations. *China Perspectives*, 2013(4), 7–16.

———., 2017. The Impact of Chinese National Identity on Sino-Japanese Relations. In G. Rozman, ed., *Joint U.S.-Korea Academic Studies*. [online] Washington: Korea Economic Institute of America, 81–94.

Available at: http://www.keia.org/publication/impact-chinese-national-identity-sino-japanese-relations [Accessed 30 March 2020].

Higuchi, N., 2005. Brazilian Migration to Japan Trends, Modalities and Impact. In *Expert Group Meeting on International Migration and Development in Latin America and the Caribbean*. [online] Mexico City: Department of Economic and Social Affairs, 1–28. Available at: https://www.un.org/en/development/desa /population/events/pdf/expert/10/P11_Higuchi.pdf [Accessed 29 May 2020].

Hyun, M., 2011. Korian nettowaku kara miru diasupora media kenkyū no chihei [The horizons of diasporic media from the viewpoint of the Korean network]. *Journal of Mass Communication Studies*, 79, 27–44.

Le Bail, H., 2013. Skilled and Unskilled Chinese Migrants in Japan: Context and Perspectives. *Les cahiers d'Ebisu. Occasional Papers* No. 3. [online] French Research Institute on Japan, 3–40. Available at: https:// www.mfj.gr.jp/publications/_data/e-CahiersEbisu3_pp03-40_LeBail_screen.pdf [Accessed 6 June 2020].

Lee, S., 2012. *Diversity of Zainichi Koreans and Their Ties to Japan and Korea*. Shiga: Afrasian Research Centre, Ryukoku University.

Leurs, K. and Smets, K., 2018. Five Questions for Digital Migration Studies: Learning from Digital Connectivity and Forced Migration in(to) Europe. *Social Media + Society*, 4(1), 1–16.

Liu-Farrer, G., 2012. Becoming New Overseas Chinese: Transnational Practices and Identity Construction among the Chinese Migrants in Japan. In C. Plüss and K.-B. Chan, eds., *Living Intersections: Transnational Migrant Identifications in Asia. International Perspectives on Migration*. Dordrecht: Springer, 167–90.

———., 2020. *Immigrant Japan: Mobility and Belonging in an Ethno-nationalist Society*. Ithaca: Cornell University Press.

Madianou, M. and Miller, D., 2012. Polymedia: Towards a new Theory of Digital Media in Interpersonal Communication. *International Journal of Cultural Studies*, 16(2), 169–87.

MIC, 2010. *Heisei 22 nen kokuseichōsa—dai 16 sho gaikokujin jinko* [2010 Population census—chapter 16: foreign populations]. [online] MIC (Ministry of Internal Affairs and Communications). Available at: https://www.stat.go.jp/data/kokusei/2010/final/pdf/01-16.pdf [Accessed 28 August 2021].

———., 2016. *Heisei 28 nen ban jōhō tsūshin hakusho* [2016 White paper on information and communications]. [online] MIC (Ministry of Internal Affairs and Communications). Available at: https://www .soumu.go.jp/johotsusintokei/whitepaper/ja/h28/pdf/index.html [Accessed 28 August 2021].

Miller, D. and Slater, D., 2003. *The Internet: An Ethnographic Approach*. Oxford: Berg.

Mizuno, N. and Mun, K., 2015. *Zainichi chōsenjin—rekishi to genzai* [Zainichi Korean—history and today]. Tokyo: Iwanami Shoten.

MOJ, 2019. *Heisei 30 nenmatsu genzaini okeru zairyū gaigoku ninsu nitsuite* [Regarding the size of the foreign population in Japan by the end of the year 2018]. Tokyo: MOJ (Ministry of Justice).

———., 2020. *Zairyū gaikokujin tōkei 2020 nen 12 gatsu matsu* [Statistics on foreign residents as of December 2020]. [online] MOJ (Ministry of Justice). Available at: https://www.e-stat.go.jp/stat-search /files?page=1&layout=datalist&toukei=00250012&tstat=000001018034&cycle=1&year=20200&month =24101212&tclass1=000001060399 [Accessed 28 August 2021].

Nishida, M., 2018. *Diaspora and Identity: Japanese Brazilians in Brazil and Japan*. Honolulu: University of Hawai'i Press.

Ochiai, M., 2010. Life and Consciousness of Foreign Trainees and Technical Interns: A Narrative. *Journal of Center for Education and Research, Gunma University* 9, 51–68.

Ong, A. and Nonini, D., 1997. *Ungrounded Empires: The Cultural Politics of Modern Chinese Transnationalism*. London: Routledge.

Pertierra, R., 2012. Diasporas, the New Media and the Globalized Homeland. In L. Fortunati, R. Pertierra and J. Vincent, eds., *Migration, Diaspora and Information Technology in Global Societies*. London: Routledge, 154–73.

Ponzanesi, S., 2020. Digital Diasporas: Postcoloniality, Media and Affect. *interventions*, 22(8), 977–93.

Retis, J., 2020. Migrations and the Media between Asia and Latin America: Japanese-Brazilians in Tokyo and São Paulo. In K. Smets, K. Leurs, M. Georgiou, S. Witteborn and R. Gajjala, eds., *The Sage Handbook of Media and Migration*. London: Sage Publications, 209–308.

Retis, J. and Tsagarousianou, R., 2019. *The Handbook of Diasporas, Media, and Culture*. Hoboken: John Wiley & Sons.

Ri, S., Funahashi, K. and Nitta, M. 2001. Ethnicity and Order: The Korean-Chinese Community in China and its Changing Identity. *Journal of the Socio-Cultural Research Institute, Ryukoku University: Society and Culture* 3 (2001), 271–88.

Saenz, R. and Murga, A., 2011. *Latino Issues: A Reference Handbook*. Santa Barbara, CA: ABC-CLIO.

Schneider, F., 2016. China's "Info-web": How Beijing Governs Online Political Communication about Japan. *New Media & Society*, 18(11), 2664–84.

———., 2018. *China's Digital Nationalism*. New York: Oxford University Press.

Sofos, S. and Tsagarousianou, R., 2013. *Islam in Europe; Public Spaces and Civic Networks*. Basingstoke, UK: Palgrave Macmillan.

Tsagarousianou, R., 2019. Beyond the Concept of Diaspora? Re-evaluating Our Theoretical Toolkit through the Study of Muslim Transnationalism. In J. Retis and R. Tsagarousianou, eds., *The Handbook of Diasporas, Media and Culture*. Hoboken: Wiley-Blackwell, 77–96.

Tsuda, T., 2004. *Media Images, Immigrant Reality: Ethnic Prejudice and Tradition in Japanese Media Representations of Japanese-Brazilian Return Migrants*. Working Paper 107. San Diego: University of California.

Vertovec, S., 1999. Conceiving and Researching Transnationalism. *Ethnic and Racial Studies*, 22(2), 447–62.

Wang, X., 2020a. *Chinese Migrants' Sense of Belonging in Japan: Between Digital and Physical Spaces*. Migration Research Series No. 61. [online] Geneva: International Organization for Migration, 1–13. Available at: https://publications.iom.int/system/files/pdf/mrs-61.pdf [Accessed 16 January 2021].

———., 2020b. Digital Technology, Physical Space and the Notion of Belonging among Chinese Migrants in Japan. *Asiascape: Digital Asia*, 7 (2020), 211–33.

Watanabe, M., 1995. *Dekasegi nikkei burajirujin—shūrō to seikatsu* [Dekasegi Brazilians—work and life in Japan]. Tokyo: Akashi Shoten.

Index

#

8/12 *Renrakukai*, 23
37 sekanzu (37 Seconds), xxiii, 172, 173, 179–83

A

Abarenbō (Roughneck) series, 66, 72
advertising: and models of gender, 187; and
    referent systems, 194; context and practice,
    187; discourse, 187; *Dō iu wake ka*—Kirin
    Beer, 190; expenditure, 187; exposure to,
    218; gendering role of beer, 188; *kōkoku
    kiji*, 205, 208; *Otoko-wa damatte...* Sapporo
    Beer campaign, 186–97 passim; reach and
    influence, 187
Ainu, 68, 69, 71
Akagi Keiichirō, xix, 65, 66, 67, 72, 73
*Akagi Keiichirō wa ikite iru gekiryū ni ikiru otoko
    (Akagi Keiichirō is Alive: A Torrent of Life)*, 66
Akai kōya (The Crimson Plains), 71
Akai yūhi no wataridori (Rambler in the Sunset),
    69
Akasen kichi (Red Light Bases), 48–60 passim
Akmareul boatda (I Saw the Devil), 93
Akutagawa Ryūnosuke, 158
All-Japan Karaoke Industrialist Association, 240
All You Need Is Kill, 129
Ama-chan, 33–34, 143, 144, 145, 146
American Idol, 238
American Occupation, xviii, xix, xxv, 8, 47,
    48–49, 55, 56, 58, 60, 66, 220–22, 227, 228,
    230
An An, 206
anzen shinwa (myth of safety), 36
aragoto, 125, 137
*Arashi o yobu yūjō (The Friendship that Started
    a Storm)*, 72

asadora (morning serial drama): and contents
    tourism, 144, 145; and disabilities, 149–50;
    and diversity, 144–45, 147, 150; and "female
    orientation", 142; and LGBTQ, 149–50; and
    local/regional identity, xxii, 141, 143–45; and
    place branding, 145; and "real Japan", xxii,
    144; and social media, 143; and the "triple
    disaster", 145–46; as "secular morning ritual",
    143; as institution of collective memory,
    141; as national drama, 140–41; effects of
    COVID-19 pandemic, 141, 146; fans of, 142–
    43; plot lines, 141–42; portrayal of resident
    Korean minority, 148
Asahi Beer, 191
Asahi no ataru ie (House of (the) Rising Sun),
    40–41, 42
audience(s): and censorship/media-shaping
    policies, xxiv, 218, 220, 221–22; and
    memories, xxv, 221, 225, 227; and scholarship,
    217; as fans, 223–24; as indicative of historical
    periods, 218; as indicators of consumption,
    xxiv, 218; characteristics of, 219; experiences
    and attitudes of, 226; gender and age profiles,
    xxv, 227–28; in studies of society, 220;
    replaced by *tarento*, 7; studies, 217–21, 223,
    225, 227, 228
authenticity, xvi, xxv, 22, 23, 144, 179, 237–38

B

*Baribara~Shōgaisha jōhō baraetii~ (Barrier-Free
    Variety Show)*, 177
Beautiful Life, 149
Beruseruku (Berserk), 126, 129, 132
BiDaN, xxiv, 207–211
Blackboard Jungle, 72
*Boksuneun naui geot (Sympathy for Mr.
    Vengeance)*, 93

Buhwal (Resurrection), 93

C

Cameron, James, 19
censorship, xvi, xxvii, xix, xxv, 48, 49, 91, 203, 218, 220, 221–22, 228; self-, xxvii, 8, 9, 13
Chibi Maruko-chan, 116, 120
children/mixed-race children 34, 37, 38, 41, 49, 51, 52, 58–59, 94, 97, 108–9, 172, 175, 191, 203, 222
Chinjeolhan geumjassi (Lady Vengeance), 93
Chūō kōron, 204
Cold War, 48, 62, 70, 71, 73, 74
Conde, David, 220, 222, 229
constraint: and heteronormative roles, 183; and masculinity, 191, 211; and performativity of gender, 180; and progression to violence and freedom, 162, 168; and women and minorities, xxii, 160–62; as literary theme, xxii; as marginalization, 162; at home, 160–61; dualism with freedom, 164, 165, 166, 173; in feminist Japanese popular fiction, 159; in Japanese society, 160–61, 166; male/female hierarchy, 160, 163, 166–67; passivity/violence, 160, 162, 163; psychological constraint, 161
contact zones: and base towns, 60; and gender politics, 59; definition of, 47; female body as, 55–56
Cool Japan, 159, 169n5
COVID-19, xxi, xxii, 124, 135, 141, 146, 151, 171, 254, 255

D

Daiei (film studio): and films aimed at teenagers, 63–64
Daisōgen no wataridori (Plains Wanderer), 68, 69, 70, 71
Daiyaru 110 ban (Dial Number 110), 71
dankai no sedai (baby boom generation), 63
dekadan no seishun (decadent youth), 64
Demon Slayer: Kimetsu no Yaiba, 118–19, 127
"Diamond Line", 65, 66, 67
disability: and 2020 (2021) Olympics/ Paralympics, 171; and the "ableist gaze", 175–76; and the feminist approach, xxiii, 172–73; and gender, sexuality and

reproductive rights, 171–75; and "innocent" stereotype, 174, 175, 181, 182; and "inspiration porn", 177; and intersectionality, 173, 175, 180; and Kumashino Yoshihiko, 174, 177, 179, 180; and sex education, 174; and sexual services for disabled, 174–75; Eugenic Protection Law and sterilization, 173–74; in morning dramas, 149–50; Japanese attitudes towards, 171; media representations of, 173, 175–83 passim; medical model vs. social model, 171; stigmatized in Japan, 171; visible and invisible, 178
disasters: and harmful/false rumors, 37, 41; and radiation, xviii, 35–39, 41, 42, 174; and myth of safety, 36; and trauma, xxi, 24, 25, 28, 32–35, 42; dread/threat, 20, 24–25, 127; earthquake, 32–42 passim, 108, 127 films about, (see "disaster films/television shows"); flood, 32; Fukushima, 32–42 passim; Great East Japan Earthquake/"triple disaster", (see "Great East Japan Earthquake"); nuclear, (see "nuclear power"); plane crash, 17–30 passim; survivor guilt, 33, 34, 35, 38, 42, 125, 133; television shows about, (see "disaster films/ television shows"); tsunami, xviii, 32–35, 39, 127
disaster films/television shows: and contemporary significance, 28; and dominance of male characters, 25; and focus on families, 25–26; and "hooks", 19–20, 23–25, 27; and reality, 19; and "suspension of disbelief", 19, 22; and the Tōhoku "triple disaster", 32; indirect representations, xviii, 33
diversity: and 2020 (2021) Tokyo Olympics/ Paralympics, 149–50, 171; and disability, 171; and the media, xv; and migrants, 246; and nation branding, 150; attitudes towards, 37; "cosmetic" 141, 147, 150 in *asadora*, 146; in Japanese society, 73, 141, 145; regional, xxii
Dondo hare (Happily Ever After), 148
Doragon bōru (Dragon Ball), 125

E

echo chamber, 21
Eden-ui dong-jjok (East of Eden), 93
enka (Japanese ballad), 72, 73
Ergo Proxy, 126, 129, 132

Ēru (Yell), 141, 142, 145–46, 151
ethnic/ethnicity, xix, xxii, xxvi, 71, 73, 147–48, 157, 159, 162, 163, 245–46, 249, 250, 254–55
ethno-history/ethnography, 218, 221, 222, 223, 224, 225, 226, 227

F

fake news, 17
fan(s), 73, 91–92, 93, 107–112 passim, 114, 119, 120, 121, 142–43, 158, 221, 223, 224, 225
feminine/femininity: and advertising, 187, 188, 189, 190, 192, 196; and constraint/violence, 160, 161, 162, 163; and disability, xxiii, 175; and Japanese women, 180, 181, 182; and women's magazines, 203–204, 210; contrasted with masculine/masculinity, 210–211; representation of women, 49–56 passim, 59; role in advertizing, 188; stereotype of, 182
feminism/feminist: film studies, 176; lens, 172–73, 183
film/film industry: and demographic factors, 63; and importance of Toei, 83; and Japanese aesthetic, 62; and the "kimono effect", 63; and transcultural interactions, 63, 68; and youth cinema, 63, 66; culture, 62, 68; decline in audience numbers, 78, 79, 89; First Diamond Line, 64; increase in number of films in color, 80–81; *jidaigeki*, 4, 10, 13, 62–63, 67, 68, 194; *matatabi mono*, 68–69; movies for TV from film studios, 84–85; New Diamond Line, 67; six major studios, 79; technological improvements in, 80
Fistful of Dollars, A, 67
freedom: and images of masculinity, 193; and imagination/creativity, 182; and progression from constraint and violence, 162, 168; and women and minorities, xxii; as presented by *taiyōzoku* characters, 64; economic, 165; death, the ultimate freedom, 165; dualism with constraint, xxii, 160, 164, 165, 166, 173; in feminist Japanese popular fiction, 159; individual, 66; of choice, 202, 239
Fujin sekai (Women's World), 203
Furagāru to inu no Choko (The Hula Girl and Dog Choko), 36–38, 42

G

Gaewa neukdaeui Sigan (Time between Dog and Wolf), 93
Galapagos effect, 21
Gegege no nyōbō (My Husband is a Cartoonist), 142, 143
gendaigeki (contemporary dramas), 63
gender, 150, 159–64, 166, 168; and advertising, 187; and audience, 223, 227–28; and language, 191; boundaries, 192; inequality, 157, 159–62; performance of, 161–62, 180–83, 188
Ginza senpūji (Ginza Whirling Boy) series, 66, 72
Girl Can't Help It, The, 72
Gitā o motta wataridori (The Rambling Guitarist), 72
Godzilla, 17
Gonda Yasunosuke, 219, 220, 229
Gonenme no hitori (Alone for Five Years), 34–35
Great East Japan Earthquake ("triple disaster"): 32–42 passim, 168, 252–53; and survivor guilt, xviii, 33, 34–35, 38; and TV dramas and films, xviii, 32, 38
Guitar Hero, 241
Gundam (see *Kidō senshi gundam*)
Gyakkōsen (Backlight), 64

H

Hallyu/kanryū, 91, 148
Hanazakari no kimitachi e (Hana Kimi), 96
Hanbun, aoi (Half Blue Sky), 34, 143, 144, 149
Harada Masato, 18, 21.
Hayauchi yarō (Quick Draw Joe), 71
Heibon panchi (Ordinary Punch), 204
Hell in the Pacific, 196
High culture/Low culture, xiii
Higurashi (Higurashi When They Cry), 132, 133
Hikari, 172, 179, 180, 182
Hiroshima (atomic bombing), 6, 19, 38, 39, 173
Hiroshima Shōwa 20-nen 8-gatsu 6-ka (Hiroshima 6 August 1945), 11
Hiruko (Shinto legend), 173
Hiyokko (Bloom), 145

I

intersections/interectional/intersectionality, xiv,
 xvi, xxiii, xxvi, 56, 162, 171, 173, 180, 183, 244,
 245, 255
Ishihara Shintarō, 64
Ishihara Yūjirō, xix, 64, 65, 66, 71–72, 73, 193
Ishihara Yūjirō Hour, 71
isho (notes), 25, 26, 27–28
Itō Yuna, 73
Iwahashi Kunie, 64

J

Japanese Western films, xix; and Ainu culture,
 68, 69; and direct cultural affiliation to
 the US, 67; and Kurosawa Akira, 68; in
 Hokkaido, 68; Kobayashi Akira as "lonely
 wanderer", 67
Jazu musume tanjō (Birth of a Jazz Girl), 71
JL123 crash (JAL123): and on-screen portrayals,
 17, 20–30 passim
Josei sebun (Josei Seven): and "rules" for karaoke,
 233
jūdai (teenagers), 63
Jūdai no hankō (Teenage Crime), 63
Jūdai no himitsu (Teenage Secret), 63
Jūdai no seiten (Teen Sex Manual), 63
Jūdai no yūwaku (Teenage Seduction), 63
jun bungaku (literary fiction), xxii, 158, 159
Jun to Ai (Jun and Ai), 145
Junjō gurentai (Innocent Fools), 72

K

*Kaikyō o koetekita otoko (The Boy who Crossed
 the Strait),* 71
karaoke: and identity, 235, 237–38; and
 technology, xxv, 240–41; and user
 experiences, xxv, 236–37; as "short-lived
 fantasy", xxv, 235–36; as "social lubricant",
 xxv, 232; economic impact of, 239–40;
 hitokara, 232; *honne/tatemae,* 238, 239;
 importance of "skill" and "practice", 232–34;
 importance of "taking part", 234; irony vs.
 authenticity, 237–38; *jūhachiban,* 232; karaoke
 2.0, xxv, 241; "karaoke-*dō*", 238; the karaoke
 box, 239; transposing from local to national,
 xxv, 235
Kareshi kanojo no jijō (Kare Kano), 128
Kaseifu no Mita (I'm Mita, Your Housekeeper), 33
Kawachi Tamio, 66
Kawakami Hiromi, 168
Kayama Mei, 179, 182
kayōkyoku (Japanese pop music), 71
Kazamidori (The Weather Vane), 147
keitai shōsetsu (cell phone novels), xv, 158
Kenjū buraichō (Tales of a Gunslinger), 66, 72
Kibō no kuni (The Land of Hope), 39–40, 41, 42
Kidō senshi gundam (Mobile Suit Gundam), 110,
 134
Kimi no na wa (What is Your Name?) 58–59
Kirin Beer: and "*Dō iu wake ka*—Kirin Beer", 190
Kiruto no ie (House of Quilt), 34
Kishi Nobusuke, 70
Kishida Kyōko, 190, 192
*Kizuna. Hashire, kiseki no kouma (Bonds. Run,
 Miraculous Foal),* 35
Kobayashi Akira, xix, 65, 66, 67, 68–69, 71
*Koina no Ginpei: Yuki no wataridori (Koina no
 Ginpei: Migratory Snowbird),* 68
Kokumin no tomo (The Nation's Friend), 204
Konbini ningen (Convenience Store Woman) 168
kōreikashakai (aging society), 157
Kozō series, 67, 72
Kumashino, Yoshihiko, 174, 177, 179, 180; and
 NPO Noir, 174
Kuraimāzu hai (Climber's High, book), 18
Kuraimāzu hai (Climber's High, film, 2008),
 17–18, 21–29
Kuraimāzu hai (Climber's High, NHK, 2005), 17,
 21–29
Kureyon Shinchan (Crayon Shin-chan), 119
Kuroi kiri no machi (Black Fog Town), 72
Kurosawa Akira, 62, 63, 68, 186
Kurozuka, 129
Kurutta kajitsu (Crazed Fruit), 64, 65, 72
Kyō kagiri no koi (Only Today's Love), 72

L

Laplace's demon, 129
LGBTQ, 149–50, 158
Lily Franky, 174, 178, 179
Love Me Tender, 72

M

magazines: and fashion and beauty, xxiv, 206, 207–8; and market genderization, xxiv, 203–4; content shift, 206; content specialization, 203, 205; for men/men's lifestyle, 204–7; history of, in Japan, 202–3; readership and content, xxiv, 202

Mahō shōjo Madoka Magika (Puella Magi Madoka Magica) 125, 128, 132, 133

Man in the High Castle, The, 13

Manpuku (Full of Happiness), 148

Mao (The Devil) 92, 93, 95–102 passim

Mare, 144, 145

masculinity: and *bushidō*/militarism, 55, 195–96; and contemporary lifestyle magazines, xxiv, 206; and disability, 176; and fashion and beauty, xxiv, 207–9; and heavy drinking, 188, 193; and historical and cultural messaging, xxiii, 188–90, 194; and marriage, 191; and "men are silent" campaign, xxiii, 186, 188–89; and patriarchy, 56; and "the salaryman", xxiv, 191, 193; as hybrid, xxiv, 210–11; associated with spaces, 189, 193; competing models of, 190–92; gender norms challenged, 192, 194, 201; hegemonic, xxiv, 192–94, 197, 206, 207, 208, 210, 211; herbivore men (*sōshokukei danshi*), 189; hypermasculity, xxiii, xxiv, 186, 190–94, 197; loss of, 55 notions questioned, xxiv, 207; *otokorashii,* 191; postwar, xix; prewar stereotypes, 57; rural, 193; threatened, 57; uncertainty of identity, 56; vicarious, 194

Massan, 147–48

Mawang (The Devil), 92, 93, 95–102 passim

media: and Abe Shinzō as revisionist, 6; and censorship/media-shaping policies, 218; and historical accuracy, 5; and historical narrative, 18–19; and ideology, 218; and interconnectivity, 4, 109, 158, 244, 255; and WWII, 5–6; as shaped by politics, xvii, 4; definition of, xv; digital, xv, xvi, xvii, xxv–xxvi, 118, 140, 143, 159, 217, 244–56 passim; ethnic, 249–50 ; formats, 158–59; in context and environment, xvi; media mix, see "media mix"; transnational transmediality, 62, 71–72, 90, 101

media mix, xx–xxi, 107; and convergence theory, 108; and fan production, 120; and Kadokawa

Film(s), 115; and *keiretsu* practices, 116; and licensing, 117; and *moe,* 111, 118, 121; and *moe*-element database, 111–12; and "multiple worlds", 120; and *"otaku"*, 110–11, 112; and storyworlds, 107, 120; and the video game industry, 117–18; anime as core medium, 113; centrality of industry, 114; definition of, 109; franchising, 107, 117, 119; Fuji Sankei Group, 116–17; history of, in Japan, 114–15; kinds/types/forms of, 118; merchandising, 110; postwar marketing, 114; produccers and consumers, 108; transmedia storytelling, 107, 110, 117, 119

Mekishiko mushuku (Mexico Wanderer), 71

Men's Club, 205

MEN'S NON-NO, 205, 206

Mifune Toshirō, 186–97 passim;

migrants: and digital media, xxv, 244; and ethnic/racial homogeneity, 245, 246; and globalization, 244; and identity, 249–50, 254; and "negotiated belonging", 252–53; and smartphone possession, 248; and social engagement, 251; and transnational communities, xxv, 244–45, 254–55 Chinese, 244–56 passim; diversity and complexity, 246–47; home and host countries, 247, 248; in the Japanese social context, 245; multilocality and accessibility, 247

Miseu Ripeuli (Miss Ripley), 93

Misora Hibari shō (Misora Hibari Show), 71

Miyajima Ken, 22, 23, 26

Mizuhara Kiko, 73

motherhood: representations of, 49, 51, 55, 59, 181

Motoya Yukiko, 168

Mt. Fuji, 23, 50, 60 as national allegory 58

Mugon no rantō (The Silent Drunkard), 66

mukokuseki ("no nationality") films, xix; and Cold War context, 69; hybrid fashion, 65; Japanese Westerns as, 67; Nikkatsu action/action films without nationality, 64

Murakami Haruki, xxii, 158

Murata Sayaka, 168

N

Nagaremono (Drifter) series, 66

Nakajima Ryōko, 175

Nakaya Noboru, 190, 192, 198
Namja iyagi (A Man's Story), 93
Nanao Special School Incident, 174
Nangoku tosa o ato ni shite (Leaving Tosa of the South), 66
Naruto, 125
Negishi Akemi, 52–53
NHK, xxi, 4, 8, 9, 10, 17, 21, 22, 23, 25, 27, 28, 33, 34, 35, 71, 72, 140–51 passim, 177
Night To Remember, A, 19
nihilistamina stories: and despondency, 129; and "*minna!*" moments, 132; and reluctant heroism, 125; definition of, xxi; distinguishing features, 126; hero/heroine, xvi, xxi, 125–35 passim; importance of the "Imaginary", 130; motivation and sacrifice, 130; nihilism, xxi, 125; responsibility, 130–31; *shōnen/shōjo* protagonist, 124–25; stamina, 126; survivor guilt, 125, 133; trauma, 125–129
Nikkatsu (film studio), xix, 63; and foreign film distribution, 65; and "youth star system", 65; "sun tribe" (*taiyōzoku*) films, 64
Nikkatsu akushon (Nikkatsu action), see *mukokuseki* ("no nationality") films
nikkei/nikkeijin, 147, 246, 249
Nisshoku no natsu (Summer in Eclipse), 64
Nodo jiman ("proud of my voice"), 238
NON-NO, 205, 206
Nora inu (Stray Dog), 194
nuclear power: and accidents/disasters, xviii, 32–42 passim, 108, 127, 146; and anti-nuclear activism, xviii, 40–41, 42; and media portrayals, xviii, 32–42 passim; bombs, 6–7
Nukiuchi no Ryū (Ryūji the Gunslinger), 66, 72

O

Odoru daisōsasen (Bayside Shakedown), 116–17
Ohanahan, 142
Okaeri Mone (Welcome Back, Mone), 146
Oldeuboi (Oldboy), 93
Olympics/Paralympics (Tokyo 2020), 149–50, 171, 177
One no kanata ni (Inseparable Souls: Father, Sons and the Crash of JAL123/Beyond the Ridge), 18, 21–29
One Piece, 116, 117, 125
Onna o wasurero (Forget about Women), 72

Orange Days, 149
Oshii Mamoru, 129
Oshin, 142
Osutakayama/Osutaka/Osutaka-no-One, 20–21

P

panpan: and English names, 52; and local communities, 52; and womanhood and sexuality, xviii; as "butterfly", 55, 59; as intermediary, xviii, 48; as "only", 53, 59; as "other", 49; as sexual contact zone, 48; definition of, 48; number of, 51
Pāfekuto reboryūshon (Perfect Revolution), xxiii, 173, 174, 177–79, 180
Pāfekuto wārudo (Perfect World), xxiii, 173, 176, 180
Pokémon, xv, 108, 120 and overseas markets, 160; and the Japanese publishing industry, 158–59; as mass-market product, 158; definition of , 158; reflective of changes in society, 157, 168;
prostitution: and anti-prostitution movement, 49; and brothels, 49; and the Recreation and Amusement Association (RAA), 48–49; in red-light districts, 49
Psycho-Pass, 129, 132, 133
publishing industry, 158

R

Rakkī sebun (Lucky Seven), 93
Reddo Kurosu—Onnatachi no akagami (Red Cross—Call-up Orders for Women), 11–12
Rengō kantai shirei chōkan: Yamamoto Isoroku (Admiral Yamamoto), 194
repatriated soldiers, 56–57
Ri Kōran, 11
Rio Bravo, 68
Rock Around the Clock, 72
Rock Band, 241
ryōsai kenbo (good wife, wise mother), 161, 203
Ryūsei no kizuna (Ties of Shooting Stars), 93

S

Sabakareru jūdai (Judged Teens), 63
Sabita naifu (Rusty Knife), 66
Sakura, 147

Sakuran, 119

Sakurazaka Hiroshi, 129

Sangatsu no raion (March Comes in like a Lion), 128

Sapporo Beer: and *Otoko-wa damatte...* campaign, 186–97 passim

Sawajiri Erika, 73

Sawamoto Tadao, 66

Seino Nana, 178

seishun eiga (youth cinema), 63

Sesang eodiedo eobneun ehakan namja (The Innocent Man), 93

Shane, 68–69

Shichinin no samurai (Seven Samurai), 194

Shimizu no abarenbō (Roughnecks from Shimizu), 66

Shingeki no kyojin (Attack on Titan),

Shinjitsu no shuki: BC-kyū senpan Katō Tetsutarō—watashi wa kai ni naritai (A True Record: BC Level War Criminal Katō Tetsutarō—I Want to be a Shellfish), 11

Shinseiki evangerion (Neon Genesis Evangelion), xxi, 111, 125, 128, 130, 132

Shirota Yū, 73

Shishido Jō (Joe), 67, 68; as *Ēsu no Jō,* 67

Shizumanu taiyō (The Unbroken/The Sun which Doesn't Set, film, 2009), 18, 21–29

Shizumanu taiyō (The Unbroken/The Sun which Doesn't Set, WOWOW, 2016), 18, 21–29

Shokei no heya (Punishment Room), 64

Shūkan asahi (Weekly Asahi), 92

Shūkan gendai (Weekly Gendai, lit. "modern weekly"), 204

Shūkan hōseki (The Weekly Magazine Hoseki, lit. "weekly jewel"), 204

Shūkan josei (Shukan Josei, lit. "weekly women"), 92

Shūkan posuto (Weekly Post), 204

Shūkan pureibōi (Weekly Playboy), 204

Shūkan shōnen janpu (Weekly Shōnen Jump), 124

silence, 186–97 passim

Slam Dunk, 125

Sora yori mo tōi basho (A Place Further than the Universe), 128

Spa Resort Hawaiians, 36–38

SS-GB, 13

Subarashiki dansei (Wonderful Guy), 72

Sukai kurora (The Sky Crawlers), 129

Super Mario Brothers, 120

Superman, 22

Supreme Commander for the Allied Powers (SCAP), 220, 221, 222, 228, 229, 230

Sutā tanjō! (A Star is Born!), 238

Suttobi kozō (Kind in a Hurry), 66

Sword Art Online, 121

T

Taiheiyō kiseki no sakusen: Kisuka (Miraculous Military Operation in the Pacific Ocean), 195

taishū bungaku (popular fiction), xxii, 157, 160;

Taiyō no kisetsu (Season of the Sun), 64, 65, 72

taiyōzoku ("sun tribe") films, xix, 63; and "decadent youth", 64; and *dankai no sedai,* 63; as adapted from Ishihara Shintaro novels, 64

Takakura Ken, 191, 193

Tanizaki Jun'ichirō, 158

Tawada Yōko, 168

television: and 60th anniversary of end of WWII, 10; and broadcast of American programs, 82; and broadcasting laws, 8, 9; and direct/indirect representation of disaster, 32; and "harmony of five races" (*gozoku kyōwa*), 11, 12; and history learning, 3; and limitations, 37; and minorities, 157, 159, 163, 167, 168; and NHK, 8; and popularity of "tarento", 96; and press clubs, 9; and relative costs of television sets, 81; and sports broadcasts, 82; and the Tōhoku "triple disaster", xviii, xxii, 32, 145–46; as "memory industry", xvii, 4, 7; as personality-driven, 7–8; as propaganda, 11–13; broadcast times in the 1960s, 86; broadcasters and newspaper affiliation, 9; coexistence and competition with film, xix-xx, 78–89 passim; dramas as reflective of changing circumstances, xxi; from the 1950s, 79; improved technology and cost comparisons with film, 84, 85; increase in television ownership, 80; industry, xix; *jidaigeki,* 4, 10, 13, 186; Kadokawa Shoten and visual productions, 87; Korean remakes of Japanese dramas, 91; "Korean Wave" (*kanryū*), 91; LDP and Asahi group disputes, 9; private broadcasting and sponsorship, 8; publicity posters, 95–96; *renzoku terebi shōsetsu (asadora),* xxi, 32–33, 140–51 passim;

"revenge" in television culture, 92–95, 99, 101; *taiga dorama,* 4, 10, 13, 140, 141; transnational exchanges, xx, 90, 101; trendy dramas from Japan to Taiwan and South Korea, 90, 91; use of "flashbacks", 98

Ten Urara (Urara in the Sky), 149

Thermae Romae, 117, 119

Titanic, 19, 20, 29

Toki wa tachidomaranai (Time Doesn't Stand Still), 34

Tokyo DOGS, 93

Tokyo wankei (Tokyo Bayview), 148

Tora-san (lead character in *Otoko wa tsurai yo* films), 193

transnational/transnationalism, 245–56 passim

truth: and fictionalized portrayals, xvii, 21–22, 23, 25; and JL123 crash, 20–23; "pillars of", 18, 20, 22, 29; as portrayed on screen, xvii, 17, 29

Tsubaki Incident, xiii, 9

Tsubasa, 144

Tsuma to tonda tokkōhei (The Kamikaze Pilot who Flew with His Wife), 11

U

Uchū senkan Yamato (Space Battleship Yamato), 120

Ueru tamashii (Hungry Spirit), 66

Uerukame (Wel-kame), 142

Umetsu Eri, 175

Umi kara kita nagaremono (The Drifter Returns from the Sea), 72

Umizaru, 116

Uroborosu (Ouroboros), 93

Usagi doroppu (Usagi Drop), 119

V

Vinland Saga, 126, 129, 130

violence: and the female body, 164; and progression from constraint to freedom, 162, 163, 165, 168; and sexuality, 166, 167; definition of, 162; domestic, 161; dualism with passivity, xxii, 159, 162, 164; forms of, 162; function of, 159, 162; gender and, 163; historical portrayals of, 6, 11, 12; in feminist Japanese popular fiction, 159; in Japanese

society, 157; in *taiyōzoku* films, 64; sexual, 59; victim/perpetrator, 164

W

Waga tōsō (My Struggle), 114

Wada Kōji, xix, 65, 67, 72

Waga seishun ni kuinashi (No Regrets for our Youth), 221

Wakaba, 148

Warui yatsu hodo yoku nemuru (The Bad Sleep Well), 194

Wataridori itsu mata kaeru (Return of the Vagabond), 72

Wataridori kita e kaeru (Wanderer Returns North), 69

Wataridori (Wanderer) series, 66, 67, 68

Williams, Crystal Kay, 73

Winter Sonata, xiii, 91

Wolf's Rain, 129, 132

Women of the Night, 48, 54

X

X Factor, The, 238

Y

Yoidore tenshi (Drunken Angel), 194

Yōjimbō, 68, 194

Yokoyama Hideo, 18

Yoshimoto Banana, 168

Young Man, 204

Young, Stella, 177

Yume ga ippai abarenbō (A Rampage Full of Dreams), 72

Z

zainichi Kankokujin, 148, 246, 249

Za terebijon (The Television), 92

Handbook of Japanese Media and Popular Cul